P9-AQX-762

WITHDRAWN

MAJOR EUROPEAN AUTHORS

PAUL VALÉRY
AND THE
POETRY OF VOICE

BOOKS IN THIS SERIES

Odette de Mourgues: *Two French Moralists: La Rochefoucauld and La Bruyère*

Ronald Gray: *Goethe: a Critical Introduction*

C. B. Morris: *A generation of Spanish Poets, 1920–1936*

R. F. Christian: *Tolstoy, a Critical Introduction*

Richard Peace: *Dostoyevsky: an Examination of the Major Novels*

John Bayley: *Pushkin: a Comparative Commentary*

Dorothy Gabe Coleman: *Rabelais: a Critical Study in Prose Fiction*

W. E. Yates: *Grillparzer: a Critical Introduction*

Ronald Gray: *Franz Kafka*

John Northam: *Ibsen: a Critical Study*

Geoffrey Strickland: *Stendhal: the Education of a Novelist*

Ronald Gray: *Brecht the Dramatist*

Henry Gifford: *Pasternak: a Critical Study*

Beverly Hahn: *Chekhov, a Study of the Major Stories and Plays*

Odette de Mourgues: *Racine, or The triumph of Relevance*

Peter Stern: *A Study of Nietzsche*

Gordon Pocock: *Boileau and the Nature of Neoclassicism*

C. A. Hackett: *Rimbaud: a Critical Introduction*

Sir Cecil Parrot: *Jaroslav Hašek*

W. D. Howarth: *Molière: a Playwright and his Audience*

Other volumes in preparation

BY THE SAME AUTHOR:

Paul Valéry: Consciousness and Nature (Cambridge 1972)
Paul Valéry and Maxwell's Demon: natural order and human possibility,
Occasional Papers in Modern Languages, 8 (University of Hull 1972)

PAUL VALÉRY
AND THE
POETRY OF VOICE

Christine M. Crow

Reader in French, University of St Andrew's

CAMBRIDGE UNIVERSITY PRESS

Cambridge

London   New York   New Rochelle

Melbourne   Sydney

Published by the Press Syndicate of the University of Cambridge
The Pitt Building, Trumpington Street, Cambridge CB2 1RP
32 East 57th Street, New York, NY 10022, USA
296 Beaconsfield Parade, Middle Park, Melbourne 3206, Australia

First published 1982

Printed in Great Britain by
Western Printing Services Ltd, Bristol

Library of Congress catalogue card number: 81–10069
British Library Cataloguing in Publication Data
Crow, Christine
Paul Valéry and the poetry of voice. – (Major
European authors)
1. Valéry, Paul – Criticism and interpretation
I. Title   II. Series
841'.912   PQ2643.A26Z/
ISBN 0 521 24182 0

General Preface to the Series

This series was initiated within the Cambridge University Press as an at first untitled collection of general studies. For convenience it was referred to inside the Press as 'the Major European Authors Series'; and once the initial prejudice against the useful word 'major' was overcome, the phrase became the official title.

The series was always meant to be informal and flexible, and no very strict guidelines are imposed on the authors. The aim is to provide books which can justifiably be given a title which starts simply with the name of the author studied: therefore to be general, introductory and accessible. When the series started, in the 1960s, there was an assumption that a biographical approach, or an approach via historical 'background' was old-fashioned; and in practice the student or general reader can find adequate biographies or literary histories. Yet it is still relatively hard to find books which address themselves directly to the works as literature and try to give a direct sense of particular structure or effect. So the aim has been to give a critical introduction to the whole œuvre or the most important works; to help the reader to form or order his own impressions by liberal quotation and judicious analysis; to assume little prior knowledge; and in most cases to quote in English or translate the quotations.

It is hoped that the series will help to keep some classics of European literature alive and active in the minds of present-day readers: both those working for a formal examination in literature and the educated general reader – a class which exists, though it may be small – who wishes to gain access to the best in European culture.

Dr Crow's volume is conceived within the general framework of the series; but to serve its particular purpose it must quote the original French very freely, and the depth and complexity of the argument are imposed by the subtlety and originality of Valéry's thought. To simplify, here, would be self-defeating; but the reader who follows this careful study is given access to deep insights into the nature of mind and language as well as a body of brilliantly original verse.

For my Mother and Father

Mais, *au fait, qui* parle dans un poème? Mallarmé voulait que ce fût le Langage lui-même.

Pour moi – ce serait – l'Être *vivant* ET *pensant (contraste, ceci)* – et poussant la conscience de soi à la capture de sa sensibilité – développant les propriétés d'icelle dans leurs implexes – résonances, symétries etc. – sur la *corde* de la *voix*. En somme, le *Langage* issu de la *Voix*, plutôt que la *Voix* du *Langage* (XXII, 435–6).

Contents

Acknowledgements   *page* xii
Abbreviations   xiii
Preface   xv
Introduction   1

PART ONE
1 Poetic development   17
2 Poetic theory   43
3 *La Jeune Parque*   66

PART TWO
4 *Charmes – L'Abeille – Aurore*   103
5 (*a*) *Au Platane, Cantique des Colonnes, Poésie*   131
   (*b*) *Les Pas, La Ceinture, La Dormeuse,*
         Fragments du Narcisse   146
   (*c*) *La Pythie*   166
6 (*a*) About *Ébauche d'un Serpent*   180
   (*b*) *Le Vin Perdu, Intérieur, Le Cimetière Marin*   194
   (*c*) *Ode Secrète, Le Rameur, Palme*   215

Conclusion   245
Notes   255
Bibliography   292
Index   299

Acknowledgements

The existence of this study owes much to Will Moore's tireless question, 'What *did* Valéry mean by "Mes vers ont le sens qu'on leur prête"?', and to my enjoyment of lectures in Cambridge by Lloyd Austin many years ago. I should like to express my gratitude to Malcolm Bowie for his helpful criticisms of the book in its final stages, and to Michael Black and Iain White for generous editorial understanding and advice. I am glad to record my debt to Virginia Crow for patiently deciphering and typing the manuscript, and to thank my friends and colleagues, particularly Caroline Bailey and Ian Higgins, for encouragement throughout. For generous permission to publish extracts from Valéry's collected works, my thanks go finally to Messrs. Gallimard and to Madame Agathe Rouart-Valéry.

Abbreviations

A.J.F.S.	*Australian Journal of French Studies*, Paul Valéry 1871–1971, vol. VIII, n. 2, 1971
AUMLA	*Journal of the Australasian Universities Modern Language and Literature Association*
B.E.V.	*Bulletin des Études Valéryennes* (Centre d'Études Valéryennes, Université Paul Valéry, Montpellier)
C I, *C* II	*Paul Valéry: Cahiers*, ed. J. Robinson (Collection Bibliothèque de la Pléiade, vol. 1 1973, vol. 2 1974)
C.A.I.E.F.	*Cahiers de l'Association Internationale des Études Françaises*
C.P.V., I, II	*Cahiers Paul Valéry*, I Poétique et poésie; II 'Mes théâtres' (Paris, NRF, Gallimard, 1975, 1977)
C.P.V.E.	*Colloque Paul Valéry – Amitiés de Jeunesse, Influences – Lectures*, Université d'Edimbourg, nov. 1976, ed. C. P. Barbier (Paris, Nizet, 1978)
E.C.	*L'Esprit Créateur* IV (1964)
E.M.	*Entretiens sur Paul Valéry*, Actes du Colloque de Montpellier 16–17 octobre 1971, ed. D. Moutote (Paris, P.U.F., 1972)
E.N.C.	*Entretiens sur Paul Valéry*, ed. sous la direction d'É. Noulet-Carner (Décades de Cérisy-la-Salle) (Paris, Mouton, 1968)
F.M.L.S.	*Forum for Modern Language Studies*
F.S.	*French Studies*
M.L.N.	*Modern Language Notes*, French issue, 'Paul Valéry', May 1972, vol. 87, n.4
M.L.R.	*Modern Languages Review*
P I., P II	*Paul Valéry: Œuvres*, ed. J. Hytier (Collection

	Biliothèque de la la Pléiade, vol. 1, 1975 [1957] vol. 2, 1977 [1960])
Poétique et Communication	Paul Valéry, Colloque international de Kiel 19–21 oct., 1977, Actes publiés par K.-A. Blüher et J. Schmidt-Radefeldt (Cahiers du 20ᵉ siècle II [Paris, Klincksieck, 1979])
P.V.C.	*Paul Valéry Contemporain*, Colloque de Paris et de Strasbourg, nov. 1971, ed. M. Parent et J. Levaillant (Paris, 1974)
R.H.L.F.	*Revue d'Histoire Littéraire de la France*
R.L.M., I	*Revue des Lettres Modernes*, I, lectures de 'Charmes', sous la direction de H. Laurenti, 413–18, 1974 (6)
R.S.H.	*Revue des Sciences Humaines*
Y.F.S.	*Yale French Studies*, Paul Valéry, 44 (1970)

Throughout this book roman small capitals followed by arabic numerals refer respectively to volume and page of Valéry's *Cahiers* (facsimile version in 29 volumes (Paris, C.N.R.S., 1957–1961)).

Square brackets within quoted matter indicate either ellipsis by the author of inessential words of phrases, or enclose explanatory or other interpolations by the author.

Preface

'O pour moi seul, à moi seul, en moi-même,
Auprès d'un cœur, aux sources du poème...'

'Le Moi, c'est la Voix' (xiv, 390)
'La voix, clef de la poésie' (vii, 164)

Like most readers, I first became acquainted with Valéry's poetry through *Le Cimetière Marin*, his most famous poem. I remember above all the sense of order it conveyed: not simply a logical order, but a deep, alert, intensely expressive order, miraculously maintained through shifts and divergencies of tone and meaning, a strangely familiar 'voice' which spoke with an assurance all its own about the less assured nature of human experience – life and death, sunlight and shadow – and which seemed to issue, not from that fictitious narrator one imagined musing in a hillside cemetery overlooking the sea, but from a source deep inside oneself, 'heard' only now that the poem brought it alive or reminded one of it.

Had I understood *Le Cimetière Marin*? Obviously not in one sense, for it is a poem which repays acquaintance over a long period of time, seeming to provide the more openings the more its 'secrets' as a formal system of words are revealed. Perhaps, on the other hand, in a mysterious way yet to be changed into conscious knowledge, *Le Cimetière Marin* had understood part of me.

At the risk of writing a study less technically detailed than might otherwise have been possible, and in the hope that I had found a subject sufficiently central to provide the newcomer with a general introduction to Valéry's poetry[1] while still sufficiently neglected to be of interest to the specialist, I decided to try to track down and appreciate more fully the particularly expressive order which these poems so compellingly convey. For, as I soon found confirmed in Valéry's comments on the type of poem truest to the essence of poetry as an art of language, an action of expressive communication[2] is their deliberate centre despite – or perhaps even because of – his more famous stress on a pure, would-be self-sufficient universe of form. The poem communicates an intimate 'voice' shared by poet and reader alike. For the human 'Self' in Valéry's thought is not an essence but a unifying *capacity*, contingent upon dialogue with the body, the mind and the world. Hence such important propositions in Valéry's poetic theory as that the Self is the Voice, and 'voice' being the key to poetry, that poetry offers a key to the action creative of Self.[3]

Not to squander creative energy on the vain attempt to express experience in language, but to attempt instead to re-stimulate the sources of expressive experience to which language itself has access: here, I felt, is a poetics as radical in its attitude to the problem of crossing from the 'reality of the poem' to the 'poem of reality'[4] as any *avant-garde* aesthetic aimed at disrupting traditional poetic means. (One does not have to read far in Valéry's comments on poetry to realise the central rôle played by an analysis of the problems of traditional poetic rhetoric.) Yet here, too, is a poetics which by consciously making accessible the operations of the creative mind made possible through language, would seem to radicalise the notion of meaning, at least to demand a different approach to hermeneutics than other forms of poetry based on the primacy of language – Mallarmé's poetry being not the least of these identifiably modern forms.

There is a certain belief that poetry inspired by the formalist muse works only through the releasing of the reader's powers of free association. Valéry might even appear to uphold this view by his constant scepticism about the whole process of interpretation in poetry, his insistence that there are as many meanings to a poem as there are readers, even that a true poem has no meaning at all. What if the unifying action of the voice itself is taken as the 'meaning' of a poem, however? My first experience of *Le Cimetière Marin* had begun to confirm for me that a certain type of communication can be achieved when the poet discovers how to weave back into a poem the multiple patterns of response generated in the reader's mind (the famous comment 'Mes vers ont le sens qu'on leur prête' seems capable of this double interpretation). Indeed, Valéry is as insistent on the potential of a certain type of poem to overcome the purely personal and indeterminate as he is on the plurality of associations it makes possible, going so far as to set as his ideal the incarnation in the reader of a living soul or, more appropriately, 'mental body'.[5] Here, surely, is an appeal to our need to create unity without sacrificing diversity and, to meet its challenge, a highly controlled transference between the spoken and the silent or unsayable which I have come to believe Valéry's poems accomplish to an unusual degree.

By concentrating on poetic ambiguity from this integrative point of view,[6] I hoped to be able to come to terms with several apparent contradictions still haunting Valéryan criticism, not the least of these being the paradox just suggested of a poetry in which unity and plurality, precision and indeterminacy, communication and the impossibility of definitive production so powerfully co-exist, a paradox closely related in turn to the problem of reconciling expressive and formalist aims. How is it that a poet who so often advocates the exclusion of all subject-matter can produce poetry so rich in recognisable human experience: consciousness in all its emotional, sensorial and intellectual confrontations with the physical world? Or – a critical issue currently much debated: who speaks in a poem? Can such radical impersonality as Valéry's be reconciled with the notion that poetry is the expression of an individual subject? In these areas, and particularly with regard to the 'Fallacy of Intentionalism' identified by New Criticism in America and taken to an extreme by contemporary French Structuralism, I felt that Valéry's work could be expected to produce surprises. So, too, the question of his affinity with Symbolism and with Mallarmé himself, so readily described by the textbooks as 'le Maître' while Valéry is thought to remain in the discipular rôle.

In contrast to Mallarmé's 'la Voix du Langage', Valéry characterised poetry as 'le Langage de la Voix'. In choosing to reflect the phrase in the title of this book, I have made the possible strength and originality of Valéry's transformation of Mallarmé's poetics one of my principal concerns. By Voice in this total sense, I shall attempt to show that Valéry meant something much more complex than the speaking voice alone, yet much more closely related to the living psycho-physiological action of speech than the notion implies in theories of narrative point of view.[7] Something of a portmanteau term, the concept remains, in my opinion, rationally coherent and convincing, permitting the integration of a theory of poetic 'fabrication' with the powerfully moving expression of individual consciousness as a universal mode of being, and perhaps even inviting the reconciliation of 'Hermetic' and 'Orphic' conceptions of poetic art.[8] Rather than attempt to describe Valéry's comprehensive theory of Voice as such,[9] however, it is the voice or discourse of poetry in this last sense on which I have chosen to concentrate: voice as a model informing the expressive action of poetry and raised to the status of a self-aware poetic myth.[10]

Having described Valéry's theory of consciousness and language in the way most likely to highlight a 'poetics of voice', I approach the poetry of *La Jeune Parque* with its aid and, in Part Two, each individual poem of *Charmes*. To say that the book is primarily designed to invite the reader to enjoy the power of the poems themselves is not the obligatory post-script it might at first appear. The idea of the mind – the reader's mind, his own mind – which Valéry designed his poems to involve is not that of a passive receptacle, yet neither is it that of an interpreter of symbolic messages. It is rather a dynamic source to be stimulated through contact with the creative virtualities activated through language, to greater and greater recognition of its own potential for change: what language alone cannot say, but consciousness without language cannot know it contains. Hence the extraordinary way in which Valéry exploits the self-referentiality of language in order to escape the self-referentiality of literature – for such, it seems to me, is the 'subversive' aspiration of a poetry conscious of its own self-affirming presence as creative desire: 'Fais que ma soif se fasse source.' How else can we account for the fact that this 'magnifique cerveau toujours en éveil',[11] a serious thinker in a variety of disciplines and well-known for his often violently 'anti-literary' attitudes, can give to poetry a supreme place in the hierarchy of human experience and thought?

St Andrews, 1979   C.M.C.

Introduction

La Littérature ne m'intéresse [...]
profondément que dans la mesure où elle
exerce l'esprit à certaines transformations,
– celles dans lesquelles les propriétés
excitantes du langage jouent un rôle
capital.   (P ɪ, 1500).

[...] il me suffit de vous voir parler,
d'entendre votre timbre et vos attaques
de voix. La façon de parler en dit plus
que ce que l'on dit...Le fond n'a aucune
importance...essentielle./ – C'est
curieux. C'est une théorie de la poésie.
                              (P ɪɪ, 273).[1]

La voix sort de l'instant et vient de la
totalité du temps; Elle paraît dans
l'intervalle, dans la coupure de la
conscience, dans ce qui sépare le sentiment
de l'acte, et ce qui oblige à parler de ce
qui s'attend à comprendre. Mais ce qui
demande à comprendre oblige à parler. (vɪɪ, 643).

Truly instrumental self-knowledge needs to be complemented by
the possession of natural models, Valéry felt (xxɪ, 743). In attempting to show how one of the most precious of these models, the
human voice, acts formally, ethically and emotionally at the heart
of his poetic theory, the aim of this book is to deepen appreciation
of the unity of analytic and creative procedures which underlies
his poetic universe. 'Poète, prends ton luth' and describe Nature,
says Musset's Muse; but for Valéry it is the Voice itself that the
Poet is exhorted to analyse and use as a natural principle:

Poète, attends – accueille – la *voix*/Regarde la Voix totale et analyse
la voix/Flux et modulation/Energie et fréquence – Passage de
l'émotion à l'expression/Délivrance – Charge/Acte – construction
[...] Bornes et registre/Continu et discontinu [...] Comment cette
liaison et construction s'organise?   (xvɪ, 395).

The human voice is a natural agent for giving form and continuity to the human organism in the face of the inexpressible experience of being alive.

Whether we see Valéry's quest for the poetic utilisation of this mystery as 'literary' is ultimately a question of definition. In his own opinion, his achievement derived from his non-literary or even anti-literary research into ways of representing the resources of the mind as part of a living organism – 'les connexions et définitions issues de mes recherches sur la vie, les fonctions Ψ' (xxiv, 117). In the field of poetic composition he attempted to evolve a form of 'harmonics'[2] by which the poet-craftsman could play on the natural resonances of the sensibility. Yet the notion of harmonics is based on a far less vulnerable foundation than a purely symbolic exchange of responses between the reader and the poem. Valéry's notion of harmonics is invigorated by his conception of language as a gesture or modifying action related to self-awareness on the level of being, our capacity as language-users internally as well as externally to 'hear ourselves speak'.[3]

At the risk of using certain concepts prior to their detailed clarification in later chapters, the present Introduction is intended to provide a general framework which will allow some of the epistemological consequences of this striking phenomenology of language to be related more closely to the subject of poetic Voice as the goal and method of Valéry's poetic practice. In particular it is designed to enable Valéry's 'poétique du langage' to be compared and contrasted with the linguistically inspired poetics of contemporary Structuralism.[4] For I believe the notion of the subject to be an aspect of literary communication[5] with which he was actively concerned, conscious as he was of the impoverishment of humanist values in any form of thinking which denies individual consciousness exchange with the world, yet also of the impoverishment caused by any essentialist thinking, humanist or otherwise, which refuses to relate individual consciousness to the limiting conditions responsible for its potential, be they biological or social in kind.

Valéry by no means confined himself to poetry. He was the author of the novel-like *La Soirée avec Monsieur Teste* (published in 1895) and the drama *Mon Faust* (1940), to name only two of his imaginative adventures in different literary genres. He wrote countless essays on subjects ranging from education and economics (a frequent source of analogy in his poetic theory) to physics and politics. Above all, he pursued for the greater part of his life – from 1894, aged twenty-three, right up to his death in 1945 – in the form of hundreds of notebooks, his study of the human mind in terms of three finite variables: 'Corps', 'Esprit' and 'Monde' ('CEM').

Largely written in the solitude of dawn, his most treasured 'point ému' of concentration before the more dispersed public activities of the day, the *Cahiers*, as they are now called,[6] offer an at first bewildering diversity of themes and areas. There are pages of mathematical jottings; reflections on problems in modern physics and biology; meditations on the nature of human love and sexuality; fragments of intense, often heart-rending prose poetry; impressionistic water-colours of human figures, marine landscapes, trees; moral and social aphorisms; meditations on the different forms of language – philosophical, religious, artistic, mathematical and scientific – by which human beings shape and express their relationship with the world.

Yet even without the help of Valéry's keenly developed insights into the nature of his own intellectual preferences, it is obvious that the thread linking these teeming pages is neither scientific enquiry nor literary creation. Valéry is concerned above all with the capacity we share for individual consciousness and, through that consciousness, for the development of our natural bodily resources for purposes of knowledge and harmony with ourselves. He was preoccupied by the possibility of converting a sense of the finite[7] into a source of intellectual energy, of harnessing the capacities of creative sensibility available to the mind for its own inner use.[8]

The ways and means by which Valéry pursued his enquiry into individual human potentiality – Monsieur Teste's 'Que peut un homme?' or the Greek 'épuise le possible' used as epigraph to *Le Cimetière Marin* – naturally varied at different stages of his life according to the status he gave at the time to different forms of discourse. The famous intellectual crisis of 1892,[9] for example, led him to reject his early verse and to devote himself instead to a form of abstract analysis by which he hoped to express the operations of the mind in the most general language possible – the language of mathematics.[10] The urge for representational precision – description of the mind as a finite totality – continued to haunt Valéry long after his famous 'return' to poetry in 1912, when he began to re-fashion his old verses and embark on the vast new enterprise of *La Jeune Parque* (where the poem is the visible fruit of the mental 'exercise' producing it).

Yet we should not accept the temptation to equate the gradual resurgence of poetry in Valéry's life with a corresponding decline in the urge to analyse and represent the human being in its potential totality, despite his growing disillusionment about the possibility of describing the mind precisely by mathematical means. We should look more closely at the terms in which that first overriding urge to understand the limitations and potentialities of human consciousness is set up, particularly from the point of view of the rôle allowed to the notion of Self. (And here it must be stressed to the newcomer to Valéry's thought that the Self to which he refers is never a purely personal one, in the sense that we may speak of character or personality to be approached by confessional self-analysis, but rather the capacity for self-awareness – 'Moi = Homo' – that we share with other human beings by virtue of our common power of detachment from the content of our emotions and thoughts.)

Valéry's enquiry into human possibility has its centre in the conviction that the mind can be approached meaningfully only from a formal point of view and by observation of the changes and transformations ('la self-variance') in relation to which individual consciousness is constantly lost and reformed. And because such knowledge of the living instant at the birth of thought could be realised only within an individual experience of the relationship between permanence and change, Valéry felt that the unique method required by his formal endeavour required him to take a finite consciousness – his own – as material and testing-ground – – 'le système en principe consiste à rattacher tout à *un* esprit *déterminé* – au mien' (I, 824) – and thus to accord to the capacity for self-awareness, 'la conscience de la conscience', a privileged place at the centre of his intellectual quest.

Indeed, it must be apparent by now that an understanding of the fundamental bond in Valéry's thinking between universality and

4

individuality or between subjective experience, self-awareness and creative discovery ('créer', 'connaître' and 'comprendre') is essential to any approach to his work.[11] Not seeing the inevitable involvement of the perceiving self in its own perceptions as a stumbling-block to objective knowledge, Valéry might be said to accord to individual consciousness a privileged position by virtue of that very involvement. 'Notre connaissance, à mon sentiment, a pour limite la conscience que nous pouvons avoir de notre être, – et peut-être, de notre corps. Quel que soit x, la pensée que j'en ai, si je la presse, tend vers moi, quel que je sois' (P I, 1233).[12] The way is open for an appreciation of poetry as the natural discourse of human reality experienced through the bodily centre of our individual consicousness – poetry as the natural field of expression, development and analysis of that which creates the human Self ('fabrication, non du MOI, mais de ce qui fait le Moi lui-même' [XVII, 444]).

From the Romantics and Baudelaire onward, poetry has also been connected with 'le Moi'. To link Valéry's poetry with Baudelaire's is to remind ourselves of its roots in a cultural tradition of 'subjective universality' in literature stemming from Montaigne,[13] with its concentrated flowering in late-nineteenth-century verse. However, a further purpose in remembering this energetic literary tradition – as much the nourishing force of Valéry's writing as his scientific and mathematical background – is to suggest an important difference of orientation within the affinity. For where the Self is felt to be the expressive agent *behind* certain forms of Romantic literature, the Self, for Valéry, is inventively discovered through the action of expression. Indeed, the difficult continuation and development of the self-constituting action of inner monologue in outer form, to further and further levels of precision, is associated by Valéry with an almost ethical value: the full co-ordination and use of human faculties we owe to ourselves and others as organisms of bounded but indeterminate form.

Notre vie, nos émotions, nos passions, n'ont d'autre valeur (autre qu'instantanée et initiale) que celle que leur donnent nos actes subséquents et l'art d'en faire quelque chose – toute l'émotion du monde n'est qu'un commencement et c'est pourquoi faut-il porter au plus haut degré *l'appareil moteur* qui puisse épuiser cette 'force'

en la rendant restituable à volonté autant de fois qu'on le voudra.
(VII, 242).

This privileged 'appareil moteur' is, needless to say, the human voice, used here metonymically – the mode of desire – for the mental capacities it makes possible. For we have already anticipated through our glimpse into the quest evoked in the *Cahiers* – 'Gladiator' or 'Système' – how much more significant than the mere capacity to speak will be this concept of creative expression. It will relate to nothing less than the 'reversibility'[14] or continuity of Self and body on which Valéry founded his gymnastics of unifying self-awareness. 'L'idée Gymnastique est capitale – C'est là ma philosophie. Manœuvre constante des grandes opérations inverses: passer du conscient à l'inconscient et de l'inconscient passer au conscient' (IV, 737). It is a goal which relates back in turn to the crisis of 1892, in which Valéry felt he had discovered suffering to be the natural reality of the mind 'left to itself' and a prey to random emotions.[15] 'Voix', he writes in a notebook of 1921 at the time of *Charmes*,

> *Orphée.* L'opération qui consiste à tirer de ma douleur un chant magnifique. Cette douleur stupide a conduit mon sens à des extrêmes de détresse, et de ténèbres et de furie impuissante mais puisque je n'y suis pas demeuré, puisque je suis remonté des enfers pour pouvoir y redescendre, j'ai appris du moins, la continuité de cette chaîne de tourments, d'espoirs et de catastrophes, et donc comment le plus haut au plus bas se relie, toute la modulation de l'être et la conservation de la vie entre les bornes qu'elle ne peut franchir – c'est là le *chant*, le registre. (VIII, 41).

Orpheus may enter and return from the underworld conducted by the thread of song, the secret continuity of the creative sensibility.

The importance of this empirical discovery of the natural foundation of art in human experience was immense. It provided Valéry with the basis of a link between therapy and knowledge, and with the intellectual justification of language – the medium of the voice – as the medium of poetry, a form of discourse more meaningful and more musical than music itself.[16] Before pursuing the question of poetic discourse further, it would seem useful to suggest something of Valéry's attitude to language itself, in particular to the 'scientific' study of language as practised by the linguist or professional language-philosopher.

6

Like Bergson and, later, Wittgenstein and other twentieth-century language-philosophers, Valéry was led to a critique of language in which certain negative aspects inevitably predominate.[17] Ordinary language is dangerously vague and imprecise as an instrument of knowledge, too general for purposes of expression, and so on. How can individual consciousness in its unique instant of simultaneous subject/object, present/absent, difference and identity be communicated at all in language created before we were born and largely appropriated for mundane or practical ends? Is not conventional language ('Fiducia'), however necessary, the dictator rather than the instrument of individual thought? Even in this negative approach, however, Valéry reveals his lack of interest in the study of language isolated from its conditions of usage in the living organism. It is his preoccupation with the fate of those precious capacities made possible *through* language which differentiates him from the linguist who studies language as a self-contained system. Indeed, his hesitations in this area of linguistics have proved in many ways his strengths, notwithstanding his own ability to prefigure many advances in the field.[18]

A further attitude to language is present in the *Cahiers*, then: an attitude based not on suspicion and scorn, but on wonder at the phenomenon of language conceived as an action or event with a direct result on the pre-articulatory and post-articulatory state of the human mind (or, to use the mathematical language adopted in the *Cahiers*, the transformation of an exchange into a function [xxviii. 617]). A hindrance when we think *in* language, allowing the pre-conceived structures of public language to determine rather than organise our thought, language possesses the power to energise and transform our experience from within. The extraordinary power of observation which Valéry brought to bear on the existential nature of language, particularly from the point of view of the complementarity of phonation and audition ('Bouchoreille' as he called it), is of central significance to his poetry, not only from the point of view of suggesting techniques and themes appropriate to the poet's use of language as his material, but from the point of view of the total subject-matter – 'Poésie' – which should be the poet's goal if he remains true to the potentialities of language as a living gesture of speech, 'vox in actu'.[19] For there is no question that Valéry should assume to adequate language and reality. By seeking ways to deepen the expressive power of language as 'parole' over and above its existence as 'langue', he sets at the centre of his poetic theory the sensation of ineffability, 'l'ineffable', the rich yet finitely structured response of individual consciousness to its own virtuality. Addressing himself to *this* sensation – 'ces *choses* ou cette *chose*, que tentent obscurément d'exprimer les cris, les larmes, silences, les caresses[...]' (vIII, 846) – the poet must represent and develop its interconnections with language itself, that vast literary masterpiece which already contains the virtual continuity of 'being' and 'knowing' which consciousness finds betrayed by the language of comprehension and ordinary speech. 'Le langage s'identifie avec la connaissance. Mais la forme du langage, cette forme qui permet de concevoir des combinaisons du langage, le montre comme fonction et tenant à l'Être' (vI, 193).

Consciousness of the self-referentiality of language has become central to literature and literary studies today, some thirty years or more after Valéry's death; and any book on his poetry must refer to the movement known as Structuralism, or at least – for Structuralism is not a single phenomenon – to that aspect of Structuralism devoted to a Structuralist Poetics. Is it fair to call Valéry a Structuralist *avant la lettre*? Is he even responsible for certain contemporary developments in this field?

In its very broadest sense, Structuralism is a manner of thinking which, in order to know how meaning is possible, investigates the 'structures' through which our perception of reality is formed. In that his whole 'manière de voir' intuitively favoured an approach which placed the formation of reality in the relationships we construct between objects, Valéry might be called a natural structuralist. His passionately analytical intelligence would have found exciting and valuable the formalist impulse behind contemporary Structuralism, with its release from positivist cause and effect and from a reference-theory of meaning, its stress on the value of abstract generality, its curiosity about language and literature as part of a wider socio-cultural system of communication. Indeed, it was largely thanks to Valéry himself that the term 'poetics' came to imply more than a mere rule-book of literary devices and rhythmical recipes.[20] Intent on bringing to bear a more rigorous consciousness on the nature of the work of art and of literary criticism, Valéry developed the notion in his famous 'Cours de Poétique' (given in the Collège de France from 1937 to 1945 to a large public audience),[21] indicating the need for an evolving study of the complex mental activity which culminates in a work produced by the mind. Years of reflection on his part certainly laid the foundation of a study of literary effects in terms of the more general processes of communication which make them possible – 'la recherche des effets proprement littéraires du langage, l'examen des inventions expressives et suggestives qui ont été faites pour accroître le pouvoir et la pénétration de la parole, et celui des restrictions que l'on a parfois imposées en vue de bien distinguer la langue de la fiction de celle de l'usage' (P I, 1441). Here is a marvellous field of critical enquiry, still taking stock of its future today.

Yet what would Valéry have thought of the early Structuralists' attempt to systematise literary forms on the lines of rule-governed operations derived from models in linguistics? How would his theory of literary effects have led him to judge an approach in which the work of literature is treated as an open-ended text where the reader is free to discover every possible meaning and where meaning is not the voice of a subject speaking through language, but the voice of the play of language speaking through the text? Is there not something in Valéry's insistence on the value of approaching the mental actions behind the literary product which suggests a radical difference of aim in relation to the study of the literary work itself?

The most important trigger to contemporary Structuralist thought in so far as it derived from the linguistic model of Saussure was the idea that all language is self-referential. Its content becomes its internal relations, and to study language, in literature or otherwise, is therefore not to trace the correspondence between words and their substantive referents, but to examine instead a system of signs. Commonplace in language-study today, particularly in the field of psycholinguistics, the notion of language as structure was upheld by Valéry in an age where traditional semantic theories of meaning were largely unchallenged. We shall see that in poetically stressing the 'palpable' potentials of language neither Mallarmé nor Valéry were adhering to a purely substantialist view of language, any more than the semantic values of language are denied by rejecting a reference theory of meaning. So far, a sense of structure holds the centre of the stage.

Behind Saussure's conception of the arbitrary relationship between the signifier (acoustic image) and the signified,[22] is the conviction that the sign in which their union takes place is itself structural, and thus, say the Structuralists, that our conception of reality is linguistically determined. The conceptual processes of the mind are not given ready to mould language in a certain way, but are determined by language in advance. There is no thought and indeed no transcendental individual self but within language and its wider symbolic systems and social codes.

That the Self when described formally is purely the instantaneous centre of a system of changing relationships ('CEM') Valéry has no doubt. His poetry and thought both provide powerful expressions of this. On the relationship between thought and language he seems at first more ambivalent. Faced with the immense dynamic mass of notes in the *Cahiers*, we may find apparently contradictory statements such as, on the one hand, 'Pensée sans langage' (IV, 253), and, on the other, 'Langage, sujet d'éternelle méditation – car c'est l'univers de la pensée' (IX, 43). Yet the phrase 'Pensée sans langage' is quickly qualified by the equally important 'Sans langage du tout n'est rien', while the idea that language reveals the universe of thought is still compatible with the conviction that defiance of language (II, 77) is the secret of the thinker concerned with individual truth, 'la pensée à l'état naissant'. True thought for Valéry takes place with the aid of an inner will to expression which is only partly linguistic and whose dialectical presence ordinary language contaminates and betrays although language itself is essential to the task of understanding. Indeed, he dreamt of constructing an artificial public language founded on the inner reality of thought – 'le fait mental' – with the images of poetry and of mathematics both converging on the area from different points of view. The idea implicit in New Criticism that poetry is emotive where science is referential, or that poetry makes statements which are the rival or the superior of science, finds little or no echo in Valéry's thinking.[23] *Both* forms of intellectual discourse are cognitive and imaginative in different ways. Nor would Valéry entertain the possibility of a purely private language.[24] With the whole Structuralist enterprise he shares the sense that language is the domain of the Other in the Self necessary to our existence as individuals if only by differentiation. Without difference there can be no identity. 'Or, cette convention fondamentale, langage, exige d'autres Moi, des échanges antérieurs. Le *Moi exige les hommes*' (xi, 912).

Is the perceiving subject totally governed by language for Valéry, however? The fact that the poetic act must operate in terms of a deviation from ordinary language in order to make plain the 'fait mental' at the birth of language and thought makes this true in a sense. Yet one of the most complex and rewarding areas of Valéry's thought concerns the relationship between Self and Other revealed in the natural action of the voice. For Valéry, the movement of the voice between sound and sense becomes the equivalent of the dialectic of 'being' and 'knowing' which constitutes the individual 'moi' as presence (see p. 55). 'La présence serait-elle oscillatoire?' (xvi, 160); 'Le moi est le nom du travail perpétuel d'opposition et de résolution [...] entre le tout et la partie [...] entre la demande et la réponse' (iii, 705). To explore Valéry's vision of the subject of poetic utterance and of speech is to appreciate that the presence developed through language is not so much the voice of language, but the voice of the Self made possible in language. Where for the orthodox Structuralist a 'langage dans le langage' would imply that the 'parole' of poetic discourse is contained within 'langue', the total language system, the same phrase implies for Valéry that 'parole' deviates from 'langue'. The Voice of poetic discourse is a sign of the Self which the humanising virtualities of language reveal as for ever beyond words.

As if the more to cherish their strange normality, Valéry's awareness is often directed towards the phenomena we take for granted, language and the normal, non-dramatic register of the voice being one of the most important of these. Yet for all his extreme consciousness of language, Valéry might be felt to be radically opposed to many of the aims and methods of contemporary linguistics. There is little sense of any belief that language can be meaningfully approached as an object. On the contrary, ordinary communication is the devouring of semiotics by understanding, and poetry communicates only by producing a delay in the process of understanding. Its signs are a pathway to an action

11

of form, in turn replaced by a more complete type of thought. Valéry might even be said to rely on the poet's intuition of the universe of sound as the direction in which all the artifice of poetic craftsmanship should travel in pursuit of a prey which in objective terms can be described only as a fleeting myth on the part of the organism – a fiction to which only the action of expression in exchange with another can give presence. This is not to say that Valéry's thought is anti-scientific. It might even be described as the more scientific in that it refuses to give linguistics a scientific status. And here his concept of 'Système' with its powerful intellectual allowance for areas unknowable, might invite comparison and contrast with that of the 'post-Structuralist' French thinker Jacques Lacan.[25]

For Lacan, too, the thrust of our thought on language must be preserved from reification without falling prey to an equally naïve belief in the power of thought without theory. For Lacan, too, the individual is contained within the wider symbolic order of language, in the sense that any notion of subject must be dialectical and 'decentred'. For Lacan, too, individual creativity is not denied by this position in the way that the fashionable phrase 'the disappearance of the subject' would have us believe. Yet it seems to me that Valéry's mistrust of Freud cannot wholly be mitigated by Lacan's re-reading and that, in matters of the unconscious in relation to language, this mistrust might serve to introduce an important difference between Valéry and Lacan as well. Valéry's mistrust of Freud centres on the dualistic notion of conscious and unconscious (more precisely, unconscious and preconscious). He himself constantly referred to the total virtuality of a person, for which, with an amusingly conscious Freudian echo, he coined the term 'Implexe': 'J'appelle *Implexe*, l'ensemble de tout ce que quelque circonstance que ce soit *peut* tirer de *nous*' (xxiv, 478); '*L'Implexe* [...] est le *reste caché structurel et fonctionnel* – (non le subconscient) – d'une connaissance ou action consciente' (xvii, 63).

From the point of view of poetic composition, the notion of 'Implexe' is immensely important in that it encourages the expressive intelligence already seen in connection with Valéry's 'Orphic' discovery (p. 6) to provoke and utilise the resources of language and the resources of the mind in a two-way movement from conscious to unconscious and back, 'développant les propriétés de [la sensibilité] dans leurs implexes – résonances, symétries etc. – sur la *corde* de la *voix*' (xxii, 436). Language itself is an 'implexe fonctionnel de biréflexes composés' (xxviii, 271), which the poet can exploit artificially just as our consciousness exploits it naturally in the action of speech. From the point of view of the present argument, however, this confirms an important difference between Valéry and Lacan, for all their similarity of interests. The 'otherness' of language for Valéry is the 'otherness' not of the sub-conscious but of 'Being', defined, as we have seen, in terms of the resources of existence harnessed by consciousness itself.[26] Not for him the wooing of the unconscious, but the task of revealing and developing the essence of poetry as the voice of 'l'Être vivant ET pensant' in its most extremely contrasting as well as interrelated form. Hence Valéry's lack of interest in Surrealist 'écriture automatique'[27] and, indeed, his far less tolerant attitude to Surrealism than that which Lacan himself has espoused. For Valéry, it is not the voice of the unconscious that poetry must be encouraged to speak, any more than the voice of thought contained in language. Above all, if the unity of the ego is spurious (here Valéry would agree with Lacan), not so the unity created by the subject as a form of cognitive desire. Hence the structuring rather than 'de-structuring' emphasis of his thought. Language is called to express the experience of multiplicity from the point of view of consciousness and its own vital sense of 'l'ineffable'.

To summarise and evaluate with regard to poetry in particular: like Mallarmé before him, Valéry founds his poetic intentions on the need to create poetic discourse, that is a use of language where the immediate function of words to communicate information is held back in favour of the palpability of language itself – what modern literary rhetoric might call the foregrounding of the utterance. Leaving for later discussion the question of the crucially different tasks to which the two poets set the powers of expression released by this attempt to speak by means of rather than despite language, let us assert that this aim in itself has much in common with that of the Formalist–Structuralist movement discernible in the Prague Linguistic Circle, the Russian Formalists and – with

its debt to Saussure and, indeed to Mallarmé and Valéry themselves – contemporary French Structuralism. From the point of
view of the notion of perceptible form (not necessarily the same as
the 'displaying of the device')[28] and from the point of view that
the meaning of a work of art is contained within its coherence as a
total structure, the spirit behind this sense of the primacy of
language is the same.

How far do the similarities go, however? Strikingly far if we
take the notion of the impersonality of literary form. Valéry never
tires of arguing that the literary work, the poem *par excellence*,
must be judged independently of the observable personality and
ideas of its author, and that, for this impersonality to be accomplished, the poem must be founded on the essential properties of
language itself:

> La tentative de rendre une œuvre indépendante de la personne
> observable de l'auteur pour qu'elle se rapporte comme d'elle–même
> à l'esprit créant en toute généralité, en plein possible 'universel' –
> conduit à la *fonder sur* ou la *déduire des* propriétés essentielles du
> langage.   (XXIII, 879–80).

Frequent formulations of the notion that the poem must appear to
be spoken by the voice of nobody,[29] give rise to the over-all
proposition 'Le point délicat de la poésie est l'obtention de la voix'
and 'cette voix ne doit faire imaginer quelque homme qui parle.
Si elle le fait, ce n'est pas elle' (VI, 176). Close to the spirit of New
Criticism in his denial of biographical and psychological intentionality, Valéry may seem close at the same time to the spirit of
radical Structuralism ('New New Criticism') which, questioning
the veiled ideological stance behind this would-be impartial whole-
ness, maintains that the text is the de-centred locus of meanings
which the reader is free to create ('re-write')[30] in any number of
ways. 'Mes vers ont le sens qu'on leur prête' (P I, 1509), said
Valéry with a Barthes-like ring,[31] or, 'Le poème est une abstraction, une écriture qui attend, une loi qui ne vit que sur quelque
bouche humaine, et cette bouche est ce qu'elle est' (P II, 1255).

But is the notion of polyvalence and reader-freedom really
involved here? It was not in language but in the action of speech[32]
that for Valéry the poet could best experience and observe the
marvellous properties of transaction possible between conscious-

ness and 'Being' – so much so that the poet does not create but inventively *discovers* through poetic composition the virtuality of a universal Self:[33] 'La joie de trouver en soi-même – des choses inattendues, imprévisibles – et précieuses – desquelles il semble que nous soyons composés, pénétrés, *capables* et inconscients' (xvii, 262). Far from presenting an emptiness to be filled by the reader's own freedom of association, the poem conceived with this action of inventive discovery as its subject and goal constrains the reader to create and recognise the plurality of meanings involved in its action of form.[34] The impersonal voice speaking in the poem becomes the discovered Self of poet and reader alike, a form of secondary intentionality in which an intense communication takes place as a reciprocated gift through the power of the poem to create multiplicity of meanings 'tout en demeurant elle-même'.[35] Beginning his poetic theory with an art of calculated effects inspired by Poe, Valéry certainly evolved to a position where greater ambiguity enters his poems; yet precisely because of the rôle of this ambiguity in allowing the reader to participate in the creation of a predetermined subject – 'Poésie' – poetry remains what he called in 1916 a conquest of the reader's attention. 'Lui faire sentir et le risque et la sécurité; conduire où l'on ne veut pas aller, arrêter sur l'obstacle, au point marqué.../L'art grossier émeut, bouleverse, enchaîne – mais ne sait pas donner et retenir' (vi, 150). Describing the marvellously free yet controlled flight of a bird, the passage is at the same time reminiscent of the poem *L'Insinuant*, evoking the art of seduction – 'Je sais où je vais,/Je t'y veux conduire' – where it is nonetheless ironically unclear whether the 'victim' or the 'seducer' pronounces 'le mot le plus tendre'. Similarly Faust and Lust in Valéry's mature drama of human love,[36] *Mon Faust*, lose track of whose thoughts are whose. In *Chant de l'Idée-Maîtresse*, Valéry suggests that the presence of 'le même' and 'l'autre' deep within the 'Colloque' of the individual self is the same as is present between poet and reader: 'Ma voix est la tienne et tu distingues/Ma volonté. Mais tu veux MOI! L'Idée!' (P i, 358). A poetics of reading spirals through Valéry's thought, as it does through contemporary Structuralism, but it is one in which the poem preserves and intensifies the same self-constituting individual dialectic as the action of speech: 'Le Moi est bien la Personne qui parle. [...]

Cet acte excite à son tour, comme en demande rétroactive, quelque chose – ou présence – ou besoin et c'est là la place du Moi. Ainsi est-il *trouvé* (xx, 190).[37] .

With this precious closure of the text on to individual consciousness in its power of exchange with another, we seem to be at a far extreme from the kind of closure Barthes opens to the play of the world. To return to the central difference between Valéry and Mallarmé, we appear also to be at a far extreme from the kind of poetics where the effacement of the author is replaced by the voice of language. For Valéry it is replaced by the discourse of 'l'Être vivant ET pensant [. . .] poussant la conscience de soi à la capture de sa sensibilité [. . .] sur la *corde* de la *voix*' (xxii, 436). Perhaps the supreme irony of his position here is that he has come closer in essence to the powers of poetry of which Mallarmé dreamed than those which the proponents of Structuralism have had in mind in making Mallarmé their champion.[38] 'On eût dit qu'il pressentait ce qui se découvrira quelque jour', he wrote of Mallarmé,

> et dont on voit déjà plus d'un présage: que les formes du discours sont des figures de relations et d'opérations qui, permettant de combiner ou d'associer les signes d'objets quelconques et de qualités hétérogènes, peuvent nous servir à nous conduire à la découverte de la structure de notre univers intellectuel.   (P i, 685–6).

Here, surely, speaks the true 'structuralist' in Valéry, but one with a very different idea from Mallarmé of what constituted the means to the poet's one true commandment: 'donner à la voix en acte une sorte de vie propre, autonome, intime, impersonnelle. . . faire de la parole un résonateur de l'esprit' (vii, 71). Wishing to substitute research into language for the whole of philosophy (xxvi, 627), it is to the power of the mind working through and in language that he turns as poet/analyst:

> O Langage!
> Personne n'a fait pour Toi
> Ce que je vois être fait
> En Toi –
> Et nécessairement par Toi.   (xxvi, 334).[39]

16

PART ONE

I

Poetic development

A un certain âge tendre j'ai peut-être entendu une voix, un contr'alto profondément émouvant...Ce chant me dut mettre dans un état dont nul objet ne m'avait donné l'idée. Il a imprimé en moi la tension, l'attitude suprême qu'il demandait, sans donner un objet, une idée, une cause (comme fait la musique). Et je l'ai pris sans le savoir pour mesure des états et j'ai tendu, toute ma vie, à faire, chercher, penser ce qui eût pu directement restituer en moi, nécessiter de moi – l'état correspondant à ce *chant de hasard*; – la chose réelle, introduite, absolue dont le creux était, depuis l'enfance, préparé par ce chant – *oublié*.   (IV, 587).

It seems important to appreciate that for Valéry there are two basic urges in the creative sensibility: the one towards externalisation and the other away from it; the one towards spontaneous expression in response to an emotion (not necessarily the expression of the emotion), and the other towards the checking of that emissive aspiration in favour of the listening equilibrium of inner monologue. Where Monsieur Teste represents the thinker who chooses complete outer silence in relation to these two conflicting impulses, the poet might be thought to choose a compromise. He will attempt to simulate in outer language the dynamic voice of that 'silence au tumulte pareil' where the two impulses towards speech and secrecy balance each other. The position is not quite equal, however. For the will to speak is already contained in the language of inner monologue, and the language the poet uses is already responsive to the quality of that inner silence where we 'hear' the world in the 'miroir parlant' of our own consciousness, emotion and thought.

This first chapter provides a brief survey – recollective or informative according to the reader's prior knowledge – of the main emotions and influences, of landscapes as well as of people, through which Valéry came to develop the full resonance of his Testian preference for the secret inner process of the mind over

17

and above its outer products: the artistic resources of his 'anti-literary' attitudes. We shall notice in particular the way in which suspicion of the arbitrary became fused in Valéry's mind with the need to keep his own literary works in touch with the sensation of the provisional nature of all definitive 'statements' other than those relating to the finite processes of communication by which human beings relate to the multiplicity of their experience. For it is in this context that the human voice makes its impact in Valéry's poetic universe: 'La *voix* est elle-même un signe, – qui crée à soi seul ou institue l'état langage – Elle ouvre le jeu, annonce que l'on va jouer à communiquer, à correspondre, qu'il faut se souvenir des conventions' (x, 568). The paradox is complete when we discover at the same time that the voice for Valéry is the guarantee of human presence at the heart of emotion:

> Toute poésie gît dans le commencement, ou plutôt est tout le temps un *commencement*. [...] *Car* (dit le voyant) – au commencement est la *Voix*. Et la voix *dit d'abord* être *voix* – *Événement*. Signe, trace d'homme et d'homme *en émoi*, de présence sans distinction de son et de sens, de Musique et de Connaissance/ Présence = résonance = identification. (xxiv, 862).

It is from the basic, irremediable emotion of the power attached to beginnings that Valéry 'begins': not simply from the urge to write, but from the sensation of richness – a sensation limited in itself – which gives rise to thought and to the need to express.

The active part of Valéry's sustained intellectual life could be said to have spanned nearly sixty years (he was born in 1871 and died in 1945). He began to send his poems to friends – as any biographically detailed study will confirm[1] – between the ages of sixteen and nineteen, continuing to write poetry long afterwards (the most fruitful creative period was that spent composing *La Jeune Parque* [1917] and *Charmes* [1922]) and showing a sustained interest in the nature of poetry to the end of his life. The rhythms of this long 'Faustian' development are underscored by three major initial influences or 'actions', as he preferred to call them, which helped provide the formal and thematic impetus of his work. The first was the Mediterranean landscape of his childhood and adolescence (he was born at Sète, where the hillside cemetery overlooking the sea helped inspire in memory *Le Cimetière Marin*); the second was the crisis of 1892 through which he formed his intellectual method in relation to the emotional and arbitrary; and the third was the poetry of Mallarmé which, together with excitement about the writings of Poe and the music of Wagner, helped inspire his passion for psychological generality and rigorous composition in matters of poetic form.[2] I shall look briefly at all three 'actions' while tracing the outer steps of Valéry's development as a poet.

Valéry grew up in the rich yet clear landscape of the Mediterranean: on the one hand, bright burning sea and rock, and, on the other, lavish vegetation – palm tree, eucalyptus, plane tree and pine – stirred and rustled by the hot tramontane wind and taking their place as actors in many of the poems. Indeed, Valéry tells us in his essay 'Inspirations Meditérranéennes' how he felt this landscape not simply to have surrounded, but to have moulded his consciousness. The three pagan divinities of sea, sky and sun are hailed as the physical ingredients of his thought. This whole essay – an indispensable introduction to Valéry's poetic universe – is far more than a mere autobiography inviting us to relate the Mediterranean imagery of his poems to elements of landscape personally cherished in his youth. It reminds us how closely connected in Valéry's thought are abstract and physical, subjective and universal; how easy it was in such an archetypal setting to sense the processes of differentiation and identity which form the basis of the action of human thought whatever its content; how close we are in moments of relaxed yet mentally alert absorption in nature to the genesis of thought in its most universal, preconceptual state: 'la philosophie à l'état naissant' (P I, 1093). Language itself reflects the physical experience at the root of mental operations, Valéry points out (P I, 1094). So closely interwoven for him are processes of pure thought, bodily gesture and visual perception, that a glance over the sea becomes in the same moment a glance over human possibility, the essentially Mediterranean experience by which man is the measure of all things.

> Dire que l'homme est mesure des choses, c'est donc opposer à la diversité du monde l'ensemble ou le groupe des pouvoirs humains; c'est opposer aussi à la diversité de nos instants, à la mobilité de nos

impressions, et même à la particularité de notre individu, de notre personne singulière et comme spécialisée, cantonnée dans une vie locale et fragmentaire, un MOI qui la résume, la domine, la contient, comme la loi contient le cas particulier, comme le sentiment de notre force contient tous les actes qui nous sont possibles.
Nous nous sentons ce moi universel [. . .]   (P I, 1092).

It is not difficult to relate Valéry's 'Mediterranean' reflections to poetry. As many of the lyrical jottings and prose poems – 'Poésie brute' – scattered throughout the *Cahiers* and published works confirm,[3] he never lost, despite his overriding interest in mental phenomena, the basically simple and naïve artistic impulse to catch and render in language the poignantly fleeting aspects of the natural world. Yet is there necessarily a contradiction even here between the aims of external realism and the expression of inner states of mind? 'Délicieux pays, îles de roche bleue sur la mer – finesses infines et éloignées' (I, 688); Valéry can conjure up the qualities of a scene through the emotion by which individual consciousness sustains or loses a sense of the reality of form and substance outside itself, that precious power to keep alive the strange, distinct presence of the external world on which our sense of identity depends.[4] 'Tu m'étonnes, donc tu es' (VII, 31).

'A chaque instant [. . .] nous sommes enfermés dans notre vue par les objets proches ou lointains qui en constituent la composition. Le "monde extérieur" nous contient et nous sommes prisonniers du *changement fermé. La seule issue* est. . .*intérieure*' (XXIX, 99). There is nothing anthropocentric about Valéry's interpretation of the Greek 'Man is the measure of all things.' Human experience is limited to the sensations of reality produced by individual consciousness as an instantaneous centre of its own perceptions, a situation of which we are made aware through a process of rational thought which produces its own sensations in turn. Nor, for Valéry, is pure solipsism involved. 'Nous nous sentons ce moi universel.'

Again it is not difficult to see the relevance of this philosophy of human reality to poetry. With the protagonists of Valéry's poems we enter the inner space of this universal 'Egosphère', the delicately fluctuating distance between consciousness and its objects of perception through which our sense of human identity is constantly shaped and re-born (Baudelaire's 'vaporisation et centralisation du moi'). 'Tout l'univers chancelle et tremble sur ma tige', says the Parque. Indeed, many of the poems might be said to take as invisible subject the processes – of imitation, differentiation, projection, metaphor and metonymy[5] – through which we relate to the world. Whether he wishes to convey the sensation of being immersed in a cherished visual reality of immeasurable worth to the mind in its repetitious circles of thought, or whether he wishes to convey the converse sensation of the worth and fragility of the mind's own internality when measured against the blindly repetitious presence of nature – 'La seule issue est...intérieure' – it is still always the reality of the outer world which Valéry sets at the centre of awareness and the centre of his poetic universe.

Yet there is a further result of Valéry's Mediterranean experience, of great relevance to his poetry. The sensation of being consciously alive in a landscape of space, light, transparency and depth provided the model of a preferred, however fleeting, state of harmony between body, mind and outer world. 'Où l'amertume est douce et l'esprit clair' from *Le Cimetière Marin* is perhaps the line which comes to mind most readily to denote this perfect balance of mental faculties, and perhaps it is through *Le Cimetière Marin* above all that we are led to the heart of the Mediterranean 'action' for Valéry: the sensation of an inner monologue where the continuity of the body checks and distances both the need for outer speech and the need for abstract thought forgetful of its source. In *Le Cimetière Marin*, Valéry draws on imagery of actual Mediterranean-type landscape to help conjure up this experience of human possibility ('c'est qu'un regard sur la mer, c'est un regard sur le possible' [P i, 1093]). Poetry speaks the voice of human possibility and human possibility depends in turn on the capacity for voice, more important than any one thought. Yet there is a sense in which the same landscape and its effects on the mind is the model of the Voice of a poem even when no such landscape is present in imagery, and even when the mind of the protagonist is totally out of harmony with the outer world. We shall see in the following chapter how the poetic state – 'l'infini esthétique' – set by Valéry as the poet's goal is designed, particularly through the 'enchantment' of its phonetic dimension, to reawaken in the reader (and in the poet enriched by the goal of exchange with another) the potential continuity of the mind with its physical roots.

Why should so much responsibility for the creation of this precious continuum devolve to the phonetic? Part of the answer must lie with the nature of existing language as a sound/sense phenomenon. The sound of words must be emphasised to allow sense to enter a structural relationship necessary to the 'flow' of consciousness as voice (see p. 55). Yet there is also a sense in which the deep rôle played by acoustic sound in our sensibility relates to poetry. Where sight is the privileged intellectual faculty relating us to the outer world, the ear for Valéry is the preferred organ of inner attentiveness: 'Elle garde, en quelque sorte, la frontière, du côté où la vue ne voit pas' (P II, 705). Above all, sound awakens in us a sudden awareness of our physical existence in time – 'le *son pur*, qui éveille l'*âme instant*' – precisely the sensation of an 'autre univers' which poetry can harness and humanise in relation to things. For Valéry's response to the external world becomes of the most intimate relevance to poetry in terms of the relation between sound and sight which the experience of inner monologue increases and which the voice of poetry mimics and reveals in outer form. In a certain state of visual sensibility, things become signs engendering the will to expression, signals through which to listen to the voice of our own inner silence, Faust's 'voir et savoir que l'on voit' (equally mysterious in presence as the sound of his own breath).

The poet has the natural sound/sense dimension of language with which to develop and celebrate the physical quality of conscious existence amongst things. The possibility was undoubtedly deepened in Valéry's case by emotional sensitivity to the sound of the human voice. Mingled with the almost mystical Mediterranean experience of his early years was the sound of a voice – 'un contr'alto profondément émouvant' (see p. 17) – and one which later became fused in his mind with the musical arias of Gluck and, at the time of writing *Charmes*, with an overwhelming experience of love.[6]

Genius might be said to create the myths of its past in order to enter, fully self-aware, the landscapes of the future. To look at Valéry's Mediterranean experience in terms of the 'myth' of that early experience of voice is to appreciate – from an aesthetic rather than psychological point of view – that here above all was the death of descriptive rhetoric and of the aims of naturalistic Realism. Valéry had discovered above all the 'singing' state of inner monologue as the natural goal of the poet through the art of composition (a word infinitely preferable to poetic creation or self-expression in the purely lyrical or personal sense): 'Les choses comme merveilleuses et parfaitement incompréhensibles mais parfaitement expressives, les mots comme des créations de position' (xvii, 440). The natural attitude of the poet vis à vis language, his medium, was to be that of the creative sensibility in its double relation to the world of things and to the world of words.[7]

Valéry happened to be born, he says, in the landscape he would wish to have been born in. It is not difficult to see the whole of his poetry as an action on language designed to re-discover creatively the cherished unity of mind and body, intellect and emotion, thought and silence associated with the shimmering talismanic landscapes of his youth. 'La mémoire et la voix: leurs exigences coïncident' (xxv, 789). Valéry's insistence on the signifying action of form is to be taken quite literally. It is the Mediterranean relation of 'forme' to 'fond' he had in mind when he wrote years later that when composing *Le Cimetière Marin* the ideal of contrast and continuity

> exigea bientôt que le poème possible fût un monologue de 'moi', dans lequel les thèmes les plus simples et les plus constants de ma vie affective et intellectuelle, tels qu'ils s'étaient imposés à mon adolescence et associés à la mer et à la lumière d'un certain lieu des bords de la Mediterranée, fussent appelés, tramés, opposés...
>
> (P i, 1503).

The second main influence in Valéry's early life was undoubtedly the famous intellectual crisis centred on the year 1892, a crisis important here both because it gave rise to a 'method' of self-analysis and because the dualism which he discerned then as a potential of consciousness provided many of the images and myths he was to treat in poetry. The elements of a universal psychodrama of 'being' and 'knowing' are always in some way present in his protagonists, the Parque, Narcisse and so on, and always fundamental to his conception of expressive composition. Indeed, '1892' – a period of many years, and of increasing importance in retrospect – was of crucial significance for Valéry's

development as a poet. It caused him to reject his early verses on
the grounds that they were insufficiently demanding intellectually,
and also to return to poetry later when he could justify himself on
the grounds of the rigour of the techniques and aims he imposed.
For these reasons, it is necessary to spend some time examining
'1892', not in an attempt to psychoanalyse Valéry, but in order to
indicate his own attitude to self-analysis – 'curieuse de sa propre
essence', in the words of the Parque – the drive which he felt to
be a natural response to conflict and disturbance, or even a
creative form of anxiety in itself.

'Toute ma "philosophie" est née des efforts et réactions
extrêmes qu'excitèrent en moi de 92 à 94, comme défenses
désespérées', he wrote in his notebooks under the rubric 'Ego',
and he goes on to instance:

> 1° l'amour insensé – pour cette dame de R que je n'ai jamais connue
> que des yeux –
> 2° le désespoir de l'esprit découragé par les perfections des poésies
> *singulières* de M[allarmé] et de R[imbaud], en 92 – brusquement
> révélées.   (XXIII, 842).

The event situated by Valéry in 1892 was a night of great
stress – the 'nuit de Gênes' – when, lying awake in a violent
thunderstorm, he felt himself torn in two between the sensation
of being on the one hand passively imprisoned in his own uniqueness and, on the other, an observer, free to look on: 'Je suis entre
moi et moi' (P II, 1435). It was during that night that he came to
his famous decision to 'defend' himself consciously from the painful effects of his own sensibility. Why submit to the distressing
oscillation between different selves, the tug-of-war between preferred and rejected states of mind brought about by the power of
thought to disobey the rational intellect (XXIX, 584)? Instead he
would turn from the painful *content* of thought to the perception
of its *structure*, the laws of succession which seemed to govern
mental states. He would substitute for the painful sense of discrepancy between cause and effect in matters of emotion, the
reassuring certainty of identification with self-awareness (P II,
1512–13): 'me tirer de tout par production d'*idées*. Cette sécrétion
[...] est mon arme naturelle, et j'ai trouvé dans la notion de
conscience-de-soi, une excitation merveilleuse de cette fonction
naturelle' (XVIII, 105).

'Méthode' and 'manie' are very close, as Valéry always realised. Nor did it escape him that self-awareness is often very close in its defensive procedures to a further form of increased suffering, the circularity sometimes represented in his poetry by the image or associated emblem of a snake biting its own tail – the Gnostic 'ouroboros'. There comes a point where consciousness seems to destroy its own life from within. Yet Valéry's at first instinctive and then more and more deliberate withdrawal into the fortified 'island' of self-awareness became for him a creative instrument totally distinct from merely circular introspection. He began to discover, as did his Monsieur Teste, '*Mystique sans Dieu*' (P II, 34), that from the point of view of an intense awareness brought to bear on itself, thought has its own rewards, not least the creative pain and pride of penetrating its own rituals, limitations, illusions of centricity, and so on – all those intricate patterns so finely brought alive in *La Jeune Parque*. Indeed, what was the 'nuit de Gênes' but, in the words he used to describe that great poem, 'la *modulation* de toute une vie pendant la durée d'une nuit'? It is only when we begin to hear the harmony of different tones in *La Jeune Parque*, splendidly confident and flowing in the heart of the anxieties it is describing,[8] that we begin to appreciate the difference: the universalising rôle of expression itself in widening the gap between 'méthode' and 'manie', and hence the potential power of self-awareness in transcending the sensation of impasse. 'Se contempler, *se connaître* est une tentative pour être' (x, 782).

As his own comment shows, it was to the conflation of two separate sources of emotional disturbance that Valéry attributed the conflict and increased lucidity of this period: one was an experience of unrequited love with its attendant strengths and strains for the sensibility; the other was personal discouragement in the face of the poetry of Mallarmé and of Rimbaud, poetry so disturbingly perfect that it seemed to exacerbate the sense of imprisonment in an individual yet, so far, impotent self. Valéry's later notes show that the two experiences held for him a common sense of inferiority ('impuissance')[9] closely connected in turn with a sensation of unused possibility. In the first case – the experience of passion at a distance – he had become sharply aware of the way in which unwanted mental images have the power to over-

25

whelm our sense of autonomy: 'Fait énorme: il y a des imaginations désagréables' (ɪ, 134). And that such mental images can feed
on themselves obsessionally, resulting in turn in *bodily* sensations
which regenerate their mental causes (xxɪx, 839–41) was a discovery he was never to forget, using it 'redemptively' as the
foundation of a deliberate method of poetic effects. In the second
case – discouragement at the poetry of Mallarmé and Rimbaud –
he had been made similarly aware that his sense of detachment
rendered him vulnerable from the point of view of creative desire
of his own: 'Trait essentiel de cette époque, Insularismes,
despotisme absolu. Rien d'assez *moi*, et ce moi – était une extrême
puissance de refus appliquée à tout – et surtout à ce qu'il pouvait
véritablement *être, faire ou espérer* !' (xxɪɪ, 843). It is this mingled
'orgueil' and 'impuissance' which Valéry was to place at the
centre of his journey of *expressive* discovery into the nature of
human consciousness.[10] For his work is not confined to abstract
analysis of mental mechanisms on the one hand and to confessions
of personal idiosyncrasies on the other. It takes us into a realm
where the most intricate intellectual sensations are approached
from the point of view of their greatest power of communicative
generality.

This highly conscious sensitivity[11] is at its most poetically and
abstractly intense in the jottings in Valéry's notebooks under the
rubric 'Narcisse'. Narcisse knows himself to be both universal and
unique, detached from and yet part of his body: indeed, capable
of an almost inhuman detachment from the finite and yet aware
that he must remain always somebody, a particular self:

> Narcisse. Chaque homme fait peur à son moi. Être *quelqu'un*
> étonne, émerveille, désespère l'organe universel de ce quelqu'un, ce
> en quoi il n'est pas quelqu'un, et qui se voit, lui Tout, contenu dans
> sa partie, et *propriété de sa propriété. Verbes réfléchis.*   (x, 401).

And by 'verbes réfléchis' Valéry is obviously thinking in particular of verbs like 's'entendre parler' and 'se voir'[12] – to hear
oneself speak or to see one's own body – which relate in turn to
the uniquely human faculty for self-awareness or 'dédoublement'
with which he was so deeply concerned:

> Je ne me suis jamais référé qu'à mon MOI PUR, par quoi j'entends
> l'absolu de la conscience, qui est l'opération unique et uniforme de se

dégager automatiquement de *tout*, et dans ce tout, figure notre personne même, avec son histoire, ses singularités, ses puissances diverses et ses complaisances propres. Je compare volontiers ce MOI PUR à ce précieux Zéro de l'écriture mathématique, auquel toute expression algébrique s'égale. Cette manière de voir m'est en quelque sorte, consubstantielle. Elle s'impose à ma pensée depuis un demi-siècle [...]. (P II, 1506).

This capacity for reflexivity becomes externalised in the poetic image of the pool in which the Narcisse of the poems gazes at his own reflection. It is not simply an allegorical symbolism, since the actual experience of seeing one's own body in a mirror is allowed to add its own particular *presence* to the theme of internal self-mirroring in the invisible sense. It is this same theme, raised to its highest point of universality, which Valéry treats in the prose-poem *L'Ange*, written in 1912 and re-touched just before his death almost half a century later:

Une manière d'ange était assis sur le bord d'une fontaine. Il s'y mirait, et se voyait Homme, et en larmes, et il s'étonnait à l'extrême de s'apparaître dans l'onde nue cette proie d'une tristesse infinie. [...]

'Ô mon étonnement, *disait-il*, Tête charmante et triste, il y a donc autre chose que la lumière?'

Et il s'interrogeait dans l'univers de sa substance spirituelle merveilleusement pure, où toutes les idées vivaient également distantes entre elles et de lui-même, et dans une telle perfection de leur harmonie et promptitude de leurs correspondances, qu'on eût dit qu'il eût pu s'évanouir, et le système, étincelant comme un diadème, de leur nécessité simultanée subsister par soi seul dans sa sublime plénitude.

Et pendant une éternité, il ne cessa de connaître et de ne pas comprendre. (P I, 205–6).

L'Ange has as one of its main themes the potential suffering within consciousness at the discrepancy between the realm of pure knowledge and the mysterious fact of being: 'être' and 'connaître'. Yet at the same time the tone is one of almost mystical calm and unity.[13] Someone, a third power – 'la conscience de la conscience' – is beyond this dualism at the same time as it is experienced, someone whose emotion is that of not being able to coincide with suffering or happiness, but whose voice is full of 'presence' in the poem itself. It is precisely because of the precious distinction between knowing and understanding that the Self for Valéry continues to survive: the mysterious existence of the creative sensibility.[14]

Valéry had begun to write poetry at a relatively early age,[15] attempting, like Rimbaud, to master the styles of many masters: Baudelaire, the Parnassians – Leconte de Lisle in particular – Verlaine and the Symbolists, or, even further back, Villon, Ronsard, Malherbe, Racine, Chénier. Many of these styles can be found woven mimetically and allusively into *Le Cimetière Marin* as the 'voices' of a common poetic heritage. It was the pull of a poetic mysticism somewhat similar to that of the English Pre-Raphaelites (writing at the same time as the French Symbolists) which seemed most to exert a hold on him at this time. He wrote in 1890:

> Je sens que le parnassien qui a d'abord été Moi se dissout et s'évapore...Il me semble que ce n'est plus l'heure des vers sonores et exacts, cerclés de rimes lourdes et rares comme des pierres! Peut-être faut-il écrire des choses vaporeuses, fines et légères comme des fumées violettes et qui font songer à tout, et qui ne disent rien précisément et qui ont des ailes...[16]

By 1892, it was the Symbolist mode of expression which seemed to prevail. Valéry began to publish – in the review *La Conque* run by his friend Pierre Louÿs – poems with titles like *Rêve*, *Élévation de la Lune*, *Fleur Mystique*, *La Suave Agonie*, *Le Jeune Prêtre*, where the words and properties used – fleeting veils, angelic choirs, marble and moonlight – denote suggestiveness rather than lead the reader to create it. This is not his 'natural' style, and he is quick to describe himself as 'pré-raphaélite malgré moi'.

The immediate result of '1892' was that Valéry turned his back on literature. It required, to use Monsieur Teste's words, a veritable 'sacrifice de l'Intellect'.

> Le littérateur – le plus grand – *pense*, au fond, comme qui que ce soit, malgré habileté, abondance, inventions. Il diffère par là du philosophe vrai, du savant, du saint – de tous ceux qui ont attenté à leur pensée en géneral et deviennent un système... (II, 626).

Only the poetry of Mallarmé with its finely discriminating economy of words used almost as if they were mathematical

symbols could escape Valéry's scorn for the vagueness and personalised subjectivity of 'Literature' in general. He turned instead
to the *Cahiers* and a 'Système' of his own. This is the period,
from 1892 to 1912, in which he published no more poetry, and
which has so often been referred to misleadingly as a period of
silence.

Valéry once described 'la Poétique' as a general study of
creative fabrication ('Faire') 'qui a pour application et dérivation
celle de faire des *œuvres de l'esprit*. Inutile et arbitraire traité en
utile et nécéssaire' (xxiv, 801). In order to examine the way in
which this interest is relevant to the poetry he wrote at the end of
the long preparatory and in its own way richly productive period
of the so called 'Silence', two further influences remain to be
introduced: that of Poe and that of Mallarmé. Their poems were
the 'stars' in the night sky of his creative ambition, as we see in
'Poème' – the points of perfection contemplated by the Angel we
have just seen seeking its 'cause' in vain in the 'ciel clair':

> Là brillait l'Hérodiade
> Là la pâle Ulalume
> Et là des Idées – Ô mon ciel – et ces nébuleuses de créations non
> realisées.   (viii, 441).[17]

It is noteworthy that conversations with close friends, such as one
with Mallarmé about Poe, are described as the most intense
experiences of these years:

> C'est un mélange de haine et amour, une intimité sans merci – avec
> une croissance de divination mutuelle, d'approximation, une fureur
> d'aller plus vite et plus à fond de l'adversaire cher, que lui. Tient du
> combat, de la course réduite à deux, du coït. [...] Preuve de
> l'existence de l'homme. – Écrire ce colloque serait un projet plus
> digne que toutes ces littératures sans force.   (iv, 908).

Valéry never lost the urge to measure himself in dialogue with
another human being and poetically to recreate the excitement
and joy of sensing the invisible 'tree' of the human voice grow
from direct interaction with another mind, a form of creative
exchange he considered to be richer in creative energies than
passionate love:

> L'inflexion, la plénitude, le timbre sans prix, le dessin miraculeux de
> la forme interne à la fois désir et possession, regret, espoir, durée,
> mouvement et ce qui meut et est mû, avec le plus haut et le plus bas,

arbre gigantesque de la Voix, arbre sacré, poussé dans la chair, chargé
des idées, Poésie même, dont le corps et les rameaux sont les
certitudes et les puissances de la Veille, mais la matière est rêve
[...]   (VIII, 38).

'Tout ceci, en présence des 2 ou 3 idées de première valeur que
je trouvai dans Poe. (Self-consciousness)' (XXII, 842), Valéry
wrote, looking back on the period from 1892 to 1894. Mallarmé
and himself alone had isolated, dissected, hoarded and adored in
secret the abstract idol of the perfect self, 'c'est-à-dire de la *self-
consciousness,* héritage de Poe' (XXIX, 536).

What were these 'two or three' ideas and their relevance
to poetry? Valéry's most frequent reference to Poe concerns
a phrase, 'Ce merveilleux cerveau toujours en éveil', which
Baudelaire had used of the American writer. Together with Poe's
own idea that 'man' is far from having realised in any genre the
perfection of which he is capable, it made a catalytic impression
on his mind: 'Ceci agit comme un appel de cor – un signal qui
excitait tout mon intellect – comme plus tard le motif de Siegfried' (XXII, 489). In fact it was through his personal interpretation of Poe's idea of unrealised human potential that Valéry
came to channel his adolescent and somewhat mystical idea of
perfection into the notion of an unrealised intellectual power
always greater than the productions through which it is achieved
(XXIII, 188).

The way in which Valéry took over and transformed this idea
confirms and echoes the extraordinarily fruitful effect Poe had on
many French Symbolist writers, despite frequent discrepancies
between his own meaning and the ideas to which he helped give
rise.[18] And since it was Baudelaire's enthusiasm which had made
Poe's ideas popular in France in the first place, it confirms at the
same time the close bonds of literary admiration or like-minded-
ness which Valéry was developing even at a time when literature
was alien to him. Indeed, it is significant that his admiration for
Baudelaire should be expressed in terms of praise for 'une intelligence critique associée à la vertu de poésie' (P I, 599). Without
critical intelligence brought to bear on language, poetry would
remain far behind music in the art of formal composition and
continuity of effects (XXIII, 273).

In the light of what we have seen of the intellectual feelings of vulnerability or even inferiority brought to a head in the crisis years, it is not difficult to understand how Poe's idea of unrealised potential encouraged Valéry. It did so in an obvious sense, in that it helped him to believe himself still capable of creating works worthy of those he admired – Mallarmé and Rimbaud. But in a much more subtle sense it helped crystallise the idea of capitalising creatively as the material of his own poetry on those very feelings of unrealised potential – the emotional resonance of 'effets sans cause' – which had so disturbed him previously. Poe's idea of the universality of this notion encouraged Valéry to concentrate on it as his own particular intimation of an important humanist and psychological truth. Poetry, accordingly, would be the discourse or actualisation of the *possible*, the voice of that part of ourselves which refused the confinement of definitive judgements, and which – unlike Gide with his trust in the unity of personality (xv, 648) – Valéry saw as the only true source of our creative individuality.

At the same time, Poe's thought was directly responsible for enabling him to relate to poetry the intellectual interests of the *Cahiers*. 'Poe le premier a songé à donner un fondement théorique pur aux ouvrages' (xii, 703), he writes, 'Et puis l'idée: on ne vit qu'une fois – Effectuer le maximum de combinaisons – Daimôn' (xxiii, 188). There are several ideas from the *Philosophy of Composition* which could not but impress someone who had tended to think of poetry as the mere expression of vague and arbitrary ideas. In the first place, poetry for Poe was based not on 'inspiration', but on formal composition. In his account of the genesis of his poem *The Raven* he even suggests that he had calculated all its effects on the reader in advance, an idea which became of great importance to Valéry. In the second place, poetry for Poe was founded – at least in Valéry's eyes – on a form of psychological analysis, on analysis of the laws of the mind rather than on the expression of mere personal states. The notion that poetry, by means of the skill and judgement brought to bear on language during the process of composition, might relate to something 'real', some subject outside the domain of the arbitrary content of the imagination already appealed to Valéry above all else. Confirmed by his reading of Poe, he went on to make it the basis of his own approach to poetry, where he saw himself as

31

possibly the first to close his mind to traditional notions of expression and to begin all over again on a purely analytical foundation (XII, 703). At the same time he was able, as he says later, to formulate clearly his notion of 'Poésie' as a general problem surprassing in interest and complexity the study of all particular poems:

'Je me mis à considérer la Poésie en tant que problème général – production complexe où tous les constituants de l'action à conditions psychiques, conscientes ou semi-conscientes, ou inconscientes, devaient figurer [. . .] Je voulais savoir ce que je faisais.'   (XXVIII, 252).

The famous notion of poetic composition as a lucidly conceived 'exercise' of mind, valuable as a form of self-construction through awareness, obviously has its roots in this kind of practical research. Poe was for Valéry one of the few thinkers who suggested that one might try in some field to travel 'jusqu'au bout',[19] to the limits of self-analysis and thus to the threshold not of the unconscious, but of the conscious mind itself: 'jusqu'à un certain mur – et la certitude que là commence vraiment l'infranchissable. Je me parcours indéfiniment. Je me regards me parcourir – et *ainsi de suite*' (I, 809).

But there is another side to Poe's writings which attracted Valéry as a young man and to which he seemed to return from a different intellectual perspective nearer the end of his life. I am thinking here not of *Tales of Mystery and Imagination* – whose macabre anecdotes appealed more to Baudelaire's taste for the exceptional than to Valéry's taste for the universal – but of *Eurêka*.[20] Here Valéry found the exciting notion of 'consistency', according to which the universe is constructed with a deep symmetry present in the structure of our minds: 'L'univers est construit sur un plan dont la symétrie profonde est, en quelque sorte, présente dans l'intime structure de notre esprit' (P I, 857). And from this notion it was but one step to the vindication of poetic intuition as a means of knowledge: 'L'instinct poétique doit nous conduire aveuglément à la vérité' (ibid.). No mere adolescent idealism, this sense of symmetry remained basic to Valéry's whole notion of poetic 'harmonics', helping him to transpose the spiritualist metaphysical conception of Poe into a materialist vision of his own where the transcendental potential of the individual mind is preserved without recourse to anthropocentric values – 'Tout aspect réel se présente donc comme *désordre* d'un ordre lié à l'être pluriel' (xɪ, 257). The 'figure' of the universe cannot escape from the 'figure' of language within the sensibility, and in the 'figure' of the poem this relationship is revealed.

'L'influence de la mer natale sur mon esprit' was not the only major influence on Valéry's mind and poetic development during the formative period of his life. It was during this early period that he was persuaded by his friend Pierre Louÿs to send some of his sonnets – *Le Jeune Prêtre* (P ɪ, 1578), *La Suave Agonie* (P ɪ, 1585) and, a little later, *Narcisse parle* (P ɪ, 82–3) – to the older poet, Mallarmé, then at the height of his career.[21] Mallarmé's response was encouraging and the beginning of a personal friendship continued until his death in 1898. Both as person and poet he provided the model of an affection and respect which was to become deeply ingrained in Valéry for the rest of his life. Does this mean that Valéry is to be seen simply as the follower of Mallarmé? Notes and letters of the period reveal a deeply ambivalent attitude, confirmed intellectually as Valéry looked back on the experience,[22] and one which it seems important to pursue further if we are to appreciate what lies behind the apparently opposite definitions of poetry attributed by Valéry to Mallarmé and himself: in the one case the 'Voice of Language', and in the other the 'Language of the Voice'.

Undoubtedly Mallarmé's poetry made an overwhelming impression on Valéry. Here was a poet who had turned his back on Lamartine and Musset – so often scapegoats for Valéry in his disillusionment with 'Littérature' – and who had produced instead a finely wrought 'alchemy' of words based on an attempt to understand language itself, the substance of literary form:

> Mallarmé, le premier, ou presque, se voua à la fabrication de ce qu'on pourrait nommer les *produits de synthèse* en littérature, par analogie avec la chimie, – c'est-à-dire des ouvrages – ou *plus exactement* des *éléments d'ouvrages* construits directement à partir de la matière littéraire qui est langage – et par conséquent impliquant une idée et des définitions du langage et de ses parties. Idée 'atomique'.
>
> (ɪx, 206).[23]

This same attitude to poetry as a craft of language became a central part of Valéry's poetry likewise, and he was certainly influenced by Mallarmé in attempting to separate the language of poetry from the language of ordinary discourse (p. 51). Valéry's mistrust of Romantic poetry had been only partly assuaged by his discovery of Baudelaire, whose poetry he felt lacking in harmonic density of effect. It was an impression which seemed expressly made to create 'le besoin, ou plutôt la *nécessité* de Mallarmé' (P II, 1532). Yet where Poe was a revelation to Valéry, Mallarmé was a problem. There were certain aspects of Mallarmé's poetic aims of which he felt intellectually uncertain and which gradually revealed the differences he felt he should develop from the point of view of a distinct poetic theory and practice of his own. 'J'attachais un grand prix à *une partie* de l'esprit de S.M. – pas à tout'; 'J'ai développé ma différence.'

One of the most problematic areas of Mallarmé's life and thought for Valéry was the unswerving faith on which it seemed to rest:

l'étrange et inébranlable *certitude* sur laquelle M[allarmé] a pu fonder toute sa vie [...] son entreprise si heureusement réussie de se recréer, de se faire, en un mot, l'homme même d'une œuvre qu'il *n'a pas accomplie* et qu'il savait ne pas pouvoir l'être.   (XXIV, 283).

This artistic perfectionism Valéry admired and envied while fearing in a sense the void at its heart, the vertiginous gratuity of a universal system made from the formless which must itself return to chance. It was from precisely the same sensation of thoughtful anxiety that Valéry created his own sense of poetry – '*Mystère, Hasard.* Ces deux aspects de la transformation du *rien* (mental) en *objet* (vers)' (XXV, 707) – yet in his own case he is wary of placing so much weight on the work itself. 'Pour lui l'œuvre. Pour moi, le moi'; 'Mallarmé ne s'occupait guère que de la forme' (XXIV, 117). Poetry is important only as the instrument of self-awareness and for the transformation of the reader's mind. In fact Valéry attempts to enchant us through the musical modulation of poetry, causing it to become permeated with the emotion of its own 'fiction'. Never does he attempt to construct within it a system of pure thought. 'Mais il y a autant de poésies que l'on veut',[24] he writes of that form of poetic discourse isolated by Poe, Mallarmé and Verlaine,

Mais, quant à moi, – ne voulant cependant renoncer à ma manière assez serrée de voir les choses, et surtout les êtres (qui s'était faite et développée hors et *contre* toute poésie), j'ai pris le parti singulier de donner à la musique et aux modulations et inflexions presque toute la fonction d'enchantement, réservant le fond à ma pensée – et l'exprimant quand je ne pouvais le laisser dans les coulisses du poème – dirigeant sans se montrer.   (xxi, 479).

We come, then, to the paradox which perhaps reveals most clearly the contrast at the heart of the two conceptions of 'Poésie'. For Valéry, influenced by his knowledge of science and mathematics, poetry is but one form of metaphorical language vis à vis the 'reality' of mental experience, where for Mallarmé poetry itself is the only true reality. For Valéry – and here is the paradox – poetry must create its own presence by appealing to the laws of being governing the sensibility outside itself. For Mallarmé, poetry must present the sensuous reality of the void introduced by consciousness into the material universe. 'Tout au monde existe pour aboutir à un beau livre.' From the point of view of the self-referentiality of poetic language, two basically different attitudes are once more revealed. For Valéry, the substance of language must be increased in order to reveal the laws of being outside language ('Faire de la parole un résonateur de l'esprit'); for Mallarmé, the same process leads to the manifestation of language itself ('La pensée exprime la parole').[25] Or, to return to our central thesis, for Valéry poetry is the voice of the living and thinking being; for Mallarmé, poetry is the voice of language. The poet's task is to allow language to reveal its relationship with the universe, where for Valéry the poet's task is to use the creative virtualities within language to reveal the creative virtualities of the human sensibility. Poetry could never contain within itself except in terms of desire the definitive link of mind and universe to which he felt Mallarmé aspired.[26]

The difference between the two forms of poetry is not that between sensuality and abstraction. Both poets are equally sensual and abstract in their different ways. Nor is it one of consciousness of language. Both place the highest value on language as form conserved in a self-referential state; and Valéry could just as well be thinking of his own as of Mallarmé's poetry when he writes

.. Alors apparaît un art du langage à l'état pur et une combinatoire ou spécieuse poétique qui a sa fin en soi-même – les objets visés par le discours n'étant que pour lui permettre d'exister (suivant la tradition qui veut qu'il ait un sens et à peu près un seul) et non plus lui pour eux. (IV, 782).

Where the conceptions of 'Poésie' show most difference in practical terms is in the amount of emphasis in Mallarmé's poetry on structural images relating to the action of writing,[27] where the imagery of Valéry's poetry relates to the universe of sound, sight and breath. Indeed, the 'music' of the two poets is totally different: in Mallarmé's case an abstract music of structural relationships;[28] in Valéry's case a music of the living being created in response to the reader's living organism (see Preface, n.5). For Valéry, the poem is a falling-short of what we are in potential when we speak; for Mallarmé a revelation of what we can now be. For Valéry, 'une parole de modulations et de relations internes – dans laquelle le physique, le psychique et les conventions du langage puissent combiner leurs ressources' (XXII, 435–6); for Mallarmé a perfect microcosm of form, refracting like a diamond the facets of universal beauty. For both poets impersonality, but for Valéry the re-simulation of the subjective; for Mallarmé, the voice of impersonality itself.

Valéry became more and more aware of the differences between Mallarmé and himself in the course of his career. He has his own aesthetic, certainly no imitation or less timid version of Mallarmé's extreme form of art. Yet as he gained confidence in his own identity as a poet, he might be said to have become equally convinced of the rôle of Mallarmé in revealing him to himself. Valéry's poetry is full of the emotion of the distinct worth of Mallarmé,[29] and it would seem fitting to end this brief discussion of their possible differences – the differences which Valéry found so vital to friendship – with the free-verse poem of 1912, *Psaume sur une voix*, inspired by Mallarmé's own voice:[30]

> *A demi-voix,*
> D'une voix douce et faible disant de grandes choses:
> D'importantes, d'étonnantes, de profondes et justes choses
> D'une voix douce et faible.
> La menace du tonnerre, la présence d'absolus
> Dans une voix de rouge-gorge,
> Dans le détail fin d'une flûte, et la délicatesse du son pur.
> . . . .
> Qui n'eût saisi les mots, qui l'eût ouï à quelque distance,

Aurait cru qu'il disait des riens.
Et c'étaient des riens pour l'oreille
Rassurée.
Mais ce contraste et cette musique,
Cette voix ridant l'air à peine,
Cette puissance chuchotée,
Ces perspectives, ces découvertes,
Ces abîmes et ces manœuvres devinés,

Ce sourire congédiant l'univers!...

Je songe aussi pour finir
Au bruit de soie seul et discret
D'un feu qui se consume en créant toute la chambre,
Et qui se parle,
Ou qui me parle
Presque pour soi.   (P ɪɪ, 682 [ɪv, 684]).

The quietness of this voice is like the tone of voice which Valéry requires in the reader of his own poetry, a tone haunting 'Ni les abîmes, ni les sommets' (p. 60) so that the Voice of the poem may speak through it and by means of it. Just so the reticence of Mallarmé's voice in relation to the universal discoveries he had made. And yet we find in this passage the emotion of the living voice as a creative principle in its own right which Valéry set at the heart of his experience of poetry and of love as a potential 'music of being' through which not merely sound but the whole personality of the speaker is brought alive. One cannot be everything. Valéry chose to be a poet 'limited' to the expression of the sensation of potentiality in the face of the finite, a poetry of possibility synonymous with the experience of conscious love. So deeply moved was he by the rich, abstract intelligence of another human being that his whole poetic quest – 'le Langage issu de la Voix' – might be seen in part as a homage to Mallarmé the person, a friend who had become the voice of poetry itself. For what Valéry admired above all in Mallarmé was the ability to be a complete human being and to relate art to the difficult intellectual task of drawing out capacities for wholeness which one would not otherwise know one possessed. Of the expression of this human plenitude in a work of art, he felt Mallarmé had dreamed without necessarily accomplishing it himself:

Synthèse de la faculté d'observation immédiate, non secondaire mais primitive, de la conception de l'homme, de la capacité com-

binatoire et logique – et de la plus intense individualité, particularité,
sensibilité sensorielle et sentimentale –

Voilà un être complet.

Poe, Lionardo – et aussi Mallarmé ont songé cela. [. . .]

Métaphysique ruinée – Certitude = Beauté. Mais œuvre doit ne
laisser aucune faculté libre de ruiner le reste.   (xxiv, 438).[31]

Valéry returned to poetry publicly in 1912, when Gide and the
publisher Gallimard attempted to persuade him to publish a
volume of some of his early poems and related writings. It was to
be a step of far greater significance than he at first realised, for,
after looking back on his early poems with the initial sensation of
being an 'enemy' father estranged from the children he had
produced, he began to rise to the challenge of revision and modification, changing many of the poems into virtually new ones, or
finding himself working into the primitive thread of the old the
innovations made possible by a more mature technique. It was
the unevenness of quality and the lack of musical substance in
the earlier verses which challenged him most. The revised poems
were published as *Album de Vers Anciens* – the first version in
1920, and an extended version in 1926. So began Valéry's second
poetic Spring, a period of intense creative renewal in which, in
his late forties, enriched by the intellectual gains of the preceding
years of abstract research, he renewed contact with an earlier
creative self.

The final *Album de Vers Anciens* consists of such poems as *La
Fileuse, Orphée, César, Un Feu distinct, Narcisse parle, Épisode,
Vue, Valvins, Été, Profusion du Soir, Anne* and *Air de Sémiramis*
(P i, 75–95), all of which contain elements of poetic craftsmanship
which show Valéry to be already a poet of emotional and intellectual skill. If any main difference distinguishes the 'poèmes de
jeunesse' from the 'poèmes de majorité' now found grouped
together in the volume, it might seem to be that the first are more
'Parnassian', reminiscent of Heredia,[32] while in the second,
Valéry is developing a form of expression closer to that which
made him famous later. This produced more musicality of
language, a greater power to weld the inner moods of the poem
into a melodic unity while conveying the separate nature of the
mind even in its points of closest interaction with a natural scene.
There is also, through greater emphasis on the experiences of

language in the poem, a different blend of naturalness and 'préciosité' – for there is always a deliberately stylised element in Valéry's poetry which prevents us from identifying with the voice of the speaker to the detriment of the Voice of the poem in ourselves (see p. 14). The 'precious' element has been transferred from recherché Symbolist words to imagery and syntax; while naturalness is present in the way in which fluctuations of landscape appear to determine as well as to reveal psychological fluctuations of mood.[33] Valéry moves further from external narrative and descriptive elements for their own sake, towards intensification of the inner reality of the mind, particularly from the point of view of the mental co-ordinates of privileged moments unstable in themselves (x, 487), 'Purs drames' as he calls them revealingly (P I, 1605). This is so not only in the increased prominence of compositional elements of the poems – studies of their variants show the variety of verbal and rhythmic possibilities through which he was constantly working to achieve such effects[34] – but also in his growing preference for a relatively small number of themes and images which he aimed characteristically to modify and develop in depth.

Despite the diversity of the poems, the imaginative universe of *Album de Vers Anciens* has a striking unity. The reader's predominant impression is of a world of intense, cherished sensations: the sight of the setting sun, the surfeit of sense-impressions on Summer days; the rich, languid landscape of the moon; fresh water on gravel; the fierce, liquid, and yet almost solid-seeming qualities of space and light; the sight of trees consuming themselves like flames or undulating like tresses of hair; naked skin like the fruit in Renoir's paintings; caressing hands; forms and shapes gathering, fading, delicately poised before loss. It is a landscape of intense intellectual sensuality, a landscape where things constantly hover and dissolve more because the mind cannot statically sustain them in their beauty as through natural processes of loss and decay, or, in *César, Un Feu distinct* or *Air de Sémiramis* – the latter included in the original version of *Charmes* – a landscape of things almost obliterated in their own exactitude by an intense upsurge of imagination. Valéry has the power to conjure up impressionistically the most overwhelming sensations, for instance the buzzing, porous nature of the Summer in *Été* – yet at the same time the power to reflect the distinct world of the mind savouring or fearing or rejecting the wealth of sensations it enjoys.

> Été, roche d'air pur, et toi, ardente ruche,
> Ô mer! Éparpillée en mille mouches sur
> Les touffes d'une chair fraîche comme une cruche,
> Et jusque dans la bouche où bourdonne l'azur; (P I, 85).

Before the more vocally 'biological' poetry in *Charmes*, we may discover here, hovering between the two proverbial extremes of the precision of the Realist and the mystical suggestiveness of the Symbolist, a particular quality which brings to mind the phrase 'mystique de la réalité pure' or 'La Voix des Choses' (P I, 1601).[35]

At the centre of Valéry's poetic universe is analogy, the gift on which Mallarmé once complimented him. Yet analogy must be extended far beyond isolated similes and metaphors, to include the complex web of relationships and equivalences governing the use of language on every possible level of its existence. For poets use analogy, the harvest of Baudelaire's 'correspondances' in infinitely different ways. It is here that crucial shifts of balance can be discerned within theories of the creative imagination and of the relationship between language, mind and world. For the Romantic poets, Nature was, in Valéry's opinion, 'un matériel immense de mots' (XII, 256), its vulnerability a tendency to rely on a mosaic of images alone. The importance of Symbolist poetry lay for him in its stress not on the one-to-one relationship of words and objects, but on the meanings *between* words and thus the multiplicity of impressions they evoke (VII, 633).[36] Yet at the same time as it imbibes the suggestive techniques of Symbolism, nothing is further from Valéry's poetry than pure impressionism or symbolism of an allegorical kind. In fact nothing is further from a symbolic use of analogy. Throughout his rich spread of writings,[37] Valéry can be found developing a method of his own where style and substance are one and in which the analogies between inner and outer world crucial to Baudelaire's poetry are related to a form of harmonic composition involving the reader in the musical virtualities of the living organism: 'Je me suis proposé d'aller un peu plus avant [que Poe, Baudelaire, Mallarmé, Rimbaud] en essayant de me faire une idée plus précise [de la poésie] dont les conditions devaient être une théorie de l'esprit, comprenant une théorie de la sensibilité' (xxvii, 194). Indeed, if Baudelaire's poetry is 'the pivot on which European poetry of the nineteenth century turns towards the future',[38] it is indicative of Valéry's own part in that development that he should single out for admiration the 'vocal' qualities of such poetry, 'la plénitude et la nettêté singulière de son timbre': its capacity, despite sometimes yielding to the temptation of 'éloquence,' to develop a pure melodic *line* (P i, 611).

This notion of a melodic 'line' capable of extending the instantaneous complexity of an impression – something which the explosive quality of Rimbaud's equally influential poetry sometimes failed to do (xxvi, 871–2) – seems first to have been brought home to Valéry through Gluck's opera *Orfeo*, which he heard in 1901. It was an experience which reminded him overwhelmingly of the 'divine' power of the creative imagination, whose source had seemed to have dried up in him since Mallarmé's death. Together with Wagner's music dramas, Gluck's arias were to become one of the inner models of *La Jeune Parque*, the famous long poem begun in 1912 and completed in 1917, and which he intended in some ways as a 'Tombeau de Mallarmé'. It was to be a kind of swan-song in which Valéry welded together the emotion of breaking with a cry the silence of his earlier renunciation of poetry and the emotion of discovering a voice with which to express that 'betrayal'.[39] Far from being his last work, the long exercise of *La Jeune Parque* led in turn to the poems of *Charmes*, published in 1922 and partly inspired by an emotional renewal through love which acquired almost the same significance as '1892'. Indeed, the experience re-united Valéry with the early emotional plenitude 'banned' from direct use at the time of 'Mme R' and of the discovery of the poems of Mallarmé and Rimbaud.

If one of the marks of an artist is the search to create that which would 'explain' the works of the creative mind (xxv, 169) – to seek 'Poésie' – then it is significant that Valéry should link the ambition of his whole poetic quest with the desire to create a musical phrase 'parlée-en-vers': a phrase which in its turn would reconstitute poetically the emotion of that lost human voice of his youth:

Toujours poursuivi par l'Idée de cette phrase musicale – parlée-en-vers que je veux insatiablement faire...Seule phrase – un seul jet ou dessin, sans nulle *fatigue* – Comme je comprends *souvent* qu'un artiste puisse toute sa vie refaire, recommencer la même figure, chercher la même figure toujours plus approchée...*de quoi?* Et je voudrais y arriver par une analyse de plus en plus fine de mon désir [...]. L'œuvre doit être (et n'être que) la maturité du désir même. [...]. Au lieu d'écrire le poëme de suite, écrire le désir, le retarder, le vivre. (VI, 663–4).

2

Poetic theory

La voix intérieure est une oreille qui parle. Entendre parle. La conscience est une bouche qui écoute. Parler écoute. (viii, 378).

Il faut écrire comme on voudrait se parler toujours à soi-même. Mais alors il faut donc surtendre et surélever ce soi-même. (iii, 882).

Le poète a pour fonction de célébrer en même temps qu'il l'illustre cette invention étonnante, le langage. (vi, 923).

Les qualités que l'on peut énoncer d'une voix humaine sont les mêmes que l'on doit étudier et donner dans la poésie. (vi, 732).

While hoping to remind the reader of some of the most famous reflections to emerge from Valéry's poetic theory – largely the heritage of the anti-Romantic position of Baudelaire intensified by Mallarmé – the main aim of this chapter is not to duplicate existing studies,[1] but to discuss the notion of Voice as it relates to this field. I shall suggest that it is in this powerful and self-ramifying area of Valéry's thought, not always obvious if we remember him primarily through his aphorisms on the need for detachment and control in matters of poetic 'fabrication', that we find a 'sensibilité sémantique' (viii, 654) relating to the very notion of poetic utterance and thus helping to reconcile the formal, referential and expressive elements with which any serious theory of poetry must be concerned. It is true that the formalist muse with its apparent denial of subject-matter remains supreme in this theory of poetry, together with its attendant virtues of detachment and control. Yet Valéry's part-intuitive, part-analytic theory of Voice leads us to appreciate the overwhelming rôle of the sensibility in his poetry and, within the sensibility, of a form of expressive desire which virtually becomes the subject-matter of poetry itself. 'Poète-Pianiste', he writes of the processes of 'listening' which lead to the detection of this inner material then to be

43

'heard' by the poem, 's'attendre et s'écouter comme un instrument; comme résonateur d'un désir, comme présence, imminence de choses désirables' (VI, 824), or, 'Comment concevoir ce travail paradoxal? – Écrire ce qui restitue ce qu'on n'a pas donné. Le vers attend un sens – Le vers *écoute son lecteur!*' (VI, 195). A poetics of fabrication, yes, but one in which the poet fabricates linguistic receptivity to the creative desires already abundant in the rich, unconsummated material of reality: 'Se faire source de ce que l'on reçoit' (X, 375).

The subject can be divided into five main topics: the natural relation between language and self-awareness (pp. 44–47); the poetic state – 'Poésie' – both in nature and as the goal of the poet's art of language (47–49); the relation between sound and sense in ordinary language and in poetic discourse (49–55); poetry as the music or song of conscious being (55–62); and, finally, the concept of musical 'figure' in which Valéry's two poetic rhetorics of expression and construction seem to me to fuse in an action or gesture of form, 'la Voix totale' (58–65). Full discussion of the fundamental notion of poetic silence will be left until the end of Part II, for Valéry's poetic theory is to be appreciated as a metalanguage containing the poems through which it was created, poems created in turn from 'une idée aussi nette que possible des moyens et de l'objet d'un art de vers' (XVIII, 233).

We could not begin to understand the living thesis behind the themes and techniques of Valéry's 'poétique du langage' without reference to the human capacity for self-awareness, 'dédoublement', and its relation to inner monologue. There is a popular tendency to think of our inner division or sense of being 'two in one' in terms of a disastrously split self or biological failing. Yet, painful anomaly or not,[2] it is this very 'dualité fonctionnelle' which a 'surprised' thinker like Valéry experiences as responsible for our sensation of self-identity in the first place. Without the duality of self-awareness, there can be no individual 'Moi' (XXVII, 797).

How does Valéry arrive at this affirmation? Significantly enough, through the notion of inner monologue – strictly speaking 'monodialogue' (XIII, 147) – as a form of differentiation enabling us to become aware through the division within. 'Parler,

c'est entendre' (P I, 1488); '[...] point de "moi" sans "toi".
Chacun son Autre, qui est son Même. Ou bien le *Moi est deux* –
par définition. S'il a *voix* il y a *oreille*' (xxii, 304). To speak is
also to hear oneself speak. Even when we do not speak aloud –
perhaps especially when we do not speak aloud – we entertain a
form of rudimentary speech or 'voix intérieure de source' which
increases our sense of conscious bodily existence. 'Par les mots
intérieurement soufflés et ouïs, j'explore ma pensée, ma possession,
mon possible – je me parcours mot à mot; et sans eux, rien ne
serait net intérieurement' (C I, 396). The question just how far
inner monologue depends on the conventions of public language
is a constantly debated one, and Valéry shares the controversy to
a certain degree. A point on which he is quite clearly convinced,
however, and one essential to his theory and practice as a poet,
concerns the difference between internal and external language –
language as it is heard by the subject, and language as it is heard
by the separate listener or even by the listener within the subject's
own consciousness.[3] '*Intérieurement*, s'il y a voix, il n'y a pas vue
de qui parle', the remark on voice and ear relationships continues,

> Et qui décrira, définira la *différence* qu'il y a *entre cette phrase même
> qui se dit* et *ne se prononce pas*, et cette *même phrase sonnante dans
> l'air*? Cette identité et cette différence sont un des secrets essentiels
> de la nature de l'esprit – et qui l'a signalée? Qui l'a "mise en
> évidence"? De même pour la vue.   (xxii, 304).

Taking our cue from this last question – as much a challenge
by Valéry to himself as an indication of his own achievement –
let us summarise the importance of inner monologue from the
point of view of its potentiality for the creative artist (it would
almost be more appropriate to talk of the creative discoverer in
Valéry's case). The first point to notice is the sheer fascination
which Valéry obviously felt at the discovery of what he calls
'Bouchoreille',[4] the inner circuit between speaking and hearing
vital to human consciousness and self-identity. We shall see
shortly how, as a practising poet experimenting with the 'lignes
auditivo-sympathiques-*motrices*' (xv, 173) of the reader, he
arrives at the striking formula 'C'est l'oreille qui parle / C'est la
bouche qui écoute' (vi, 823) to describe the natural treasures
provided by 'Bouchoreille'.

The second point – which helps to explain why sensitivity to inner monologue makes the poet's task an inversion – concerns the relationship between consciousness and the capacity to speak. 'La personne qui parle est déja autre que moi', Valéry notes, '– et je suis fait autre qu'elle, par cela seul que cette *personne qui parle m'*engendre *personne qui entend*' (xx, 15). In insisting that the presence of the conscious subject is dialectical rather than contained within language (see p. 11), he is reinforcing that same sense of difference between the Self and spoken language which we have already observed as offering a challenge to the potential poet/analyst, and which he constantly singles out as being of far greater significance than words in themselves ('La *Personne qui Parle* n'est pas CE qui n'est pas Personne, et qui *Sent* et ne sait *Parler*' [xvii, 742]; 'Il faut chercher, chercher indéfiniment ce de quoi tout ce que nous disons n'est que traduction' [vi, 762]). From this sensitivity to the self-constituting action through and behind words comes the notion – central to this study – of the human voice as a *sign* of the individual human being: 'Le *Je ou Moi* est le mot associé à la *voix*. Il est comme le *sens* de la *voix* même – celle-ci considérée comme un signe' (xxvii, 271). And from this same sense of the individual Self as a conscious presence at the birth of language and of thought comes the challenge to the poet artificially to invert the processes by which language moves away from the reality of the speaking/hearing subject, while respecting the laws by which thought is developed: 'Artificiel pour remonter le sens de la génération ordinaire des paroles; naturel pour observer profondément les lois de leur addition et de leur édification' (iv, 652). It is this total Voice, 'simulation aussi savante que l'on peut de la pensée à l'état naissant' which we shall hear 'sonnant dans l'air'.[5]

Before turning to the poetic state itself, there is one further point to notice in connection with inner monologue. Through an unusual awareness brought to bear on this region of pre-conceptual sensation, Valéry became convinced of the transformational rôle of language in our experience.[6] Whether or not it results in the structures of speech, the action of inner monologue revealed the potential of an expressive energy with the power to stimulate self-awareness as an almost physical self-presence.[7] It was this transformational potential which Valéry felt he could trigger in the reader the other way round, by choosing sounds which would stimulate the mind's ear by stimulating the mouth and lungs in the action of reading (not only reading aloud, although that was preferable). But above all, it was this trans-formational potential which he related to the whole notion of poetry as an art of language designed to communicate by awakening the reader's own need to express. For if poetry for Valéry included practical appreciation of the mysteries of the human speech chain in all its aspects, psychological, physiological, acoustic,[8] it was still devoted above all to the task of increasing self-awareness by manipulating the mental capacities made possible through speech. Discussion of the relation between language and consciousness placed by Valéry the 'Poète-Pianiste' at the service of Valéry the analyst, and by Valéry the analyst at the service of Valéry the poet-craftsman – three vital stages in the process of creative invention – must end, then, on a paradox. By using language outwardly to express the difference between language as speech and language as inner action, the poet is bringing to bear on the process of poetic communication the expressive virtualities of the sensibility already contained in language. That this form of self-referentiality involves neither poetry about poems nor poetry about language should become clearer as we turn to Valéry's vision of 'Poésie', goal and subject-matter of poetry conceived in this light.

In his famous essay 'Poésie et Pensée Abstraite' (P I, 1314–39), Valéry introduces the notion of states of mind as specialisations or departures ('écarts') from the normal state of 'disponibilité' of the nervous system, 'l'état moyen de notre être, l'état d'indifférence des échanges' (P I, 1320). The state of mind to which he refers as the 'natural' poetic state – a state we can experience when in love, listening to music, before a landscape, hearing a pure sound,[9] and so on – is characterised by a sensation of changed inner relationships (Baudelaire's 'correspondances'), a sense of increased exchange between ourselves and the world. Things, ideas, beings, all become as if *'musicalisés* [. . .] résonnants l'un par l'autre, et comme harmoniquement correspondants' (P I, 1321).

However close this description of the natural poetic state to Valéry's requirements concerning the artificial poetic state to be engendered in the reader by the language of a poem,[10] it is crucial to his view of the nature of poetry as a craft of language that the two states are totally different from one another as well. The most obvious difference relates to the poet himself in the process of poetic composition. It is no good simply describing such a state, for then it will not be experienced by the reader. The poet's task is to 'make' rather than to 'say'. Indeed, Valéry went so far as to characterise the act of poetic fabrication as one which turned the poet into a machine for causing inspiration in the reader rather than feeling it himself.[11] Shocking only in their context of standard literary theories of lyrical emission, such aphorisms are based on precisely that sense of the difference between outer language and inner monologue examined above. But there is a further difference between the natural poetic state and the poetic state sought by the poet as gift of the inspiration induced in the reader. Deeply related once more to the specific nature of the poet's verbal medium, this difference concerns the effect of the artificial poetic state itself. Not only is the poem the means to a privileged state of the sensibility more durable and less randomly organised than the fleeting privileged moment in nature – here Valéry joins Baudelaire, Proust and Mallarmé – but, by virtue of its unique relationship to language as a mode of communication capable of self-referentiality, it leads the reader to a state of self-awareness more richly co-ordinated than any other form of art. 'Songez aussi qu'entre tous les arts', writes Valéry with an enthusiasm proportionate to his sense of the difficulties of a verbal medium,

> le nôtre est peut-être celui qui coordonne le plus de parties ou de facteurs indépendants: le son, le sens, le réel et l'imaginaire, la logique, la syntaxe et la double invention du fond et de la forme... et tout ceci au moyen de ce moyen essentiellement pratique, perpétuellement altéré, souillé, faisant tous les métiers, le *langage commun*, dont il s'agit pour nous de tirer une Voix pure, idéale, capable de communiquer sans faiblesses, sans effort apparent, sans faute contre l'oreille et sans rompre la sphère instantanée de l'univers poétique, une idée de quelque *moi* merveilleusement supérieur à Moi.
>
> (P I, 1339).

To draw from common language a pure Voice: with this injunction to the poet concerned with the aim of creating 'Poésie', we have reached perhaps the most fruitful overlap between the

intellectual ethic of a poetry of voice and the question of technique. For while removing poetic discourse as far as possible
from the commerce of ordinary language, it is still to the conventions of ordinary language that Valéry will attend for his action
of poetic purification, and it is still to the expressive action of
speech itself – 'la voix en action' (I, 1332) – that he will look for
stylistic inspiration as that purification takes place.

Many of the literary essays in *Variétié* (P I, 1314ff.) are devoted
to describing the closed but 'infinite' effect sought by the poet
who wishes to create with language a field of relationships capable
of stimulating the laws of demand and response in the reader's
sensibility.[12] Leaving until later the question of how this harmonic
resonance and its organisation is achieved, let us simply note that
poetic discourse is thus both more meaningful and more musical
than language in ordinary usage (P I, 712); that compared to
non-poetic prose, it is as sound to mere noise (P I, 1326) or as the
purely practical and mundane activity of walking to the gratuitous and joyful activity of dance (P I, 1329–30).[13] And what of
meaning in relation to poetic discourse? How at least – for the
notion of meaning is one which concerns the total Voice of poetry
to which this chapter is leading – should the poet relate to the
already double existence of language as 'forme' and as 'fond'?
Unlike the language of ordinary speech – prose in its purely
informational sense – poetic discourse is obtained when form
does not die away as it does when a message like 'Vous avez du
feu?' is transmitted and understood. Like a phoenix perpetually
reborn from its own ashes, it creates the desire to be heard over
and over again – a mnemonic need which is intensified when we
fail to understand what somebody says.
  When Valéry writes of prose as if it is automatically distinct
from poetry, he means an ideal prose constructed for purely
informational ends. *All* language has a double function of 'son'
and 'sens', 'forme' and 'fond', 'inutile' and 'utile'. In fact
Valéry centres his approach to language on a sense of astonishment that so much of its rich potential is redundant in ordinary
speech. Meaning in practical communication is achieved through
a kind of speed in which an action of understanding annuls the
multiple possibilities opened by words themselves and prevents

our falling into the abyss which would open if we lingered too long.

In contrast to this perhaps deliberately over-simplified theory of communication in ordinary language usage (its closeness to the extremist view of Monsieur Teste 'Qui se hâte *a compris*' [P ii, 53] reinforces the impression of its reductiveness), Valéry elaborates his more sustained and complex theory of communication in a poetic use of language: 'L'art de poésie consiste dans le développement des caractères *inutiles* du langage exploités en vue d'un certain effet. Ces caractères inutiles sont ceux qui disparaissent par la compréhension' (xvi, 841). In bringing about the increased reality of language necessary to this exploitation, the poet is in a sense reversing the transitive function of language, 'abusing' the power it makes manifest (xxiii, 228), thwarting the tendency of the mind towards comprehension in the immediate sense. Now, encouraged by the substance of form to linger within the universe of language, we are no longer protected from the ambiguity and multiplicity natural to its being. 'Le sentiment artiste et poète en littérature consiste à percevoir la pluralité de valeurs de chaque mot ou expression, et à essayer de se servir de cette multiplicité' (xi, 172).

To *develop* the useless characteristics of language which have been exploited for a certain effect; to try to *use* this multiplicity: there are certain important qualifying phrases in Valéry's comments which are sometimes overlooked when we are allowing him simply to contrast for us the intransitivity of poetic discourse and the transitive nature of purely informational prose. In fact the action of comprehension is annulled by the poet only temporarily and on one level of language. Having released certain effects of ambiguity and polyvalence, the poet uses and develops their potential in the communicative action of the poem as a whole. Then once more, like the language of prose when it has achieved its purpose, the language of the poem is silent: 'Un bon poème est silencieux' (ix, 342). It seems essential to remember the presence of this secondary form of communication – 'l'acte du langage' – when Valéry's poetic theory is charged with the denial of meaning or, conversely, when his poetry is charged with failure to fulfil an impossible purity of theoretical intent. As we have already observed, poetry for Valéry is *more* meaningful than ordinary language. The confusion arises only through a misunderstanding of the nature of meaning in poetry and, as we shall see in connection with sound/sense values, through a misunderstanding of the range of linguistic elements included in the action of form.

Many of Valéry's comments on the difference between a poetic and an informational use of language are obviously re-statements in his own terms of Mallarmé's already famous insistence on the two distinct functions of language, 'informative' or 'essential' (poetic), and of what Mallarmé called the undeniable desire of his times to separate these two functions as far as possible.[14] Yet is the foregrounding of the substance of language an aim in itself in Valéry's case? Does he use the poetic act to dislocate everyday meaning with the same result? Valéry's constant reference to the action of speech as potentially more valuable than language itself suggests that this is not the case, and that the time has come to examine his theory of the aims of poetic practice from the point of view of the possible original use to which he put his Mallarméan sensitivity to poetry conceived as a 'saying' through the 'doing' of form. We have reached the question of sound/sense relationships in Valéry's theory of poetic communication.

> La poésie, peut-être, c'est toute l'âme, – toute la parole, tout le dictionnaire possible de l'être, tout l'être en tant qu'appels, réponses, actes, émotions, considérés comme un instrument. Telle est la lyre et non autre chose. Parcourir d'autorité, avec liberté totale, sauf les propres règles de l'instrument, ce registre, clavier universel, aux cordes innombrables – Mais chaque fois il faut créer la corde – Montage de la lyre [. . .].   (VII, 425).

Like so many of Valéry's meditations on the total action of poetic invention, this one is packed with suggestions which reveal greater and greater precision in connection with different parts of his thought. Here we find that 'Poésie', the aim of the poet, is no less than to render eloquent the creative sensibility itself, a universal virtuality to be awoken and played on in the reader, and one which is also that of the poet in the process of composition. His own sensibility provides the chords of the lyre on which the poem must play.[15]

'Montage de la lyre': it is characteristic of Valéry's startling control in matters of poetic composition that his own sensitivity to the transformational relationship between consciousness and the action of speaking should have become the initial basis of the process of fabricating a poem – a poem begun, that is, by the need to express the possibilities of speech. Often a poem would originate in a pleasing or intriguing combination of words of random origin (the 'vers donné') which would be followed up artificially by allowing other combinations to form, so far with no other arbiter than the psycho-physiological circuit of 'Bouchoreille' itself.[16] 'Je sens [...] assez nettement se former ou se chercher mes vers dans une région de l'appareil vocal-auditif', Valéry confided, 'et moyennant une certaine attitude de cet appareil (en tant qu'il est capable de modifications musculaires)' (xxvii, 444); 'Le vouloir intérieur requiert les mots et n'a pas de sens hors d'eux. Mais ils sont par leur nature productibles au moyen de muscles, des actes réversibles, excitateurs et excités.'[17]

For a poet whose sensibility scorned the arbitrariness of mere 'saying' and who longed to fabricate from existing language 'une Voix pure', the proven reversibility of the process from thought to mouth muscle provided a rich encouragement. Yet it is not only sounds and combinations of sounds satisfying to the sensibility which the arbitration of 'Bouchoreille' provided. Valéry speaks of the silent production of individual truth in 'ce moi plus particulièrement logé et caché à l'arrière des yeux et dans la partie du masque et de la gorge qui est faite pour parler' (xxiv, 106), reminding us of 'la voix intérieure de source'. In so avidly turning his attention to the 'empire' of 'Bouchoreille' during the process of poetic composition,[18] it is to the capacity for self-awareness through inner monologue, 'la pensée à l'état naissant', that Valéry is choosing to 'listen' as a poet. 'Fais que ma soif se fasse source. Et que mon ouïe intime écoute avec ravissement ma voix intérieure' (xxiv, 283). *This* voice with its restricted lexicon of words[19] will be simulated and retained when the poet/craftsman turns his attention to the organised form of the poem as an external object 'sonnant dans l'air' and combining the 'isolated' state of language as song with the conventions of language as public exchange (xv, 347).

Voilà le poète aux prises avec cette matière verbale, obligé de spéculer sur le son et le sens à la fois; de satisfaire non seulement à l'harmonie, à la période musicale mais encore à des conditions

intellectuelles et esthétiques variées, sans compter les règles con-
ventionnelles...
  Voyez quel effort exigerait l'entreprise du poète s'il lui fallait
résoudre *consciemment* tous ces problèmes... (P I, 1328).

The stages of the complex action of poetic composition are, of
course, overlapping or simultaneous, as Valéry suggests here.
Nor does his own attempt to approach the process as consciously
as possible preclude the resources of the involuntary. Valéry's
appeal to 'Bouchoreille' is a case in point, suggesting that the war
against Romantic 'Inspiration' was fought in the name of the
power of the poetic imagination to organise and adjust levels of
unconscious material rather than to eliminate them in favour of
calculated effect.[20] It is possible to isolate the question of sound
and sense for the purposes of discussion, however, and to use such
discussion to approach the question of overall meaning which
Valéry's poetics of vocal music finally invites us to explore.
  Linguistic sound in general – the existing phonetic sounds and
syntactical groupings of words and the additional patterns of
relationship through which phonetic and rhythmical substance can
be increased[21] – is one of the main means by which poetry makes its
entry into the reader's receptive consciousness, 'tout ce domaine
de la sensibilité qui est gouverné par le langage' (P I, 1458). Valéry
felt that the poet should give as much attention to the existing
sound dimension of language as to its semantic dimension: '...un
véritable poète, un homme pour qui les sons du langage ont une
importance égale (*égale, vous m'entendez bien!*) à celle du sens'
(P I, 1079). The 'vous m'entendez bien' is indicative of the many
misunderstandings which had often arisen in this area of poetic
theory, in particular the assumption that when a poet denies the
importance of 'subject-matter' in his poetry he is advocating the
possibility of an art of pure sound. The area is a complex one
already made famous by Mallarmé, yet it is important to sort out
its essentials with a view to determining the particular and in some
ways unusual relationship of sound/sense values in Valéry's poems.
  As with Mallarmé's poetry, the relation between sound and
sense and of the by no means totally equivalent question of form
and meaning can best be approached through the two distinct
areas of individual words or word groupings on the one hand, and
the total voice of the poem on the other.

Asked about the relationship between sound and sense in the first linguistic space, Valéry's answer would seem to be categoric. 'Chaque mot est un assemblage instantané d'un *son* et d'un *sens*, qui n'ont point de rapport entre eux' (P I, 1328). The Cratyllic notion of a primitive unity of sound and sense is never entertained. Indeed, its absence may help account for the striking refusal in Valéry's poetry to treat sound as a mere support-system of the referential values of words, even after the poet has worked on or against language in its ordinary state. In answer to a question concerning the relationship between sound and sense in the created space of the poem as a whole, however, Valéry's answer would be far more complex even than the notion of an acquired or secondary Cratyllism would imply, and to appreciate it involves looking more closely at the intentions and means of a poetics whose aim is quite literally the solicitation of the reader's voice ('Le vers écoute son lecteur').

In describing the poet as someone for whom the sound of words is equal in importance to their meanings, Valéry is referring to the existing phonetic nature of words, an element which plays as large a part in his attempt to foreground the *form* of language, veiled in ordinary usage, as the semantic dimension of words. Just as the poet accentuates the semantic yield of words by setting them in relationships which increase their power of connotation or 'resonance',[22] so he accentuates the phonetic presence of words by choosing combinations of vowels and consonants, alliterative, assonantal and otherwise, which prevent the immediate disappearance of form. Often extending far beyond the threshold past which the intellect cannot consciously recognise the rôle they play in our experience, these phonetic configurations are one of the most originally thorough features of Valéry's poetic art.[23]

Yet we have already seen that Valéry conceived the foregrounding of the natural phonetic and semantic richness veiled in ordinary language usage as a means to an end: the creation of meaning – expressive meaning – through the poem as a whole. To examine the relationship between sound and sense from the point of view of this new, finely balanced system of meaningful form is to appreciate the appropriateness of the analogy with a pendulum oscillating harmonically between the two extremes. 'Pensez à un pendule qui oscille entre deux points symétriques', writes Valéry in a passage of central importance to the idea of Voice,

> Supposez que l'une de ces propositions extrêmes représente la forme, les caractères sensibles du langage, le son, le rythme, les accents, le timbre, le mouvement – en un mot la *Voix* en action. Associez, d'autre part, à l'autre point, au point conjugué du premier, toutes les valeurs significatives, les images, les idées; les excitations du sentiment et de la mémoire, les impulsions virtuelles et les formations de compréhension – en un mot, tout ce qui constitue le *fond*, le sens d'un discours. Observez alors les effets de la poésie en vous-mêmes. Vous trouverez qu'à chaque vers, la signification qui se produit en vous, loin de détruire la forme musicale qui vous a été communiquée, redemande cette forme. Le pendule vivant qui est descendu du *son* vers le *sens* tend à remonter vers son point de départ sensible, comme si le sens même qui se propose à votre esprit ne trouvait d'autre issue, d'autre expression, d'autre réponse que cette musique même qui lui a donné naissance. (P I, 1332).

The remarkable result of Valéry's treatment of sound and sense as consciously separated variables is that it allows the semantic components of the poem to take on structural value and the structural values of the poem to take part in a semantic or signifying action in turn.[24] For the indissoluble[25] harmony between sound and sense at the heart of poetic speech has now become the invisible subject of the poem, the living pendulum of the voice with its roots in the expressive sensibility which poet and reader now potentially share.

> Le poète écoute, comprend la voix, s'en fait une cachée et essaie de la fixer par son art. [...] Le système de la voix et de l'ouïe se conjugue avec un système de l'ouïe et de la voix dans l'autre – et en celui-ci l'ouïe imprimée par la voix d'autrui doit émouvoir sa propre voix mais ne le peut que par l'intermédiaire central (VII, 6–7).[26]

It is precisely *because* sound and sense are treated and kept as separate variables that this dialectic is possible. Before finally returning to the rôle of the reader in its realisation, we need to examine the concept of music and song – poetic music – through which the total synthesis of this communicative gesture of form takes place.

The association of poetry with music is one of the commonplaces of the Symbolist period. Again Mallarmé comes to mind, with his enthusiasm for the music of Wagner – shared originally by

Baudelaire – and his determination to make poetry capable of a similar power to affect the nervous system. 'Reprendre à la musique son bien' becomes the poetic catch-phrase of the period.[27] The analogy between the two art forms is misleading if we leave out of account the specific nature of each medium: pure sounds in the case of the musician and 'impure' elements in the case of the poet. Nor does the aim of either Mallarmé or Valéry involve the mere imitation of music. In Mallarmé's poetics, it is the written word of poetry, l'intellectuelle parole à son apogée', which becomes the source of true music, the totality of universal relationships in which all existence must culminate. For Valéry likewise it is the discourse of poetry which is brought into its own through the use of non-representational techniques shared with music as an art of pure form. Poetry is more human than music, he notes (VI, 195).

In following the Symbolist idea of treating language 'musically', is Valéry using the same techniques as Mallarmé, however? Does he arrive at a similar notion of poetic discourse in relation to knowledge and universal beauty of form? We have already noticed in connection with Valéry's admiration for Wagner[28] that it was the fusion of technique with the passionate and affective resources of the living organism which appealed to him rather than any 'idea'. In any other region than that of the technical simulation of passion, it is significantly the music of Bach which he came to prefer. The 'Suite en ré majeur', for example, 'Chose sans prix. Donnant l'idée de l'exploitation totale, formelle, fermée d'un Possible commensurable. La basse représente l'attention' (XVII, 60), or, of the art of fugue,

> La *fugue*, relation entre une mélodie et elle-même, dans un champ auditif – où se distinguer et se confondre, jouent,
> Le reconnaissable –
> Le même en contraste avec le même
> Contraste du même et du même –
> L'être et son image – (XII, 527).

Valéry's appreciation for such music centred on its power to operate a kind of living analysis through which he could sense the separate self in the heart of his emotions (P I, 704): its structural equivalence with that total self-awareness which so deeply and constantly moved him as the very emblem of poetry conscious of itself. The terms of his appreciation help remind us that poetry relates to the ideal made possible by the longing produced by music: the ideal of a synthesis of 'being' and 'knowing' in the living organism.

> Entre la chose qui est ce qu'elle est et la chose dont la fonction est d'être autre que ce qu'elle est, il y a un intermédiaire.
> C'est cet intermédiaire, le moyen de la musique.
> (Entre l'Être et le Connaître, travaille la puissante et vaine Musique).
> (P II, 704).

To return to the question of comparison with Mallarmé and with Symbolism: Valéry uses all the musically inspired techniques of sound-patterning, modulation of tone, rhythmic development, suggestion and so on, which he felt to be the natural heritage of an art of language. Yet where this use differs from the Symbolist aim of fluidity or, indeed, from the graphic and spatial music of Mallarmé's equally musically-inspired techniques, is in the notion of the musical continuity of 'being' and 'knowing', mind and body, already a potential of the living organism in its relationship to inner monologue. It is *this* potential that poetry must develop and articulate. We have returned to the notion of the living voice – not music – as the model of Valéry's poetic art, a model involving expressive self-referentiality.

We know that Valéry was deeply moved by the emotive quality of the human voice, to the extent of postulating a singing voice in childhood which had imprinted his sensibility with the creative tension of a desire to reconstitute the impossible object of the need it had instilled (p. 17). It was the singing voice in particular which he held in mind as a model for the monologue of *La Jeune Parque*, and the singing voice, appreciated through the recitatives and arias of Wagner and Gluck, which he most often heard inside himself when coming to terms with modulation, one of the most striking and elaborate of his musically inspired poetic techniques.[29] 'Voix – Poésie', is thus a characteristic jotting in the *Cahiers*,

> Les qualités que l'on peut énoncer d'une voix humaine sont les mêmes que l'on doit étudier et donner dans la poésie.
> Et le 'magnétisme' de la voix doit se transposer dans l'alliance mystérieuse et extra-juste des idées ou des mots. La continuité du beau son est essentielle.   (VI, 732, P II, 550).

We are close to the 'magical' conception of poetry as reflected in the title *Charmes*. 'Le vers doit avoir un caractère *magique* ou ne pas être' (v, 585); '*paroles magiques*, des figures verbales [. . .] dont le timbre, l'ordre, le ton, les temps mesurés, les sons, comptent plus que le *sens*' (xvII, 270).[30]

Yet we have already seen in connection with the sound/sense values of words that Valéry's Mallarméan stressing of the phonetic substance of words above their referential values is a means of allowing the semantic to enter a realm of structural relationships in turn powerfully related to meaning as an action of total form. In enjoining the poet in himself to work on ideas until they are inseparable from song (vI, 725),[31] Valéry is pointing to a region of poetic invention far deeper than the mere imitation of musical techniques in order to seduce by verbal magic. It is one where the notion of song refers to a capacity of the living being, made possible through the voice, and developed in poetry itself, 'l'Être *vivant* ET *pensant* [. . .] poussant la conscience de soi à la capture de sa sensibilité – développant les propriétés d'icelle dans leurs implexes – résonances, symétries etc. – sur la *corde* de la *voix*' (xxII, 435–6). It is to *this* action of co-ordinating self-awareness that Valéry's goal of harmonic relationships is dedicated, and in which the pure expressiveness of music is transcended by a glimpse of the superior Self of which language alone makes us capable. We have finally arrived at 'la Voix totale' and the poet's synthesising attempt to replace the finite abstractions of thought *in* language by a form of discourse consciously in touch with 'le corps vivant': thought in its universal potential of 'la réponse, l'acte et l'instant d'un homme'.[32]

'Pour moi la voix intérieure me sert de repère', Valéry wrote in this connection,

> Je rejette tout ce qu'elle refuse, comme *exagéré*; car la voix intérieure ne supporte que les paroles dont le sens est secrètement d'accord avec l'être *vrai*; dont la musique est le graphique même des mouvements et arrêts de cet être. (vI, 170).

It is important to appreciate that although inner monologue determines the type of words used by the poet in his attempt to simulate the movement of inner being – 'l'être vrai' – it is not itself the goal of poetry, any more than is the fictional identity of the protagonist we find woven thematically into the narrative thread of the poem. The true subject – 'l'Être *vivant* ET *pensant*' – to be identified by poetry is one who does not exist prior to the experience of either poet or reader except as a shared capacity – 'le possible' – to be inventively discovered and made available through its speech. Hence the primacy given in Valéry's poetic theory to the action of articulation, both as a guide for the poet in the process of composition and as one of the means by which the reader enters the same bodily world.

'Si au lieu d'abstraire', Valéry writes in relation to the first of these sources of material (the process of composition from the point of view of the poet's own expressive sensibility),

> pendant le travail d'expression, je ne sais quelle présence de l'être tout entier, de sa vie sensitive et motrice, alors la participation de ce véritable *résonateur* communique au discours de tout autres puissances, lui restitue des caractères tout primitifs, le rythme, le geste la collaboration de la voix par les timbres des voyelles, les accents, introduisent, en quelque sorte, le corps vivant, réagissant et agissant – et ajoutent à l'expression *finie* d'une 'pensée' ce qu'il faut pour suggérer ce qu'elle est d'autre part – la réponse, l'acte et l'instant d'un homme.   (see n. 32).

It is *not* true that poetry for Valéry is about poems. It *is* true, as this remarkable passage confirms, that poetry for Valéry is about the expressive sensibility. And the way in which it is 'about' this subject involves its realisation during the process of its composition. In *this* sense poetry is self-referential.

Yet Valéry's poetry is also self-referential in the manner in which it involves the reader in the realisation of its subject, not least through the action of articulation involved in its existence as sound. Valéry never forgot that poetry relates to an essentially oral tradition,[33] and while he was as conscious as Mallarmé of its graphic dimension on the page as a form of music to the eye, he nonetheless set above all else the appeal of the poem to the mind's ear via the muscles of the mouth and the respiratory function of the lungs. Poetry should be read aloud. In this way we add the vibrant acoustic dimension of physical sound to our experience. Yet even when we do not read the poem aloud, we shall be responding internally to the poet's intricate care over the sound dimension both phonetic and rhythmical.

Valéry once dreamt of enticing a trained singer to read his poems aloud in order to place at the disposal of the poem a diction fully responsive to the changes of tone, timbre, pitch, inflexion, and so on, which he had tried to signal by every possible verbal means (P II, 1261). His interest in the relation between physiology and melody in theatrical voice-production proved particularly fruitful while he was composing *La Jeune Parque*.[34] Yet it is significant to the thesis pursued here that he advised the reader of pure poetry – the goal he set himself, but felt he had obtained very rarely – to approach 'la diction des vers' from a singing register slightly higher than that of the ordinary speaking voice, and to descend towards the register of the poem which lay between (P II, 1260). For to sing or declaim poetry would detract from its power to discover the 'singing being' – 'faire chanter une *Idée* de l'être vivant et pensant' (xxv, 706). To dramatise or emotively interpret one's reading would likewise damage its natural musical tones. The vocal volume which Valéry most admired was a quiet one, relatively monotonous in tone and pitch;[35] and if this seems to conflict with the active involvement of the reader in the poem as utterance, we must remember that the experience of sound which Valéry sets at the heart of his poetry is one of internal sound, sound heard inwardly as a reminder of the living body as organ of consciousness. In taking song as a model, Valéry was taking not sound itself but the continuity of the human voice as inspiration, a continuity which seemed to possess the power to penetrate the listener's consciousness with the presence of its own being:

> Le chant est plus réel que la parole plane; car elle ne vaut que par une substitution et une opération de déchiffrement tandis qu'il meut et fait mimer, fait vouloir, fait frémir comme si sa variation et son étoffe étaient la loi et la matière de mon être. (P I, 1443).[36]

As always, this power of continuity and self-presence is set at the disposal of a fully conscious action on the part of the reader involved in the physical act of articulation. Again it is not the poet or reader who must sing the poem, but the poem which must sing 'la fonction qui parle':

> Pour qu'une œuvre [...] *existe comme par elle-même*, soit 'Poésie', il faut qu'on ait trouvé et fixé le *Ton*. Alors la chose Chante. Le ton est l'essence du style et des rythmes. Il est la clef de l'état de l'homme, qui en accorde toutes les actions diverses. (xv, 46).[37]

Many of Valéry's contributions to the definition of 'poésie

pure'[38] are synonymous with descriptions of a poetry centred on the human voice. 'La voix définit la poésie pure', he states, for example: 'C'est un mode également éloigné du discours et de l'éloquence, et du drame même, que de la netteté et de la rigueur, et que de l'encombrement ou bien de l'*inhumanité* de la description' (VI, 176). One of the most characteristic modes of such poetry – in addition to its expressive subject-matter, its stress on the action of presence involved in speaking, its involvement of poet and reader in a shared action of discovery – is the primacy it accords to stylistic techniques demanding continuity: the modulation of sounds and images, the architectural balance of rhythm, the integration of strophic variation, and so on. Based on the three related abstract arts of music, mathematics and architecture, such techniques provide the natural poetic bridge between 'epos' and 'logos', 'being' and 'knowing'; yet, says Valéry, their full resources as elements of tonal variation were virtually unknown to the Parnassians and even Hugo failed to observe them, 'coupable contre la voix' (VII, 642). Oratorical poetry, descriptive poetry or poetry which sets out to surprise by a mass of unrelated images is as alien to Valéry as philosophical poetry, the mere expression of ideas in versified form. Only such 'musical' artists as Racine,[39] Chénier, Baudelaire, Mallarmé and Rimbaud have known how to utilise this deliberately restrained, almost whispering melody of form. 'La poésie n'est pas la musique; elle est encore moins le discours' (P II, 1260); 'La voix poétique est celle qui institue échange égal entre toutes les parties d'une voix...' (XVIII, 754).

The poets Valéry mentions have all put their 'musical' capacities to different purposes, however. To turn once more to the purposes to which Valéry devotes his own discovery of the musical potential of language is to discover a theory and practice of poetry which radicalises the notion of structure by allowing it to subsume all the various levels of language within itself (phonetic, rhythmic, referential and so on) until they themselves become the expressively semantic components of the poem. Valéry hints as much by characterising tone as the essence of style and of rhythm, rather than by describing tone and rhythm as devices of style.[40] In a poetry of voice it is not thoughts, but the relationships *between* thoughts that become expressive agents, while the function of the Voice of the poem conscious of itself is to communicate the expressive action involved in that form as a total figure of speech.

If discussion of the concept of figure has been left until now, it is because it is not simply a device within a poem – Valéry was scathing of the 'modern' abuse of single devices such as metaphor[41] – but a procedure which incorporates the whole poem as a gesture or expressive form of speech.

For Valéry, the figure occurs in ordinary language usage when speech manifests a certain distance from the most direct or transitive movement of thought. It signals 'le réel d'un discours', the expressive qualities made possible through the action of speaking and lost when we think of what is being said in language itself: 'Le réel d'un discours c'est après tout cette chanson, et cette couleur d'une voix, que nous traitons à tort comme détails et accidents' (P ɪɪ, 85). By multiplying figures of speech artificially, the poet has the power to increase the natural power of the figure to transgress the linguistic action by which form is veiled or destroyed. He has the power to make visible the expressive action that ordinary language usage conceals:

> Le poète qui multiplie les figures ne fait donc que retrouver en lui-même le langage à *l'état naissant*. D'ailleurs, en considérant les choses d'assez haut, ne peut-on pas considérer le Langage lui-même comme le chef-d'œuvre des chefs-d'œuvres littéraires, puisque toute création dans cet ordre se réduit à une combinaison des puissances d'un vocabulaire donné, selon les formes instituées une fois pour toutes?
>
> (P ɪ, 1440).

There has been little growth in understanding of the literary figure since its analysis in classical rhetoric, Valéry suggests. The remarkable consequence of his own usage, based as always on the conservation and development of precious classical concepts,[42] is that in relating the action of poetry to that of the figure in the action of ordinary speech, and by extending its usage to the whole poem, he is allowing the poem to fulfil the same expressive function as speech itself – 'vox in actu'. Now once more, as in ordinary language, the figures of speech by which this action is achieved can be seen as fleeting and transparent:

> Un poème doit être une fête de l'Intellect. Il ne peut être autre chose. Fête: c'est un jeu, mais solennel; image de ce qu'on n'est pas, de l'état où les efforts sont seulement rythmés, rachetés. [...]
> La fête finie, rien ne doit rester. Cendres, guirlandes foulées.
>
> (vɪ, 220).

For Valéry every action of self-definition must remain fleeting and provisional, with no other form or duration than that of the gesture through which it is made. In this sense the human voice is like a flame, a festival, a dance consuming itself from within. Yet the flame, the festival and the dance exist in our minds, as does the voice itself, as the form of an expressive gesture: 'Le ton est comme le geste de la voix' (ix, 771), '[...] une sorte de figure pour l'ouïe' (P i, 208). In making the whole poem a new figure of speech, a creative gesture, Valéry centres his poetry on an extreme paradox or tension: that of an art-form both sensuous and necessary which presents itself as provisional and illusory in the very moment of its communication. In the *Cahiers*, the statement 'Entre l'Être et le Connaître travaille la puissante et vaine musique' (P ii, 704) is followed by 'Musique très belle, je sais que tu me mens' (xvi, 395).

I shall be illustrating later how Valéry's poems convey an intricate range of emotions springing from this very knowledge: the power of the mind to pierce to the heart of its being as an organism without being able to transcend or destroy the 'limitations' of the sensibility on which that knowledge relies for its power. Indeed, poetic voice itself is described by Valéry as 'la conservation de la vie entre les bornes qu'elle ne peut franchir, – c'est là, le chant, le registre. Et la mesure de cet intervalle qui est vivre à plusieurs unités qui sont rythmes' (viii, 41). In poetry presenting itself as musical charm alone, such self-referential knowledge would be fatal. The charm would be destroyed. Yet Valéry's poetry communicates not by charm but by exchange. In poetry based on the goal of expressive dialogue, self-referential knowledge – knowledge of its own source as expressive desire – is the confirmation of the permanent note of consciousness which Valéry sets at the centre of his art.

Le Cimetière Marin sprang from 'une figure rythmique vide' (P i, 1503), its semantic content submitted at all times 'à la volonté ou à l'intention de satisfaire le sens auditif' (P i, 1675). If we have at no time referred to the content of such poetry in itself, it is because the gesture of expressive form at the heart of Valéry's poetry *is* its subject, a subject which demands in turn all the different range of tones and attitudes which themes, sounds, syntax and rhythms converge to provide. 'L'univers musical était donc en vous, avec tous ses rapports et proportions' (P ɪ, 1327), Valéry writes, or 'C'est par notre voix que nous comprenons le chant des instruments' (vɪ, 100). In this sense, the human voice provides the subject as well as the medium of the poem:

> Un poème est un discours qui exige et entraîne une liaison continuée entre la *voix qui est* et la voix *qui vient* et *qui doit venir*. Et cette voix doit être telle qu'elle s'impose, et qu'elle excite l'état affectif dont le texte soit l'unique expression verbale.   (P ɪ, 1349).

Of course this kind of poetry will be rich in themes. At the same time it will resort to symbolism less than any other modern poetic form.[43] Its themes will lead us constantly to the 'presence' of the Self at the heart of the 'absence' of thought; to the living silence and sense of the provisional[44] which underlies our consciousness hearing its own inevitable need to express and change from within.[45]

'Ne crains pas, mais écoute' is the advice of Lucrèce, the thinker, to Tityre, the lyrical artist in the *Dialogue de l'Arbre*:

> lorsqu'il te vient dans l'âme une ombre de chanson, un désir de créer qui te prend à la gorge, ne sens-tu pas ta voix s'enfler vers le son pur? Ne sens-tu pas se fondre et sa vie et ton vœu, vers le son désiré dont l'onde te soulève? Ah! Tityre, une plante est un chant dont le rythme déploie une forme certaine, et dans l'espace expose un mystère du temps.

It is precisely this action of listening to the birth of the capacity for song which Valéry/Lucrèce carries out, not only in his poetic theory, but in poetry itself. 'La poésie est – l'état chantant – [...] de la *fonction qui parle*' (xɪ, 744). Now it is Tityre the lyrical artist, who is inspired in his turn as listener, saying to his companion, 'Mais tu deviens toi-même un arbre de paroles...' (P ɪɪ, 193). For in harnessing the power of the voice to express what links our consciousness to 'ce qui n'est pas elle' (ɪɪɪ, 698), Valéry allows language to reveal the indefinable creative virtualities of 'being'. 'A quoi répond le chant? Qu'est-ce qui veut qu'on chante? La réponse contiendrait la connaissance de la poésie' (xvɪ, 75). The note on which to end this discussion of Valéry's poetic theory is thus one of both precision and mystery. The precise 'poétique du langage' he so thoroughly developed and applied is based on the mysterious power of the human voice to bring to light the nature of being, that which is always new in the instant, a perpetual dawn of individual consciousness striving towards expression and never to be confused with or confined to the content of its words. The voice is real because its attachments to the body of the mind are real; and in the indefinable and indissoluble relationship between sound and sense lies the dawn of individual consciousness. In devoting his craft of language to the articulation of this potential, the poet is loyal to the voice of poetry conceived not as the voice of language but as the voice of human totality: 'Faire de la parole un résonateur de l'esprit'. To attempt this feat means to treat language as a craft involving the most exacting balance of human faculties; for the poetic principle lies not in the natural ease of imagery, but 'dans la Voix, et dans l'union singulière, exceptionnelle, difficile à prolonger, de la voix avec la pensée même...' (VII, 71). Language is utterly inadequate *in itself* to express human experience, 'Et cependant c'est l'affaire du poète de nous donner la sensation de l'union intime entre la parole et l'esprit' (P I, 1333).

3

La Jeune Parque

Oh! faire une phrase longue en vers avec le modelé de la musique à inflexions suivant à la trace des changements de l'être voilé [...] tableau de la pensée même quel que soit l'objet.   (v, 59).

La poésie est bien plus *humaine* que la musique. C'est qu'elle est comme l'homme même, un équilibre entre les fonctions jalouses: les concepts, les images, les sons; les associations, les similitudes, les tendances, les actes [...].   (vi, 195).

Toute voix 'dit' avant tout *quelqu'un parle au Je*.   (xxvii, 271).

La parole intérieure n'est la voix de rien. Comment est-elle entendue?
                                                        (iii, 483).

'Qui pleure là', questions the voice of pure consciousness which opens the poem,

> Qui pleure là, sinon le vent simple, à cette heure
> Seule, avec diamants extrêmes?...Mais qui pleure,
> Si proche de moi-même au moment de pleurer?

Valéry called *La Jeune Parque*[1] a lyrical drama (xxvi, 706) and notes it was the shock of the power of music that led to a poem permeated with notions of musical composition and thus more conscious of its specifically linguistic difficulties, techniques and ideals. Like the first bars of a symphony, those first lines have already led us to anticipate a journey in which two sources of expression are richly interwoven yet formally separate: on the one hand the diffuse meanings of words spread out as if to isolate moments of being poignantly diverse, and, on the other, a euphonic pattern of sounds curiously equal in persuasion and rivalling the power of syntax to bind those moments together in thought. To hear within ourselves the different threads of such an overture is to participate in an experience of complex unity in which the speaking consciousness – 'la Personne qui parle' – is borne forward on a melodic continuum over and above the separate elements – phonetic, semantic, rhythmic – of which it is made up.

Composed over the period from 1913 to 1917 and the fruit of Valéry's long years of 'silent' research into the relationship between language, consciousness and Self, *La Jeune Parque* is obviously a poem of central significance to the subject of inner monologue in relation to poetic discourse; and it is on this surprisingly neglected area[2] that I shall concentrate while attempting a general introduction to the poem. At the same time *La Jeune Parque* seems strangely inexhaustible, beckoning the more tantalisingly and compellingly as one reaches the end of each new avenue. Could one of the most positive features of a poetry of voice be to open in suggestive range through the figure of the desire it so powerfully confines? 'On n'est responsable que de la valeur que l'on donne à sa pensée, et non de cette pensée', Valéry wrote in a notebook of 1906 when reflecting on the intellectual questions that the poem seems most to make visible:

> ma parole intérieure peut me surprendre et je ne puis la prévoir. Quand elle parle, j'appelle moi non ce qui parle, le tiers inconnu, mais l'auditeur de la parole intérieure. Le Moi est le premier auditeur de la parole intérieure. Non celui qui répond – mais celui qui va répondre. Dès qu'il répond il cesse d'être Moi [...] Il est lui-même un phénomène de *reconnaissance*.   (III, 832).[3]

The true subject of the poem is self-awareness, he tells us categorically on more than one occasion.[4] And already in those opening lines a dense poetic texture is filling the space between 'me' and 'je': 'Dès qu'il répond il cesse d'être Moi.' But first we must turn to the voice of the Parque's own immediate consciousness, descending with her into the labyrinth of self-analysis as she experiences 'une suite de substitutions psychologiques, le changement d'une conscience pendant la durée d'une nuit' (P I, 1622).[5]

To take first the bare, 'fictional' evidence that can be pieced together from the poem, we are led to imagine a young woman, the Parque or Fate – at first no more identifiable as a particular being than is Proust's narrator exploring the virginity of nocturnal consciousness – waking at night, in tears, within a rocky marine landscape and tormented by what amounts to a question concerning her own identity: 'Qui pleure là...?' At first not recognising – or knowing but not feeling? – the tears as her own, trembling,

and having left the bed where she was asleep, she addresses the
stars – rather as the speaker in *Le Cimetière Marin* takes the sky
as arbiter of his changing experience – and tries, in their keen,
tormenting presence (the sharpness of her own questioning mind
and the glittering tears it has not been able to shed?) to find out
the cause of her body's expression of her own tantalisingly mysterious grief. Did she harm herself in some way ('Quel crime par
moi-même ou sur moi consommé?...') or was it some fantasy of
desire she had left out of account when, blowing out the lamps
('Au velours du souffle envolé l'or des lampes'), she had encircled
her head in her arms and looked deep into the forests of herself:

> Je me voyais me voir, sinueuse, et dorais
> De regards en regards, mes profondes forêts.

Yet perhaps at that stage – the separated line 'J'y suivais un
serpent qui venait de me mordre' provides a subtle transition into
this tautology – she had not been so much in charge of herself as
she had thought. The urge to know, which she had taken to be the
whole of herself, her total possessor, had stung her with its bite as
if she were a separate entity, drawing from a still unknown part of
her being the poison of unfulfilled desire:

> QUEL repli de désirs, sa traîne!...Quel désordre
> De trésors s'arrachant à mon avidité,
> Et quelle sombre soif de la limpidité!
>
> Ô ruse!...A la lueur de la douleur laissée
> Je me sentis connue encor plus que blessée...

Could it be that an unknown part of her being, a secret sister, was
pulling her away from her more vigilant self:

> Dieux! Dans ma lourde plaie une secrète sœur
> Brûle, qui se préfère à l'extrême attentive.

She had been able, nonetheless, in hesitant words she now triumphantly recalls, to dismiss this 'dear' serpent, being no longer
tempted by the persuasively sensual shape it had assumed to
seduce and deflect her from knowledge:

> VA! je n'ai plus besoin de ta race naïve,
> Cher Serpent...Je m'enlace, être vertigineux!
>   [...]

'Sensualité, souvenirs, paysages, émotions, sentiment de son
corps, profondeur de la mémoire et lumière ou cieux antérieurs

revus, etc. . . . . Cette trame qui n'a ni commencement ni fin, mais des nœuds [. . .]' (P I, 1636): in the course of the monologue which Valéry describes in this way, various further sections (marked by initial capitals and separated by typographical blanks of more or less relative importance) suggest the various ideas or mental 'incidents' in the course of which this constantly re-established urge towards knowledge and detachment continues to unfold.

The Parque is led to remember, for instance ('profondeur de la mémoire et lumière ou cieux antérieurs revus') the golden (perhaps only retrospectively golden) state of mind in which she had lived ('Harmonieuse Moi, différente d'un songe') before self-consciousness with its stinging and shadowy awareness of mortality had entered her thoughts:

> Tous ces pas infinis me semblaient éternels.
> Si ce n'est, ô Splendeur, qu'à mes pieds, l'ennemie,
> Mon ombre! la mobile et la souple momie,
> De mon absence peinte effleurait sans effort
> La terre où je fuyais cette légère mort.
> Entre la rose et moi, je la vois qui s'abrite;
> Sur la poudre qui danse, elle glisse et n'irrite
> Nul feuillage, mais passe, et se brise partout. . .
> Glisse! Barque funèbre. . .

Again *Le Cimetière Marin* comes to mind with its similar image of shadow as the inevitable counterpart of the light of pure thought: 'Mais rendre la lumière suppose d'ombre une morne moitié.'

In yet another main passage, she reflects – proudly? – on the dangers of self-knowledge. It produces a sensation of total detachment from life, a kind of anticipation in which the past, present and the future seem to converge in total predictability:

> Ô DANGEREUSEMENT de son regard la proie!
>
> Car l'œil spirituel sur ses plages de soie
> Avait déjà vu luire et pâlir trop de jours
> Dont je m'étais prédit les couleurs et les cours.
> L'ennui, le clair ennui de mirer leur nuance,
> Me donnait sur ma vie une funeste avance:
> L'aube me dévoilait tout le jour ennemi.
> J'étais à demi morte; et peut-être, à demi
> Immortelle, rêvant que le futur lui-même
> Ne fût qu'un diamant fermant le diadème [. . .].

In this bleakly prophetic state – 'ennui' at its most piercingly devoid of Romantic masochism – would even the capacity for memory be able to work its magic and conjure up visions of a lost evening of love?

After challenging memory itself ('Souvenir, ô bûcher, dont le vent d'or m'affronte') to cause her still to blush, the Parque recalls a state of would-be absolute consciousness in which she desired to be transformed into a pure, exemplary state of being by the activity of thought alone:[6]

QUE DANS LE CIEL PLACÉS, MES YEUX TRACENT MON
TEMPLE!
ET QUE SUR MOI REPOSE UN AUTEL SANS EXEMPLE!

and there follows the famous sequence where she is torn between the claims of, on the one hand, thought itself, leading to rejection of life and the possibility of suicide as an action of her own chosen destiny; and, on the other, life, with its promise of creation and maternity, symbolised by the passionate, burgeoning trees of Spring. Yet Spring too leads to death and she refuses to think of giving birth to more mortals to suffer and die...

It is to the human presence of her own slowly forming tear that the Parque now returns at this pitch of her dilemma – the lovely passage beginning 'Je n'implorerai plus que tes faibles clartés' – and to the assurance of the earth – '...Dureté précieuse...Ô sentiment du sol'. Tempted, perhaps, to dream of transcendant absorption in another – 'Où traîne-t-il mon cygne, où cherche-t-il son vol?'[7] – she knows at the same time that the earth, too, is treacherous beneath, and that she walks fragile and mortal on its surface, leaving no trace:

> Mais sous le pied vivant qui tâte et qui la crée
> Et touche avec horreur à son pacte natal,
> Cette terre si ferme atteint mon piédestal.
> Non loin, parmi ces pas, rêve mon précipice...
> L'insensible rocher, glissant d'algues, propice
> À fuir, (comme en soi-même ineffablement seul),
> Commence...Et le vent semble au travers d'un linceul
> Ourdir de bruits marins une confuse trame,
> Mélange de la lame en ruine, et de rame...
> Tant de hoquets longtemps, et de râles heurtés,
> Brisés, repris au large...et tous les sorts jetés
> Éperdument divers roulant l'oubli vorace...

70

Hélas! de mes pieds nus qui trouvera la trace
Cessera-t-il longtemps de ne songer qu'à soi?

Terre trouble, et mêlée à l'algue, porte-moi!

This whole first movement of *La Jeune Parque* (lines 1–324) takes, place, we imagine, in the darkness of night with only the blinding mental imagery of the two 'nature' passages to lighten it: in the first, visions of the Parque's firm and radiant body striding through golden cornfields in the wind and sun; and in the second, the tossing trees of Spring churning their branches against the blue of the sky like oars on the sea.[8] In the second and final 'movement' (P I, 1626) beginning:

MYSTÉRIEUSE MOI, pourtant, tu vis encore!

the natural light of the sun is beginning to rise, as we feel from the images of rosy light on the islands and on her body which the Parque greets as harbingers of the new day:

SALUT! Divinités par la rose et le sel,
Et les premiers jouets de la jeune lumière,
Îles!...Ruches bientôt, quand la flamme première
Fera que votre roche, îles que je prédis,
Réssente en rougissant de puissants paradis;
[............]
Rien n'égale dans l'air les fleurs que vous placez,
Mais, dans la profondeur, que vos pieds sont glacés!

The last line, with its characteristic 'but', suggests that she is still locked in the claims of interiority; and the last movement, in a different key from the first, is still punctuated with echoes in memory of the darkness of the night before. Should she not, after all, have chosen to destroy herself and thus to refuse to capitulate to the claims of the relative?

Ô N'AURAIT-IL fallu, folle, que j'accomplisse
Ma merveilleuse fin de choisir pour supplice
Ce lucide dédain des nuances du sort?

This natural mental process of retrospective questioning and recapitulation of her visions and dilemmas from a point of greater calm and drowsiness – the passage most consistent with Valéry's aims (P I, 1630) – leads the Parque to consent gently to abdicate her vigilance in sleep and in the near-death of language itself:

> Doucement,
> Me voici: mon front touche à ce consentement...
> Ce corps, je lui pardonne, et je goûte à la cendre.

And from this new position she knows, wakeful again, and exploring with astonishment the persistence of life within her, that she must despite herself accept joyfully, with the rough sting of her bitter awakening to the light and the wind still biting her skin, the streaming sunlight of the unavoidable new day:

> ...Alors, n'ai-je formé, vains adieux si je vis,
> Que songes?...Si je viens, en vêtements ravis,
> Sur ce bord, sans horreur, humer la haute écume,
> Boire des yeux l'immense et riante amertume,
> L'être contre le vent, dans le plus vif de l'air,
> Recevant au visage un appel de la mer;
> [.............]
> Alors, malgré moi-même, il le faut, ô Soleil,
> Que j'adore mon cœur où tu te viens connaître,
> Doux et puissant retour du délice de naître,
>
> Feu vers qui se soulève une vierge de sang
> Sous les espèces d'or d'un sein reconnaissant!

An attempt to summarise this fictional continuity is useful up to a point. Where it is inadequate is not only in the obvious sense that any paraphrase of poetry is inadequate, but in its failure to account for the psychological complexity of the monologue itself as a mode of being. 'Il faut chercher, chercher indéfiniment ce de quoi tout ce que nous disons n'est que traduction' (VI, 762): there is a sense in which Valéry's advice applies as much to our interpretation of the Voice of the poem as to that of ordinary speech. Only if we seek expressive continuity below the surface referentiality of language and in this case apart from the literary device of the speaker as fiction, do the conventions of poetic discourse become transparent and we recognise the experience of the Parque as our own – a process Valéry refers to humorously in his fable *Le Philosophe et la Jeune Parque* (P I, 164).[9]

Take, for instance, the notion of a 'character' whom we call the young 'Parque' (Fate). The title of the poem with its flavour of Classical Antiquity is a purely literary means of introducing the universality of consciousness and its destiny of being perpetually re-born to itself. Those images of sea, rock and light recall in sometimes bitter key the universality of Valéry's Mediterranean landscape already discussed (p. 19). To confine the poem to the experience of a 'character' would be to lose its power to involve us actively in the relationship between consciousness and Self which is being presented as the total subject of the poem. (Valéry had considered other titles such as 'Pandora' and 'Psyché' before deciding on the present one [P ɪ, 1626].) Nor should we suppose that the element of 'character' is increased because Valéry has chosen the image of a young woman through which to project the self-awareness which is the subject of the poem. The popular cultural tradition has been preserved by which female gender is associated with the nervous system – 'Anima' or 'l'Âme'[10] – to which, like child to parent or part to whole, consciousness is functionally subordinate for all its illusions of hegemony, while the image of refusal to give birth increases the potential tension in the poem between 'consciousness' and 'life'.

The use of particularised gender – maleness would be equally particular if it could be distinguished from the use of impersonal pronouns – emphasises the capacity for detachment from the 'accidental' self. Yet is there not a further reason for Valéry's choice of the female in the notion of voice – 'Mlle Âme' – which we have seen him associate with poetry itself?[11] Is it not fitting that, remembering the contralto voice he had heard in his youth and had associated with lack or longing, Valéry should now re-create, embodied in female form, the 'song' of what was lost? The body of the Parque is as elusive to herself as it is to the poet/lover, her creator: a presence perpetually to be re-created as her own through acts of memory and anticipation made possible through inner speech. Yet the reconstituting process of mono-dialogue by which she survives and fills her own lack of longing is the perfect equivalent of that Pygmalionism of literary form by which the poet creates a work of art as voice.[12] While not suggesting that the poem is in any way limited to this form of self-referentiality, I shall return to the subject of poetic voice conscious of itself as one of the exciting areas of meaning available when we move beyond the fiction of 'character' into the total action of the poem as expressive form.

A further objection to a purely narrative approach to *La Jeune Parque* is that an attempt to fit the events described by the Parque – as it is convenient to call 'la Personne qui parle' – into a linear or extra-textual sequence prevents the appreciation of Valéry's skill in evoking the perceptual present of consciousness in the heart of its sensations of present, future and past. Yet should we go to the opposite extreme and deny all representation of the inner time-scale in which, at least for the perceiving consciousness of the speaker, distinction is made between before and after? This would surely diminish the power of the poem to draw on the resources of fiction – our belief in the presence of a living subject – at the same time as we are actively encouraged to see through that fiction, as does the Parque's consciousness her 'personality', into the space where the poet communicates with us in relation to its power.[13] When Valéry referred to the structure of his poem as 'cette trame qui n'a commencement ni fin, mais des nœuds' (P I, 1636), he was surely referring not to the a-temporal experience of pure textuality such as we experience in certain extreme forms of the New Novel, but to the coincidence of textual time with the thread of conscious-ness as it is woven 'sur la corde de la voix'.[14] It is true that Valéry's experiments in non-representational literary form are sometimes described in terms which sound very like those of Robbe-Grillet. He confides, for example, that it would be interesting 'de faire *une fois* une œuvre qui montrerait, à chacun de ses *nœuds*, la diversité qui s'y peut présenter à l'esprit, et parmi laquelle il *choisit* la suite unique qui sera donnée dans le texte' (P I, 1467). Yet the vital distinction in the case of *La Jeune Parque* is the presence of a vocal continuity related to the 'éternel présent' (III, 882) of the living being at whatever moment of consciousness is evoked, what we saw Valéry call 'une suite de substitutions psychologiques, le changement d'une conscience pendant la durée d'une nuit'.

Valéry was characteristically clear about what he had wished to achieve in his poem. In 1935 he wrote, looking back,

> J'ai essayé de faire venir au monologue [...] ce qui me semblait la substance de l'être vivant, et la vie physiologique dans la mesure où cette vie peut être perçue par soi, et exprimée poétiquement.
>
> (XVIII, 533).

and, in 1937,

> Dans la Parque et la Pythie, seul poète qui, je crois, l'ait tenté, j'ai essayé de me tenir dans le souci de suivre le sentiment physiologique de la conscience; le fonctionnement du *corps* en tant qu'il est perçu par le Moi, servant de *basse continue* aux incidents ou idées. Car une idée n'est qu'un incident.
>
> (XX, 250).

74

Such comments are by no means essential keys without which *La Jeune Parque* could not be appreciated and understood. They are ones we might be led to formulate for ourselves once the experience conveyed by the poem has been, not paraphrased, but analysed in terms of the relation of the conditions of language governing poetic discourse to the conditions of consciousness governing inner monologue and the birth of self-aware thought. For the *tour de force* achieved in *La Jeune Parque* as a work of art of great expressive unity in complexity is to have integrated in a single thread of discourse at least three recognisable levels of experience: immediate consciousness, bodily sensation, and self-awareness, 'la conscience de la conscience'. None of these levels is self-contained. Each modifies the others, to produce a continuous form which becomes in turn the self-aware voice of the poem. 'C'est une rêverie qui peut avoir toutes les ruptures, les reprises et les surprises d'une rêverie. Mais c'est une rêverie dont le personnage en même temps que l'objet est la conscience consciente' (P I, 1626).

When Valéry describes *La Jeune Parque* as 'une rêverie', he is referring, of course, not to its genetic nature, but to the living continuum achieved by the poet's realisation of 'une œuvre de volonté', an immense task combining 'les idées que je m'étais faites sur l'être vivant et le fonctionnement même de son être en tant qu'il pense et qu'il sent' with 'une langue aussi imagée que possible et aussi musicale que possible' (P I, 1623). In looking at some of these combinatory methods in the rest of this chapter, I shall concentrate above all on the power of a poetry of voice not simply to use symbolic devices with which to simulate its subject-matter, but to involve the reader's sensibility in the creation of that subject-matter, and to do so by appealing above all to 'les machines de la voix', the link between our own use of inner language and thought. For *La Jeune Parque* challenges critical techniques if we are not to respond inadequately to one or other of the two equally important worlds of textuality and psychological realism. At the same time as it presents us intellectually and emotionally with an overwhelmingly rich and forever changing experience, it seems to offer a curiously simple logic on the level of its construction, reminding us of Valéry's remark 'Les grandes œuvres sont filles de leur forme qui naît avant elles.' In the first place 'le fonctionnement du corps en tant qu'il est perçu par le Moi' can imply only the narrative mode of first-person speaker. In the second place, the most readily accessible example of 'le sentiment physiologique de la conscience' is provided by the 'transition' experience of sleeping and waking.[15] And, last, the 'contradiction' of a 'rêverie' both continuous and discontinuous, the object as well as the subject of 'la conscience consciente', cannot but suggest a form of expression similar to modulation in music, a technique which will involve a sense of continuity in change not only in relation to the sound elements of language, but in relation to the continuum of 'Corps', 'Esprit' and 'Monde' handled by the poem semantically. Indeed, it is in the all-embracing nature of modulation as it is conceived by Valéry that we can expect to understand the reconciliation brought about in the poem of formal and semantic, representational and creative elements: how the poem can dispense with characterisation and linear chronology while retaining the whole rich world of literary mimesis in relation to subjectivity and time.

> Qui pleure là, sinon le vent simple, à cette heure
> Seule, avec diamants extrêmes?...Mais qui pleure,
> Si proche de moi-même au moment de pleurer?

– the first lines of the poem take us indeed into a first-person monologue, but one scarcely at first recognisable as such; one where, with its 'who goes there?' directed towards a source of sound strange to the speaker, the conditions of 'monodialogue' seem to have become curiously explicit. It is not until many lines later that the first-person pronoun, 'Je', with its main verb 'scintille' is allowed to appear. '*Se parler*', Valéry wrote in his notes as part of his reflections on the way the living being thinks and feels,

ce fonctionnement étrange, immédiat qui témoigne de la grossièreté de notre idée du Moi, de l'insuffisance des notations 'psychologiques'. Comment peut-IL SE dire quelque chose? Et qui est MOI, du parleur ou de l'auditeur? De la source ou du buveur? – Quelle relation entre ces membres de l'instant?/[...]/

Parfois, quand ME attend, il fait parler en JE son attente! Tous nos personnages intimes n'ont à eux tous qu'une bouche et qu'une oreille – quoique plus d'un *langage* – c'est-à-dire d'une accommodation – cf. Poésie.   (xxvi, 159).

All internal monologue implies a distance between the different 'speeds' of the mind – 'vivant' and 'pensant' – and it is in this vital interval or 'coupure' that our conscious identity is formed. In making these different speeds and voices 'visible' in language, the poem is increasing our sense of how the human 'Moi' is formed. The cry the Parque hears as separate from herself and indistinguishable from the sound of the wind, provides at the same time a source of drama and pathos whose tension and emotional resonance can be poetically exploited. The 'personnages intimes' created by the Parque's self-listening questioning weave their voices throughout the poem in the rôles of 'secret sister', 'serpent' and so on. For although the outer thread of the monologue is always given cognitively to the syntactical structures of thought in its retrospective mode of self-analysis, it is the semi-autonomous presence of the mythical protagonists within it whose voices determine its different registers, inflections and tones. In the apostrophe to the serpent, the voice of 'l'extrême attentive' is uppermost, for instance – a pure search for knowledge which justifies even lapses, fatigues and fantasies as part of its own overall integrity of design:

69 Je sais... Ma lassitude est parfois un théâtre.

82 Mais avec mes périls, je suis d'intelligence,
Plus versatile, ô Thyrse, et plus perfide qu'eux.

In the 'Primavera' passage, on the other hand, the voice telling the Parque to 'hear' the force of life that her intellect rejects is that of the 'secrète sœur/[...]qui se préfère à l'extrême attentive'. By a marvellous application of its own natural expressiveness to the capacities it makes possible, language has been used by the poet to speak what the conscious mind cannot otherwise know it contains.

For it is not simply the mechanism of inner monologue that is revealed in *La Jeune Parque*. Valéry simulates and exploits the sense of fluctuating certainty at the heart of self-identity, taking us, from the unresolved question at the opening of the poem in all its existential anxiety, on a journey of self-expression in which the speaking consciousness grows in confidence and self-identity through the action of language itself. In terms of a specific answer, the question is unresolved. The whole structure of the poem revolves around it in a simultaneous zone of awareness. It is a question asked anew in terms of each 'physiological' event of the sensibility, so that the poem almost passes through an Ouroboros-like phase or circle, from zero to zero.[16] From the point of view of its power to contribute to the modulation of awareness, however, the question acts as a catalyst. We see the Parque recognising the dualism within her as the source of her own individual consciousness, and gradually moving from the sensation of bodily strangeness:

> 4 Cette main, sur mes traits qu'elle rêve effleurer,
>   Distraitement docile à quelque fin profonde,

to triumphant identification with her body as the source of her own mental power:

> 333 Regarde: un bras très pur est vu, qui se dénude.
>   Je te revois, mon bras...Tu portes l'aube...

That strangeness and dualism is still present in this action of identification, with its change from third to second person ('Cette main', 'Je te revois') is one of the most expressive accomplishments of the poem. These fragile yet precious moments of self-recognition through the monologue of memory – 'MYSTÉRIEUSE MOI, pourtant, tu vis encore!' – are all the more moving in that they are set in the context of intellectual detachment from their emotional origins.[17] For the reader they radiate their light through the whole poem, while for the purely present consciousness of the Parque they are moments alone. The action of memory and the action of voice clothe them in the sustained self-awareness reflected in poetic form.

'*La Jeune Parque* fut une recherche, littéralement indéfinie, de ce qu'on pourrait tenter en poésie qui fût analogue à ce qu'on nomme "modulation", en musique' (P I, 1473). Any approach to poetic form in *La Jeune Parque* leads immediately to the subject of modulation – the technique through which Valéry approached the central problem of uniting the two modes of consciousness, 'être' and 'connaître'; or, as we saw him put it, 'le fonctionnement du corps en tant qu'il est perçu par le Moi, servant de *basse* continue aux incidents ou idées' (xx, 250).

A specific source of inspiration in composing the poem was the music of Gluck and of Wagner, particularly the vocal recitative: 'La notion de récitatifs de drame lyrinque (à une seule voix) m'a hanté [...]. J'avoue que Gluck et Wagner m'étaient des modèles secrets' (P I, 1636).[18] Gluck's recitatives Valéry considered in turn as transformations of the poetic voice in certain passages of Racine (for example, the 'songe d'Athalie' [P I, 1632]).[19] The element shared by these sources is obviously continuum of form: modulation in music being the action of passing from one key to another (or the management of melody and harmony in a particular key). Valéry can be said to have achieved his ambition of making *La Jeune Parque* sound like a single phrase from beginning to end (P I, 1620). Yet it is not only formal continuity but the symphonic *depth* of musical modulation which appealed to Valéry in relation to poetry. He admired Wagner's music for 'l'enregistrement par timbres et combinaison de divers *plans* de la conscience-sensibilité et des modulations psych-physiques qui les joignent comme soudures de Riemann' (XVIII, 78), in short for the creation of a 'monologue-volume' (XXI, 390).[20] To turn to the presence of modulatory techniques in *La Jeune Parque* is to sense the conjunction of these two formal principles of change and continuity, depth and directionality: the flow of the discourse and its power to integrate diffuse and instantaneous detail as well as changes of tone, mood or key.

Valéry associated his modulatory 'obsession' with the musical sequence of syllables and lines and with the shifting substitution of idea-images following the consciousness and sensibility of 'la Personne-qui-parle' (XXIX, 92) (a person who is in part the reader, as we are beginning to see). It was the 'passages' or transitions between the various 'tableaux' of the poem which caused him the most difficulty (P I, 1636). Here changes of tone must be very carefully controlled.

Confining discussion of modulation to these two areas,[21] let us look again at the opening sections of the poem, through the prelude of lonely self-questioning and address to the (Pascalian?) stars, to the wondering description of the serpent with its painfully stimulating bite of intensely human concern:

> Qui pleure là, sinon le vent simple, à cette heure
> Seule, avec diamants extrêmes?...Mais qui pleure,

Si proche de moi-même au moment de pleurer?
Cette main, sur mes traits qu'elle rêve effleurer,
Distraitement docile à quelque fin profonde,
Attend de ma faiblesse une larme qui fonde,
Et que de mes destins lentement divisé,
Le plus pur en silence éclaire un cœur brisé.
La houle me murmure une ombre de reproche,
Ou retire ici-bas, dans ses gorges de roche,
Comme chose déçue et bue amèrement,
Une rumeur de plainte et de reserrement...
Que fais-tu, hérissée, et cette main glacée,
Et quel frémissement d'une feuille effacée
Persiste parmi vous, îles de mon sein nu?...
Je scintille, liée à ce ciel inconnu...
L'immense grappe brille à ma soif de désastres.

Tout-puissants étrangers, inévitables astres

A richly textured organisation of sound plays an immediate part in our experience of these lines. With its emphatically varied 'coupes' and 'rejets', its rich rhymes, its startling use of space and capitals, above all its voluptuous phonetic appeal to the mouth ('bouche, but' [xx, 429]), it is as if *La Jeune Parque* has the articulatory and acoustic physiology of the speaking voice and the mechanism of our memory and anticipation as the centre of its being, offering the reader a precise vocal score with pitch, tempo and intonation carefully suggested and controlled. 'Obliger le lecteur à tendre vers le chant' (xv, 299) was the kind of goal which Valéry set himself at each stage of the poem's elaborate four-year genesis, a goal closely connected with the achievement of 'la continuité du beau son'. We have already noticed that the solicitation of 'les machines de la voix' is a goal which far surpasses the production of a certain type of diction oriented towards a further listener. The voice is 'un moyen qui rend sensible [...] l'accommodation immédiate de l'être [...] à la profondeur intérieure qu'on veut toucher en lui' (vii, 6). By appealing to the voice, Valéry is appealing to the 'profondeur intérieure' of the reader's own sensibility. The musical continuum of the poem takes place in that region of interiority 'behind the eyes and in the throat' (p. 52) – another way of saying that, irrespective of identification at the level of surface experience, we hear the voice of the Parque and its capacities for the unification of 'being' and 'knowing' as our own:

Et par elle (la musique) je vois que le plus profond – ce qui se
prétend tel, le plus chatouillant, le plus terrible, – la *chose même* . . .
est maniable. Entre la chose qui est ce qu'elle est, et la chose dont la
fonction est d'être autre que ce qu'elle est, il y a un intermédiaire.
C'est cet intermédiaire, le moyen de la musique.   (P II, 704).

Attentiveness to sound for purposes of musical continuity is most
obviously achieved in the passage by the symmetrical or nuanced
repetition of single vowels or consonants ('intrasonance' and
'multisonance' were Valéry's own terms).[22] In the first three lines,
for example, the three consonantal sounds 'p', '[s]' and 'm' are
allowed to achieve through repetition a presence of their own far
greater than in the random spread of sound in ordinary language
use: '*p*leure', 'sim*p*le', '*p*leure', '*p*roche', '*p*leurer'; '*s*inon', '*s*imple',
'*c*ette', '*S*eule', '*S*i'; '*s*imple', 'dia*m*ant', 'extrè*m*es', '*M*ais', '*m*oi-
même', '*m*oment'). Yet it is not only the foregrounding of
individual consonants that dominates, but the relationships between the favoured phonemes[23] – as if Valéry wishes to stress both
the instantaneous and the continuous qualities of sound. Other
phonetic relationships are equally at work even in these few lines.
The plosive 'p' is linked to 'l' or 'r' and echoed within a word or
adjacently, and the assonance of 'i' and 'eu' is also present ('Qu*i*',
'*si*non', 'd*i*amants', 'qu*i*', 'S*i*'; 'pl*eu*re', 'h*eu*re', 's*eu*le', 'pl*eu*re',
'pl*eu*rer'). Emphasised yet further by their positions as end-rhyme
('heure'/'pleure'; 'pleurer'/'effleurer') or as internal rhyme ('Qui
pleure'/'heure'; 'extrêmes'/'moi-même'), these configurations of
sound are distributed and focused with marvellous precision and
density, reaching the mind by the inner ear whether or not we
distinguish their full range at the time. 'C'est cette indétermination
qui est la clef de la prestige', Valéry had written paradoxically
about the precise form of music with its power to operate a form
of 'analysis' within the nervous system: 'Il y a donc une partie
séparable dans mes actes et mes émois' (P II, 704).

To continue to pick out only the sound patterns nearest the
surface of the passage is to discover that the light but persuasive
'i', so beloved of Mallarmé,[24] flickers its way through the whole
prelude, reminding us constantly of the initial question, 'Qui . . . ?',
and culminating in the no longer interrogative but still question-
conscious affirmation 'Je scintille, liée à ce ciel inconnu.' This itself
is an intricate sequence of open and closed vowels – in particular

the modulation [i], [e], [œ] which Valéry felt peculiarly his own and which he linked to the intimate italianate flexion of voice associated with his youth. Note, too, how the repeated sibilant [s] is carried down by the bearers 'Hérissée', 'frémissement', 'effacée', 'persiste', 'sein', 'scintille', 'immense', 'soif', 'désastres', until it reappears on the other side of the space in 'Tout-puissants étrangers, inévitables astres', ready to modulate into a further sequence of its own. Nor is rhyme allowed to dominate over other devices, despite Valéry's bold subordination in its favour of surface semantic principles. Prepared for within the line – by half-rhyme, internal rhyme and simple homophony – it seems to greet and extend the principles of repetition and anticipated change involved in other types of sound-pairing.

Rhythm can scarcely be discussed separately from these strikingly self-conscious principles of phonetic modulation in *La Jeune Parque*. Valéry's classical alexandrine with its Racinian sensitivity (p. 61) is both self-contained, with its carefully varied patterns of stresses, and prompt, with its varied use of 'rejets' and overrunning phonemic patterns, to take part in the grouping of lines into statuesque and musically linked masses, contributing in their turn to what Valéry called 'une composition musicale à plusieures parties'.

> $\overset{4}{\text{Qu}}$i pleure là/sinon le vent simple/$\overset{5}{\text{à}}$ cette $\overset{3}{\text{heure}}$
> $\overset{1}{\text{Seule}}$/avec diamants $\overset{8}{\text{extrêmes}}$?. . ./Mais qui $\overset{3}{\text{pleure}}$,
> $\overset{}{\text{Si}}$ proche $\overset{6}{\text{de}}$ moi-même/au moment de $\overset{6}{\text{pleurer}}$?

Standing emblematically apart, yet still organically related to the total overture, these lines offer a controlled experience of acceleration, deceleration and re-acceleration[25] which is both flexible and yet urgent, seemingly inseparable in its total context from the consciousness and breath of the speaker, the articulatory presence of the reader, the idea of the sound of the wind and the image of the ebb and flow of the sea.

Yet what is the overall function of sound in *La Jeune Parque* and how are we to relate it to the poem's overall meaning? In what sense, if at all, is it necessary to have recourse to critical concepts of mimesis, psychological symbolism, and so on?

The function of sound is easily established in relation to the formal design of the poem. Phonetic interlacing contributes to cohesion and harmony, 'l'allure enchaînée-enchaînante du langage poétique' (XIX, 152). Whatever themes and tones are present in the poem, however diverse its 'tableaux', all are related and moved forward by 'la continuité du beau son', 'l'onde porteuse' of a poetic utterance simulating phonetically the magic will to self-existence of the human voice. Since the whole poem is presented through first-person monologue, it is certainly not a transgression into the domain of spurious sound/sense equivalence against which Valéry warns us (p. 54) when we relate the flow of this principle to the flow of consciousness of 'le personnage fictif'. Musical modulation is the architectural bridge between the continuity of conscious awareness and the continuity of poetic form. The sound 'i' of 'Qui pleure?', for instance, might be said to be given a double function in the poem, both 'formel' and 'significatif'. On the one hand it provides auditory continuity with the ensuing passage in which it is so often repeated, and on the other it contributes to meaning through association with the plaintive question in whose semantic context it first so predominantly occurs. With a fleeting lightness of its own – Mallarmé's famous example of the light word 'nuit' and the heavy word 'jour' serves to remind us of the arbitrary nature of sound[26] – the 'i' sound is repeated in the lovely 'HARMONIEUSE MOI' section of the poem where a 'golden' tonality quite different from the crisply anxious beginning is felt. Likewise the word 'ordre', from which Valéry said that the image of the serpent and its bite was derived, passes from the rhyme 'ordre/mordre' – why should a rhyme not create an idea? – into this same 'golden' section where its homology, 'or', is picked up in a multitude of homophones: 'adorée', 'dorée', 'trésor', 'or', 'poreuse', 'enclore'. Now, associated with pleasure, warmth, light and self-harmony, the high occurrence of bi-labials and labio-dentals – 'p', 'b', 'm' – are all the more heavily voluptuous in contrast to the light, hard 'i' which keeps them tonally alert and reminds us semi-consciously of the for ever detached observer – 'la basse continue' – to which they still belong.

A decision to treat sound and sense for what they already are: totally separate variables, has not precluded the use of imitative sound on Valéry's part: the hiss of the serpent with its repeated sibilants, the ebb-and-flow rhythm of the sea in the alexandrine.

Even here, however, onomatopoeic uses of language are more likely to enter the poem indirectly, at points in the monologue where images of the sea and of the serpent are absent except in the reader's own associative memory. A form of phonetic irony can often result: the intrusion of a serpentine sibilant penetrates a would-be autonomous state of consciousness on the part of the Parque. Above all, Valéry has used sound to produce changes of tone and tempo within outer continuity, richly exploiting its non-referential nature as a means of heightening the presence of consciousness as the movement of voice oscillating like a pendulum between the sound and the sense of individual words (p. 55). Through sound we are never allowed to forget the substance of consciousness as 'being': the rich and far more intricate than purely alliterative sound-patterning of a line like 'Je m'ébranlais brûlante et foulais le sol plein' filling with emotive density of substance the field of darting mental relationships it offers as thought. In this deliberately ornate architecture of sound and sense a rhyme like 'pleurer/effleurer' can create not only an associative ligature, but a new form of artistic experience in which the communicative function of language has the rôle of discovering and inventing all in one. Only art can express that grief has a kind of *touch* when experienced from within. Note, too, in a line like 'Distraitement docile à quelque fin profonde', how a word can stand out hauntingly through its escape from a surrounding alliterative pattern – 'fin' stands out here from the plosives – only to become integrated into a further network of its own (the soft 'f' of 'fin' is picked up by 'profonde', in this case, linked back in turn by its open vowel to 'docile'). Or appreciate how in 'L'immense grappe brille à ma soif de désastres', the sonorous semi-consonant [y] at the caesura seems to prolong and draw forward the initial 'i' of 'immense' until, in the context provided by the referents of the words, it scintillates like a star. These are but a few of the infinite adventures offered by *La Jeune Parque* into the ornamental and psychological riches of language which the poet is applying to its action of form. 'La forme, c.à.d. – la *Voix*, qui est l'*Unité* [. . .]. Ce n'est pas la continuité, mais la présence soutenue [. . .]' (xii, 806); 'Le style est acte [. . .] L'acte refait le corps' (vii, 681).[27]

It is not only sounds which interrelate so compellingly in *La Jeune*

Parque that we cannot but integrate them into our experience of
the subject of the poem as an artistic experience. The semantic
fields from which Valéry chooses his words are also made to
resonate, recall and resist each other according to what Baudelaire
called our immortal need for symmetry and surprise. Before
turning to the wider semantic dimension in which sound itself
becomes the total self-conscious subject of the poem as discourse,
I shall look at the rôle these also play in poetic modulation.
For to enter the universe of *La Jeune Parque* is to be reminded at
every turn that modulation is not simply a poetic device for
Valéry, but a capacity of the living being – 'le moyen de la
musique' (P ɪɪ, 704) – the very experience of life as manipulated
in consciousness which he is at pains to convey as our potential.
Around this invisible subject of 'motilité' (p. 108) the themes of
the poem intertwine.

From the point of view of words themselves, we find that the
semantic field of the poem centres on aspects of the natural world,
that whole harsh, bright, changing reality of sea, sky and rock
which has so often provided the 'stage' of human thought. Here is
the external substance of consciousness in its intentionality, and
here is the field of linguistic relationships on which the poem
draws to involve the reader in the Parque's action of mind. Here
above all is the centre of a series of metaphors serving to relate
consciousness to the body and the body to the rest of the natural
world in literary terms. When a traditional metaphor is used – the
central analogy between the sun and the light of the fully conscious mind is an obvious example – Valéry veils the abstract side of
the comparison so that we are scarcely aware of its conventionality
in ordinary language use and must retrieve it for ourselves. 'Plus
vous serez précis, plus vous donnerez au lecteur une tâche difficile
et rebutante. Or, les objets de pensée ou les états complexes d'un
être vivant sont choses mal dénommées. On ne peut les déterminer
qu'en accumulant les *relations* et les combinaisons' (P ɪ, 1621).
The semantic values and even the themes of *La Jeune Parque* are
as free as its form is disciplined and as its total subject-matter is
simple and uniform.[28] We have arrived at the glissando of 'images-
idées' of which metaphor is only the means, and through which
the structural relationships between referents acquire ethical pre-
dominance over themes and images themselves. We have arrived

at the decomposition[29] of the word in favour of its resonance in an overall action of stylistic voice.

Approached in this light, *La Jeune Parque* revolves on a series of analogies which extend structurally into every aspect of its language, referential included. In the passage already analysed in terms of sound, an analogy is immediately set in motion between the stars and tears – 'Qui pleure là [...]/Seule, avec diamants extrêmes'. It is an analogy in which neither term of the comparison resolves our anticipation of discrete units of meaning by taking precedence over the other. The diamonds are both tears and stars, and, because they are both, they are also neither tears nor stars, but points of reference in the invisible current of emotion they serve to carry between them, 'la pensée à l'état naissant'. It is this very blurring of division between inner and outer, literal and metaphorical, which allows the reader to recognise and share the paradoxically clear and universal reality of the mind in its vital capacity for subjective disorder. Ambiguity here is a precise poetic tool to dislocate meaning from a one-to-one relationship between a word and an object, so that the poet may use the qualities of words as signs in a system of harmonic relationships much more closely akin to the 'real' subjective relationship between the mind and its objects of perception: 'L'Esprit oscille entre le système des relations internes et des sensations sans significations, et la représentation des "choses" ' (XI, 257).

'Je scintille, liée à ce ciel inconnu...', says the Parque, her face, we imagine, sparkling with tears which become like stars themselves as we see the metaphor itself transformed.[30] Yet her tears have been partly caused by the stars in the first place:

> 21   Vous qui dans les mortels plongez jusques aux larmes
>   Ces souverains éclats, ces invincibles armes,
>   Et les élancements de votre éternité [...]

So dense is the network of cause and effect, and, moreover, so free from naturalistic context or fixed reference-point is the whole metaphorical figure, that we move interpretatively in a poetic space governed more by the resistance of the real world to language than by a sense of equivalence between perception, world and word. '*La perception abolit plus qu'elle ne donne*, car elle est une combinaison de ce qui est reçu par le sens avec d'autres éléments et cette combinaison *choisit*' (xvi, 841). In this perceptual field the Parque's 'Je scintille' signals itself as a linguistic choice full of the emotion of self-discovery, and the reader enters a realm where the power of language to communicate psychological actions is celebrated and embodied in the poem itself. Valéry is finding a way, as he said he wished, to simulate and develop the power of inner monologue betrayed by ordinary language. 'Au début, le mot est *phrase*, attitude. Tard, il se dégage et devient unité-objet. D'abord il fut un nom complexe d'un ensemble d'impressions, ni verbe, ni adjectif, ni sujet. Mais tout cela...' (iii, 421). Hence the curious delaying of syntactical ligature in *La Jeune Parque* and the widening of its bonds to reveal the discontinuities or mental sensations between. It is from these intensely isolated moments that the continuity of self-awareness is formed, the equivalent of poetic Voice.

A further aspect of Valéry's handling of the modulation of ideas and images concerns, then, the manner in which they themselves are integrated into the field of vision of 'la conscience consciente', both for the Parque on the level of fictional psychology and for the reader on the level of poetic symbolism, the two levels harmonically integrated in turn.

One such example is Valéry's use of the image of the serpent which, however archetypal, is not simply left as a symbol of self-knowledge for the reader's detection, but is integrated, indeed self-generated within the folds of the monologue itself, an image through which the Parque is able to represent or fictionalise her own torment, eventually to dismiss it in turn: ' "Va! je n'ai plus besoin de ta race naïve" '[31] (though with the added Racinian irony that the repetition of the event linguistically is sufficient to accentuate as well as exorcise its hold). In the passage in question we are made to feel that the 'bite' must exist in an invisible preconscious region 'before the poem opens', just as its cause must remain absent from the Parque's own consciousness except as 'cette chose' which music reveals our capacity to transform. 'J'y suivais un serpent qui venait de me mordre'. Meanwhile we have 'heard' the image of the serpent's coils in the previous lines evoking the labyrinthine depths of the Parque's attentiveness, born in turn from bodily sensations: the contraction of limbs, the pulsing of blood:

32 Toute? Mais toute à moi, maîtresse de mes chairs,
  Durcissant d'un frisson leur étrange étendue,
  Et dans mes doux liens, à mon sang suspendue,
  Je me voyais me voir, sinueuse, et dorais
  De regards en regards, mes profondes forêts.

She is the serpent which her own consciousness discovers as its nature, both active and passive, subject and object – and while still playing on the traditional resonance of the image, Valéry has allowed it to shift in psychological function within the action of inner monologue. The action of form has created its content, and the serpent is both ornamental emblem and psychological symbol in one.[32]

If the serpent-motif, with its echoes of Wagner and Gluck, provides a play of modulations called up from the depths of the mind itself, countless images in the poem are taken at the same time from the half-imagined, half-perceived world of external nature.

The first and most obvious function of these images – all fundamentally symbolical in that they concern forms of language – is to provide an impression of the reality of the natural universe in which the mental drama of the Parque is dramatically and lyrically staged. From the very first lines of the poem, with its glittering stars, its sobbing wind and swelling sea, its slippery rocks covered with seaweed, to the monstrous forms of waves dashing their white surf on the shore at the end, the strange separate reality of the landscape is always present, always changing, its pallor gradually lit by the dawn light, ready to be transformed by the golden sun. The external world is also present in the mental images conjured up by the Parque in the darkness: memories of landscapes of dazzling light filled with corn and flowers; visions of great tossing trees greeting the Spring with their thundering fleeces of leaves; tantalising previews of the still invisible islands, their contours soon to be illuminated by the rosy light of dawn, when they will be set buzzing with an animal and human activity outside the self.[33] Surrounded by water and light, these islands are deceptively stable and permanent. They rise into the sky from cold, fluid depths, and the trees too, their branches rowing like oars in the tributaries of the sky and their 'golden fleeces' suggestive of voyage, are linked with the dissolving action of water, their tender rivers of underground sap redolent with suggestions of departure and death. All is movement, all is change. Such descriptions – Ronsardian in their power to evoke movement in Nature – serve to remind us of those principles of multiplicity, change and unity at work in the natural universe 'outside' the Parque's mind. At the same time they proffer a variety of elemental motifs – wind, rock, sunlight, earth and water – which interrelate symbolically with the drama of consciousness which is the poem's true subject.[34] The Protean fluidity of the sea, the deceptive solidity of the soil, the revivifying or 'inspirational' powers of the wind, the revealing and illuminating power and intransigence of the sun: all these part-abstract themes can be constantly interwoven, together with their changing physical presence in the landscape, in ways which reveal and investigate the aims and operations of consciousness engaged in its own invisible drama of fragmentation, stabilisation, reconstitution and change.

Yet the elemental composition and substance of the outer world provides above all a source of metaphor, and thus a means by which mind and body, inner and outer world can be yet more intimately linked as part of a total 'Egosphère'. We have already begun to see in relation to the double motif of tears and stars how Valéry builds up a web of analogies between inner and outer worlds. The process becomes more and more complexly expressive as landscape is expressed in terms of mind and body, and mind and body are expressed in turn through images of landscape. In the first lines of the poem, the sea is described in human terms, for instance:

> La houle me murmure une ombre de reproche,
> Ou retire ici-bas, dans ses gorges de roche,

while the Parque's mind and body is described conversely in imagery taken from the natural world: 'Quel frémissement d'une feuille effacée', 'mes profondes forêts', 'plages de soie' and so on. Sometimes the metaphorical element is provided by straight personification or anthropomorphisation of landscape ('une ombre de reproche', in which Valéry revivifies the conventional expression by reminding us of its physicality); sometimes ('profondes forêts') the metaphor is tinged with an additional literary echo (in this case the 'forêts de symboles' of Baudelaire's sonnet). Sometimes, tempted by the fertile analogical soil of the poem, the reader's imagination is led to form analogies of its own. Because we never quite 'see' the body of the Parque – consciousness always seeking to comprehend (embrace) itself – we create her total shape from the elusive fragments of imagery we are given, a vast human form, filling the imaginary space of the poem through which we 'measure' the world. Unlike Robbe-Grillet in his early essays,[35] Valéry is obviously not against the use of anthropomorphic imagery as a traditional source of literary expression. Yet he has made visible the mental actions involved. The mental needs behind the rhetorical devices of synecdoche, metonymy, periphrasis, personification and so on, are allowed to come alive.[36] Indeed, we find them actively recognised in the self-aware monologue of the Parque: 'Îles! dans la rumeur des ceintures de mer,/[...]/Vous m'êtes à genoux de merveilleuses Parques'; '[...] et sur cette gorge de miel/[...]/Se venait assoupir la figure du monde'.

Nature in *La Jeune Parque* is not a storehouse of words, but a storehouse of *signs*: signs of the vast, inescapable disorder ('le changement fermé') from which human consciousness and its language of self-expression are formed: 'L'Homme est la mesure des choses'. It is with the reality of this discovery, both terrifying and reassuring, a source of vulnerability and a source of pride, that the Parque must come to terms if she is to be fully herself. For if the poem expresses the claim of individual consciousness to absolute purity, it shows at every stage how that purity is denied by natural experience. The voice of the wind, the waves, her own cries and changing emotions, the pulsing of her blood, repeat at every stage to the Parque the impossibility of all but interior escape from the interpenetration of consciousness and nature; while the whole poem is like a constant transmutation of categories, an expressive revelation of the delicate membrane between body, mind and world which language perpetuates and expressively dissolves. Those commentaries on the poem which refer cosily to the Parque's 'decision to reject the Spring' or to the poem's expression of 'pure intellect' forget the disturbing splendour of passages evoking violent mental sensation, where the sensibility is literally pierced with the sensation of being alive. For there are passages in *La Jeune Parque* where a very narrow borderline separates panic from ecstasy, order from incoherence, even when consciousness is at its most immune. 'Tout l'univers chancelle et tremble sur ma tige'. Here within the organised poetic form of Mallarmé, Valéry is close to the sensations conveyed by Rimbaud's poetry with its 'incohérence harmonique', while the reader is never allowed to forget the rôle of language in ordering as well as sacrificing the richness of mental experience. Where Rimbaud chooses to simulate the natural disorder of sense-impressions which impel the mind to creation – 'Le remarquable *pouvoir-excitant* d'une certaine 'incohérence' [qui] oblige à créer' (xxvi, 871) – Valéry chooses to convey the emotion of the conscious mind at the point of its knowledge of the provisional nature of language, and to do so in such a way as to make the communicative value of that act of poetic expression an end in its own right: 'Tout ce qui est verbal est provisoire. Tout langage est moyen. La poésie essaye d'en faire une fin' (xii, 673). Indeed, the sensation of the ineffable is given its fully conscious exploration and poetic justification in *La Jeune Parque*. The reader is present at the birth of the alternative pathway towards tears[37] or speech which the Parque naturally travels in the face of the pressure of existence at its most conscious and therefore unknowable: 'Connaissance = Expression. [...] *ce que tu es* en tant que *tu peux le connaître*; ce *que tu te connais* et ce que tu sais exprimer sont la même chose' (xxiii, 790); 'De l'ineffable – "*Les mots manquent*" – La Littérature essaye par des mots de créer l'état de manque de mots' (xviii, 350).

A conclusion to an appreciation of *La Jeune Parque* would seem to point in many possible directions. I have chosen to concentrate on the power of the poem to make us aware of the relationship between consciousness and language and thus of its own action as a drama of poetic voice.

To write is to take up a position from which things can be seen on one side and language on the other, Valéry suggested: a given subject immediately awakening in the poet a certain group of words (iii, 882). The 'given' subject of *La Jeune Parque*, as we have seen, is the experience of living as it is perceived by consciousness. In that inner monologue is essential to consciousness, a form of language or relationship to language is already part of this subject. Hence the many words in the poem connected with language and the voice in various stages of its relationship to physical being: 'mot', 'parole', 'parle' at one end of the scale, and 'cri', 'soupir', 'plainte', 'hoquets', 'râles' at the other.[38] 'Toute cette richesse', Valéry wrote of 'Vox', 'Le cri, le soupir, le gémissement, le roucoulement, l'exclamation, le hurlement, le sanglot, la note prolongée, le murmure, le tirade...', all have their rhetorical equivalents in 'le récit' (vii, 8). Already we can appreciate that by filling the poem with words denoting aspects of the voice, Valéry is exposing the mental and physiological 'substance' of 'le récit' rather than using it to clothe extraneous ideas. In order to convey the bodily sensations, the multiple indeterminations, the pauses at the birth of language and thought in its 'outer' form, Valéry has chosen as his model 'une espèce de "voix du sang" (en amitié de l'esprit) qui m'est chère plus que tout' (P I, 1624), a 'voix rattachée aux entrailles, aux regards, au cœur' (viii, 41).

La Jeune Parque was intended to convey a knowledge of the human organism which the reader must be drawn to *learn* rather than simply to recognise. The discourse of the poem itself must be involved in the drama of consciousness and language in which the Parque is fictionally engaged. If the phonetic sound-dimension of the poem is the main source of enchantment while ideas are kept in the wings, then this experience of enchantment too seems to be made visible in the drama of the poem. Sound is the theme of the overture, for example. The sound of the wind in its perpetually empty presence, at first indistinguishable from the Parque's own cries, seems to weave a continuous thread from the random noises of the sea – 'Et le vent semble au travers d'un linceul/Ourdir de bruits marins une confuse trame...'. The suggestive power of these images, once we apply them to the human subject of the poem, is immense. With the Parque we recognise our own need to seek meaning in the random forms of nature, and, at the same time, the freedom at the heart of such intentionality, the void related to the sensation of origin,[39] the reward and penalty of that improbable 'magic' of song by which the fictional continuity of our personality is vocally sustained. One of the finest achievements of the poem is surely its power to convey the emotion of consciousness as the intellect penetrates its own source in the sensibility, an achievement in which the mnemonic value of poetic form is allowed to play an unusually visible part. For the poem is far more complex than a purely symbolic adventure into the unificatory mental actions it is conveying through and in relation to language. References to sound are only the most obvious side of a process which extends into every level of the poem, allowing us to perceive the mental actions made possible through rhythm, rhyme and metaphor which the rhetorical devices of language deny: 'L'usage du langage rend l'esprit insensible à *la réelle condition mentale* des choses qu'il pense par paroles' (xxi, 480). We are back to the living experience of speech at the centre of the poem and which we find consciously echoed in the Parque's question ('Qui pleure?') towards the origin of her own voice, a form of 'being' she can never completely 'know': 'Et de mon sein glacé rejaillisse la voix/Que j'ignorais si rauque et d'amour si voilée'.[40] It is this rift which the Voice of the poem will unify by presenting its strangeness harmoniously, and this rift which the Parque's consciousness might be said to learn to incorporate by a form of expressive self-awareness based on the power to interpret or 're-think' as well as simply to 'hear' the division within: 'Le chant et les idées – *absorbe la parole interne*' (xvi, 75). I shall approach this area by examining the way in which the structure of the poem points towards the possible reconciliation of the two distinct tones of 'being' and 'knowing', a further compositional echo of the Bach-like art of fugue. 'L'être s'écoute – Trouve une surprenante *suite*, une continuation liée par un lien mystérieux' (ibid.).

It is part of Valéry's skill in what he called poetic communication as opposed to mere 'creativity', that he has linked private images, born on the level of the Parque's sensations, to general cultural myths. *La Jeune Parque* has thus been read at one and the same time as an evocation of waking and a Dantesque allegory of the stages of human life.[41] But how does Valéry *treat* the movement by which the Parque's consciousness is brought towards acceptance of life, symbolised by the rising sun? How do we interpret the *tone* of that finale and in what way does it illuminate the intellectual implications of the poem?

The whole poem might be said to have played out the different possible attitudes of the individual conscious mind towards its own capacity for awareness as it changes physiologically in time. In interpreting the finale where the Parque greets the coming of day, symbolic of the process of living in which she has been inescapably involved all along, it is important to realise that both attitudes to consciousness are still present. The words 'malgré moi', in the height of gratitude to the sun are an indication. It is not sufficient to say that the poem ends in a glorious sun-lit rebirth correspond-ing with self-acceptance in any absolute or permanent sense. For the same detachment from her own instinctive appetite is still present within the Parque and, however gratefully, she must recog-nise the bitter repetitiveness of her own mental states:

> 325 MYSTÉRIEUSE MOI, pourtant, tu vis encore!
> Tu vas te reconnaître au lever de l'aurore
> Amèrement la même...

Yet if the poem is based on a series of cyclical returns – as consciousness always must be in its physiologically determined response to 'le hasard' – how do we account for the two move-ments in the poem: the one, in the first part, towards the pain-fully impossible goal of absolute self-sufficiency, and the other, in the second part, towards gradual acceptance of the limitations of the mind? Valéry could be said to have achieved the feat of moving the Parque's consciousness from the anguished question at the beginning of the poem to the plenitude at the end without any apparent change of direction being involved.[42]

The key to this last transformation is provided, not by any conscious resolution on the part of the Parque, but by the body: that deep, mysteriously total Self which, even when she has not been aware of it, and even when she has intellectually rejected the consoling intellectual notion of 'being', has brought her forward from dream to waking and even from the banks of death:

> Attente vaine, et vaine...Elle ne peut mourir
> Qui devant son miroir pleure pour s'attendrir.

If the body, the total sensibility, has been responsible for her own consciousness in its movement from sleeping to waking – that 'étrange mouvement aveugle, passage du rien au désordre, du désordre à l'ordre' (IV, 496) – cannot its secret continuity be appropriated by the mind for its own ends, its own further glorious

94

illusions of power? 'Car je tremblais de perdre une douleur divine', the Parque had admitted. Must she not prolong the opportunity afforded by her anxiety to find out the secret before it is too late?:

> Cherche, du moins, dis-toi, par quelle sourde suite
> La nuit, d'entre les morts, au jour t'a reconduite?
> Souviens-toi de toi-même, et retire à l'instinct
> Ce fil (ton doigt doré le dispute au matin),
> Ce fil dont la finesse aveuglément suivie
> Jusque sur cette rive a ramené ta vie...

In one sense it is always too late. The coming of day at the end of the poem is symbolic of the 'limit' to knowledge itself. Her sacrifice incomplete ('supplice inachevé') the Parque is pulled back into the claims of contingency in time. Such, at least, are the sensations of the intellect in the critical epochs of transition provided by the phases of the body of which it is part. And we know that Valéry's own description of his 'objet philosophico-littéraire' had been

de montrer en jeu et à la fois, ces divers ordres qui font la complexité de l'homme, qui font les uns aux autres, ressorts et ressources et qui forment objectivement la condition primordiale de la pensée, son élasticité. C'est pourquoi le rêve est si important, étant un autre mode que la veille de produire ces combinaisons ou de les enregistrer. C'est pourquoi les états critiques, les 'phases' de l'être sont si captivants.[43]

'Ressorts et ressources': surely this helps explain the paradoxical union in the poem of cyclical repetition (the 'fate' of consciousness) and the transmutation of intellectual values gradually taking place at the end, indeed, picked up by the reader in the overall tonality of the language even before such values have been fully recognised by 'la Personne qui parle'. Enriched by the extreme thoughts of the night in which she has discovered the potential death inherent in consciousness – 'de mon néant secrètement armée' – the Parque has experienced the limits of knowledge, the uncrossable barrier of being and knowing, and the sense that it is in the interests of her own individual self, *not* fully to 'understand' and thus destroy sensibility with its life-giving sting. A similar experience was expressed in *L'Ange* (p. 27) and is the fruit of Monsieur Teste's skirmishes with the dark:[44]

95

Donnez, ô Noir, – donnez la suprême pensée…Mais toute pensée
généralement quelconque peut être 'suprême pensée'.

  Si'l en était autrement, s'il en fût une *suprême en soi* et *par soi*,
nous pourrions la trouver par réflexion ou par hasard; et étant
trouveé, devrions mourir.   (P ii, 37).

To return to the final lines of the poem, it is now possible to
suggest that two tonalities, negative and positive, are both vital to
the movement by which the Parque's consciousness retains its
individual identity, and 'life must go on'. Far from 'capitulating'
to life, she has retained in the heart of that acceptance the power
of conscious separation – 'malgré moi' – necessary to human
individuality. Her very act of alignment with necessity ('il le faut,
ô Soleil') is as much an intellectual as an instinctive one. Life
itself is now the source of consciousness. Consciousness is now the
life-giving sun. To model the demands of the mind on those of the
body is the ultimate wisdom of self-awareness, the only possible
extension of its power, and in this creative achievement, this
acceptance of the necessity of dualism, resides paradoxically the
only possible unity of the self. Surely it is the discovery of this *new*
source of being which is reflected in the harsh yet joyful tone of
the lines where the Parque accepts the finiteness of her own body
and the full risk of human life. Now once more, but this time in
full possession of the idea of mortality, the body will be felt to
support the consuming rays of the sun. The circular modulation
of the poem is *almost* complete.

Poetry should offer the reader 'une pensée singulièrement achevée'
(P i, 95), one in which no faculty is left unsatisfied to ruin the rest
(p. 38). The reason why the Parque's monologue is *almost* complete is ultimately to be sought in the nature of poetry itself. For it
is not the voice of consciousness as it is lived that the poem celebrates and makes visible, but the Voice of consciousness as it could
be, once expressively complete. Here the poem turns a perfect
circle on itself.

  'Je pense donc que la sérénité de l'œuvre ne démontre pas la
sérénité de l'être' (P i, 1638), Valéry wrote, having produced *La
Jeune Parque* 'dans l'anxiété, et à demi contre elle' (P i, 1637).
The poem was composed during the First World War. And
whereas the long years of preparation represented by the *Cahiers*

seemed to Valéry then an almost shameful activity, the task of completing a poetic work subject to such strict linguistic conditions – 'formel', 'significatif' and 'accidentel'[45] – began to seem to him a kind of duty, that of saving the French language in its hour of defeat. In speaking of the difference between the serenity of the work and the anxiety of being, Valéry is drawing attention to the power of the poem to create a state of aesthetic harmony: the changed intellectual values of existing 'dans un tout autre mode et comme dans un tout autre *temps*' (P I, 450), a feeling of intense yet alert absorption where our minds may experience, fully awake, the fluidity of relationship between subject and object present in the autonomy of dream.[46] For the Parque herself, this urge towards autonomy is perpetually thwarted, only temporarily realised in states of memory or longing ('HARMONIEUSE MOI, différente d'un songe...'). Perhaps her 'crime' was to identify with just such a preferential state of emotional plenitude at the expense of other necessary states of being in time: the 'hard' sense of control as well as the 'tender' sense of defeat.[47] For the reader, however, the poem makes this privileged state of harmony perpetually present: a state bathed not in the light of memory but in the light of Voice.[48]

When Valéry writes of the aesthetic experience as giving the reader access to 'un tout autre *temps*', he is largely thinking of the rhythmical and sonorous power of poetic language to defy finite reduction to thought, the aim of 'poésie pure'. Yet this is not enough to account for the power of *La Jeune Parque* to radiate meaning with each new reading, its power constantly to reward our desire to watch ourselves live. It was Valéry's aim to give language its *full* application in poetry, to create the sensation of human nature enchanted and enslaved by the cognitive as well as creative possibilities of the word ('Faire chanter une idée de l'être vivant et pensant'). The unusually complete action on and through language carried out in *La Jeune Parque* involves us in the emotion of *knowing* the drama of the creative sensibility – the drama of voice – in which the Parque and, through her image, the poem itself is engaged.

'L'opération qui consiste à tirer de ma douleur un chant magnifique', Valéry had written in connection with his discovery of the 'Orphic' nature of the Voice in its relation to time (p. 6),

[...] j'ai appris du moins la continuité de cette chaîne de tourments, d'espoirs et de catastrophes, et donc comment le plus haut au plus bas se relie, toute la modulation de l'être et la conservation de la vie entre les bornes qu'elle ne peut franchir, – c'est là, *le chant*, le registre. Et la mesure de cet intervalle qui est vivre à plusieurs unités qui sont rythmes.

Il faut que le chant, suprême don, adieu suprême au passé, éternel présent de ce qui fut... (VIII, 41).

The experience of time is a complex one in *La Jeune Parque*. It involves the reader in both the continuity and the change of a human consciousness, its urge to escape the confines of being and the necessity of return to the source of its own life: 'voix rattachée aux entrailles, aux regards, au cœur et ce sont ces attaches qui lui donnent ses pouvoirs et son sens – Voix, état élevé, tonique, tendu, fait uniquement d'énergie pure, libre, à haute puissance, ductile' (ibid.).[49] By comparing Valéry's description of voice with the Parque's own experience, we can see how the poem has expressed the meaning of its own action of form. In the heart of human consciousness is awareness of the passing of time and the coming of death, the total image of the processes of diffusion and disorder against which it forms its freedom to express. '[...] que l'adieu le plus déchirant soit aussi et en même temps l'extrême du bonheur de l'expression', Valéry's analysis of 'Voix' continues, – 'voilà, voilà le divin mystère...Mais je rencontre ici cette vieillerie qu'on appelait le chant du Cygne' (VIII, 41). In personal terms, *La Jeune Parque* is a farewell homage to Mallarmé and the necessary re-assertion of Valéry's voice as a poet in his own right. In literary terms, the poem gives voice to the fact that expression is always a swan-song on the part of the human being knowing it will die.

The complex resonance given to the theme of consciousness of time and of death in *La Jeune Parque* cannot be explored fully here. I have introduced it in order to suggest how the themes of the poem perfectly suit and draw out its mental substance as an expressive action, what Valéry called, still without confining the process to the personal, 'une autobiographie, dans la forme' (P I, 1631–2). By choosing adolescence and puberty as the 'age' of his heroine, Valéry is bringing alive that dualism of 'being' and 'knowing', life and death, central to his exploration of the drama of the human voice and of art. Adolescence is the *lived* symbol of the conflict between life and death which must enter the conscious-ness of the Parque if she is to become fully human. Consciousness must assume awareness of death if it is fully to speak the voice of the human Self in its longing for the lost but re-affirmed timelessness of youth, 'adieu suprême au passé, éternel présent de ce qui fut'. It could be said that the motifs of suicide, memory, immortality, sexuality, grief and re-birth which run throughout the poem are all rich orchestrations of one invisible subject: the instinctive desire to *know* as a means of increasing the sensation of creative auton-omy, and, as an unavoidable part of that desire to know, the drama of difference and identity provided by speech ('Ce qui veut comprendre demande à parler'; 'Toute voix "dit" avant tout *quelqu'un parle au Je*').

The imaginary nature of certain fears caused Valéry himself a particular type of suffering: the feeling that although central to self-identity, knowledge is impotent in eliminating the suffering it has foreseen: 'Pourquoi me dévores-tu, si j'ai prévu ta dent?'.[50] 'Qui sondera ma bêtise', he notes of this sensation, '[. . .] Qui voit mieux que moi la nullité de mes maux atroces?. . . Je souffre aussi de la Vanité de mes douleurs, autant que de leurs morsures incon-testables. *L'imaginaire mord et déchire le réel*' (VIII, 466). The experience is also central to the Parque's thirst for self-knowledge – 'curieuse de sa propre essence'. Indeed, much of the poem can be read as a marvellously recognisable evocation of the sensations of consciousness from this point of view: the 'suicide' implicit in the intellect as it attempts to cling to its own illusion of elimin-ating life through self-expression[51] ('Parler, c'est prévoir' [XXVIII, 617]); the feeling of fear at losing the validity of the grief caused by its self-protective but painful hold ('Car je tremblais de perdre une douleur divine' [see Ch. I, n. 8]), and so on. One of the most striking expressive effects of the poem is to give voice through tone to the note of constant emotion as the Parque observes within herself the change from identification with this form of intellectual suffering, to identification with the experience it is designed to avoid.

For the most courageous and life-affirming 'message' of *La Jeune Parque* is not the inevitable survival and continuity at the end of the poem, but the confirmation, through its own richly interlocked and self-replenishing structure, that the dualism of 'being' and 'knowing' can itself be accepted intellectually as the condition without which no creative autonomy can take place. 'J'interroge mon cœur quelle douleur l'éveille', says the Parque, 'Quel crime par moi-même ou sur moi consommé?...'. No answer to the question can put an end to its form. It must constantly be asked and re-asked as the expression of the limits of her own self-knowledge constantly re-formulated by the action of speech. Yet the asking of the question also points to the constant discovery and re-discovery that there is no 'crime' at the root of the experience of mental suffering; that in its self-alerting signal lies the 'sting' of consciousness itself. In this partially linguistic exorcism, we find perhaps more than anywhere else in Valéry's poetry 'l'éducation et l'espèce profonde de la voix de l'auteur. La voix intérieure' (vII, 70), its capacity raised through the discriminatory action of poetry to a superior state of power.[52]

Is *La Jeune Parque* an obscure poem? It has often been classed as such, taking its place with Mallarmé's *L'Après-Midi d'un Faune* and *Un Coup de dés* as the archetypal 'obscure' poem of the Symbolist epoch. Neither excusing nor denying the presence of difficulty,[53] Valéry analyses instead the types of condition responsible for the feeling: first the difficulty of the subject-matter from the point of view of expressing inner experience in words, especially where sensations are concerned; secondly, the independent formal conditions imposed by the poet – harmony, continuity of effects, elegance of syntax, and so on – leading to a density of experience which may demand a tension disproportionate to the reader's curiosity concerning a literary work; and third – the general effect of the two previous conditions – 'l'accumulation sur un texte poétique d'un travail trop prolongé' (P I, 1621). But to read *La Jeune Parque* is a never-ending source of self-discovery. It is an obscure poem only if we forget that for Valéry there is no finite meaning to a text. A poem is an object or event of the senses, whereas the interpretations it suggests cannot alter its material capacity to produce quite different ones. I have tried to suggest that the 'quite different' meanings we shall find when we return to *La Jeune Parque*, the difficult and rewarding anxiety of seeking its linguistic thesis once resolved, are possible only because it has a fixed and finite subject containing within itself the reason for its existence as art. For the process of thought is infinite, incoherent, provisional. Only a work capable of sacrificing its riches can reach that region of ourselves where unity inhabits and all that is not expressed is once more 'purement possible' (P I, 453). The conventions of ordinary language are opposed to this poetic paradise where thought and sound are as united as body and soul (P I, 457). Where *La Jeune Parque* affects us most deeply is in its power to express the hopes and the price of that poetic union, one which extends beyond the concept of a privileged moment of harmony into the whole experience of human life in its awareness of death. The question 'Qui pleure...?' is the shape of individual consciousness aware of its contradictory capacity for emotion and yet objective insignificance in the natural world:

> Hélas! de mes pieds nus qui trouvera la trace
> Cessera-t-il longtemps de ne songer qu'à soi?

> Terre trouble, et mêlée à l'algue, porte-moi!

Not simply a few symbolic images, but every line of *La Jeune Parque* refers, through the metaphor of language, to a conscious instant of human life described from the point of view of the desire to express and to know: 'Ce qui se forme et vient prendre figure de pensée de moi, sur mes lèvres, – est-il de moi avant que je l'aie repensé, reconnu?' (XI, 670). The unifying emotion of recognition is at the heart of *La Jeune Parque*: recognition of the dualism involved in the action of inner monologue,[54] recognition of the Self as something wider and more unknowable than consciousness – 'MYSTÉRIEUSE MOI, pourtant, tu vis encore!' – and above all recognition that the action of language is necessary to continue that action of unification until it is fully understood and can once more become silent. It is this action which poetry continues and completes, an action confirmed when as with a musical melody, we 'remember' the words of the poem as part of our own experience. It is not every day that we hear the 'figure' of our own desire.[55]

> Attente vaine, et vaine...Elle ne peut mourir
> Qui devant son miroir pleure pour s'attendrir.

The sensibility, like the poem, its mirror, is always born anew in its 'sentiment d'actuel éternel' (xviii, 533), lost and re-discovered as the mind experiences and manipulates the sensation of time. It is not only physical death which is present in the poem, but the potential death of consciousness in life without the sting of the sensibility to keep it alive.

PART TWO

4

Charmes – L'Abeille – Aurore

La poésie peut-être, c'est toute l'âme – toute la parole, tout le dictionnaire possible de l'être, tout l'être en tant qu'appels, réponses, actes, emotions considérés comme un instrument. Telle est la Lyre et non autre chose. (VII, 425).

C'est trop peu d'être poète, l'objet du poète est le poème. Et le poème n'est que l'enchantement et le remuement du prochain. (X, 850).

En toute chose, il faut trouver la *Musique des actes* et, elle *rencontrée* – tout chante et se fait merveilleusement. (XII, 657).

Composing the first poems of *Charmes* after the long, slow effort of *La Jeune Parque* seemed to Valéry like fencing with a foil after a bar of lead (P I, 1623). The reader also senses the relative ease of this hard-won freedom. To come upon these dancing structures full of humour, movement and light is like stepping out into the landscape of intellectual possibilities the Parque achieves as the result of her struggles with the dark. Indeed, the notion of taking a step and of dancing is a frequent image of the poetic principle in Valéry's thought. By 'taking a step' in the mental space of rhythm and memory, we achieve an increased sense of self-aware-ness, a sensation which the language of poetry makes available to the mind: – 'La durée est un accroissement de présence' (VIII, 862). In the composition of *Charmes* Valéry was celebrating not only a hard-won skill in matters of verbal discipline, but also a hard-won truth of intellectual experience: the incarnation of mental energy in a disciplined action releases freedom of exchange and recon-nects the mind with the world. '*Tenir* l'être même [...] Car je vous invente – Moi, *l'inventeur de ce qui est*, Orphée!' (VIII, 362).

Charmes, the poems of Valéry's maturity – published first as a collection in 1922, when he was fifty-one, and thereafter in slightly revised versions until 1942 – were indeed born from the Parque

103

('*Charmes* naquit ou naquirent de la Parque'),[1] and in the course of this analysis we shall find many echoes of the previous long poem in the form of motifs and images separately expanded or treated in a different key. The dawn of *Aurore*, the serpent of *La Pythie* and *Ébauche d'un Serpent*, the marine landscape of *Le Cimetière Marin*, the sleeping woman of *La Dormeuse*, the caryatides of *Cantique des Colonnes*, the constellations of *Ode Secrète*, the turbulent plane tree of *Au Platane*: all emanate from the earlier poem, as if Valéry had prepared there a vast dictionary of elements to be placed at the disposal of a language more and more conscious of its own varied possibilities. For if *La Jeune Parque* is 'une autobiographie par la forme', *Charmes* is 'le drame de l'Intellect', a verbal pageant where that same basic drama of the invasion of the human sensibility by its own passion for self-knowledge is explored from the point of view of the different tones or moments of consciousness to which it can give rise. An essential part of this expressive exploration is use of the greatest possible range and variety of metrical forms. And Valéry did not simply pay lip-service to traditional forms (adopted as a reaction against what he took to be the vagueness of much contemporary poetry). He displayed and utilised each in an individual way.

'*Charmes*: c'est-à-dire *Poèmes*', Valéry entitled his 1942 edition,[2] reminding us that all true poems have the power to enchant; and in 1941 'Deducere carmen' (P I, 1644); 'Carmina – Chants magiques – Liturgia'.[3] Hymns, incantations, magic songs, drawing the reader into a 'musicalised' state of mind in which sensibility and intelligence act as one. Despite the stress on 'magic' and the appeal to areas of necessary ignorance where we cannot follow how and why such language affects us, there is to be nothing lulling or soporific about these enchantments: festivals of the intellect, delights of the mind fully awake. Valéry's notes suggest the aim of sharpening the intellect by teasing it with a buzz of fermenting ideas, enticing it more lucidly to appreciate that only via the body, the centre of all values, can will-power act on mind. Although it may appear pure delight a fruit is nourishment in disguise. Thought should be present in poetry in a similar way (P I, 1452). Already there is a hidden barb to the title, *Charmes*. All is not what it seems. The seductive art of the poem may even be presented ironically from within, the fragility of its harmony exposed at the very moment of its birth. The tiny poem *Le Sylphe*, so often quoted in the context of critical approaches to the ambiguity of *Charmes*, puts us on our guard not simply against treating the poems too heavily and definitively, but also against treating them flippantly.

> Ni lu ni compris?
> Aux meilleurs esprits
> Que d'erreurs promises!

Chance and error have their rôle in true thought. It is possible to read *Le Sylphe* as a poem about pleasure itself, about the inspiration of the privileged moment, light and passing, beyond the problems of lucidity, yet deeply related to our instinct of curiosity towards the intermittences of the heart. In that the evanescence of such inspiration is given a voice, we are alerted to expect from *Charmes* a discourse opposed as much to the incoherence of spontaneous inner monologue as to the surface rigidity of external thought 'in' language. The popular expression 'Ni vu ni connu' is expanded in a series of metaphors which make visible the mental sensations and actions behind language and allow these patterns to be transposed to the play of the poem itself. A work which could not be further from *La Jeune Parque* in length, range and tonality, *Le Sylphe* epitomises the sense in which the poems of *Charmes* can challenge the ingenuity of our imagination however tauntingly slight in form. No poetry could be further than *Charmes* from moral didacticism, yet no poetry could be closer to the equivalence of delight and instruction aspired to by classical art. To discover how such poems expressively break as well as still formally contain the spell of enchantment within them, is one of the critical tasks in which the reader becomes more and more engaged through contact with the increasing aesthetic pleasure of the work.

It is not only between *La Jeune Parque* and *Charmes* that we can expect to find links. Many of the poems of the collection overlap with one another too. The opening and closing poems of the volume, *Aurore* and *Palme*, had a common genesis which is still reflected in their shared heptasyllabic line and sustained fruit imagery. The fact that Valéry chose to separate them and to develop the harsher side of the fruit image in the one (the thorns and bees round the fruit-gatherer in *Aurore*) and its gentler side in the other (the slow, patient ripening of fruit in *Palme*) confirms that the poetic effort of *Charmes* is directed towards simplicity in complexity: 'La plus véritable profondeur est la limpide' (P II, 593). A surprisingly small number of themes are treated in the greatest possible variety of *tones*, and the reader's mind is invited to form the greatest possible number of inter-connections. Three of the main poems – *Aurore*, *La Pythie* and *Palme* – were originally published under the title *Odes* in 1920, forming the living pillars of this musical forest or temple, while a few basic themes and images co-existed in Valéry's mind with the actual composition of *La Jeune Parque*. He was staying at the time near Avranches: a tree-filled landscape by a tidal river, a lush region of white earth with groves of great purple beeches and limes where he would walk barefoot at dawn, and of which he wrote in a letter of 1918: 'Tu ne peux imaginer quelles matinées j'ai passées pendant ces deux ou trois mois d'été, dans cette riche région où le grand arbre pousse comme l'herbe...' (P I, 1655). The particular effect of dawn on Valéry's sensibility – sadness, enchantment and lucidity combined; the stimulating presence of great trees; an intoxicating yet also disturbingly arbitrary sensation of mental vitality and will-power; acute awareness of the cycle of the sun and the corresponding limitations of the body – 'Le Jour et le Corps, deux grandes puissances...' (P II, 810): there could scarcely be a better description of the mental landscape of *Charmes*.

Yet it is not simply for its potentially poetic motifs that the letter of 1918 is revealing – dawn, the tree, the cycle of the sun and its subtle coloration of the joint energy of body and mind. Experience of these privileged moments of beginning became closely related in Valéry's mind to the capacities he wished to cherish and provoke in his reader: capacities of transparency and resonance in which the barrier between inner and outer world seems to be dissolved and the mind experiences itself as both instrument and source. 'Le matin premier existe comme un uniforme son' (P II, 588), Valéry writes of this acute sensitivity to the porosity of mind and nature – 'l'âme instant' or 'l'attente événement' – and a stanza added to *Aurore* in 1920 (and subsequently eliminated) expresses this sensation of mingled knowledge and creativity in 'Orphic' terms:

Immobile, tête fée,
Ta substance de cristal,
Matière même d'Orphée,
Rayonne le jour total.
Dans la vibrante demeure
Il n'est de souffle qui meure
Sans avoir semé l'amour.
Je suis cette créature
Dont la fatale nature
Est de créer à son tour.   (P I, 1658).

The sensibility is described here in an elusive combination of partly sexual and alchemical images which helps Valéry convey the ceaseless creativity of its response to the world ('donner/ recevoir') and the 'fatality' of the creative response of consciousness in its turn. Yet the productive energy of mind which Valéry links to the main period of composition of *Charmes* is seen in the letter as precious and fleeting. The reader senses the emotion with which these capacities are shared and celebrated in poetic language in relation to their very impermanence in immediate experience. The ease of composition of the poems is purely relative.[4] The natural, self-consuming incoherence of the creative imagination has been channelled by disciplined effort into a conscious dialogue which includes the challenge of the reader in its action of love (see Part One, p. xvii). It is through this deflection into an art of communicative magnetism through language that the overwhelming power of the sensibility in its 'Orphic' response to nature is utilised and contained.

It is easy to discover more specific links between the poems of *Charmes* and the circumstances of their composition. The response of the mind to the living tree is explored in *Au Platane* and extended into analogy between the growth of a tree and the vitality of the human sensibility in *Ébauche d'un Serpent*; the fertility and solitude of the mind at dawn is present in *Aurore*; response to the cycle of the sun is the basis of *Le Cimetière Marin*: images of the physical world transposed into the drama of the mind, not simply symbolically but as a means of conveying the transformational nature of thought itself. The unity of mind and body from the point of view of the sensibility, was confirmed for Valéry at the time by an overwhelming experience of love which he came to see as an 'event' of comparable magnitude to

107

that of '1892'.[5] Yet more important than any *theme* in the poetry of *Charmes* is the sense of a potential for creative detachment in the heart of experience and with it, a power to modify the experience of living through a form of awareness – 'la puissance de motilité' (xxii, 304) – with passions, values and sensations of its own. Present in love, which Valéry saw as a potential masterpiece of human experience were its energies utilised rather than dissipated, this note of possibility sounds throughout *Charmes* in the heart of the different voices of the sensibility conveyed within it, even dominating the musical enchantment of language itself, though perfectly contained within the experience of form. Poets should be encouraged to produce, like musicians, said Valéry, a diversity of variations or solutions to the same subject (P i, 1501). *Charmes* can be approached as marvellous Bach-like exercises in every possible scale in the relation between expression and thought.

Yet how far is the collection, *Charmes*, to be credited with a deliberate architecture, and what critical approaches are the most appropriate to its spirit as a volume? Ever since it was first published in 1922, *Charmes* has aroused a variety of critical attitudes towards its possible coherence. Some have considered the volume as a deliberately organised work with an inner architecture (any modifications of design on Valéry's part being interpreted as attempts to deepen and improve the original plan).[6] An approach of this kind has been taken to imply in its turn allegorical significance. Single poems have been interpreted as expressing moments in a drama of poetic inspiration unfolding progressively through certain stages (the birth of a poem, and so on).[7] An alternative approach has been to envisage the collection as totally random other than as a series of poems interrelated through formal principles such as length of line. In all successive versions of *Charmes* Valéry does seem to have maintained a grouping in which long poems are interspersed relatively evenly between clusters of short ones, and in which metrical diversity is stressed to its maximum ('J'ai tenté d'utiliser pour chaque poème un rythme différent').[8] This is so from the heptasyllables of *Aurore* and *Palme*, through the octosyllables of *La Pythie*, the decasyllables of *Le Cimetière Marin* 'raised to the power of twelve' (P i, 1503), to the alternating alexandrines and hexasyllables of *Au Platane*, the rapid pentasyllables of *Le Sylphe* and *L'Insinuant* and the alexandrines of *La Dormeuse, Fragments du Narcisse* and *Le Rameur*, all with their varied internal forms and technical challenges.

Yet it is now possible to suggest that *Charmes* is organised neither with a deliberately fixed architecture, nor as a mere album of unrelated pieces; certainly that an allegorical interpretation distorts the nature of its suggestive power. *Charmes* is a volume of poems with a unity, but one in which, unlike *Les Fleurs du Mal* – deliberately organised to give the outline of a human destiny –[9] any thematic coherence likely to detract from fully *poetic* coherence is deliberately dissolved. The unity of *Charmes* lies not in its themes, but in the creative principles affirmed through the treatment of similar themes and images in different tonalities and their further integration into the 'music' of thought. It is a collection arranged so as to allow the reader's mind maximum freedom in appreciating the poems as self-sufficient entities and as works rich in relationships with one another – relationships which are by nature varied and infinite, as Valéry's own re-grouping of the poems served to emphasise.[10] That the type of symbolism which follows from this principle of the activation of the 'laws' of the imagination through the dense constraints of the poem is not allegorical and certainly not justifiably confined to the type of self-referentiality which implicates poetry itself, say the birth of a poem, is easily demonstrated as a result. It is the adventures of 'l'esprit créateur' in its relationship to language which Valéry festively celebrates and explores in *Charmes*.

L'Abeille

Of the twenty-one poems of the final version of *Charmes*, six are much longer than the others, their titles distinguished in capitals in the previous edition of 1926, and it is these six major poems: *Aurore, Fragments du Narcisse, La Pythie, Ébauche d'un Serpent, Le Cimetière Marin* and *Palme* which I shall discuss in greater depth, weaving the shorter poems around them as Valéry intended in his own plan, and dwelling on a poem like *Ode Secrète* only in order to make explicit the metaphysical aesthetic of Symbolism which I have taken to provide the counterpoint to the concept of poetry developed throughout the book. However there is one sonnet, *L'Abeille*, the position of which I have altered in order to highlight the drama of language, thought and sensibility orchestrated in the volume as a whole. Indeed, Valéry's own original placing of *L'Abeille* as the opening poem of the collection[11] confirms its power to act as epigraph to the drama of pain and pleasure illustrated in the different pieces such as *Aurore* (the opening poem proper, with its treatment of the same subject from a different mental 'moment' of the body's response).

To remind ourselves of this central drama – the drama of 'being' and 'knowing' at the heart of Valéry's conception of conscious experience – is to sense, as we did in *La Jeune Parque*, the power of the intellect to mingle with the obscure emotions and sensations of life. Hence, for Valéry, the experience of oscillation when the sensation of living becomes 'opposed' to the intellect; but hence, too, the paradoxically welcome sensation of being bitten or stung into awareness by the stimulus of an emotion or sensation which wakens our conscious selves from partial sleep and sets us towards the creation of a 'substitutional' continuity of our own:

> Ô ruse!...A la lueur de la douleur laissée
> Je me sentis connue encor plus que blessée...
> Au plus traître de l'âme, une pointe me naît;
> Le poison, mon poison, m'éclaire et se connaît:

The bite of the serpent was provided for the Parque by her own truth-seeking sensibility, allowing her to suffer *because* she is unable to embrace or 'comprehend' with the 'arms' of her mind the whole bodily self of which knowledge is but part.

Valéry's poems are not Romantic glorifications of mental suffering. There is an extreme point in this delicate pain/pleasure circuit where creative communication springs from the fused sensation of knowledge and of life. Held within the individual mind at an extreme point of silence and solitude, such exquisitely regenerative pain is also close to the emotion of love, of finding oneself modifiable through a process of exchange in which the intellect, contrary to popular assumption, plays the highest, most 'resonant' part (not only in disciplining the energies involved, but in releasing them for use). 'Vol vers l'aigu [...]', says Valéry's Faust of this strange abundance of emotional energy,

Quelle plénitude, et quelle approche extraordinaire...de l'éclair...
C'est le degré suprême de la Parole. Car, n'est-ce pas un échange de
mystères et la limite de l'entente et de la compréhension immédiate?
Quel poème pourrait-il articuler, ce Bien Souverain?[12]

Without claiming that Valéry's poems succeed in presenting
this 'Bien Souverain' of expressive self-awareness – ineffability is
after all proposed as its essence – I shall suggest that the sensation
of its imminence and lack are conveyed as one of the most creative
aspects of human individuality. 'Et ne parlons pas de "plaisir"'...
Il s'agit de bien autre chose', the notes to 'Faust IV' continue,
'[...] Un gain sublime dans la quantité quotidienne des parties
nulles ou perdues, qui sont la vie'. There are many close links
between this concept of intellectual desire ('Vol vers l'aigu, Danse
dans l'Être, et tendre lutte et choc des plus sensibles armes de la
vie...') and the poem *L'Abeille* with its at first sight straightforwardly erotic imagery of unprotected breast and illuminatory
pain. Yet comparison with the Faust 'letter' serves to remind us
that the erotic imagery of *Charmes* is at its most suggestive when
we allow it to relate at one and the same time to the desire of
consciousness to transform its own uniqueness[13] through the
communicative processes made possible by language. Neither a
poem about sexuality nor an allegory of poetic creation, *L'Abeille*
treats both these areas of experience through the more general
patterns of creative desire shared by the intellect in poetic communication and in love. 'Créer une sorte d'angoisse pour la
résoudre...': it is to this rich mental drama of thirst and source,
desire and anxiety, pain and enchantment in time to which the
metaphor of the bee's sting acts as epigraph: 'Le Temps! il bat
dans la douleur entre la connaissance et la volupté' (vii, 362).

> Quelle, et si fine, et si mortelle,
> Que soit ta pointe, blonde abeille,
> Je n'ai, sur ma tendre corbeille,
> Jeté qu'un songe de dentelle.

L'Abeille: the title of the poem seems to warn us that whatever
intricate patterns of suggestion branch out from the linguistic
ambiguities within, the subject is simple and self-contained: the
bee, one of those living things external to ourselves whose existence
never ceased to haunt and fascinate Valéry himself.[14] Yet the title
of a poem refers to a linguistic reality. How can language do more

than embody the desire to render the living, always supposing that an artist so conscious of the transformation rôle of language retains this impulse at all? The bee as 'signifiant' has meanwhile a literary resonance drawing us to the subject of Inspiration as treated in classical Antiquity and the Renaissance. How will a poet as alert to these dimensions as Valéry deal with the play of naturalistic, formal and lyrical possibilities involved in making with words?

As with so many of the poems of *Charmes* whatever their further yield, the precise, immediately recognisable characteristics of a natural object or phenomenon never cease to be present in some form. Here the universal qualities of a bee are conveyed impressionistically in the manner of a La Fontaine[15] by direct but evanescent references in the words themselves: its potentially lethal sting ('Quelle, et si fine, et si mortelle,/Que soit ta pointe...'), the visual effect of its body in movement ('blonde abeille'), and, through a periphrasis which brings together all the previous characteristics, its capacity to strike the mind of the beholder in a minute flash of sound, colour and warning ('alerte d'or'). Hard consonants (there are as many as eight '[k]' sounds in the poem) reinforce the idea of sharpness, in contrast to the soft 'm' and 'r' sounds associated in the context with voluptuousness, sleep and death. The speaker, a girl or woman like the Parque but more obviously the pure 'Anima' of the sensibility, implores a bee to sting her lightly covered breast so that her mind through her senses may be awakened from sleep: a piece of erotic badinage in Classical and Ronsardian form in which an allegory of Poetic Inspiration is distantly involved (the breast of the Muse, the sting of the inspirational bee). Already the naturalistic elements of the poem are absorbed without visible transition into a symbolic frame of reference. We may recall, too, that Valéry frequently uses the image of the bee as part of the central metaphorical apparatus of a poetry of voice: words seducing and seduced by the receptive 'corolla' of the ear; pain changed poetically to nectar; thoughts buzzing with speech, and so on.[16]

Yet from the very first words of this tantalisingly Sylph-like structure,[17] it is clear that any passive viewpoint will fail to exhaust the dynamic symbolism involved, whether it be representational description on the part of the speaker or allegorical interpretation on the part of the reader. Valéry's symbols always actively involve us on more than one level, precise and suggestive, physical and abstract in one. From the first words of the poem it is through syntax, a deliberately self-conscious, Mallarméan syntax, that the universe of the poem is presented. The purely notional presence of the bee is challenged and rivalled by the vigour of the monologue in which it is addressed, a voice asserting itself as conscious desire, as unmistakable presence in lack. 'Whatever the nature of your sting, even if it should involve death, yet I have taken only minor steps to protect myself; is my reckless daring not worthy of reward?' says this intellect of the sensibility. As for the Parque, the pride of this instinctive enquiry is already acting to the mind as a source of return. ('Fais que ma soif se fasse source' [xxiv, 283].)

In the second quatrain this same ego-filled syntax takes the form of an explicit command ('Pique du sein la gourde belle'), savouring, in the form of periphrasis, the sensation of self-presence which use of language has increased. In the first tercet it moves away from affront on its object to break out instead in a simple statement of need ('J'ai grand besoin d'un prompt tourment'), again an egoism proudly in touch with its power to recognise its exchange with the world. 'Un mal vif et bien terminé/Vaut mieux qu'un supplice dormant' is a generalisation based on past experience and thus a sign of the ability of the intellect to transcend the closure of the present moment. Finally, the jussive subjunctive of the last tercet, 'Soit donc mon sens illuminé', is the grammatical shape of an attempt to summarise, redeem, abridge, perhaps even – for the poem ends with a meditative repetition, 'Sans qui l'Amour meurt ou s'endort' – an attempt to use the present instant to escape the flow of time (an attempt Valéry named 'une fois pour toutes', the instinctive urge of the intellect to exhaust in a single moment all the possibilities of life).

This is not a philosophical poem, yet it is a poem which explores the 'cogito'[18] of philosophy at its birth, the apostrophic logic of intellectual desire. Such is the circle of fascination to which desire is inevitably condemned, and with it the corresponding self-referential image of the bee's illuminating and lethal sting. The bee *is* desire, the image desire creates of itself.[19]

There are, of course, many other ways through which we can

approach meaning in *L'Abeille*, particularly if we are to make more of the controlled ambivalence at its centre between subject- and object-relationships, seducer and seduced – a region of great importance in Valéry's poetics and one which he frequently introduces into the themes and subject-matter of his poems through the image of sexual desire. Take, for example, the central meta- phor of the breast as fruit ('tendre corbeille', 'gourde belle') on which the invisible analogical links between bee and lover, body and sensibility, bee and intellect, and in turn, intellect and pain, might be said to depend. In that it is presented by the speaking voice itself in its campaign of seduction in order to break free from seduction, this image takes on, like an illusionist drawing which invites oscillating interpretations, the function of express- ing on the one hand an autonomous self (Moi^1) at the centre of its experience, and, on the other, (Moi^2), a self submitting to its experience without apparent control, the seducer seduced. The partly humorous and precious image of the girl talking to the bee becomes transformed on the level of the deeper logic of the poem into an expression of the variable relationship between subject and object at the heart of all inner monologue. The wider drama of Tantalus and Narcissus is not far away.

Yet if thought and perception betray inner ambivalence, so, of course, does language, and the preciosity of treatment in a poem like *L'Abeille* never allows us to forget the presence of language itself as a tantalising and creative 'game'. Language cannot but be a form of seduction, the Poet appears to say, as he plays with words, complicating the 'natural' flow of a sentence ('Quelle, et si fine, et si mortelle'), varying the rhythm of the octosyllable, unexpectedly displacing an adjective ('la gourde belle') or even evolving a form of linguistic pun as the action of the girl covering herself with flimsy lace – to hide but the more to reveal – is paralleled in the rhetorical device (*occupatio*) by which the poet 'veils' the idea of the breast in metaphor ('tendre corbeille') only to reveal it the more sensuously later on ('Pique du sein la gourde belle').[20] Preciosity makes language visible, too, in the paradoxical linking of opposites, pleasure and pain, life and death – never allowed to remain completely antithetical ('mal vif', 'supplice dormant') – from which so much of the poem's curiously enforced mobility is derived (enforced in that the poem actively causes us to supply further associations between, say, Eros, the winged archer and the bee's sting). The sting itself is an instrument of pain ('tourment', 'mal') desired as a form of pleasure, a positive stimulus to the mind and senses. Yet at the same time as it is life-giving and regenerative ('mal vif', 'Sans qui l'Amour meurt ou s'endort!'), it is also the harbinger of a new form of death and danger ('mortelle', 'infime alerte d'or'). Release from circularity on one level is replaced by circularity on another. Each stanza reiterates in slightly different form[21] and in a single self-contained sentence the central theme of desire or impatience[22] which generates and closes the form as a whole – a ballet of verbal modulations and relationships similar themselves to the sustained mobility of desire.[23]

However much the preciosity of its treatment may make us aware of the presence of language in this ballet of symbolic relationships, the overriding effect of *L'Abeille* is not that of a purely flippant game of seduction and wit. It is rather an expression of the emotion of enchantment, the emotion of discovering the mechanism of 'charm' – 'poésie' – and its power to bewitch as well as awaken the mind.[24] The bee is eponymously the poem *L'Abeille* whose tiny linguistic structure acts as the 'infime alerte d'or' by whose 'pointe' – a rhetorical term now for the sharpness of wit – our sensibilities awaken to the pain and pleasure of their own 'literary' being as desire for surprise. Behind the apparent casualness of *L'Abeille* is the drama of creative anxiety at the heart of Valéry's vision of the intellect, the drama, even, of intellectual influence where one either rejects what is alien or transforms it into one's own further identity if one is not to 'die' (P II, 1511). 'J' espérais de vous, Maître', says Faust's disciple to his master, 'comme une morsure du serpent de la sagesse dans la chair de mon esprit, une piqûre d'un poison de transformation profonde et merveilleuse...' (P II, 313). How can thirst become a source? How can my own language, self-seduction, retain its links with knowledge of the outer world? It is from a perspective where for Valéry to emit and to receive, to create and to understand are synonymous that we can turn to the true overture of *Charmes, Aurore.*

Aurore

On a first reading, even after we have become aware of the potentially disturbing elements within it, *Aurore*[25] appears to be an ecstatic hymn to the pleasures of waking and the promise of a new day. Rose-pink light, buzzing bees, silken spiders' webs, shadowy vines laden with fruit: the imagery immediately suggests a warmth and appetite for life absent from the sharp-edged monologue of the Parque. Where she had accepted the coming of the day and the rising sun only from necessity, here the mind advances with a fierce confidence and joy. Is it simply that the Parque enters a new day from a vantage-point of painful lucidity as to its repetitive nature, whereas the speaker in *Aurore* is sufficiently befuddled with drowsiness to experience hope, the pleasure of the organism confused with rational belief? Simple enough to possess this undertone – or complex enough to remind us of it – *Aurore* still invites a very different reading and one which, never leaving behind the simple theme of waking after sleep with its fund of physiological imagery, expresses nonetheless a second and different form of waking – a waking within lucidity itself.

Take, for instance, the opening stanza in the monologue:

> La confusion morose
> Qui me servait de sommeil,
> Se dissipe dès la rose
> Apparence du soleil.
> Dans mon âme je m'avance,
> Tout ailé de confiance:
> C'est la première oraison!
> À peine sorti des sables,
> Je fais des pas admirables
> Dans les pas de ma raison.[26]

It would be difficult to justify an interpretation of the poem as a paean of praise for the glories of nature, when the natural dawn is touched on so briefly: 'la rose/apparence du soleil', or when even this brief impression of the natural sun is revealed retrospectively to depend on a hidden analogy with the 'light' of human reason. The growing light is the light of the mind. The word 'apparence' has in its context the double meaning of both 'manifestation' and 'deceptive reality',[27] while 'La confusion morose/Qui me servait de sommeil' suggests in turn, empowered by the double meaning of 'morose' as both taciturn and reluctant (Lt. 'morare', to dawdle or delay), that consciousness is waking not only from the drowsiness of natural sleep, but, as in *L'Abeille*, from a less alert state of awakeness, mental lethargy or lack of self-awareness in its fully developed sense. The first poem of *Charmes* evokes the song of the conscious mind 'waking' to the understanding of its own capacities, including, as we shall see, the capacity for language itself. Nor is it the birth of language but the birth of *awareness* of language which is conveyed: the mind becoming aware, through the dualism introduced by language, of its own creative relationship to the sensibility, source of exchange with the world.

Where the Parque had feared the treacherous ground on which she trod, mortal and vulnerable, the speaker in *Aurore* advances from the shifting sands of the sensibility with buoyant and confident steps. With reason as guide – not mere rationality, but that full, luminous light of self-awareness with its power to dispel the monsters from which it is formed – even the sands themselves ('A peine sorti des sables') can be appreciated as making the confidence of the present firmer by comparison. From the platform provided by nascent self-awareness, the mind in *Aurore* – unlike that of the Parque, hurtled from one side to the other of her inner dualism – has a glorious sensation of option: to explore either the joys of ideas or the mental sensations at the root of ideas, forms of thinking both offered by reason as sources of pleasure and power. Having listened to the first possibility and marvelled and enjoyed its potential, it is the second possibility, with all its greater risks and difficulties, which the voice of creative self-identity chooses in *Aurore*:

> Leur toile spirituelle,
> Je la brise, et vais cherchant
> Dans ma forêt sensuelle
> Les oracles de mon chant.

'Quelle, et si fine et si mortelle/Que soit ta pointe': is not the ability to choose difficulty and risk the essence of confidence devoid of naïve hope? Was not the Parque's torment caused by lack of this option, a lack which called up images of suicide and her reluctant choice of life as something inescapable? Perhaps,

after all, the two protagonists have much in common; but with
the difference that the Parque had not yet fully consciously discovered the void at the centre of herself as a source of creative
power, the delights of 'l'informe'. Or again, is the creative hope
at the end of *Aurore* – expressed by means of the movement
through time of the previously absent Mallarméan swan[28] – a
naïve 'waking' illusion which the Parque's nocturnal lucidity
would quickly destroy? To find oneself unable to answer such
questions definitively is to realise just how much the meaning of
Valéry's poetry depends on *tonality*, the different poetic stress
given to areas of experience thematically similar in themselves
and with no solution other than in existential terms.

Aurore, in monologue form, is composed of nine ten-lined stanzas
which seem to echo with their regular progression the confident
affirmation of the voice they bear as a source of presence to itself.
Yet this very regularity is composed, we find, of a multiplicity of
quivering movements rather than of reflective statements neatly
contained within each verse.

What may appear calm blocks of words are woven together
from questions, enjambements, changes of register – from the
intimate to the gravely, though still excitedly, proverbial – and
above all, from exclamations: statements transformed by the
characteristic exclamation marks of *Charmes* into urgent, lyrical
apostrophes. The bold regularity of the stanza form is meanwhile
belied by the uneven measure of the heptasyllable, seven measures
where the ear expects an eighth, restlessly moving on as each new
element is introduced.

> Tout calice me demande
> Que j'attende pour son fruit.

Even the internal rhyme reinforces here stylistically the linguistic
message that reward comes from movement in similarity, that to
wait is itself a hoping and a listening, a vast impatient luxury of
controlled yet eager thirst: 'vouloir, vouloir...Et même ne pas
excessivement vouloir' (P I, 480). And this is not the only instance
in the poem of a form of 'en abyme' or stylistic echoing, by
which the reader's experiences are picked up thematically within
the text itself. Should we feel that something about the poem

– its imagery of thorns, pain, blood – curiously belies its at first sight drowsy, humorous sun-lit tone, then our sense of deceptive simplicity, of challenging inner complexity, is expressed for us explicitly in the image of transparent water revealing infinite depths. But which came first, the experience or the textual echo? Such an image obviously helps form our receptivity to textual patterns in the first place, just as mental imagery for Valéry, is more than a mere reflection of the mind's contents, indeed, our strongest reality. Such poetry is not without links with that mental plenitude for which the Parque still half-consciously longed even at the height of her happiness – a happiness incomplete since it failed to contain the notion of mortality, its portion of shade: 'Je regrette à demi cette vaine puissance'.

The plenitude evoked in *Aurore*, on the contrary, contains the idea of thorn and shadow. It is a more integrative state of consciousness, its tone of joyfulness more precious accordingly; and in that it coincides with the incorporative ideal of poetry, it is indeed 'une pensée singulièrement achevée', containing and accepting its own risks and shadows, defending itself from within from its own power to charm. The consciousness of poetry – 'Poésie' – and the light of self-awareness – 'l'Âme' – could be said to coincide. But to trace this thesis further will involve discussing the rôle in the poem of language – sound – as a consciously expressed experience and theme.

> Salut! encore endormies
> À vos sourires jumeaux,
> Similitudes amies
> Qui brillez parmi les mots!
> Au vacarme des abeilles
> Je vous aurai par corbeilles,
> Et sur l'échelon tremblant
> De mon échelle dorée,
> Ma prudence évaporée
> Déjà pose son pied blanc.

'Le mot est le mouvement de *salut*!' (x, 4), Valéry wrote, using once more the characteristic exclamation mark which turns a statement into surprise. 'Salut! Divinités par la rose et le sel, [...] Îles!', the Parque had said to the buzzing islands of the dawn, and 'Salut! [...]/Similitudes amies/Qui brillez parmi les mots!', says the speaker in *Aurore* 'seeing', and thus remembering, the intellectual pleasures of language, the links between words. To greet is to recognise, to name and to remember all in one, and it is this language-linked capacity for self-identity which Valéry seems to be evoking by the self-referential device of greeting or celebrating in language the capacity to greet and celebrate made possible by words. If the word is the movement of greeting, it is also – to take the other sense of the word 'salut' – the movement of salvation, the movement by which, in naming the world, we identify ourselves.[29] And perhaps we should not be too ready to conclude that those 'similitudes amies' are best confined to the kind of phonetic similarities which the poet *par excellence*, the poet of 'poésie pure' in particular, sets at the centre of his craft. The double meaning of the word 'salut' itself invites 'friendly similarity' – friendly because to perceive a relationship is to be greeted in turn by a smile – and this capacity for recognition is at work in all mental activity where conscious awareness is involved. The poem is surely concerned with this general capacity for self-recognition through memory: the capacity to generate and appreciate ideas. To be able to perceive similarities and differences between words is to be able to think creatively, and it is towards this 'golden' capacity that the mind of the speaker gradually climbs, already recklessly posing a 'white foot' on the 'ladder' of the intellect. Language here is at its most delightfully rewarding for the reader too. As we ourselves perceive more and more relationships, we feel proud and confident in our own advance. 'Ma prudence évaporée', for example – a characteristic periphrasis for temerity in which mental sensation replaces the abstract – invites us to call to mind the potential threat of the bees: by a process of metaphorical deduction, ideas, with the vital power to sting the mind awake. Similarly, the whole stanza contains the impressionistic, never quite finalised image of someone climbing a ladder to gather basketfuls of fruit. In the course of relating this visual image to the abstract idea it expresses metaphorically (the mind gradually climbing to higher and higher levels of conscious awareness), we find ourselves creating further images: a golden vertebral column (Mallarmé's 'désir et mal de mes vertèbres' may be partly responsible),[30] a trembling ladder of invisible mental being with physiological shape through which is expressed the hope of universal form. And perhaps, too, in response to that lovely modulation from the

rosy light of the dawn in the first stanza to the fuller golden light
in the second, with its corresponding mental modulation from confused half-sleep to full waking and from mental confusion to
reason, the further physiological image comes to mind of the rose
tinge of blood up to the 'golden fleece' of the head – a resonance
which derives, together with its further erotic and mythical connotations, from reading *Aurore* in conjunction with *La Jeune
Parque* and other poems in *Charmes*, in particular *La Pythie*.
Such is the exciting power of Valéry's poetry to give 'visible'
expression to mental impressions naturally rich in physiological
sensations of their own:

> Quelle aurore sur ces croupes
> Qui commencent de frémir!
> Déjà s'étirent par groupes
> Telles qui semblaient dormir:
> L'une brille, l'autre bâille;
> Et sur un peigne d'écaille
> Égarant ses vagues doigts,
> Du songe encore prochaine,
> La paresseuse l'enchaîne
> Aux prémisses de sa voix.
>
> Quoi! c'est vous, mal déridées!
> Que fîtes-vous, cette nuit,
> Maîtresses de l'âme, Idées,
> Courtisanes par ennui?

Imagery in these stanzas is humorously domestic, taken from
everyday realities of waking: yawning, combing the hair. It dazzles
by its fusion of the banal and abstract, by its presence not simply
as a device, but as a sign, like humour, of the virtuoso capacity for
analogy, which is here the theme of the poem. Meanwhile the
animality of 'croupes' and the reference to the Ideas as courtesans
keeps alive metaphorically the still developing notion of reciprocity between consciousness, language and self. Without the
presence of consciousness, they became bored, 'courtisanes par
ennui´, 'maîtresses de l'âme',[31] and now they themselves speak –
a certain piousness is the risk of the virtuoso performer? – flaunt-
ing their own miraculous persistence during the interval of the
night:[32]

> – Toujours sages, disent-elles,
> Nos présences immortelles

Jamais n'ont trahi ton toit!
Nous étions non éloignées,
Mais secrètes araignées
Dans les ténèbres de toi!

The tone of these lines and of the following stanza ('Ne seras-tu
pas de joie/Ivre [...]') is simple: a lyrical apostrophe to the
mysterious process of maturation by which ideas form in the
shadows of the mind – in sleep or in an interval of conscious
thought – ideas which seem strangely powerful by virtue of their
close cohabitation with nature. Something of the joy and power of
this process, proof of the roots of the intellect in processes more
comprehensive than those relating to its own subjective sensations
of autonomy, is conveyed in the mixed metaphors of roof, spiders'
webs, shadows, silken suns: linked in turn to the still main but
now implicit metaphor of Ideas as 'Maîtresses de l'âme', courting
the soul with their 'tremblants préparatifs'. Yet, simple and lyrical
in tone, these lines still play a complex rôle in the structure of the
poem. Taken together with the following stanzas in which the
speaker's consciousness rejects this offer of inspiration, they introduce perhaps the most important paradox at the heart of the
poem and at the heart of Valéry's theory of the creative imagination. How is it that although courtesans of the soul, the Ideas have
remained faithful to the speaker's consciousness ('Jamais n'ont
trahi ton toit!')? How is it that they are spiders spinning webs of
being – Mallarmé's image for the creative imagination[33] – yet that
they themselves are subordinate to the overriding consciousness of
the speaker, who even eventually rejects them? How is it that they
themselves 'speak' within the total monologue of 'la Personne qui
parle'?

Such reflections draw our attention to the complex structure of
the poem, where the total voice of the speaker is logically included
in the analogies it makes, speaker and proposition knowingly part
of the same system (III, 707). It is the consciousness of the speaker
which endows the ideas with speech and thus with retrospective
insight into the lost unity of self for ever to be restored. It is the
consciousness of the speaker which is both the spider catching the
sensibility in its own metaphorical nets and the nets themselves.
Hence, to use the précieux image, the paradoxical faithfulness of
the courtesans in the heart of their adultery. Hence the para-

doxical joy and benefit from what must be rejected now in order to be enjoyed more meaningfully later on. 'Leur toile spirituelle,/ Je la brise [...]' – the movement that follows is not, then, as it is so often taken to be, a movement of rejection of the intellect in favour of the senses. It is rather a movement towards discovering and restoring the primitive totality of the mind which the Ideas themselves proclaimed at birth: that very same, forward-moving confidence and trust in the unknown on the basis of present sensation which has been there in the poem since the very first verse.

A passage in Valéry's Dialogue *Eupalinos ou l'Architecte* can be used to confirm and clarify conceptually the important mental structure which he is celebrating analytically and lyrically in *Aurore*. 'Je sens mon besoin de beauté, égal à mes ressources inconnues, engendrer à soi seul des figures qui le contentent', says Eupalinos:

> Je désire de tout mon être...Les puissances accourent. Tu sais bien que les puissances de l'âme procèdent étrangement de la nuit... [...] Les voici, toutes chargées de clarté et d'erreur. Le vrai, le faux, brillent également dans leurs yeux, sur leurs diadèmes. Elles m'écrasent de leurs dons, elles m'assiègent de leurs ailes...

and yet, Eupalinos continues,

> Ô moment le plus important, et déchirement capital!...Ces faveurs surabondantes et mystérieuses, loin de les accueillir telles quelles, uniquement déduites du grand désir, naïvement formées de l'extrême attente de mon âme, il faut que je les arrête, ô Phèdre, et qu'elles attendent mon signal.

And, to his listener's question concerning the cruel force of this rejection or postponement of completion:

> – C'est qu'il m'importe sur toute chose, d'obtenir de *ce qui va être*, qu'il satisfasse, avec toute la vigueur de sa nouveauté, aux exigences raisonnables de *ce qui a été*. (P II, 96–7).

To return to the poem, we can see how Valéry is exploring that urge towards the total expression and understanding of experience, that hope of self-replenishing form, which leads the mind away from its own immediate gifts – away from Ideas – only the better to capitalise on their strengths creatively, on their miraculous birth in the heart of the wider sensibility of which they are part: a paradoxical movement of refusal of the intellect by the intellect, which contains in itself an exultant, risky feeling of freedom, a feeling of relying on the body as a wider principle for inspiration than the intellect alone. It is this creative principle, one which we saw the Parque painfully discovering as a natural necessity of the creative mind before fully aligning herself with it intellectually, which is given its full emphasis in:

> Être! Universelle oreille!
> Toute l'âme s'appareille
> À l'extrême du désir...
> Elle s'écoute qui tremble
> Et parfois ma lèvre semble
> Son frémissement saisir.

These lines and those of the following stanza ('Voici mes vignes...'), perfectly integrated into the poem, yet self-sufficient in their microcosmic powers of suggestion, take us, then, to the heart of *Aurore*, to the heart of *Charmes*, to the heart of the experience of creative invention on which Valéry based his theory and practice of poetic composition. Through the image of the deliberately broken web of ideas and the daringly difficult search in the sensual forests of the mind for the oracles of song, he introduces the theme of 'Being' as a vast, listening ear: 'Être! Universelle oreille!',[34] to which the sensibility, 'l'âme', the total nervous system, is creatively attuned by desire, an ear listening to its own trembling movements which the lips of consciousness – language – seem sometimes to seize. Here, then, are the shady vines, the cradles of the precious sense of newness paradoxically necessary to the mind for its sense of identity. Here consciousness is in perfect reciprocity with those creative principles of the natural universe within its own substance. Where the intellect alone was incapable of finding a cause in the heavens, to use the words of *L'Ange*, the sensibility, inclusive of the intellect, offers via the reason a purpose for the intellect to adopt as its own.

> Je fais des pas admirables
> Dans les pas de ma raison.

It is the reward of this anti-rationalist but still predominantly intellectual certainty of the fertile and cohesive values of 'l'informe' which the two final stanzas of the poem appear to affirm and recapitulate in a yet higher key or tone of rational self-awareness:

> Je ne crains pas les épines!
> [. . .]
> Il n'est pour ravir un monde
> De blessure si profonde
> Qui ne soit au ravisseur
> Une féconde blessure,
> Et son propre sang l'assure
> D'être le vrai possesseur.

And in the final stanza with its almost mystical imagery of swan and deep water, it is in the context of reason itself that hope is felt to exist, a sensation of presence and futurity all in one – 'l'attente événement' – with its characteristic physiological shudder from the neck to the tip of the toe:

> J'approche la transparence
> De l'invisible bassin
> Où nage mon Espérance
> Que l'eau porte par le sein.
> Son col coupe le temps vague
> Et soulève cette vague
> Que fait un col sans pareil...
> Elle sent sous l'onde unie
> La profondeur infinie,
> Et frémit depuis l'orteil.

In a sense, *Aurore* is Valéry's *Art Poétique* – a reason for discussing it here at relatively great length. It evokes the creative principles – 'Poésie' – on which we have seen him base his theory of poetry as the celebration and application of the properties of language. The poet's initial impetus must be away from ordinary language usage – which entices thought in a direction far from its unified intellectual and physical origins – and back instead to the potential unity at its roots, 'la philosophie à l'état naissant'. 'Être libre', Eupalinos had continued, 'Il y a bien des choses, [. . .] il y a... toutes choses dans cet instant; et tout ce dont s'occupent les philosophes se passe entre le regard qui tombe sur un objet, et la connaissance qui en résulte... pour en finir toujours prématurément' (P II, 97). Just such a deliberate bifurcation of response is clearly present in the poem.

How closely, too, the lines beginning 'Être! Universelle oreille!' can be related to that attitude of 'acoustic' expectancy or 'atten-

tion' (the root of 'attente'), which for Valéry characterised intellectual sensibility in the state of resonant self-awareness necessary
for the first stages of poetic composition: that reversed relationship
between the mouth and the ear ('l'oreille parle, la bouche écoute')
to which he so often refers. For example:

> Un homme qui fait des vers, suspendu entre son beau idéal et son
> rien, est dans cet état d'attente active et interrogative qui le rend
> uniquement et extrêmement sensible aux formes et aux mots que
> l'idée de son désir, reprise comme retracée indéfiniment, *demande à
> inconnu*, aux ressources latentes de son organisation de parleur, –
> cependant que je ne sais quelle *force chantante* exige de lui ce que la
> pensée toute nue ne peut obtenir que par une foule de combinaisons
> successivement essayées.   (P I, 212).

Is it *so* misleading to interpret *Aurore* and the companion poems
it heralds as the symbolic description of poetic inspiration, the
speaker as the poet awaiting the privileged form of the work, and
so on?

The answer to this question should contain, I think, an equally
large element of yes and no. If we interpret the symbolism of the
poem in too narrow a sense, we may fail to do justice to its power
to explore the sensations of consciousness in its general relationship
to self-unity: the subject which never ceased to interest Valéry,
and which gives rise in his poetry to the metaphorical expression
of an immense range of feelings of general human relevance.
The experience of song – 'Poésie' – is an experience of mental
unity unrelated to specifically linguistic or musical contexts,
although never unrelated to the capacity of consciousness for inner
dialogue, 'la parole intérieure'.

The implied comparison with poetic composition has nonetheless served to remind us that for Valéry interest in the generation
of the poem was inseparable from interest in the functioning of
the living being in general. It was the interdependent relation
between the self-governing operations of the intellect and the sensibility ('parler/entendre'), in turn dependent on the body as a
whole, which the process of creative invention in poetic composition more than any other activity of thought made graphically
and dramatically visible, particular, in his case, in relation to
sound. To state that the symbolism of *Aurore* relates to the process
of poetic composition is essentially to state that it relates to that

intrusion of knowledge into the process of living, that discovery of the resonant nature of the sensibility, which, for Valéry, is the essence of consciousness as a form of self-listening exemplified in the capacity for inner monologue. 'Cet hymen de pensées qui s'est conclu de soi-même sur tes lèvres, comme l'acte distrait de ta voix', says Eupalinos:

> [...] tient à une nécessité admirable, qu'il est presque impossible de penser dans toute sa profondeur, mais dont tu as ressenti obscurément la présence persuasive. Imagine donc fortement ce que serait un mortel assez pur, assez raisonnable [...] pour méditer jusqu'à l'extrême réalité, cet étrange rapprochement des formes visibles avec les assemblages éphémères de sons successifs; pense à quelle origine intime et universelle il s'avancerait;...' (P II, 96).

Yet a more serious consequence of confining the symbolism of a poem such as *Aurore* to the idea of the poet rather than to the relationship between consciousness and the sensibility in general is that it tends to underestimate that whole region of poetic composition specifically related to the process of communication and language as a craft of form. The poet's specific work begins for Valéry when the process of creative sensibility he refers to in *Aurore* is adjusted to the universe of language itself, a process of infinite judgement, willpower and control where the mind must once more move away from its united intellectual and physical origins in order to communicate and extend them in verbal form, Looking again at *Aurore* from this point of view, we discover, to our surprise, that its theme is almost an anti-'Art Poétique'. For the poem could equally well be interpreted thematically as a rejection of poetry, a rejection of the whole definitively formalised universe of words and a violently affirmed 'return' to the forests of the sensibility where, as in Baudelaire's *Correspondances*, the 'egality' of the mind and nature is enough: 'Voici mes vignes ombreuses/[...]/A l'égal de mes regards...'.

The resolution of *this* paradox takes us back to the complex structure of *Aurore* and to the power of the images at its centre to relate outwards to contain the mind of the speaker – and thus, by implication, the mind of the poet 'imagined' within the dialogue itself. Attempting to arrive at a complete representation of the creative action of the mind exemplified in poetic composition, Valéry wrote in his essay on La Fontaine:

Désesperons de la vision nette en ces matières. Il faut se bercer d'une image. J'imagine ce poète un esprit plein de ressources et de ruses, faussement endormi au centre imaginaire de son œuvre encore incréé, pour mieux attendre cet instant de sa propre puissance qui est sa proie. [...] Là, attentive aux hasards entre lesquels elle choisit sa nourriture; là, très obscure au milieu des réseaux et des secrètes harpes qu'elle s'est faites du langage, dont les trames s'entretissent et toujours vibrent vaguement, une mystérieuse Arachné, muse chasseresse, guette.   (P I, 484).

By relating the poem to this remarkable passage, with which it has so much imagery in common, we can see that in *Aurore* Valéry has indeed 'imagined' the Poet; or, rather, that he has imagined a mind imagining the structure of its own desire in its relation to the experience of language. Rather than attribute to the speaker the image of the spider's web, he has attributed it – by the device of reported speech – to the ideas themselves, thus distancing once again the mind from its own image. The central intellectual paradox at the heart of Valéry's theory of the creative imagination is thus allowed to radiate from language itself; namely that the mind is capable of a form of attention, 'attente', readiness, which presupposes but cannot predict what it finds. It is the structure of this vital form of waiting – a paradoxically active waiting incapable of formulating its object, yet powerfully orientated and selective in its dealings with the sensibility – which the poem simultaneously analyses and lyrically evokes, linking, in the words of *Eupalinos*, 'une analyse à une extase' (P II, 96). By these 'structuralist' methods, Valéry nonetheless expresses the anti-Structuralist notion of a subject at the centre of its work, a spider or hunter whose webs of metaphor are necessary to the emergence of a form which, however separate, is nonetheless necessary in revealing that which it is not: individual consciousness. 'Le Moi est bien la Personne qui parle. [...] Ainsi est-il *trouvé*' (xx, 190).

The true meaning of *Aurore* is its total effect, the transformational action of language by which the reader in turn 'awakes' to the creative processes of the intellect activated by language.

> La confusion morose
> Qui me servait de sommeil,
> Se dissipe dès la rose
> Apparence du soleil.

To turn again to those words, having 'understood' the semantic message they contain, is to find ourselves free to set out on the journey of another poem. How the sounds of words (those persuasive patterns of 'm', 's', 'p' and 'd' and predominant 'o') create the forward moving sensation of physical continuity they describe not through any fleeting equation between the sound and referential sense of words, but through their own power to awaken the physiological roots of our mind in its 'désir de son'.

> Toute feuille me présente
> Une source complaisante
> Où je bois ce frêle bruit...
> Tout calice me demande
> Que j'attende pour son fruit.

The theme of the anticipation of sound as the source of the sensibility is no longer a metaphor external to our own experience. We too 'drink' sound and anticipate its reward from within, rhyme not the least of the experience: 'demande', 'attende'; 'bruit', 'fruit'. Where metaphors introduce a change of direction within the unity of the semantic field,[35] sound creates homogeneity. Indeed the rhythm of the poem is so insistent in its projective grouping of words – the pronounced mute 'e' often coinciding with the caesura so that the 3 + 4 division seems blurred and impetuous – that we feel the 'message' of the speaker to consist of movement itself. Nor is this process of formal transformation confined to the organisation of sound, rhythmically and phonetically. The structure of *Aurore* creates a form of progressive synchronicity, as if language is describing the unfolding of simultaneous levels of experience, each new phrase sending us back to earlier points in the poem so that we have before us eventually a complete universe, a closed system, a perfect spider's web.

In the 'Orphic' stanza omitted from the final version of *Aurore*, which is, I have suggested, relevant to the creative drama expressed in *Charmes* as a whole,[36] Valéry had referred to the 'fatality' of the creative mind which cannot but echo in turn those creative relational principles discovered on the level of the primary sensibility in its relation to sound:

> Je suis cette créature
> Dont la fatale nature
> Est de créer à son tour.

It is now possible to suggest that the stanza was omitted for reasons of scrupulous judgement relating to the power of the poem to turn back on itself and reflect like a mirror its own creative principles. *Aurore* concerns the hope injected into the mind by wilful or rationally controlled bifurcation away from the certainty of ready-made 'linguistic' thought into the uncertain system of the sensibility. To introduce a note of analytic finality would have been to destroy the poem's power to express the freedom, confidence and joy instilled into consciousness by language. '[...] il faut du travail pour faire la chasse et simuler les premiers termes de la *pensée à l'état naissant*. Simulation aussi savante que l'on peut, de la pensée à l'état naissant. C'est poésie' [vi, 469]. Valéry might just as well have added 'Poésie, c'est *Aurore*'. For it is precisely on this note – the verbal celebration of the power of language to simulate and embody the *birth* of thought – that the collection *'Charmes, c'est-à-dire Poèmes'* begins.

(a) Au Platane, Cantique des Colonnes, Poésie

'Mon âme aujourd'hui se fait arbre. [. . .] Hier je la sentis source', says Tityre in Valéry's *Dialogue de l'Arbre*, and, to the challenge of Lucrèce that he is the spirit of pure metamorphosis,

> C'est à toi de le dire. Je te laisse la profondeur. Mais puisque cette masse d'ombre t'attire comme une île de fraîcheur au milieu du feu de ce jour, [. . .] faisons entre nous l'échange et la connaissance de cet Arbre, avec la louange et l'amour qu'il m'inspire... [. . .] Tendrement naît l'aurore, et toute chose se déclare. Chacune dit son nom,[1] car le feu du jour neuf la réveille à son tour. Le vent naissant bruit dans ta haute ramure. Il y place une source, et j'écoute l'air vif. Mais c'est Toi que j'entends. Ô langage confus, je veux fondre toutes tes voix! Cent mille feuilles mues font ce que le rêveur murmure aux puissances du songe. Je te réponds, mon Arbre, je te parle et dis mes secrètes pensées.   (P II, 178).

Before its next two main poems, *Fragments du Narcisse* and *La Pythie*, *Charmes* contains seven shorter poems which can be seen to pursue the different perspectives of consciousness heralded in *Aurore*, the first of these, *Au Platane*, evoking precisely what the splendidly lyrical yet also deeply analytical passage just quoted suggests: the 'voice' of the mind as reflected and inspired by the Tree.[2]

Au Platane

Many of the images used in *Aurore* to describe the sensibility as a resonator picking up its own trembling movements and converting them into consciousness have been transferred in *Au Platane* to the great plane-tree itself, its mass of quivering leaves sounding like harps in the bitter Mediterranean wind:

> Haute profusion de feuilles, trouble fier
>   Quand l'âpre tramontane
> Sonne, au comble de l'or, l'azur du jeune hiver
>   Sur tes harpes, Platane,

and its roots deep in the dark maternal soil:

> Ombre retentissante en qui le même azur
> Qui t'emporte, s'apaise,
> La noire mère astreint ce pied natal et pur
> A qui la fange pèse.

The image of the tree's roots and white trunk as a pure nascent foot echoes the 'pied blanc' which the 'prudence évaporée' of the speaker in *Aurore* placed on the rung of the ladder of reason – consciousness in its purest, boldest, most lyrically aspiring or 'vertical' form – and the living shade of the plane tree is chosen explicitly by 'la Personne qui parle' to be the bearer of precisely that same message of the hope of song:

> Afin que l'hymne monte aux oiseaux qui naîtront,
> Et que le pur de l'âme
> Fasse frémir d'espoir les feuillages d'un tronc
> Qui rêve de la flamme,
>
> Je t'ai choisi, puissant personnage d'un parc,
> Ivre de ton tangage,
> Puisque le ciel t'exerce, et te presse, ô grand arc,
> De lui rendre un langage!

In this sense, the externally real tree evoked in *Au Platane* is chosen by the speaker as the 'oracle of song' in the same way that the 'vignes ombreuses' of inner sensibility were chosen in *Aurore*. Watching the great tree tossing in the light, its feet in the dark, its leaves sparkling with light and shade and sounding in the 'inspiring' wind,[3] the human mind is inspired in turn to detect and refurbish the principles of its own creative sensibility, re-electing them in the living tree as a source of illumination, strength and delight. 'Le rendement est preuve de la puissance de l'esprit. Que d'observations subtiles sur un arbre. Désordre local, ordre général' (xii, 365).

The act of choice stylised in *Au Platane* is, then, a complex one involving both freedom and finitude. By 'choosing' an object in the outside world to 'bear' the message of the inner sensibility it reveals, the eye and ear of the creative imagination – 'le seul poète' – is reaffirming that same preference for the pre-intellectual which we have seen at work in *Aurore*. It elects a source outside the network of its own ideas which strengthens its creative freedom by

132

contact with its limits, its inability, like the tree, to move away from its own relational principles, its own fatal 'love'.

We cannot help but see in trees our own upstretched arms, Valéry once noted (I, 334).[4] This vital limit to our perceptions is explored in the poem *Au Platane* both in the images of human shape through which the tree is evoked:

> Tu penches, grand Platane, et te proposes nu,
> Blanc comme un jeune Scythe

and, above all, in the urge towards language which the mind of the beholder cannot but attribute to the tree. Tossing and swaying, its branches appear to be communicating by their gestures, while the sound of the wind rustling the branches seems already like the intoxicating beginnings of music or articulate language. It is an impression so strong that the tree is begged eventually to formulate the language the wind appears to wring from it; to groan, to dare to express its sufferings with a voice:

> Ose gémir!... Il faut, ô souple chair du bois,
> Te tordre, te détordre,
> Te plaindre sans te rompre, et rendre aux vents la voix
> Qu'ils cherchent en désordre!

To this plea, of course, the tree does not comply. Even its apparent gesture of proud refusal reinforces that same circle of anthropomorphic images expressively projected onto it by the watching mind:

> – *Non, dit l'arbre. Il dit*: NON! *par l'étincellement*
> *De sa tête superbe,*
> *Que la tempête traite universellement*
> *Comme elle fait une herbe!*[5]

Yet we *know* we cannot but be reminded of human gestures by the shapes and sounds of the natural world. Awareness of the inevitability of the anthropomorphic provides a check on the power of fantasy to go beyond 'le vrai', that power which Tityre, the lyrical artist, fears Lucrèce, the thinker, will wish him to curb. In reality, these two strands of our perception – detachment (Lucrèce) and involvement (Tityre) – are simultaneous or oscillatory. Detachment is also present in empathy and in our use of images with which to structure reality. It is visibly present, for example, in the first-person framework of the narrative in which the speaker projects his images in the form of exhortations, comparisons, commands:

> Flagelle-toi!...Parais l'impatient martyr
> Qui soi-même s'écorche,
> Et dispute à la flamme impuissante à partir
> Ses retours vers la torche!

A comparison with a living flame is chosen to express the tree's dynamism; yet the *difference* between the flame and the tree has been used at the same time to reinforce the distinctively human, a vast, desirous impatience unheard of in nature and which recognises itself only by further differentiation from what it perceives, here its sense of what the tree cannot do, rooted as it is in the soil.[6]

'Appear the martyr': it is as if the conventions of grammar have been used in such a way as to reveal the mental processes at work in imagery – in this case the sensation on the part of the language-user that analogy is approximate and as important in its points of difference as of similarity.[7] The mode of address displays as it is used, the human freedom, power and isolation of recognising the provisional and alternative, and the knowledge that the penalty for the descriptive power made available by language is loss of union with what we perceive. To understand and to create are one, is the kind of axiom from his notebooks which Valéry might be said to have embodied in such a poem. By a curious reversal brought about by the semantic pivot in the last stanza of the poem (which retrospectively re-casts what has gone before it), the object's refusal to become what it appears to be acts as the affirmation of the very same mental freedom which language encourages: the power of the mind to distinguish itself from the imagery it projects as part of itself (xix, 543).

What, then, of the poem *Au Platane* as a totally united gesture of language? One of its most striking achievements is to make visible, as does Baudelaire's poem *Le Cygne*, the processes of detachment and involvement available to the mind in the creation of analogy – the way in which such processes can increase our sensation of being alive. How our sense of self-identity can be increased by exchange with things outside ourself both notional and present – the tree in this case is conveyed very much as a *present* tree – was to Valéry one of the most precious of intellectual discoveries and one which poetry has the task of celebrating and recording in turn. For at the same time as it finds a way to make visible as poetic presence this invisible interplay of mental faculties, *Au Platane* is a discourse in which lyricism and analysis, the responses of Tityre and Lucrèce,[8] merge into a passionate 'song' of their own, the song of a human response to nature[9] which becomes in its own turn 'un arbre de paroles' (P II, 193).[10]

Which came first in the poem's genesis: the reality of a rhythm – the alternating alexandrine and six-syllabled line mimicking the swaying and striving of a tree in the wind – or the notion of real tree suggesting a rhythm; or, again, the rhythm of an emotion striving for words and selecting the rocking tree as image of itself? Whichever way round – and the primacy of rhythm over theme is characteristic of Valéry's method of creative invention – it is the phenomenon of language as much as the phenomenon of tree which *Au Platane* 'leaves' in our memories. We ourselves are now 'inspired' by the possibilities of the creative imagination which the tree-image seems to embody as one of those 'figures de pensée' by which the poet can modify the fixed constructions of words.[11] The process is there in miniature in those 'mots-aiguillages'[12] which so often cause the ideas in Valéry's poetry to fly in more than one direction at once. The word 'Cheval',[13] for instance, at first the rearing and chafing form of the tree which the watching imagination strives in vain to possess definitively, then springs out as Pegasus, the winged horse of the gods, confirming the theme of inspiration which has been present all along in the references to music, to expression, to the breath of the wind (Lt. 'inspirare'). This being so, the reference to the poet when it comes is removed as far as possible from the scriptural notion of language or, indeed, from the metaphorical or analogical in any indirect sense:

> Ô qu'amoureusement des Dryades rival,
> Le seul poète puisse
> Flatter ton corps poli comme il fait du Cheval
> L'ambitieuse cuisse!...

Instead, the reference grows from the thirst of the narrator in touch with the limitations of perception and the provisionality of language which the tree makes him feel in exhilarating form. Tree and watcher, poet and horse, coincide associatively; and the horse, like the tree, cannot be tamed by desire[14] except in order to create further reflections of itself – 'l'esprit étant alors les variations d'une chose qui n'est pas esprit' (xix, 543). For where it cannot confine and exhaust, language has a special role in expressing the emotion of what cannot be said. 'N[ous] ne sommes pas accomplis en tant qu'hommes par la vue et le tact. Il nous faut *parler*', Valéry once noted with obvious relevance to the kind of expressive impetus – 'voice' – which the stylistic devices of *Au Platane* make curiously visible:

> faire parler la chose comme si ce fut une limite, un seuil, que *l'expression articulée*.
> C'est une éducation nouvelle et difficile que de considérer ou plutôt de *ressentir*, au contraire, que le langage est provisionnel, – que le système des mots est le *plan des échanges* avec le commun, le primitif, l'impur et l'idolâtre.   (xiii, 590).

Far from didactic in the rhetorical sense, the poetry of *Charmes* is deeply didactic in the poetic sense, imparting a knowledge of the existential relationship between language and experience which must be felt to be learnt[15] – the poet's task being to impart that knowledge by extending and applying the properties of language made manifest in speech.[16]

Once again we can see why Valéry omitted from the final version of the poem a stanza which risked making his subject too explicit. The omitted stanza in this case directly compared the dilemma of the human being to the condition of the tree:

> Ton supplice n'est pas un supplice étranger!
>   Mais, l'ornement du nôtre,
> Je t'assemble à l'horreur de ne pouvoir changer
>   Mon ombre contre une autre!   (P i, 1660).

Not only is this human comparison implicit throughout the poem in terms of the organic laws which are shared by the natural and the human organism, but by the omission of the stanza it is transposed more effectively to the presence of the human voice and its powers. The language of the narrator is the language which the tree cannot give because it is not human; while the language of the poem is the language that ordinary speech cannot give.

> [...] point de 'moi' sans 'toi', Chacun son Autre, qui est son Même.
> Ou bien le *Moi est deux* – par définition. S'il a *voix* il y a oreille.

Intérieurement, s'il y a voix, il n'y a pas vue de qui parle. Et qui décrira définira la *différence* qu'il y a *entre cette phrase même qui se dit* et *ne se prononce pas*, et cette phrase sonnante dans l'air?

(XXI, 304).

The complex refusal of voice on the part of the tree in *Au Platane* is Valéry's poetic rendering of this vital difference between external and internal language, his means of articulating the 'silence' or 'ineffability' of the mind behind speech. The paradox of *Au Platane* is thus the paradox of a poetry of voice at its most conspicuous. Flight from language as absolute coincides expressively with the natural power of words to relate creatively to what cannot be said.[17] Is *Au Platane* a poem about freedom or fatality, silence or sound?

Cantique des Colonnes

With playful humour, Valéry has transformed the 'vivants piliers' of his next poem, *Cantique des Colonnes*,[18] from the 'forests' of the sensibility in *Aurore* and from the plane tree in *Au Platane* to stone temple columns which, with their sun-topped capitals like hats trimmed with living birds, appear to 'sing' to the mind's eye with their radiantly symmetrical forms:

> Douces colonnes, aux
> Chapeaux garnis de jour,
> Ornés de vrais oiseaux
> Qui marchent sur le tour,
>
> Douces colonnes, ô
> L'orchestre de fuseaux!
> Chacun immole son
> Silence à l'unisson.
>
> – Que portez-vous si haut,
> Égales radieuses?
> – Au désir sans défaut
> Nos grâces studieuses!
>
> Nous chantons à la fois
> Que nous portons les cieux!
> Ô seule et sage voix
> Qui chantes pour les yeux!

Arranged regularly on the page like the stanzas of *Aurore* – though this time both stanza- and line-length are shorter and lighter[19] – *Cantique des Colonnes* recalls *Aurore* also through its most prominent descriptive device: that of endowing the object described with the faculty of speech. 'Pieusement pareilles', the columns, like the 'Similitudes amies' of *Aurore*, voice in a chorus their own life-principle. And that they do so in answer to a question, 'Que portez-vous si haut [. . .]?' intensifies the presence of a beholder (although this time no first-person speaker is involved in the dialogue). It is partly through the withdrawal of a first-person speaker from the description that Valéry achieves expression of such intense empathy and involvement with architectural form. The human mind, responsible for the creation of the columns in the first place, finds in their harmony and symmetry the expression of its own inner principles which it now contemplates lovingly in outer form, a form which answers a question with song. The intensity of this reciprocity is responsible for the transmutation of the third-person pronoun ('Chacune immole son/Silence à l'unisson') into the second person ('Que portez-vous si haut,/Égales radieuses?'), a distance finally swept away altogether in the supreme action of self-identification which allows the columns to speak in the first person: 'Nous'. Once more Valéry has made visible the internal creative capacities which the action of language makes available. Personification, the 'literary' device of animating an inanimate object, has been consciously explored and its latent properties accentuated in such a way as to suggest intentionality. The columns speak my delight.

The creative capacities made available to consciousness by language are in this case the capacity to relate to an object on every possible level of the mind, visual and intellectual. The regularity of the columns on the visual level, for example, suggests an experience of harmony which signals itself in the form of movement and rhythm, in turn creative of musical delight. The radiant columns 'sing' to the mind's ear.[20] Regularity and solidity suggest at the same time at a more analytic level an equation, as in *Aurore*, between movement in space and movement in time. The columns 'walk' through the centuries, a notion which gives rise to a further progression of analogies combining sensation and abstract idea: the endurance of love, the weight of the world, a stone falling through water, the hieratic footsteps of their illustrious bodies in fable and myth:

> Nous marchons dans le temps,
> Et nos corps éclatants
> Ont des pas ineffables
> Qui marquent dans les fables...

By such means, Valéry translates aesthetic experience into words, perhaps choosing the image of the columns in the first place in order to explore the mental sensations most intimately connected with architectural, mathematical and musical principles of form. The columns, like the plane tree, have been 'chosen' to bear the message of the creative intelligence and, by a stylistic transposition on the part of the poet, they celebrate in turn the joy they evoke.

There is a difference from the use of personification in *Au Platane*, then. Where the plane tree said 'no' to the message of metaphorical language, the columns seem stylistically to affirm and accept. By placing the two poems together or simply by reacting to tiny pieces of evidence within the imagery of *Cantique des Colonnes* itself, we can see the extreme conceptual control with which Valéry handles the relationship between Dionysian and Apollonian elements in his thought. The living plane tree, Dionysian in its effect, is said to cause the knees of the young virgin to bend:[21]

> Quand l'âme lentement qu'ils expirent le soir
> Vers l'Aphrodite monte,
> La vierge doit dans l'ombre, en silence, s'asseoir,
> Toute chaude de honte.

But the inanimate columns, representing principles of the pure intellect, are explicitly denied erotic appeal:

> Servantes sans genoux,
> Sourires sans figures,
> La belle devant nous
> Se sent les jambes pures.

Where the living plane tree bends and tosses in space convulsively, the columns only *walk* through time and must employ for dancers[22] the winds and the leaves:

> Incorruptibles sœurs,
> Mi-brûlantes, mi-fraîches,
> Nous prîmes pour danseurs
> Brises et feuilles sèches,

But it would be all too easy to assume that Valéry is setting up in the one poem a Dionysian principle which the mind fails to tame but needs for its growth, while in the second poem he explores an Apollonian principle which leaves the mind untouched in its emotional depths while appealing to its intellectual response to pure mathematical form. Just as the plane tree surprises us by being purer than the animal – 'Mais toi, de bras plus purs que les bras animaux' – so the antique columns surprise us by their whimsical gentleness, 'Douces colonnes', even by their deafness to the weight of the dignified responsibility they bear:

> Picusement pareilles,
> Le nez sous le bandeau
> Et nos riches oreilles
> Sourdes au blanc fardeau,
>
> Un temple sur les yeux
> Noirs pour l'éternité,
> Nous allons sans les dieux
> A la divinité!

Preventing any immobility in the description by bathing the stone columns in radiant sensations of warmth and movement, Valéry preserves in the outer form of the poem the theme of the dignity of Art as a divine, eternal principle in the manner of Classical Greek Antiquity; but only to introduce at the same time a multitude of exciting paradoxes which prevent our associating the pure, 'inhuman' side of the intellect with the unappealing and cold or indeed with the transcendental in any absolute sense. The endurance of art, the 'divine' temple of the human mind, the eternal laws of mathematics, the silent music of architecture:[23] all such commonplaces are presented in such a way as to suggest their power to penetrate the deepest, most 'corporeal' recesses of the mind. Indeed, the very beauty of the columns is wrought from hurt and effort (the stanzas on the birth of the columns chiselled from hard stone and awakened from their crystal beds by the metal claws of the architect's tools read like a poetic tribute to Gautier).[24] 'Mais le contraire d'un rêve, qu'est-ce, Phèdre', asks Socrates, 'sinon quelque autre rêve?...Un rêve de vigilance et de tension que ferait la Raison elle-même! [...] Qui sait quelles Lois augustes rêvent ici qu'elles ont pris de clairs visages' (P II, 154). The columns are 'Mi-brûlantes, mi-fraîches': artefacts capable, like the tree, of taking their share of natural light and shade, reminiscent of living beings not simply because of their bird-trimmed hats and female forms, but because they suggest the continuity of conscious and unconscious processes in ourselves.

A light, joyful poem which perfectly maintains its appeal as an evocation of the visual pleasures of architecture,[25] *Cantique des Colonnes* is nonetheless of primary intellectual importance in *Charmes* in that it conveys the unity of physiological, aesthetic and cognitive principles at the heart of Valéry's thought. We are reminded once more that his early love of architecture, music and mathematics did not simply provide an analogical basis for the techniques of poetic composition, but sent its roots deep into the experimental substance of poetry as an intellectual capacity of the conscious creative mind whose function is to enjoy. Behind the mature understatements of *Cantique* are strong echoes of the essay *Paradoxe sur l'Architecte* of 1891, in which Valéry had evoked the Orphic and Wagnerian aspect of his inspiration: the forest of silence, the 'hautes effloraisons des piliers et les colonnes liliales' bearing their universal, magic symbols like fruits on the tree of knowledge, the forest where one *listens* to the potentialities of the sensibility made available through traditional form:

> Or, celui qui entre et qui regarde, ébloui de l'œuvre tirée d'un songe, retrouve inévitablement d'héroïques souvenances.
> Il évoque, en un bois thessalien, Orphée, sous les myrtes; et le soir antique descend. [...] Le dieu chante, et, selon le rythme tout-puissant, s'élèvent au soleil les fabuleuses pierres, et l'on voit grandir vers l'azur incandescent, les murs d'or harmonieux d'un sanctuaire.
> Il chante! assis au bord du ciel splendide, Orphée! Son œuvre se revêt d'un vespéral trophée, et sa lyre divine enchante les porphyres, car le temple érigé par ce *musicien* unit la sûreté des rythmes anciens, à l'âme immense du grand hymne sur la lyre!...
>
> (P ɪɪ, 1405–6).[26]

It is Orpheus, then, Orpheus in his rôle of Amphion, mover of stones as well as charmer of beasts, architect through music, whose presence enters *Charmes almost* explicitly through *Cantique des Colonnes*; and it is Orpheus, musician and lover,[27] whose presence is *almost* made explicit in *Au Platane* in the image of the wind playing the strings or 'harps' of the leaves and branches and seeming to wring from their disorder the unity of a voice.

The two strands of architecture and music with their varying creative impulses, expressive and constructive, are brought

together in the notion of poetry as the voice of the creative intelligence, unifying 'être' and 'connaître':

> Arme-toi de la Lyre! Excite la nature!
> Que ma Lyre enfante mon Temple,
> Et que le roc s'ébranle au nom du Nom Divin!   (P I, 173).

Such is the traditional mythology of the creative mind on which
we see Valéry drawing in *Charmes* through a form of symbolism
outside the textual space of the poems and shining through into
the specific self-contained forms proposed. Yet such are those
sensually visible forms that they often modify and revivify in turn
the traditional myths on which they are based. The divine, the
eternal, the inspired, the beautiful: all begin to quiver from animal
head to foot, while that animal body begins to speak with a voice
of understanding full of the creative potentials of the natural
universe, full of the strange power, curiosity and tenderness of
finding itself mortal and alone with speaking ear and listening
tongue. 'Rien ne peut nous séduire [...] qui ne soit [...] ou
préexistant dans notre être, ou attendu secrètement par notre
nature' (P II, 114).

Aurore, Au Platane and *Cantique des Colonnes* with their
central images of the ladder of the waking mind, the stretching yet
fixed plane tree and the radiant columns bearing the temple of
the sky, already make us aware of the powerful imaginative unity
of *Charmes,* in which human limitation, desire and possibility are
constantly evoked, through sensations and objects which symbolically enact the mind's encounters with itself, the body and the
world (C.E.M.). Many of the central images of this drama relate
to archetypal metaphors already embedded in language and
thought: for example, the waters of time, the sun of reason, the
thorns of difficulty, the spirit or breath of inspiration, the roots of
being; and we have begun to see how Valéry plays on these basic
metaphors in an infinite variety of forms, invigorating their
physicality in the context of the intellect, but at the same time
using them to endow the intellect with a presence and power of its
own as a creative virtuality of the physical world. Throughout this
drama of freedom and fixity, repetition and change, detachment
and involvement, expansion and recoil, the presence of Language
constantly makes itself felt. It is not simply a vehicle of expression

on the part of the poet, but the natural stimulant and organiser of the sensibility, rendered visible at the level of subject-matter and theme. Indeed, we have seen Valéry discovering a psycho-physiological myth of his own to add to the stock of traditional metaphors he is treating poetically: that of consciousness as a listening mouth and speaking ear (VIII, 378).[28] This central metaphor of the 'listening' sensibility provides the drama at the root of his Orphic conception of poetry and is reflected within that poetry in turn. Thus, Orpheus, half god, half man, or, like language, half 'knowing', half 'being', ruptures the sleep of the animal with his singing and awakens the mind to its own dangerous divinity: 'la divinisation de la Voix' (P I, 597). It is easy to appreciate how the next two poems of *Charmes*, *L'Abeille* and *Poésie*, are generated internally by the pressures surrounding this same drama. *L'Abeille* – already discussed as a virtual epigraph to *Charmes* – took the form of an appeal by the animal sensibility to be stung to the pain of awareness by the god of ideas. *Poésie*, to which I shall turn next, affirms conversely the 'divinisation' of the human voice inspired by the muse of poetry, Intelligence, yet potentially thwarted by the force of its own desire.

Poésie

[...]
Dieu perdu dans son essence,
Et délicieusement
Docile à la connaissance
Du suprême apaisement,

Je touchais à la nuit pure,
Je ne savais plus mourir,
Car un fleuve sans coupure
Me semblait me parcourir...

Dis, par quelle crainte vaine,
Par quelle ombre de dépit,
Cette merveilleuse veine
A mes lèvres se rompit?

[...]

Mais la Source suspendue
Lui répond sans dureté:
– Si fort vous m'avez mordue
Que mon cœur s'est arrêté!

143

The traditional allegory of the Muse offering the poet the milk of Inspiration has been translated in Valéry's poem into an extended metaphor of the drama of the human sensibility as a listening mouth. Significantly, it is the *mouth*, not the ear, which is the instrument of inspiration, 'Une bouche qui buvait/Au sein de la Poésie'; and it is to the mouth, on whose lips it depends, 'Que seras-tu sans mes lèvres?', that the source of poetry replies.[29]

> Toute feuille me présente
> Une source complaisante
> Où je bois ce frêle bruit…

In *Aurore* the sensation of creative virtuality made possible by the temporary reciprocity of nature and the sensibility flooded through the whole body in the same image of sonorous liquidity – 'l'onde' – and with the same evanescent image of the swan which here in *Poésie* is seen in negative form:

> À peine sur ta poitrine,
> Accablé de blancs liens,
> Me berçait l'onde marine
> De ton cœur chargé de biens;
>
> [...]
>
> Le silence au vol de cygne
> Entre nous ne règne plus!

The privileged state – 'poésie' – evoked in *Poésie* is one of fusion, harmony, timeless self-possession; a state of child-like happiness, of liquid and refreshing shadow. Yet in the context of the whole poem, it is important to see that this state is presented as lost, and recaptured only through memory.[30] The poem begins with the idea of a movement of disruption in which the peaceful, drinking mouth is separated from the breast by surprise. By following through the intellectual and physiological 'logic' of such imagery, we see that the lost happiness – a half rhythmic, shadowy state of womb-like and unreflective self-unity – is only fully resurrected and illuminated when the speaking mouth has recapitulated and expressed it.

> À peine, dans ton ciel sombre,
> Abattu sur ta beauté,
> Je sentais, à boire l'ombre,
> M'envahir une clarté!

It is not the sensation of disruption itself that fills the poem, but the sensation of happiness replenished ('A peine...A peine') in language itself.

> Revenir *à soi* [...].
> Au moment de la jouissance de l'entrée *in bonis*; à la mort du désir; et quand s'ouvre la succession de l'idéal se fait une oscillation, une balance, entre le plaisir de mettre la main sur le réel et le déplaisir de touver ce réel [...] moins délicieux que sa figure.
> Je dispose de ce bien [...].
> Mais il y manque pourtant quelque chose. – Son absence – cette force de se faire imaginer. (P II, 647).

The poem begins, as did *La Jeune Parque*, with an analytic question: what negligence caused the marvellous flow of pleasure to cease? And it is the unravelling of this question with the help of language which brings the final illumination at the end of the poem as a further source of happiness and strength: the strength to understand and accept the transitoriness of the poetic state, a random phase of the sensibility itself, 'cette force de se faire imaginer'.

Valéry has used the possibilities of poetic language to explore the different levels of consciousness: the possibility of an arbitrary and mysterious fusion of discontinuous selves; the childlike resentment at the cessation of the mystery; and the new happiness to be gained when the past is resurrected and its loss understood: the two major faculties – memory and analysis – of poetic imagination itself. Yet it is to the integration of these levels of mental being in self-awareness, the muse of total, incorporative Intelligence, that poetry looks for its inspiration; and we are reminded of Valéry's refusal to identify creative values with language or sensibility alone.

Poésie is no more a mere theory of the poetic state than is Baudelaire's *Correspondances*. It is a true poem, and one where an allegorical or proverbial exterior is belied by a powerful expressive complexity. Built up through an interplay of light and shadow, liquid and solid, this complexity is the product of a constant process of insinuation, modification and paradox which stimulates the mind to imagine and invent further ideas. The phrase 'sans dureté' in the last stanza, for example, suggests the persistence of a secondary form of inspiration within the intellect itself, a trust capable of accepting the pain and anxiety of an interlude as the necessary condition of transition from the hypnotic flow of the poetic state into its conscious assessment (and perhaps recreation and extension in a poem). That same acceptance of the 'bite' of the sensibility was the theme of *Aurore*. The total 'message' of the poem – 'vouloir, vouloir, et même ne pas excessivement vouloir' – is meanwhile one of the most penetrating comments in Valéry's thought on the paradoxical and self-replenishing relationship between human creativity and desire when properly 'used'. Desire passionately, but desire even more passionately to know when to cease desiring so that your desire will be rewarded in time!

These patterns of intellectual suggestion are permitted by the transposition in *Poésie* of images of extreme sensuousness into the realm of the intellect. And, by a creative irony often achieved in Valéry's poems, the images which flood the mind of the reader as the most privileged state of being available to the intellect, are images of silence: a silence – 'poésie' – whose strange, liquid, non-verbal qualities we now 'hear'. The interruption of silence by the intrusion of words is thus a further invisible theme of the *Poésie*. Yet silence, like innocence, like snow – 'sans visage et sans voix' (P I, 326) – is an ambiguous, part-negative quality when language and thought are not involved in seeking it; and it is a typically Valéryan paradox that it needs a poem called *Poésie* to point expressively to that strange source of human pleasure 'où cesse même un nom', a source so cruelly arbitrary and elusive in its offer of joy.[31]

(b) Les Pas, La Ceinture, La Dormeuse, Fragments du Narcisse

Les Pas, La Ceinture and *La Dormeuse*, the three brief poems immediately preceding *Fragments du Narcisse*, were kept together in all successive versions of *Charmes* in what might be seen as the Narcisse cycle,[32] each poem pursuing the silent attentiveness of the mind in the face of something outside itself, the object of its love, the source and revelator of its power.

Les Pas

'Voici l'instant [. . .], l'instant le plus délicieux peut-être quand il précèderait le bonheur même, et que le bonheur même ne vaudra pas', wrote Gide in *La Porte Étroite*, making Jérôme walk slowly towards Alissa, delaying the moment of arrival, the sky pure and delicate as his inner joy.[33] It is through the same image of the lover approaching the beloved – 'Personne pure, ombre divine' – that Valéry explores the theme of potentiality in his poem *Les Pas*.[34] Fear of disillusionment or of the too rapid passing of the longed-for experience – 'cet acte tendre', the presence, the touch, the kiss, the 'gifts' of love[35] – whatever psychological patterns are implied (and these are more the province of Gide than of Valéry), it is the state of anticipation itself, ('attente'/'attention'), the savouring of the moment in advance, which provides here the source of exquisite delight and inner calm.

> Ne hâte pas cet acte tendre,
> Douceur d'être et de n'être pas,
> Car j'ai vécu de vous attendre,
> Et mon cœur n'était que vos pas.

Reflection on the complex structure of so simple a poem reveals further levels of implication specifically Valéryan in tone. Whereas in Gide's novel it is the narrator's own footsteps which approach the beloved, here it is the narrator who perceives the approaching footsteps:

> Tes pas, enfants de mon silence,
> Saintement, lentement placés,
> Vers le lit de ma vigilance
> Procèdent muets et glacés.

This is a narrator who perceives the footsteps and yet who nonetheless still feels in control of happiness, first in the form of a plea – 'Ne hâte pas cet acte tendre' – yet above all (for reliance on external compliance with one's inner wish is obviously no source of certainty) by a form of self-awareness. Recognition that anticipation alone is the source of the mind's deepest pleasure, proffers a form of affirmation temporarily invulnerable to pain:

> Car j'ai vécu de vous attendre,
> Et mon cœur n'était que vos pas.

Surely Valéry is expressing our pride in the power of our own minds to accentuate natural capacities – this emotion as much as

147

our sense of humble gratitude for the external source on which such capacities depend. The placing of the explanatory analytic clause at the end of the poem suggests that self-awareness frames as well as concludes the response.

No mood, be it pride or otherwise, is allowed to exist unmodified in Valéry's poetry. Subtle choices of words in *Les Pas* express movement and temporality, even a fundamental plurality of interpretation within the outer framework provided by evocation of the 'laws' of the mind. Modulation from 'tu' to the conventionally yet not necessarily more distant 'vous' in the last two lines of the poem; the use of the imperfect tense for the already receding footsteps – 'Et mon cœur n'était que vos pas'; the possibly imagined or at least internalised nature of the footsteps in the first place ('enfants de mon silence'; 'muets et glacés'; 'pas retenus'): all these devices introduce elements of obliqueness and intangibility into an otherwise definite evocation of event. Even the expectancy of the kiss is in the form of a tentative hypothesis allowing for chance and surprise in the manufacture of joy:

> Si, de tes lèvres avancées,
> Tu prépares pour l'apaiser,
> À l'habitant de mes pensées
> La nourriture d'un baiser, [...]

Moreover the whole poem revolves on ambiguity of tone, a constant flickering from joy to wistfulness within an interpretationally fluid (though structurally definite) imagery of movement and suspense. Is the experience the affirmation of individuality in the face of inevitability – pleasure in advance of what will inevitably come – or is the futurity on which that pleasure is based itself unreliable, in which case the experience is defensively substitutional in kind? Is it pleasure at all, now that analysis of the nature of that pleasure has intervened? Is there anything concrete for the imagination to postpone and savour, or is the imagination itself a process of postponement designed to savour what never need exist? 'Ici les délices sont cause/Suffisante au cours des choses', we read in *Ébauche d'un Serpent*. We are invited to the heart of 'la sensibilité de l'intellect' and to the heart of a form of consciousness which is both the potential destroyer and the source of emotion and love.

'[...] *les Pas*, petit poème purement *sentimental* auquel on

prête un sens intellectuel, un symbole de "l'inspiration"' (xxvIII,
427), Valéry wrote. A love-poem rather than a symbol of inspiration, yet our efforts to keep in mind the poet's intention without
belying the total effect of the poem should not encourage us to go
to the opposite extreme and trivialise a work whose very simplicity
of theme – the waiting lover – is treated in so beautifully resonant
a way. The bed which is approached is conveyed as the 'bed' of
the mind – 'le lit de ma vigilance' – and the kiss which is prepared
is designed for 'l'habitant de ma pensée', the inner Self. Those
mute, frozen footsteps are themselves the children of silence, their
real or imagined reality echoing in the consciousness which receives
them, and so on. Sensuousness is distanced and increased through
perception. And what *is* love – the 'sentimental' – for Valéry, but
an experience of consciousness able to preserve through its own
solitude or 'silence' the distinct individuality of the other and of
the self, a vital space or distance without which communication
and exchange cannot exist.

It is the perfect, measured presence of this mental space or
interval, the inner silence of emotion which we 'hear' in *Les Pas*
however we interpret it. With its perfect balance of phrasing,
accelerating and decelerating on either side of its controlled yet
fluid caesura (2/6, 3/5, 3/5, 2/6 in stanza one and 4/4, 3/5, 1/7,
4/4 in stanza two), its delayed syntax, its appositions, its homo-
nyms (the central image of withheld or negated footstep appears to
spring from the negative 'pas'), its favourite alliterations (labials
and open vowels in particular), *Les Pas* speaks the message of
form, the message of poetry and the message of emotion all in one.
'Et mon cœur n'était que vos pas'. For the voice of poetry, too, is
made of measured tread, of heartbeats,[36] of a system of anticipation, which half creates what it finds ('attente/événement'). To
draw an analogy between the 'voiced' emotion of poetry and the
'silent' emotion of love is not to turn the poem into an allegory of
inspiration. Instead, we are rediscovering the notion of inspiration
within the notion of love itself, a state of resonance and exchange.
For if *Aurore*, at the beginning of *Charmes*, had expressed a desire
through an image of *hope* – 'Toute l'âme s'appareille/À l'extrême
du désir' – there is no such fierce movement in *Les Pas*. Desire has
been transferred from futurity to the inner trust on which movement depends in advance. The more cosmic intellectual themes of

Le Cimetière Marin are not far away from this tiny, intimate poem where life itself is felt to be suspended fleetingly and consciously before death. Here, however, a precious, living image is suspended by anticipation alone, 'Entre le vide et l'événement pur'. And as so often in Valéry's poetic universe, the privileged source of consciousness, however silent, is sound ('s'entendre parler'), the beat of inner time: 'donner/recevoir'. The presence of the 'Other' has the same inner resonance as the presence of the Self.

La Ceinture

The same power to cherish an external source on which the Self depends for its own fragile sense of presence is expressed from a different perspective in the even shorter poem *La Ceinture*, where a mysterious shadow dances in the evening light, its girdle-like shape the only bond of the mind with the world before evening and death. Again, as in *Les Pas*, the present is cherished – this time the sunset – as a moment exquisitely poised before loss. And again, as in *Les Pas* and in the longer poem *Profusion du Soir*[37] which it recalls in themes and imagery, the lonely presence of consciousness in the heart of its perception is accepted as the condition of beauty and life:

> Quand le ciel couleur d'une joue
> Laisse enfin les yeux le chérir
> Et qu'au point doré de périr
> Dans les roses le temps se joue,
>
> Devant le muet de plaisir
> Qu'enchaîne une telle peinture,
> Danse une Ombre à libre ceinture
> Que le soir est près de saisir.
>
> Cette ceinture vagabonde
> Fait dans le souffle aérien
> Frémir le suprême lien
> De mon silence avec ce monde...
>
> Absent, présent... Je suis bien seul,
> Et sombre, ô suave linceul.

With its extraordinary economy of suggestion – vast abstract themes such as love, consciousness, beauty, vision and death condensed into its miniature frame – *La Ceinture* is one of the most moving poems Valéry ever wrote. It conveys a mood of poignancy which transforms the fleeting, visible shape into a source of joy, while at the same time remaining distant from joy and its possible fluctuation into sadness (something of the same perspective as in Baudelaire's prose poem *Le 'Confiteor' de l'Artiste*).[38]

'Un homme contemplait entre ciel et Soi une figure mystérieuse dont il ne voyait qu'une face, et *on* lui disait que c'était la figure de sa vie à demi figée, à demi informe' (P II, 813), is a commentary Valéry might have written. But also, in the words of Faust to Lust:

> Ce moment est d'un si grand prix. [. . .] Il me possède comme ses accords de sons qui vont plus loin que la limite du désir de l'ouïe, et qui font tout l'être se fondre, se rendre à je ne sais quelle naissance de confusion bienheureuse de ses forces et de ses faiblesses. [. . .] Le plus beau de ce jour chante avant de mourir.   (P II, 319).

Without allegory of any kind, the poem seems to weave its emotion from the sensation of sight alone; that intensely pure, almost mystical experience of mind and eye – 'VOIR [. . .] et savoir que l'on voit' (P II, 322) – which provides the silent, 'listening' receptivity to the world and the self which the poet's ear translates into verbal form: '[· · ·] *je suis ce que je suis, je suis ce que je vois*, présent et absent sur le Pont de Londres' (P II, 514), Valéry wrote of this fleeting reciprocity with the real. The flimsy shape – perhaps the floating dress of a nymph-like, dancing figure as in Corot's *Plaisirs du Soir* – is at the same time unspecified, called up from the faintly changing patterns of the sunset, the horizon suffused with colour, and transformed into an image through the trembling filter of desire between the self and the world. Silence, sight, movement, breath are the ingredients of the inner 'voice' of individual consciousness which the poem 'recalls'.

'Pour qu'une œuvre [. . .] soit Poésie, il faut qu'on ait trouvé et fixé le *Ton*. Alors la chose chante' (xv, 46). If *La Ceinture* 'sings' as it does, it is surely because the tone, so important a source of unity in Valéry's poetry, is never broken, whatever complex modulations take place within. 'Au point doré de périr' – the physicality of colour breaking into the abstract prepositional phrase[39] – sets this tone here as one of pleasure in beauty and anguish in loss, the two held together as the different elements of its harmony modulate from plenitude to rupture, from joy to sadness and solitude, from solitude to tenderness. One way in which such unity is achieved is through the balance of the melodic movements in the strict quatorzain form. The melodic upsurge of the first strophe corresponding with the vision of the setting sun, is paralleled by a movement of descent in the second, corresponding in turn with the appearance of the shadow, while the same pattern is then exactly repeated in the second part.[40] The final couplet might be said to act as both an echo and a transposition of the whole previous structure into a poignant new key.[41] Such is the perfect orchestration of even this brief poem. Unity of tone is maintained as well through choice and position of words. The adjective 'suave' – 'ô suave linceul' – prevents the idea of death from disrupting the mood of tenderness,[42] and recalls the ambivalence of consciousness in its dual position of 'force' and 'faiblesse', its solitary awareness of the imminence of death.

Where *La Ceinture* might be thought most striking, however, is in its precisely expressive use of ambiguity. The dancing shape is at the same time a woman, a cloud, a floating girdle or belt, an image of death, an erotic fantasy – all these and at the same time none of them – Dionysius being always the 'lack of a name' (IV, 736). By seeming to trace ambiguity to its source in the mind of the beholder, Valéry has poignantly evoked that state of desire in which mobility is conferred on external surroundings, making the world seem both harmonised with the mind and at the same time distant; eloquent and at the same time mute: 'qui parle et qui ne parle pas' (I, 626). The mind in *La Ceinture* seems distanced from the nature of its own imagination with its 'fatal' law of creativity, and yet vulnerably exposed to the minutest idea and sensation provoked by the scene, a reminder of the way in which the sensibility for Valéry – 'l'informe' – is the prime mover of thought. Sunset, in this context, cannot but trigger images of human limitation, the disappearance of the mind in forthcoming death. Yet *La Ceinture* is still not a poem where the attentive mind has forfeited its vital 'puissance de motilité' (XXII, 304). One of its most intricate modulations is from the silent, speechless pleasure, 'le muet de plaisir', to the voicing of the idea of separation itself, a modulation which moves from the affirmation 'mon silence' to the divided 'Je suis bien seul', with its distinct first person pronoun, the highest point of objectivity and dualism within the single system of Self (III, 707). The introduction of language ('Je/ME') coincides in this way with a form of tragic consciousness 'Absent, présent' which only the voice can exemplify as unity. The supreme bond of human silence and the world is the voice of individual consciousness, its image stirred and threatened by the 'breath' of the evening breeze.

It is at points like these that Valéry's poems most differ from those of Mallarmé, despite the fact that *La Ceinture* is full of Mallarméan echoes, even perhaps the image of the 'ceinture' itself, part of the erotic fantasy in *L'Après-Midi d'un Faune*:[43]

> [...] je vais parler longtemps
> Des déesses; et par d'idolâtres peintures,
> À leur ombre enlever encore des ceintures.

For while the lovely line 'Dans les roses le temps se joue' suggests, in its context of cherished cheek and feminine presence ('La fin de jour est femme' [P I, 303]), an image of erotic pleasure and deceptive mask, it occurs in a context where no triumphant, redemptive power of art is symbolically portrayed to replace the setting sun and its associations with solitude and death. All the skill of the poem goes instead towards expressing the quality of a fleeting instant which the mind cannot hold except as an image with the same duration as the voice itself, part of the physical world.

La Dormeuse

'Souffle, songes, silence [...]', these are also the poetic ingredients of the final poem in the trilogy, *La Dormeuse*, where, this time through the theme of watching a sleeping woman, the 'eye' of the beholder reflects on the human form before it, questioning its secrets, empathising with its longings, and is finally drawn through that very action of looking to renewal of conscious self-presence, 'la conscience consciente':

> Dormeuse, amas doré d'ombres et d'abandons,
> Ton repos redoutable est chargé de tels dons,
> Ô biche avec langueur longue auprès d'une grappe,
>
> Que malgré l'âme absente, occupée aux enfers,
> Ta forme au ventre pur qu'un bras fluide drape,
> Veille; ta forme veille, et mes yeux sont ouverts.

Again language discovers and prolongs the instantaneous

sensations of sight, 'la pensée à l'état naissant', and we may think again of Valéry's reference to the Self as a form of pendulum: 'Notre pendule poétique va de notre sensation vers quelque idée ou vers quelque sentiment, et revient vers quelque souvenir de la sensation. [. . .] Or, ce qui est sensation est essentiellement *présent*. [. . .] Entre la Voix et la Pensée [. . .], entre la Présence et l'Absence, oscille le pendule poétique' (P I, 1332–3). It is just this oscillation between various degrees of self-presence, detachment and involvement, that all three of these poems delicately describe as the point of greatest creative virtuality:

> Quels secrets dans son coeur brûle ma jeune amie,
> Âme par le doux masque aspirant une fleur?
> De quels vains aliments sa naïve chaleur
> Fait ce rayonnement d'une femme endormie?

An interrogative form is established within a descriptive mode. If meaning in language involves obtaining the hearer's or reader's recognition of the intention to produce certain effects,[44] then Valéry's description of a sleeping woman is made complex by the linguistic devices through which he invites us to experience the mystery rather than the encapsulation of form. The poem points to form as an achievement of wondering involvement and astonishment on the part of the silent, contemplative mind. It revolves on the dynamic paradox of 'absence' and 'presence', the essence of consciousness interpreting the changing 'signs' of its past and future world.

Her own consciousness absent in sleep but busy in dreams, 'l'âme absente, occupée aux enfers', the woman's sleeping form awakens the consciousness of the beholder. The skill of the poem lies not in the précieux paradox, but in the way in which metaphors taken from the natural world – the delicacy of a flower, the gravity of water, dappled light, an animal with fruit – are woven into the part physical, part abstract texture in a way which suggests their purely tentative equivalence to reality, their powerlessness to take us further than the solitary passion of a mind filled with the tender, inquisitive sensations of sight. Sensuality, aggression, solemnity, irony, peacefulness: all these moods are held together, in a richly alliterative language locked in its own substance as the sleeping woman is in hers, and imitative of the rhythms of breath. 'Dormeuse, amas doré d'ombres et d'abandons': the solid presence of language acts as rival power to that 'invincible accalmie', the radiant mask behind which the sleeping mind also meticulously works. The whole poem turns on itself, as is the essence of the sonnet, challenging us with its own deceptively peaceful form.

'.[....] Veille; ta forme veille, et mes yeux sont ouverts'.

In the trilogy of poems *Les Pas, La Ceinture* and *La Dormeuse* with their shared imagery and themes, we have seen how Valéry uses poetry to penetrate and convey the intimate and mobile relationship of individual consciousness to itself and the world. Whether an inner or outer relationship predominates, he is concerned with expressing the fluctuation within consciousness of two states or phases, 'absence' and 'presence' and the corresponding reciprocity – 'une sorte de liaison harmonique et réciproque' (P II, 1317) – between these states and the impressions from which they are formed or create in their turn, 'une correspondance mystérieusement exacte entre les *causes* sensibles, qui constituent la *forme* et les *effets* intelligibles, qui sont le *fond*' (P II, 1317). Valéry prefaces his comment by the reflection that the term 'Poésie' has come to designate not only an art of linguistic effects but the state of *'invention par l'émotion'* which a poem supposes and wishes to communicate. It is easy to see how, particularly in *La Ceinture*, this desire for form provided the themes of the poem itself. The moment of sunset offers a moment of transition in which the mind moves from sensation to thought, from experience of the world to experience of the Self, the same perceptual pattern as is expressed in *La Dormeuse*.

A further theme shared by the three poems is that of another person – 'l'Autre' – seen from the point of view of inner separation and solitude – the same distance governing the 'Je/ME' relationship within the Self. From solitude and separation comes a movement of reaching out towards the Other's similar position, and with the discovery of a threshold of shared limitation, comes a movement of retraction, creative in turn of fresh desire.

Similar in theme, each poem rings the changes, by some slight modification of tonality and structure, on the essential mobility of self-awareness, its relatively autonomous power to postpone, to reflect, to renew. Each, like *Aurore* and *Poésie*, conveys as part of the dynamism by which it is motivated, a passionate urge to learn

from experience, to draw the 'moral' from every new confronta-
tion of the self and the world. And in each poem the theme of
privileged silence precedes the separation of consciousness and its
subsequent pressure to speak. Never as in these 'poems of silence'
was there such an extreme expressive tension between language
and the action of poetry itself.

'Un amour d'un certain genre doit se nommer enchantement,
charme' (xv, 423), Valéry wrote. Leaving aside here his life-long
attempt to understand the nature of love and its potential rôle in
the conscious mind,[45] we can still see that a central part of this
analysis is concerned with analogy between the state of harmony
or 'song' produced by a certain form of direct emotion, and the
state of musical resonance of effect aspired to by poetry. And it is
not only on a comparative plane that Valéry links Éros and
Psyché. As we saw in *L'Abeille*, the drama of the mind itself is
seen as a drama of erotic desire, desire for fusion yet with power
and mobility retained by individual consciousness. This concept is
present in the exploration of consciousness and creativity embodied in *Charmes*, and we have already noticed this source of
analogy in many of the poems: the tremulous moment of self-
possession at the end of *Aurore*; the sense of division and amorous
desire for poetic re-unification in *Au Platane*, 'Ô qu'amoureuse-
ment des Dryades rival'; the beatific devotion 'Sur la table
d'amour' in *Cantique des Colonnes*, and so on. All three poems
contain images of seducer and seduced and set up an ambivalent
transference of power and creativity, 'thirst' and 'source', of great
relevance to the theme of poetic voice. All lead to a multiplicity of
metaphors transposed from the human body to the outside world
or vice versa, and conveying the drama of the creative sensibility
in erotic or sexual terms. The plane tree offers its naked white
body like a young Scythian athlete; the breasts of the 'absent'
woman in *La Dormeuse* are evoked in terms of her own desire for
thirst-quenching fruit. The same image of Tantalus is used in
La Jeune Parque to express the thirst of consciousness for total,
embodied knowledge of life, and the same image is elusively
present in *Aurore*: 'Voici mes vignes ombreuses,/Les berceaux de
mes hasards!'. It is through the erotic as well as childhood image
of mouth and breast, too, that Valéry presents in *Poésie* the concept of Intelligence. Such imagery does not indicate sexual or

erotic experience as the subject of the poems any more than sexual imagery is used as an allegory of poetic creation.[46] It relates to the sensations and aspirations of individual consciousness inventively discovering what is (the same emotions that inform sexual love). The omitted Orphic stanza of *Aurore* makes this relationship quite plain (see p. 107). And with the myth of Orpheus there enters the rôle of selective self-awareness in transposing the natural relationship between Self and universe into song (xvi, 506). From its earliest beginnings in his thought in the context of Wagnerism and the unity of so-called 'male' and 'female' principles of mind, the theme evolves poetically from the idea of the divine human temples made 'au moyen de la parole' (P ii, 113) – the poetic principle given flesh in *Cantique des Colonnes* – to the gesture by which Orpheus' lyre is finally taken from his hands and gently thrown into the fountain, image of love, death and poetic substance itself. Once more, the Orphic urge to construct and to sing is expressively mingled in *Charmes* with the movement of the mind away from its own architecture and will-power, to culminate instead in a form of tenderness (see Chapter 4, n.12), the magical rôle of the voice over and above what is said.

Fragments du Narcisse

Ô douceur de survivre à la force du jour,
Quand elle se retire enfin rose d'amour,
....
Quelle perte en soi-même offre un si calme lieu!
L'âme, jusqu'à périr, s'y penche pour un Dieu
Qu'elle demande à l'onde, onde déserte, et digne
Sur son lustre, du lisse effacement d'un cygne...

Where *La Jeune Parque* and *Aurore* took their themes and images from the dawn, *Fragments du Narcisse*[47] relates to the evening, the time when consciousness is at its most relaxed yet vulnerable, as it prepares for night and the fading of its own links with the external world. Evening here is the time of the body, deliciously fatigued by the movements of daytime and slowly taking consciousness to task. Centred on one of the most constant and thoroughly developed themes of Valéry's thought as a poet, the work offers one of the richest and most poignantly beautiful poems of *Charmes*. Dramatically lyrical[48] in its intensity, it is a monologue of which

Valéry insisted on the simplicity of form and the comprehensibility – different in this respect from *La Jeune Parque* – and where his compositional effort concentrated on the harmony of the language itself (P I, 1672). Indeed, it is the simulated presence of a living voice, sustained throughout the poem as a single flow of euphonic sound, which most impresses the reader, reminding us of Valéry's ideal of poetry as a complete language where 'la *forme*, c'est-à-dire l'action et la sensation de la *Voix*, est de même puissance que le *fond*' (P I, 1336). Within this continuous vocal flow, complex sequences – semantic, syntactical, phonetic and rhythmic – shift and re-echo each other melodically and symphonically, providing the substance of the poem. I shall try to suggest that the achievement of linguistic harmony is not simply a means of clothing the poem's most obvious subject – the dualism of consciousness and the Self – with musical enchantment, but that it provides and transforms the experience of that subject itself. '[. . .] ce corps et cet esprit, [. . .] s'ils échangent entre eux de la convenance et de la grâce', writes Valéry in the words of Eupalinos, '[. . .] c'est donc qu'ils auront découvert leur véritable relation, leur acte. Qu'ils se concertent, qu'ils se comprennent au moyen de la matière de mon art!' (P II, 100).[49]

The Narcissus theme frequently recurred in Valéry's writings. Taking from the Greek legend the name of the youth condemned – for rejecting the love of the nymph Echo[50] – to love the reflection of his own image in the pool, he used it to refer to the inner dualism of consciousness: 'Être et connaître. Âme et corps. Général et particulier. Moi et personnalité. Visible et voyant. Tout et partie.'[51] The myth thus appears in the *Cahiers* in a context quite different from that of its popular associations with bodily beauty and negative self-love ('narcissism'). Stripped of its moral and sensual overtones – partly connected in Valéry's mind with Gide's very different treatment of the same theme – the Narcissus motif is a ready-made emblem for the faculty of 'dédoublement' which Valéry pursued throughout his life. The treatment of a theme in abstract thought and in poetry is very different, as Valéry insisted with reference to this subject in particular. Yet before attempting to see where that difference lies in relation to *Fragments du Narcisse* (there was a previous poem *Narcisse Parle* of 1920 and a further poem, *Cantate du Narcisse* of 1939),[52] we should recall a further dimension to the Narcissus theme as it is pursued in the *Cahiers*, and one which relates to the fundamental reciprocity in Valéry's thought between inner and outer world. 'Narcisse –/Miroir parlant/ Ce que je vois me parle/par quoi il est Moi' (see Part I, p. 22) he wrote of this reciprocity – a formula pinpointing once more the relationship between sound and sight central to a study of the subject of poetic voice.[53]

'La proximité est chose extraordinaire. Je n'ai pas su le dire dans le Narcisse dont c'était le vrai sujet, et non la beauté revenant sur elle-même' (VII, 627). But is it so certain that Valéry has failed to achieve his aim in *Fragments du Narcisse*? Temporarily leaving this question aside, let us try to isolate the concept of 'proximity' itself. In relation to the analysis pursued in his notes, 'proximity' would seem to be the sense on the part of consciousness that Self – epitomised by our power to hear ourselves speak and to see our own bodies – is spontaneous and elusively different at the same time as part of the perceiving subject:

> Le moi est aussi le sentiment: que toute connaissance est partielle (et ce sentiment exagéré fait l'émotion parfois de qui se regarde dans un miroir et s'étonne de *se voir particulier, se sentant universel*, ou de se voir, lui tout, dans son aspect partiel [chose dans mon reflet et tout dans mon idée]; et s'il y avait un miroir qui permette de réfléchir l'être mental – ce serait le même sentiment, et la peur d'être plus restreint, plus petit qu'on ne le voit. Se voir quelque chose, soi qui se sent La Chose, toute chose).   (III, 780).

Where the poetic treatment of this theme – brought alive by the interwoven literary images of Narcisse seeing his image in the pool and hearing the echo of his voice in the woods and fields – may reveal important differences from its treatment in abstract analysis is in the positive rôle given in the poem to that sense of revelatory difference or otherness, and above all in the expressive closing of the distance between consciousness and its sense of the body's separate identity. A continuity of being is musically established between 'être' and 'connaître', endowing with vocal presence the 'absence' which is Self. Hence the further rôle of poetic enchantment – 'l'harmonie même de la langue' – in leading the reader to experience the same conscious interdependence of mind and body that the poem orchestrates as its subject and theme. To support this argument we must turn to the poem itself.

Once more the title of the poem seems to possess a double existence, as a reference to the imagery within it – the 'fragments' of Narcisse's body reflected in water and sound – and to the 'fragments' of the poem in its inevitably unfinished state. The poem's very being is elusive as Valéry attempted to deepen a subject of so much intimate appeal to his mind: the elusiveness of the human Self in its most universal form. For all its separately composed pieces,[54] *Fragments du Narcisse* achieves, however, a remarkable poetic unity. The opening line, 'Que tu brille enfin, terme pur de ma course!', is the overture of an ever-widening set of variations on the theme of intellectual thirst for self-knowledge and self-unity – variations which modulate through the three separate parts of the poem with growing tragic intensity until the final lines evoking the coming of the night and the disappearance of the image in the pool:

> Hélas! corps misérable, il est temps de s'unir...
> Penche-toi...Baise-toi. Tremble de tout ton être!
> L'insaisissable amour que tu me vins promettre
> Passe, et dans un frisson, brise Narcisse, et fuit...

The whole poem, with its quivering décor of light and shade, sound and silence, is based on a series of echoes and reflections not only in imagery – the physical world of nature – but in the manner in which these elements are related one to another in a vast network organised to convey the sensations and tonalities of inner experience. Any possible monotony in the monologue is alleviated, meanwhile, by the dramatic organisation of the poem into three parts (making its ending more inevitable while deepening the implications of the note of loss and silence on which the poem ends). In the first of these, Narcisse invokes the nymphs of the pool, silencing their voices in order to pursue his solitary contemplation of Self:

> Nulle des nymphes, nulle amie, ne m'attire
> Comme tu fais de l'onde, inépuisable Moi!...

In the second part ('Fontaine, ma fontaine, eau froidement présente'), he addresses the pool itself, taken as witness – a frequent rhetorical/psychological device in Valéry's poetry – of the vanity of love for another, and leading to an urgent plea to his image to reply to his desire:

> Quitte enfin le silence, ose enfin me répondre,
> Bel et cruel Narcisse, inaccessible enfant,
> Tout orné de mes biens que la nymphe défend...

And in the third and last section ('...Ce corps si pur, sait-il qu'il puisse me séduire?'), Narcisse leans towards his fading image in the pool, turned once more towards his own potential unity by the double theme of the vanity of nature and of love. The poem lyrically and thematically emphasises his position of solitude by incorporating in its second section a powerful critique of sexual attraction, seen from the intransigent position of Narcisse as a monstrously deceptive and fleeting union, and presented at the same time as an ironic 'Tristesse d'Olympio' where the Romantic dreams of lovers remembering are seen as inevitably falling short once more of the mind's desired fusion with itself and the world. All is change and movement, pulling Narcisse away from the possession of this peaceful lucidity and happiness – yet everything in the poem seems at the same time to provide just such a possibility, making it impossible to decide whether the tone is tragic at all. How to capture intellectually the paradox at the root of this ambivalent poetic power to enchant?

One of the poem's most striking aspects is its use of sound: not only phonetic sound as a source of enchantment for the reader (Valéry has produced here some of his most intricate systems of 'multi-' and 'intrasonance'),[55] but sound as an integral part of the subject of the poem, treated as the source of consciousness of 'la Personne qui parle'. Sound and sight are intimately mingled thematically as Narcisse fears to trouble the calm surface of the water with his breath, hears the very grass grow in the calm silence, senses the swelling noises of the natural world as if they too are voices, and turns to the sight of his image with lips outstretched as if both to speak and to kiss. The experience of reflexive sound – 's'entendre parler' being for Valéry the not quite symmetrical equivalent of 'se voir' – reaches its most dramatic linguistic moment in the sequence of the echo, in which Narcisse is seemingly mocked by the sound of his own voice thrown back by the rock:

> Les efforts mêmes de l'amour
> Ne le sauraient de l'onde extraire qu'il n'expire...

PIRE.
> Pire?...
>> Quelqu'un redit *Pire*...Ô moqueur!
> Écho lointaine est prompte à rendre son oracle

In a purely literary sense, the 'event' is ironic in that the nymph Écho – her presence stylistically reinforced by the 'e' of 'lointaine' – emphasises the impossibility and vulnerability of this solitude even at the point of its greatest intensity. There is also a baroque shift and play of perspectives as the device of rhyme is allowed to penetrate the semantic space of the literary fiction itself. We may be reminded, too, of the seriously playful values of Molière's *Amphytrion*, as Narcisse speaks to his double as to a more perfect self ('Ô semblable!...Et pourtant plus parfait que moi-même'). Yet the myth of Écho slips perfectly into the terminology of 'dédoublement' and 'identity in difference' basic to the drama of consciousness and Self – 'proximité' – which Valéry intended as the 'real subject' of his poem. To hear sound is a threat to self-unity, since it depends on the detachment of the conscious subject from its experience. Yet sound at the same time generates the self-awareness without which the sensation of self-identity – 'Re' – could not exist. '*on* se retrouve. RE – on se fait Je. *On* trouve Je' (XV, 134). *This* is surely the paradox at the heart of the poem and one which I believe accounts for the ambivalence between pain and pleasure, triumph and tragedy, of which its 'charm' is composed. Unlike Molière's Amphytrion, Valéry's Narcisse *knows* the nature of his dualism. From that knowledge – consciousness of consciousness again – comes the power to treat the mind as a total system in all its discontinuities. It is this 'ars magna' of conscious living which Valéry had in mind when he wrote in the context of poetic composition:

> Écrivain. Le violiniste, l'oreille couchée au bois, et conduisant son archet amoureux, ne fait qu'un avec l'instrument et le son même. L'instrument de bois se perd, s'oublie, il se fait entre le son et l'homme un échange direct. C'est un cycle fermé, un équilibre entre les forces données et les sensations reçues [...]. *C'est un Narcisse ce violiniste*. (my italics). (VII, 668).

Separation is necessary to the creation of unity. Without dualism there would be no individual 'Moi'. 'L'être complet est double' (VII, 627).

The Narcisse of Valéry's poem accepts this condition when he refrains from uniting with the image he so desires:

> Mais, pour désaltérer cette amour curieuse,
> Je ne troublerai pas l'onde mystérieuse:

It is often overlooked that the theme of the poem is not one of tragic frustration alone, but one of the vitality of desire approached as a source of being in itself. The fact that the voice, and thus the individual consciousness, of Narcisse is silenced with the fading of his separate image is but a further expression of this. As at the end of the closely related poem *La Pythie* (which Valéry wrote at the same time as the main part of the *Fragments*), the third-person form – 'brise Narcisse' – is sufficiently ambiguous to be spoken by a further level of Self – 'on' – still continued within the monologue. And if the speaker implies by 'Narcisse' the image of himself – the source, as in *La Ceinture*, of his fragile sense of existence in the waking, living world – then the device serves to convey at the same time the creative as well as tragic contingency of consciousness, the mingling of 'force' with 'faiblesse' which Valéry so frequently explores. The main values of the poem are not to be sought in the 'sayings' of the speaker – a shadowy protagonist born like *La Jeune Parque* from the literary appeal of an intellectual subject – but from the poem as a whole in its power to suggest the potential unity of the composer in action – the unity made possible by dichotomy, which we see in the gestures of the violinist and hear in the music of Bach.

One of the poem's most considerable feats lies, then, in its power to make present in the reader's imagination an awareness of sound as the source of 'dédoublement'.[56] The term 'voix' occurs more than once in the context of the natural world external to Narcisse, so that we become conscious of both the preciousness and the fragility of his own voice, threatened and submerged in its limited sphere. 'La voix des sources change, et me parle du soir', he says of the 'listening' evening calm, or, of the coming night, 'Sa voix fraîche à mes voeux tremble de consentir'. Soon the landscape is indistinguishable from the echo of his own being:

> Antres, qui me rendez mon âme plus profonde,
> Vous renflez de votre ombre une voix qui se meurt...

Vous me le murmurez, ramures!...Ô rumeur
Déchirante, et docile aux souffles sans figure,
Votre or léger s'agite, et joue avec l'augure...
Tout se mêle de moi, brutes divinités!
Mes secrets dans les airs sonnent ébruités,
Le roc rit; l'arbre pleure; et par sa voix charmante,
Je ne puis jusqu'aux cieux que je ne me lamente
D'appartenir sans force à d'éternels attraits!

This passage recalls not only the experience of sound in *La Jeune Parque* – symbol of the permeation of the sensibility by the natural universe – but also the famous image of *Le Cimetière Marin* where the mind is a sonorous gulf, 'sonnant dans l'âme un creux toujours futur'. Closely founded on Valéry's analysis of the relationship between consciousness and inner language – 'Parler écoute' – such imagery has an evocative resonance of its own. Complex moods and sensations verging from exaltation to panic are contained within the intense lyricism of the monologue, the deliberate syntax and frequency of pauses on stressed syllables giving the alexandrine a gravely dramatic force. To say that Narcisse 'hears the grass grow' is too literal to account for the sense of mystical absorption created by the mixed imagery of a line like 'J'entends l'herbe des nuits croître dans l'ombre sainte'. Such imagery is both more subtle, more symbolic and more precise in its rendering of tonality and mood. We are not far from the carefully composed yet fluid passage ('Ô douceur de survivre à la force du jour...') which Valéry singled out for its success in being 'absolument vides d'idées' (P I, 1662) (empty of the abstract ideas which have no direct place in 'poésie pure').

It is not only the *theme* of sound which leads to the contemplation of the body – the mysterious total Self always out of reach on which Narcisse depends for his preservation in a changing, dissolving world. The sound-architecture of the poem also draws the reader to experience a unity always out of reach of analysis, but always physically present to the mind through resonance and echo. By appealing so strongly through sound to our 'besoin phénix', Valéry is appealing to the same source of fascination and enchantment which draws Narcisse to the idea of the living body – not merely its reflection – as the only possible continuity on which the mind can base its love:

> [...] Et qui donc peut aimer autre chose
> Que soi-même?...
>   Toi seul, ô mon corps, mon cher corps,
> Je t'aime, unique objet qui me défends des morts!

A complex poetic alchemy has made the continuity of bodily awareness and poetic discourse appear to coincide. Nor could that voice exist without the presence of the world.[57]

We have already noticed that the poem ends on an image of dissolution which is double-edged in implication. On the one hand it suggests the doubt and destruction of the mind as it loses its vital power of exchange with the separateness of external reality; on the other, affirmation of the never-ending dualism of 'être' and 'connaître' as the condition which makes possible consciousness itself. The poem is a fragment in the further sense that Valéry had intended to write a lengthier finale where the starry night sky alone would be reflected in the mirror of the pool (P I, 1674):

> Visage, beau visage, il est temps de périr.
> Mille dieux contre toi occupent cet azur.
> . . . .
> Ta fontaine n'est plus qu'une splendide nuit
> Et cette profondeur pure et désespérée
> Tout entière parfois tremble et meurt vaguement.
> . . . L'univers qui s'y voit tombe éternellement.   (P I, 1674).[58]

Closely linked to the prose poem *L'Ange* (P I, 206),[59] where the self-questioning mind reaches a point of mirrored purity of similar intensity, this projected finale is also closely related to Mallarmé's poetry, in particular the sonnet 'Ses purs ongles...', where the stars shine out in the mirror after the death of the 'Master', as if to suggest the prolonging through language of the beauty of form achieved in art. Yet the heavily qualified words presenting the image in *L'Ange* – 'dans une telle perfection de leur harmonie [...] qu'on eût dit qu'il eût pu s'évanouir, et le système, étincelant comme un diadème, [...] subsister par soi seul [...]' (P I, 206) – suggest that for Valéry the living human voice alone is necessary to the art of language. This crucial concept is similarly reflected at the end of *Cantate du Narcisse* (P I, 420): in the line spoken by the choir 'Elle n'est plus que la voix de Narcisse', and in the Nymph's adjoinder – 'Il fait battre mon cœur; il fait trembler ma voix' –

165

where even the final disappearance of Narcisse is followed by the
resurrection of emotion in the face of the turbulent and enchant-
ing world of nature. For Valéry the voice is as necessary to the
poem as the universe to the Self – 'Il y a autre chose que moi, s'il
y a moi, et réciproquement' (VII, 31). *Fragments du Narcisse* as
we know it, ends not with the death of Narcisse and his reappear-
ance as a flower as in the legend, but with the dynamic ambiguity
of a refusal to become one with the calm, unified image of death.
Narcisse remains Proteus, 'inépuisable Moi'.[60] In this sense Valéry
has preserved for the reader, the full dramatic irony and doubt of
a voice set in the context of its always imminent silence in death.[61]
That the basic impetus behind the whole Narcisse cycle in his
poetry and thought is one of expression through communication
is confirmed by the following comment:

> Quand j'aime quelqu'un, je le traite comme moi-même, c.à.d.
> très mal, très soigneusement, très intimement durement. Je me rende
> insupportable – mais le sujet ne sait pas combien je parle, et je pense
> avec lui, avec quelle franchise! [...]
> Pour moi, le comble de l'art serait de faire un dialogue où *cela*
> se parlerait tout seul – mais si j'en possède le frémissement et cette
> fixité extraordinaire – je n'en vois pas les portes, et il n'y en a
> peut-être pas. J'appelais cela Narcisse (il y a 14 ans).[62]

Fragments du Narcisse poetically mirrors this perpetual quest for
the truth of the individual self hearing itself speak and knowing
that its form is the body alone. 'La proximité est chose extraordinaire.' Is it so certain that this rich poem with its stylisation
of enchantment has not succeeded in making some of its intentions
present in transparent form? The voice trying to express itself can
only enchant, the poem tells us lucidly, a 'système fermé' like
poetry itself. Solitude is the truth without which there cannot be
love.

(c) **La Pythie**

Immediately after *Fragments du Narcisse*, Valéry has placed a
further long poem, *La Pythie*, a 'fontaine de noirceur' erupting at
the centre of *Charmes* and in relation to which the other poems
seem to receive something of their magical power to enchant.[63]
I shall suggest that *La Pythie* is not, as has often been supposed,

an alien interlude in the volume. It is a poem which takes us once more to the heart of Valéry's conception of the sensibility, introducing this time an important ambivalence towards the impersonality of language as reflected in poetic discourse itself (see Part I, p. 176).

One of the original poems of *Charmes* of 1917, *La Pythie* was composed in the landscape of gigantic trees – Avranches – at the same time as Valéry was completing *La Jeune Parque* and meditating more and more deeply on the nature of 'inspiration' (P I, 1655). Its links with that poem and the landscape of their common genesis can easily be perceived. Valéry's Delphic Pythoness or priestess of Apollo,[64] racked and tormented by the 'divine' force – Language? – seething within her body, is like one of the great trees of *La Jeune Parque* bursting with the force of Spring. 'Le printemps vient briser les fontaines scellées!', cried the Parque, 'N'entends-tu pas frémir ces noms aériens', and the Pythia, too, appeals to herself to hear the rivers of inner sound coursing in her veins as she anticipates with both desire and dread the birth of Voice – a form which will overcome the contradictions of her urge both to submit and to recoil, musically uniting her intellectual and animal selves:[65]

> Entends, mon âme, entends ces fleuves!
> Quelles cavernes sont ici?
> Est-ce mon sang?...Sont-ce les neuves
> Rumeurs des ondes sans merci?
> Mes secrets sonnent leurs aurores!
> Tristes airains, tempes sonores,
> Que dites-vous de l'avenir!
> Frappez, frappez, dans une roche,
> Abbatez l'heure la plus proche...
> Mes deux natures vont s'unir!

The reader already experiences the motivating force of a rhythm combining impatient anticipation with deliberate measure,[66] and savours the presence, through metaphor and metre, of the pressure of pre-articulate verbal form:

> Ah! brise les portes vivantes!
> Fais craquer les vains scellements.

I shall suggest that Valéry has brought together in the poem the most basic concepts and metaphors from the drama of consciousness, language and 'being' which he experienced and analysed so thoroughly in the course of poetic composition: the mind/body relationship as a cavern of inner sound (Part One, p. 107); the creative sensibility as a lyre (p. 285); the 'irrational' as a bounding horse which the intellect must learn to harness and ride (p. 258, n.8); poetry as a total 'Voice' co-ordinating all our faculties as one.

'Pâle' profondément mordue', the Pythia has been bitten, like the Parque, by the serpent of self-awareness (the python is the very emblem of the priestess with her 'trépied qu'étrangle un serpent'). Like the Parque, too, she instinctively turns to the joy of the past (and eventually to tears) in an attempt to escape the painful experience of dualism thrust upon her by the 'Puissance Créatrice' seeking outlet through her being. In the heart of the violence of her monologue, not without its own complex changes of tone in response to the mental effects of the body,[67] the invocation to the state of physical oneness she feels to have been hers ('Mon cher corps...Forme préférée...' [stanza 9]) offers us a sense of freshness and peace predictive of the relief and harmony of expression to come. Yet the irony for the reader here is that the lost paradise (before the advent of the 'prophetic' power of consciousness and language) reveals itself linguistically to be the very image of death:

> Douce matière de mon sort,
> Quelle alliance nous vécûmes,
> Avant que le don des écumes
> Ait fait de toi ce corps de mort!

It is the strength of this image of mortality, so closely interwoven with the capacity to participate in human destiny through language, which – snake herself in this Valéryan viperology of the intellect – the Pythia feels bending her to its will:

> Ô formidablement gravie,
> Et sur d'effrayants échelons,
> Je sens dans l'arbre de ma vie
> La mort monter de mes talons!
> Le long de ma ligne frileuse,
> Le doigt mouillé de la fileuse
> Trace une atroce volonté!
> Et par sanglots grimpe la crise
> Jusque dans ma nuque où se brise
> Une cime de volupté!

La Pythie is a poem which risks being either reduced to tameness by literalism concerning its central symbol or underestimated in its expressive precision. Its unashamedly mixed metaphors – taken here from the architectural, the vegetable, the sexual, the psychological and the mythical – are controlled with a logic centred on the 'propriétés logopsychiques' (xxix, 339) of language in its drama of flesh made word and word made flesh. For it is the drama of Voice itself which gives unity and meaning to the action of the poem, taking us far more deeply into the relationship between emotion and rationality, or between consciousness, language and bodily sensation than could a poem based on a purely allegorical treatment of 'Inspiration'. 'Voix rattachée aux entrailles, aux regards, au coeur', Valéry wrote in connection with the theme of the necessary descent by the poet/musician, Orpheus, into the underworld: 'et ce sont ces attaches qui lui donnent son pouvoir et son sens – voix, état élevé, tonique, tendu, fait uniquement d'énergie pure, libre, à haute puissance, ductile'.[68] All through the poem, images of musical sound[69] allow us to relate the experience of the Pythia to the drama of 'être' and 'connaître' which for Valéry, the Voice of self-knowledge harmonised and developed in poetry, and which he advised the poet to seek to understand as the basis and goal of a poem:

> Tirer le poème de réflexions sur la poésie, d'une forte imagination de la Poésie. Ne pas trouver la Poésie à la suite d'un incident qui va à un état, mais partir de l'état vers les incidents, le créer d'abord par connaissance de sa nature et structure. Voilà mon 'idéal' de 'poète', c'est aussi le comble de l'intellect   (xvii, 870).[70]

La Pythie still richly qualifies as one of Valéry's sustained monologues based on the pursuit of expressive self-awareness through different stages of being:[71]

> Hélas! ô roses, toute lyre
> Contient la modulation!
> . . . .
> Le temple se change dans l'antre,[72]
> Et l'ouragan des songes entre
> Au même ciel qui fut si beau!

Yet because of the violent sensation of dualism involved in this particular moment of being – the painful process of conscious creativity in which the inner workings of the mind seem to be made cruelly transparent – a way must be found to suggest the sensations of strangeness and inevitability involved. Hence the central metaphor of the Delphic priestess, oracular medium of an intransigent god. Hence, too, the separate narrative framework of the monologue. The first two and a half stanzas are spoken by an impersonal narrative voice (it may feel to the reader like the voice of an objective but purely external awareness) which leads us into the trance-like vociferations of the Pythia ('La Pythie exhalant la flamme [...] Vocifère [...] – Ah! maudite!...Quels maux je souffre!), finally to return us, in the penultimate stanza, to the third person perspective with its relative security:

> Telle, toujours plus tourmentée,
> Déraisonne, râle et rugit
> La prophétesse fomentée
> Par les souffles de l'or rougi.
> Mais enfin le ciel se déclare!
> L'oreille du pontife hilare
> S'aventure dans le futur:
> Une attente sainte la penche,
> Échappe de ce corps impur.

Not the least of the many ironies of this cleverly deceptive poem is the disproportion between that 'voix nouvelle et blanche' and the monologue itself – over eighteen full ten-lined stanzas and not perhaps as 'unreasonable' ('déraisonne') as the narrator's voice would make out. The main body of the poem is taken up by the Pythia's graphic analysis of the sensations of the intellect seemingly forced to abdicate its control – sensations of protest, fear or reasoned acquiescence evoked from the very standpoint of lucidity the Pythia fears she is being forced to abdicate. (No mood is without dualism of some degree, pleasurable or otherwise, and Valéry makes us feel that the 'irrationality' of the 'unconscious' is a function of reason itself, perhaps an area where he differed from Freud.) Notwithstanding Valéry's own dissatisfaction with the poem as over-hasty by his meticulous standards, the reader cannot but sense, in the light of this disproportion, a certain irony concerning, after so much labour and anguish, the 'transcendental' calm grandiloquently proclaimed in the final stanza, its origin appropriately obscure:

> Honneur des Hommes, Saint LANGAGE,
> Discours prophétique et paré,

Belles chaînes en qui s'engage
Le dieu dans la chair égaré,
Illumination, largesse!
Voici parler une Sagesse
Et sonner cette auguste Voix
Qui se connaît quand elle sonne
N'être plus la voix de personne
Tant que des ondes et des bois!

Could it be that the wisdom the Pythia has achieved is recognition that the monster within her is a fiction produced to intensify her individuality in the face of the idea of death? Could it be that the god tormenting her body is none other than conscious intelligence with its power to illuminate its own source in the sensibility and to express its findings through language for purposes of rational truth? 'Imagine donc fortement', Valéry wrote in *Eupalinos*, 'ce que serait un mortel assez pur, assez raisonnable, [. . .] pour méditer jusqu'à l'extrême de son être, [. . .] pense à quelle origine intime et universelle il s'avancerait; et à quel point précieux il arriverait; quel dieu il trouverait dans sa propre chair!' (P II, 96).

Raped by the god, Language, with the forcible entry of human universality into her subjective being, the Pythia loses her bodily oneness and privacy:[73]

Toute ma nature est un gouffre!
Hélas! Entr'ouverte aux esprits,
J'ai perdu mon propre mystère!
Une Intelligence adultère
Exerce un corps qu'elle a compris!

The paradox at the heart of the relationship between language and the sensibility, and one which the poem splendidly exploits with its own exhilarating tone and linguistic self-consciousness is that through this 'rape' the Pythia is empowered to give birth to a unique form of unity: the unity of Voice with its power to express individual experience in universal form. This is the power we feel magnetising the Pythoness in the heart of her torments, allowing her to express her recoil from the symbolic in violent, physiological metaphors, and to inspect with a rational curiosity equal in force to any Dionysian panic, the conflicting urges with which she is beset. Before the birth of language, the threat of the overpowering richness of experience within her – the inverse of the delight felt by the speaker in *Aurore* – can only cause her to cry for the death

of the monstrous serpent into which she feels she has been transformed, for its head to be held up, like the head of Medusa, so that
the whole world be turned to stone (stanzas 6 and 7).[74] The
imagery at the end of the poem is wide enough to suggest the
waves of sound coursing through the body – that 'voix du sang',
as Valéry once called it – and, with its classical resonance ('ondes'),
to denote the waves and waters of the natural world.[75] The
Pythia's sensibility is the lyre played by the natural universe whose
sounds the intelligence alone can harmonise to universal form.
Always in the background of the poems of *Charmes* is the drama
of Orpheus with his new-found power of musical enchantment
through expression:

> Ai-je blessé, heurté,
> *Charmé*, peut-être,
> Le Corps secret du monde?
> Ai-je sans le savoir,
> Ému la substance des cieux [. . .]?
> . . . .
> Me voici plus puissant que moi-même,
> Voici que je me trouve étrange et vénérable
> Pour moi-même,
> Égaré dans mon âme, et maître autour de moi!
> Et je tremble comme un enfant
> Devant ce que je puis!   (P i, 176–7).

The voice of wisdom at the end of the poem contains these contradictions serenely and majestically, enriched by a balance of
humility and pride.

La Pythie is obviously a 'poème ludique', a symbolic play in
language of the sensations and possibilities of language usage,
'la parole'. I have introduced it in somewhat unorthodox fashion
(stressing the rôle of the rational and conscious mind in emotion)
in order to stress the breadth of symbolism I feel to be involved.
Of course the poem relates to Inspiration in a way which makes
it applicable to poetic discourse – poetry being an intensified use
of the 'belles chaînes' of language through which the 'god', intelligence, has wandered into the flesh ('en qui s'engage/Le dieu dans
la chair égaré'). Yet Valéry's approach to poetic composition
always centres on the mental processes revealed in the creative
sensibility. Although the metaphor of the medium and the god

relates traditionally to the birth of the poem in its most mysteriously intuitive aspects, its treatment here allows it to acquire a much more general power of suggestion, particularly in relation to the processes of difference and identity manifested in self-awareness and speech.

One of the mental sensations conveyed most effectively in *La Pythie* is in fact that of 'depersonalisation', the painful feeling Valéry referred to as 'Non sum quit suis' (see Part I, p. 26). Far from being associated with trance-like loss of self-awareness, this sensation is bound inseparably to individual consciousness. It is *because* of consciousness that the Pythia feels as if a tempest of disorderly imagery – in turn the sensations produced by the body – has taken over her rational mind ('l'ouragan des songes'), splitting her being in two. It is *because* of an acute form of inwardly-directed consciousness that the sound of her own voice strikes her as strange and unacceptable, the produce of an alien as well as separate Self.[76] The words

> Qui me parle, à ma place même?
> Quel écho me répond: Tu mens!

take us close to the loss of self-identification associated with what is commonly called madness, but also to the drama of consciousness and language which Valéry associated with the ordinary phenomenon of speech. The poem's most disturbing and yet reassuring moments are ones which evoke the transition from fear to acceptance as the conscious mind re-establishes its self-trust in the face of these phenomena, loyally reasserting their necessity as part of the dualism from which its own continuity is dynamically formed. On the one hand the power of speech makes the Pythia feel as though her tongue were being hacked to pieces by the convulsive words breaking from the disorder within her (stanza 5); on the other, the power of speech enables a vast herd of monsters foddered in the unconscious to surge into the light of day:

> Ah! brise les portes vivantes!
> Fais craquer les vains scellements,
> Épais troupeau des épouvantes,
> Hérissé d'étincellements!
> Surgis des étables funèbres
> Où te nourrissaient mes ténèbres
> De leur fabuleuse foison!

Bondis, de rêves trop repue,
Ô horde épineuse et crépue,
Et viens fumer dans l'or, Toison!

Here Valéry's imagery is at its most fantastic yet controlled,
stimulating the reader to create constant associations between
rational and irrational categories, and expressing the power by
which the mind 'hits back' at chaos with an order of desire
nurtured by the original source, 'l'informe'. By making us aware
of the linearity of ordinary language compared with the multiple
discourse of inner monologue, Valéry is describing what he felt to
be one of the essential secrets of the mind: its power of self-
identification through the difference between inner and outer
speech: 'Et qui décrira, définira la *différence* qu'il y a *entre cette
phrase même qui se dit* et ne se prononce pas, et cette *même phrase
sonnante dans l'air?*' (xxii, 304). Are we not reminded here of the
discrepancy between the long, tortured monologue of the Pythia
and 'la voix nouvelle et blanche' which emerges at the end of it?
The discrepancy between a legend and its birth in the travails of
experience seems a central concern of Valéry's and one which
revealed itself to him particularly sharply through poetic composition, where the process and the product struck him as being
totally distinct.[77] By making the Pythia 'speak' of this difference,
Valéry could be said to be partly redeeming it poetically: forcing
the poem to reveal the difference between inner and outer worlds
vital to its existence.

Who, then, do we feel speaks the proclamation of the power of
'Saint LANGAGE' in the last stanza of the poem? Are the words
to be interpreted as part of the narrative voice at the beginning
and end of the monologue? Are they spoken by the euphoric
'pontif', his ear eagerly and somewhat ridiculously attending the
voice issuing from the mouth of the Pythia as that of a god?
Are the words spoken by the Poet drawing the moral of the
monologue?[78] By the new voice itself? While the poem is sufficiently flexible to allow all these interpretations on a purely fictional
level, it seems essential that we should at least in some way
attribute the utterance to Language itself speaking through the
Pythia's torments (the device of projecting words into a silent
phenomenon – the columns in *Cantique des Colonnes*, the 'Ideas'
in *Aurore*, the sensibility in the case of the Pythia herself is a

frequent one in *Charmes*). '[. . .] chez Hugo, chez Mallarmé et quelques autres', Valéry wrote on the subject of poetic impersonality,

> paraît une sorte de tendance à former des discours non humains, et en quelque manière, *absolus*, – discours qui suggèrent je ne sais quel être indépendant de toute personne, – une divinité du langage, – qu'illumine la Toute-Puissance de l'Ensemble des Mots. C'est la faculté de parler qui parle; et parlant, s'enivre; et ivre, danse.
>
> (P II, 635).[79]

The final stanza of *La Pythie* refers to the potential self-referentiality of language which he felt to be epitomised in poetic discourse itself.

Throughout this study we have seen how, despite his admiration for Mallarmé's type of poetry with its use of this power of impersonality to express 'la Voix du Langage', Valéry preferred to think of poetry as 'Le Langage issu de la Voix'. In my opinion it is precisely this difference that the ambiguity of the poem reflects. However vainly, the Pythia struggles to *refuse* the universality represented by Language which at the same time she knows is necessary to self-realisation. The expressive direction of the poem is devoted to sharpening our awareness of the discrepancy between legend and reality as well as to the affirmation of its magnificence, thus preventing us from unequivocally accepting a cult of Art based on 'la divinisation de la Voix' (P I, 597).

The original title of *La Pythie* was, in fact, 'Le chansonnier des ombres', and one need not read far to sense echoes of the poetry of Hugo, in metre, stanza-form and in imagery – trembling light, vast fantastic shadows, demonic horses, prophetic depths:

> Ô profondeurs épouvantables,
> Qu'est-ce donc que vous me voulez?
> . . . .
> Quels chevaux entend-on hennir?
> Quel fantôme erre en nos décombres?
> Quels yeux voit-on par tes trous sombres,
> Masque effrayant de l'avenir?[80]

The question: homage or parody, is over-simplified, however. Valéry's attitude to Hugo's poetry reveals both admiration and dislike. That he found Hugo 'coupable contre la voix' (VII, 642) brings us back finally to the poem's ambivalence towards impersonality of discourse, 'la Voix du Langage'.

On ne sait pas quel personnage est celui dont la *voix* est le vers de
Victor Hugo. Il faut toujours faire des vers en songeant à celui dont
ils seraient la parole – naturelle; et qui doit être une sorte d'unité
vivante – d'individu. (VII, 210).

We have seen throughout the first part of this study that this
unified voice was not, for Valéry, that of the author (approached
biographically), but that achieved in the work of art itself. The use
he wished to make of the impersonality of poetic discourse was
that of simulating the unity of a living being: '[. . .] écrire ce qui
suppléera à l'absence de l'auteur, au silence de l'absent, à l'inertie
de la chose écrite' (XII, 10). It is a further irony of this rich,
Rabelaisian work that it approaches this anti-Hugolian position
with such exhilaratingly Hugolian imagery, and that the mask of
Apollo and Dionysius become so strangely interchangeable. 'La
forme, c'est-à-dire – la Voix, qui est l'*unité*', Valéry wrote appropriately, ' – c'est cela qu'il faut trouver chaque fois et qui ne se
donne pas toujours – il y a bien des œuvres sans voix [. . .] alors
s'impose à l'autre l'acte tien' (XII, 806).

I have suggested that the subject of *La Pythie* is the creative
unity of the mind through the most disturbing moments of its own
unavoidable self-investigation, 'être' and 'connaître'. It is not by
accident that the image of Medusa or Hecate, goddess of the
moon, takes its place in the mythology of the poem. The famous
lines of *Le Cimetière Marin* – '. . . Mais rendre la lumière/Suppose
d'ombre une morne moitié' – receive here powerful orchestration.
The intellectual strength of *La Pythie* does not lie in its presenta-
tion of a purely rational transposition of conflict into value. It
is rather the deep-rooted power of rationality itself which the
poem treats as a source of expressive experience, a power related
in its turn to the 'double' nature of language. The Pythia's refusal
to acquiesce in her linguistic destiny[81] is presented as both the
death and the triumph of individual consciousness, a feat of
linguistic expression which the eulogy to Language at the end of
the poem allows us to inspect in all its paradoxical force. The
human sensibility is a tree played on by the winds of Consciousness
and Nature[82] and it is this dualism which Valéry makes the ever-
present source of self and, correspondingly, the ever-present centre
of what Language cannot say.

If *La Pythie* is often considered to introduce a jarring note into *Charmes*, this opinion largely relates to its stress on 'Inspiration' as an overpowering force it is felt difficult to reconcile with Valéry's belief that nothing of worth in art can be achieved without critical judgement and will. He stated that he would rather write nothing at all than something of genius produced under the power of a trance. 'Rougir d'être la pythie' (P II, 550). It has not been difficult to suggest that, on the contrary, *La Pythie* is perfectly at home in *Charmes*, its implied attitude to 'Inspiration' perfectly consistent with Valéry's own poetic theory and practice.

In the first place, Valéry denied the value of certain involuntary states of mind only in that they were not intrinsically related to the means of expression or to the intellectual developments of the Self through the exercise of the mind. It was in relation to precisely this experience of 'effets sans cause' that in '1892' he elaborated his 'method' of thought with its attempt 'musically' to 'cut the roots of pain' (v, 309). (Part I, p. 6). The same recoil from emotional wastage is reflected in the Pythia herself. Indeed it is through her mouth that we receive what could be seen as a scathing indictment of the popular Romantic notion that emotional delirium is akin to genius. A donkey's carcass would do just as well to receive the message of the gods (stanza 13). Such an interpretation of the state of Inspiration reduces the poet's rôle to a miserably passive one,

> Table ou cuvette, en somme, mais point un dieu, – le contraire d'un dieu, le contraire d'un MOI, (. . .). Il est étrange que plus d'un poète se soit contenté – à moins qu'il ne se soit enorgueilli, – de n'être qu'un instrument, un *médium* momentané. (P I, 1376).

Valéry himself was far from content with this definition of poetry, of course, turning it, as we have seen, into a highly conscious craft of language, and insisting in turn that this craft should allow the poet to range communicatively and expressively (as he has done himself in *La Pythie*) over a whole scale of emotions and sensations from the most highly conscious to the most involuntary: 'comment le plus haut au plus bas se relie'. 'Inspiration' should be transposed from the poet to the reader, who experiences through the poem a 'larger-than-life' consciousness, a Voice appearing to emanate from a more complete Self.[83]

How, then, are we to accept that so direct a link is established in *La Pythie* between the overwhelming disorder of the sensibility when 'être' and 'connaître' oppose each other and the voice of order at the end? Valéry's own recoil from certain antagonistic states of mind – 'quand les fantômes sont contre moi' (v, 309) – was based on the paradox of being unusually capable of the integrated emotion of 'la sensibilité intellectuelle'. The Pythia fears likewise that she will drown in those 'ondes sans merci', her own potentials for mental imagery, without the help of Language with its strange security of control.[84] It is in the face of the sensibility – 'mon plus cruel don' as he once called it – that critical control and attention to the separate universe of language is necessary in the first place. 'La Pythie ne saurait dicter un poème./Mais un vers – c'est-à-dire une *unité* – et puis un autre./ Cette déesse du Continuum est incapable de continuer./C'est le Discontinuum qui bouche les trous' (P ΙΙ, 628). The poem *La Pythie* itself is proof of the fact that a long poem can be created 'artificially', born from the sonorous 'vers donné' ('Pâle, profondément mordue') which the poet then sought to surround with 'vers calculés' worthy of the initial effect. It was precisely because of its never-ending riches and terrors that Valéry elaborated his craft of poetic composition, a means of mingling the animal and the intellectual world – 'être' and 'connaître' – in a way which exploited the musical capacity of the expressive intelligence, 'l'unité de la Voix'. This ideal of unity is perfectly consistent with the remark made by Valéry at the time of composing some of the early poems of *Charmes*:

> L'idée d'inspiration, si l'on se tient à cette image naïve d'un souffle étranger, ou d'une âme toute-puissante [...] peut suffire à la mythologie ordinaire des choses de l'esprit. [...] Mais je ne puis arriver à comprendre que l'on ne cherche pas à descendre dans soi-même le plus profondément qu'il soit possible.   (P Ι, 1665).

The octosyllable of *La Pythie*, dithyrambic yet calmly ordered, is proof of the unity of the creative sensibility at the heart of this quest for self-knowledge, confirming for both Pythia and Poet that for all the experience of dualism between 'being' and 'knowing', 'Il y a contradiction à dire que l'on conçoit un autre *Moi*' (xv, 586). Just as form is the poem's true subject, so the perceiving self is presented as part of the bodily sensibility in its naturally intoxicated, emissive relationship with the world:

> La poésie peut-être c'est toute l'âme – toute la parole, tout le dictionnaire possible de l'être, tout l'être en tant qu'appels, réponses, actes, émotions considérés comme un instrument. Telle est la Lyre et non autre chose. Parcourir d'autorité, avec liberté totale, sauf les règles seules de l'instrument [...], ce registre, clavier universel aux cordes innombrables [...]. L'univers, instrument de musique, moyen d'expression...moyennant un état spécial – de tension, d'ivresse, de désordre fécond et de mouvement.   (VII, 425).[85]

6

(a) About 'Ébauche d'un Serpent'

If *La Pythie* took us deep into the caverns of the sensibility from which emerges the song of the Voice – knowledge of death transformed into musical form – then the remaining major poems of *Charmes* – *Ébauche d'un Serpent, Le Cimetière Marin* and *Palme* – might be said to develop this 'myth' from the point of view of its maximum generality: the mind open to its own creative potentiality and 'style'.[1] Again there are many detailed studies of the poems from the point of view of technique and general interpretation. I shall simply suggest their possibilities as poems of voice.

Ébauche d'un Serpent

Ébauche d'un Serpent was composed at the same time as *La Pythie*,[2] once more in the Hugoesque ten-lined stanza. Another tree, another serpent or, as the blasé Méphistophélès puts it: 'Encore une affaire de Frruitt' (P II, 331). Yet this time it is the serpent himself who speaks – to the sun, to Eve, to the tree of the garden – offering the tempting fruit, seducing with his voice as does poetry itself, and even confident enough to give the game away at the same time:

> Le plus rusé des animaux
> Qui te raille d'être si dure,
> Ô perfide et grosse de maux,
> N'est qu'une voix dans la verdure!

This time it is the whole Biblical myth which seems to have been waiting to take its place in Valéry's poetic drama of intelligence and creativity, his 'jardin spirituel' of the pleasure-seeking mind.

> PARMI l'arbre, la brise berce
> La vipère que je vêtis;
> Un sourire, que la dent perce
> Et qu'elle éclaire d'appétits,

> Sur le Jardin se risque et rôde,
> Et mon triangle d'éméraude
> Tire sa langue à double fil...

The first, indeed the only narrative voice in the poem is that of the serpent – Satan, Lucifer, Méphistophélès – who spits out his hatred of creation in general and of man in particular (stanzas 1–12), brings all his verbal powers of persuasion to bear on the temptation of Eve (13–26), and, finally, evokes the Tree of Knowledge through which is prophesied the destiny of the human race. His argument, vibrant with images of light and shadow traditionally used to evoke moral dualisms of 'good' and 'evil', and strongly flavoured with tones of nineteenth-century occultism, proclaims that God created 'Man' simply for His own glorification, while he himself, the Serpent of Knowledge, can modify this state: changing the hearts of human beings by playing subtly on their propensity for self-love. Creation is thus the Fall rather than the triumph of God:[3]

> Ô Vanité! Cause Première!
> Celui qui règne dans les Cieux,
> D'une voix qui fut la lumière
> Ouvrit l'univers spacieux.
> Comme las de son pur spectacle,
> Dieu lui-même a rompu l'obstacle,
> De sa parfaite éternité;
> Il se fit Celui qui dissipe
> En conséquences, son Principe,
> En étoiles, son Unité.
>
> Cieux, son erreur! Temps, sa ruine!
> Et l'abîme animal, béant!...
> Quelle chute dans l'origine
> Étincelle au lieu de néant!...
> Mais, le premier mot de son Verbe,
> MOI!...

The serpent's seduction of Eve as representative of the human race in its urge for knowledge will be a means of revenge on God, which he proceeds triumphantly to announce with hissing, alliterative scorn:

> En vain, Vous avez, dans la fange,
> Pétri de faciles enfants
> [...]

181

> Sitôt pétris, sitôt soufflés,
> Maître Serpent les a sifflés,
> [...]

And the poem ends with a hymn to the great Tree of Knowledge itself:

> Ô Chanteur, ô secret buveur
> Des plus profondes pierreries,
> [...]

> Tu peux repousser l'infini
> Qui n'est fait que de ta croissance,
> Et de la tombe jusqu'au nid
> Te sentir toute Connaissance!
> Mais ce vieil amateur d'échecs,
> Dans l'or oisif des soleils secs,
> Sur ton branchage vient se tordre;
> Ses yeux font frémir ton trésor.
> Il en cherra des fruits de mort,
> De désespoir et de désordre!

Finally Valéry added yet a further stanza to give weight to what is already implicit in the 'logic' of the poem. The serpent offers to God the *triumph* of his sadness, his revenge being contained in the immense hope for the bitter fruits of knowledge which drives human beings ever on and on. It is their thirst for knowledge which makes the tree so gigantic, raising the omnipotence of nothingness to the power of being and thus overshadowing the power of God himself:

> Beau serpent, bercé dans le bleu,
> Je siffle, avec délicatesse,
> Offrant à la gloire de Dieu
> Le triomphe de ma tristesse...
> Il me suffit que dans les airs,
> L'immense espoir de fruits amers
> Affole les fils de la fange...
> – Cette soif qui te fit géant,
> Jusqu'à l'Être exalte l'étrange
> Toute-Puissance du Néant!

For all its circularity of imagery – the serpent biting its own sparkling tail – the poem thus ends on an image of ironically exultant creativity and growth.

'J'ai toujours ramé dans mon esprit [...] contre la puissance valeur des imageries à une dimension' (XVII, 205), Valéry wrote, and, similarly, no reader of his poetry will expect an abstract argument to be more than a framework, least of all an argument in theological terms. From those very first insinuating lines,

> PARMI l'arbre, la brise berce
> La vipère que je vêtis;

we are conscious of something else, an unalleged enjoyment on the part of the serpent himself and a sensuous linguistic presence which gives just too much weight to its own power to enchant and become self-enchanted, to be concerned with philosophical or theological niceties other than as a mask. The not always negative power of deception is, after all, a central theme of the poem, as we are reminded by the serpent's own address to the sun:

> Soleil, soleil;...Faute éclatante!
> Toi qui masques la mort, Soleil,
> [...]
> Par d'impénétrables délices,
> Toi, le plus fier de mes complices,
> Et de mes pièges le plus haut,
> Tu gardes les cœurs de connaître
> Que l'univers n'est qu'un défaut
> Dans la pureté du Non-être!

How beautifully double-edged these lines! In the mouth of the Testian serpent – negation in the light of the abstract intellect alone – they appear to be bitter and cynical, the denial of the presence and substance of nature as all but illusory. Yet they present to the reader the inverse of that very argument: the possibilities offered by the emptiness of nature as the condition of human creativity and worth.[4]

> Fauteur des fantômes joyeux
> Qui rendent sujette des yeux
> La présence obscure de l'âme,
> Toujours le mensonge m'a plu
> Que tu répands sur l'absolu,
> Ô roi des ombres fait de flamme!

Having once identified a certain level of his own abstract thought with the philosophy of the serpent, Valéry expresses the same sceptical attitude towards the 'charm' of nature and of poetry, another form of 'mensonge'.[5] Yet the 'lies' of metaphor with their golden honey have a further use in the garden of the mind than simply to provide material for more despair.

Let us look more closely at the 'style' of the serpent. Valéry named it 'le style Beckmesser', a style modelled on the carping critic in Wagner's *Meistersinger*,[6] a style so full of alliterations – 'Dore, langue! – dore-lui les/Plus doux des dits que tu connaisses!' – that it becomes almost a pastiche of his own techniques. Indeed, many a philosophy and literary tone is parodied – Bossuet, Pascal, Schopenhauer, to name only the most obvious. 'Tout le travail très difficile de ce poème a porté sur les *changements de ton*. J'ai exagéré exprès assonances et allitérations', Valéry wrote,[7] and it is surely the abundance of alliteration, particularly the gentle 'bs' and 'ls' of lines like the opening, which are responsible for a singing or voice-accentuating impact on our minds quite alien to any message of emptiness and bleakness that the serpent's words may semantically contain. This is the paradox, the wit and the self-aware meaning of the poem. The serpent, a burlesque character, a destructive spirit phonetically creaking with all the apparatus of deliberate disguise, is himself seduced by the language he uses to tempt Eve, is himself moved by the beauty of her body dappled with sunlight: 'Jusques à moi tu m'attendris'. He is forced to recognise the power he has invented through language, with its pleasure-making laws of slowness, pause and contrast, the 'harmonics' of the emotions made to vibrate and sing through skill. '(La superbe simplicité/Demande d'immenses égards!...)'. What more perfect example than this seduction-scene of the relationship between reader, poet and voice in poetry (the poet seduced by the gift of self he discovers through the reader), and of the model of the body on which Valéry's art of poetic resonance is based ('En toute chose, il faut trouver la *Musique des actes* [...]' [XII, 657]). Orpheus both invents and seduces, and *Ébauche d'un Serpent* is a poem ironically conscious of this power.

But we are going too fast, lured by what Valéry would call the temptation of abstract argument with its premature conclusions ('Si tu es vif, le lent t'échappe'). To appreciate how he turns a Schopenhauerian philosophy of nihilism to its own disadvantage while making use of its destructive energies, we must pause like Eve within the 'quasi éternel' (XII, 579) of the poetic state itself.

The serpent is a formalist, his physical presence merely evoked 'amongst' the great tree, his essence rocked by the breeze – 'La vipère que je vêtis'. A smile, a tooth, a triangle of emerald with a literally forked tongue – his venom is yet never so vile as wise hemlock which actually kills.[8] He is a mere 'sketch' of a serpent, a system of smiles and appetites impressionistically conveyed to our imaginations, as present and yet absent as the smile of the Cheshire Cat. The comprehensive preposition 'parmi' curiously used of a single noun, 'l'arbre', is the stylistic signal of a process of creation which the poem embodies with marvellous linguistic alacrity. The spirit of evocation with his 'innombrable intelligence', the serpent evokes himself as a verbal presence, a form of synechdoche, a voice in the verdure with the musical power to create experience in turn:

> – *Siffle, siffle!* me chantait-il!
> Et je sentais frémir le nombre,
> Tout le long de mon fouet subtil,
> De ces replis dont je m'encombre:
> Ils roulaient depuis le béryl
> De ma crête, jusqu'au péril!

By such humorous, allusive language, the reader is engaged as a conscious yet unwitting accomplice in the power of poetry knowingly to create what it desires us to hear and see.[9]

'PARMI l'arbre' has a further function. It calls to attention the indivisibility of the three protagonists, Serpent, Eve and Tree despite their fictional independence, thus preparing the symbolic transition, from the serpent to Eve and from Eve to the tree, in which all three personae are ultimately contained. For Eve herself, a 'masse de béatitude', is totally engaged in the lure of knowledge itself.[10] It is into her ear with its receptive corolla that the honeyed words fall, in turn to nourish the bee (stanza 20), and it is her mouth which thirsts for the deliciousness of the fruit with its characteristically Valéryan promise not of immortality but of the savouring of mortal life (stanza 21). The forked tongue, the drinking of ambrosia-like words and other such dead linguistic metaphors are revivified as part of a poetic symbolism of song, while vibrant pictures of the outer world are themselves rendered erotically in words. The form and texture of human flesh quivering in the light as it is about to cede to desire is made ironically proverbial:

> Génie! Ô longue impatience!
> À la fin, les temps sont venus,

Qu'un pas vers la neuve Science
Va donc jaillir de ces pieds nus!

Nor is the image of trembling marble inappropriate to the always underlying theme of artistic creation, when we remember that the lyre of Orpheus made rock forms[11] tremble and take female form. 'Masse de béatitude' or not, it is through the poetry of words that Eve is awakened to intelligence, and it is perfectly fitting that the 'te' of the final stanza refers no longer simply to her, the pure human sensibility, but to the tree itself, the great tree of combined emotion and intellect which, like the Parque or the Pythia, she has ultimately become. Through the image of the tree, symbol of creative unity at the heart of so many of Valéry's works, all the themes and tonalities, negative and positive, woven through the poem combine in a single image of possibility and growth:

Arbre, grand Arbre, Ombre des Cieux,
Irrésistible Arbre des arbres,
Qui dans les faiblesses des marbres,
Poursuis des sucs délicieux,
Toi qui pousses tels labyrinthes
Par qui les ténèbres étreintes
S'iront perdre dans le saphir [...]

Through the Tree of Knowledge, now symbolic of the 'musical' unity of human intellect and sensibility, the desire to understand and to create become one. The tree, like poetry, opens vast pathways of possibility, 'arbre de paroles'.

'Nihilisme bizarrement constructeur' (P i, 352), Valéry once said of his intellectual scepticism. In *Ébauche d'un Serpent* the serpent's negative voice acts almost despite itself as that of an 'agent provocateur', the poisonous but vital element of thought. Like the bee in *L'Abeille*, it is 'celui qui modifie', and with modification comes self-awareness, creativity and change, a fuller intelligence than the purely rational or avidly logical alone.[12] It is the voice of *this* form of intelligence, 'la sensibilité intellectuelle', which the whole poem orchestrates, reminding us once more of Valéry's conception of poetry as the expression of a totally unifying Voice.

'Comme en delice il change son absence': in showing how the Voice of 'l'être vivant et pensant' can 'raise nothingness to the power of being' – the drama of *La Pythie* with its discovery of death as the 'empty' form of the Self and, as we have still to see, the drama of *Le Cimetière Marin* – *Ébauche d'un Serpent* reaches a complex form of expression where poetic communication takes place through parody – almost parody of the principle of Voice itself. The extreme detachment of the mind towards its creations is contained in a structure of words which expressively denies and reaffirms its enclosure in the enchantment of form, mirror of the inescapable 'délice' of being alive. From this important poem, many of the smaller works on either side appear to stem. *L'Abeille*, *Les Pas* and *La Dormeuse* could be said to relate respectively to the serpent's bite, to the moment of potentiality before Eve takes the fruit, and to the beauty of Eve's form with its mysterious mingling to the eye of the beholder of the poetic ingredients 'lumière', 'ombre' and 'sommeil'. 'La "création poétique" – c'est la création de l'attente' (xii, 660), Valéry wrote. The remaining poems *L'Insinuant*, *La Fausse Morte* and *Les Grenades* seem equally closely related to the drama of the main poem.

L'Insinuant

Employing a five-syllabled line as short and light as *Le Sylphe*, *L'Insinuant* is a veritable exposé of the elusive magnetism of voice. It is as if the serpent of *Ébauche* is continuing his campaign of seduction (once more in the conventional guise of active male and passive female persona, seducer and seduced). Again play is set up between the sensuousness of language – verbal 'insinuation' – and the sensuousness of physical form, while the paradoxical line 'Mon dessein mauvais/N'est pas de te nuire' delightfully illustrates the power of language to communicate by presenting as a source of freedom what is essentially closed.

> O Courbes, méandre,
> Secrets du menteur,
> Est-il art plus tendre
> Que cette lenteur?
>
> Je sais où je vais,
> Je t'y veux conduire,
> Mon dessein mauvais
> N'est pas de te nuire...
>
> (Quoique souriante
> En pleine fierté,

Tant de liberté
La désoriente!)[13]

Ô Courbes, méandre
Secrets du menteur,
Je veux faire attendre
Le mot le plus tendre.

Again the theme of art and deception; again the fusion of
intellect and sensibility; again the symbolic mingling of the sexual
and poetic, the ironic compliance of seducer with the deliciousness
of his aim. With its preciosity, its wit, its 'double entente',
L'Insinuant creates a taut, paradoxical context in which Valéry
can evoke the potential seduction of the mind by its power to
anticipate what it expects to find – the 'resonant' capacity already
explored in Narcisse. Who speaks, meanwhile, 'le mot le plus
tendre' – its tenderness placed in a position of intriguing prominence by the break in the previous pattern of the rhyme scheme?
Is it the seducer or the 'victim'; or, in terms of the inner voices of
the dialogue of consciousness, the willed or relaxed self? The at
first sight outwardly representational imagery of the poem soon
begins to reveal the same ambiguity between inner and outer, Self
and Other, will and relaxation so effective in *Les Pas*. 'Je veux
faire attendre': will-power, like consciousness, is a deceptive
faculty in the mental universe explored by Valéry's poetry, its
dominance proudly or fearfully eroded by the involuntary nature
of deeper desires. Once more the structure of the poem catches
and delights intellectually in the paradoxes of a moment of
potentiality, source of unified action on the part of the mind
before words.

La Fausse Morte

La Fausse Morte, in some ways one of Valéry's most conventional
poems, based on the précieux paradox of love and death, takes on
new significance in the total poetic context of *Charmes*. For in the
image of the illuminating 'bite' as the sleeper awakes – only an
apparent 'Dormeuse', despite the same acoustically appealing
'ombres' and 'abandons' – comes the resonance of all those images
by which Valéry expresses the vital invasion of 'être' by 'connaître', or, in this case, of 'connaître' by 'être':

HUMBLEMENT, tendrement, sur le tombeau charmant,
  Sur l'insensible monument,
Que d'ombres, d'abandons, et d'amour prodiguée,
  Forme ta grâce fatiguée,
Je meurs, je meurs sur toi, je tombe et je m'abats,

Mais à peine abattu sur le sépulcre bas,
Dont la close étendue aux cendres me convie,
Cette morte apparente, en qui revient la vie,
Frémit, rouvre les yeux, m'illumine et me mord,
Et m'arrache toujours une nouvelle mort
  Plus précieuse que la vie.

The power of *La Fausse Morte* to evoke patterns of illumination relating to the sensibility is in no way detrimental to its existence as a poem based primarily on the act of love, the only poem of *Charmes* with a direct sexual theme. It refers to the act of love with a self-conscious tenderness which derives far more from its use of sound and rhythm than from précieux imagery. Yet précieux imagery is still more than purely decorative. It provides the distance of tone necessary to save from banality the central conceit through which love and death are compared. The poem contains more ambiguity than is at first apparent. How does that 'nouvelle mort' more precious than life (with its corresponding change of sound and tempo) relate to the theme of enjoyment in the poem? Does it offer renewed pleasure or, on the contrary, an awakening from the closed world of pleasure itself? There is the same ambivalent attitude towards 'charm' that we have found throughout Valéry's poems, reminding us, as in *L'Abeille*, that the harmony desired by consciousness is far from the half-oblivion of sleep or sensual repose. The lure of deception signalled in the title leads to a region where mental and physical sensation is approached simultaneously through the paradox of pleasure and pain, intellectually so close.

Les Grenades

'Une science vive crève/L'énormité de ce fruit mûr!', quipped the serpent of *Ébauche* of the fruit of the Tree of Knowledge, and it is as if *Les Grenades*, with its striking analogy between ripe pomegranates and the brows of thinkers bursting with thoughts, prolongs this concept in sensorial form. The initial impression given by this sonnet, beloved of anthologies for the economy of its suggestion, is of linguistic mimesis: the poetic imitation of the presence of fruits, their hard skins cracking with the pressure of luscious red seeds within:

> Dures grenades entr'ouvertes
> Cédant à l'excès de vos grains,
> Je crois voir des fronts souverains
> Éclatés de leurs découvertes!
>
> Si les soleils par vous subis,
> Ô grenades entre-bâillées,
> Vous ont fait d'orgueil travaillées
> Craquer les cloisons de rubis,
>
> Et que si l'or sec de l'écorce
> À la demande d'une force
> Crève en gemmes rouges de jus,
>
> Cette lumineuse rupture
> Fait rêver une âme que j'eus
> De sa secrète architecture.

The qualities of an object cannot exist independently of perception, and Valéry has chosen characteristically to present the sensations of sight through the voice of a first-person speaker. More than this. The theme of perception becomes explicit. The speaker is brought to increased self-presence through the perception of something outside the Self – '*Le réel est mon équivalent*' (VII, 31) – and finally to consciousness of the nature of perception. The theme of the final tercet is literally a memory of self brought about through the sensation of sight, a poetic demonstration of the manner in which we move to self-awareness through intentionality, the perpetual sight of ourselves through what is lost.[14]

Yet one of the most remarkable differences between *Les Grenades* and poems conveying the modulations of consciousness confronted by external reality is its stress on the similarity between processes in nature and processes in the mind in which an action of self-revelation through language takes place, a similarity which even extends into the 'separation' or 'absence' of consciousness itself: 'Fait rêver une âme que j'eus/De sa secrète architecture'. Leaving aside detailed study of the sound and imagery of the poem, I shall concentrate on the possible contribution of *Les Grenades* to a poetry conscious of itself.

It is not only the visual sensation of pomegranates which we find played on thematically in the poem, but their existence as a gesture of form available to the understanding. Their form is a *sign* of the slow, invisible process of ripening which has led to their explosive shape in the present. Their spatial structure is perceived as a dynamic function of time.[15] It is through abstract concepts – maturation, structure, potentiality, duration – born on a level of visual experience in which sight and knowledge constantly check and reinforce each other, that the central analogy is shown to arise. The hard, bulbous fruits ripened by the sun are *like* the rounded foreheads of thinkers whose discoveries have also matured through slow processes in time, and whose explosive thoughts have violently burst open their brows to reveal the structure of thoughts within. On the disturbing physical appearance of this 'rupture' we are not allowed to dwell, for Valéry's alert sense of timing has deflected us already into the abstract connotations of the analogy: 'Cette lumineuse rupture'. It is thoughts rather than brain cells which we 'see' through language, while the strongly meditative direction of the final tercet confirms the existence of the creative sensibility – 'l'âme' – as the invisible potential involved in the transaction throughout. The sight of the fruit has stimulated in the watching mind the same invisible processes of discovery attributed to the thinkers. The process of description has reminded the speaker of 'le Moi' ('La mémoire et la voix: leurs exigences coincident'). Could it have done so without the presence of inner monologue with its tentative distance from sensation at the same time as its immersion? 'Je crois voir...' simulates what is essentially an action of speech.

Many of the stylistically expressive procedures of this sophisticated poem – particularly its use of metonomy – involve the reader in an experience of language of a satisfyingly self-referential kind. By virtue of the interplay of tenor and vehicle in the central metaphor[16] we participate in an action of imagination in which 'la philosophie à l'état naissant' is involved. Abstract and physical, visible and invisible, natural and artificial interplay and unite for us too. If the pomegranates are like minds, so also do certain concepts such as pride, lucidity, effort and endurance acquire, through association with the natural world, a vigour and inevitability not available before. 'Dures grenades', at first read as an

address to the 'signifier' changes within this widening circle of
analogical relationships into a metaphor of mind. Now the whole
poem is a gesturing form, a figure, ready to evoke and contain
further analogies in turn. We awaken – as does the beholder to
the potentiality of the mind in the presence of the fruit – to the
presence of language: its nature as a transformational action
which the 'luminous rupture' of the poem makes visible in turn.

Language undoubtedly makes itself felt in the expressive qualities
of sound chosen to reinforce the sensuous reality of the pomegranates – a rare case of phonetic mimesis on Valéry's part.[17]
In the lines

> Et que si l'or sec de l'écorce
> À la demande d'une force
> Crève en gemmes rouges de jus,

we 'hear' the cracking skins in the hard consonants, sense the
corresponding changes to contrasting softness of sound in the
references to the succulence of the fruits within. To make such a
link between sound and meaning involves our minds in a further
kind of analogy – the highly complex metaphorical process of
language itself – and one whose artifice we are not allowed to
forget in the highly stylised pattern of the two sounds in a sonorous
architecture of their own. In the final transaction between what
Valéry called 'l'accord exact de la Voix qui est un acte et de
l'Ouïe qui est sensation' (P 1, 596), sound is far from onomatopoeic.
We are asked to make the transition from the sensation of sound
whose total presence is the medium of the poem, to the visual
sensation which sight supposes as an intellectual theme – the
inverse procedure from the transition from sight to sound in 'la
Personne qui parle'. The presence of language is no longer
'transparent' but demands association with the themes and images
the poem has proposed.

Take, for example, the movement from inside to outside or
from invisible to visible made present in the image of the fruit
whose secrets lie revealed – ('Mes secrets sonnent dans l'air' is the
Pythia's equivalent in the world of external speech). Analogy with
abstract thought-processes and the physical brows of thinkers has
already encouraged the movement from inside to outside to work
on two different levels at once. Our imaginations are primed for

the final transfer as we associate language too with the image of fruit. We 'think we see' in the ripe seeds ready to tumble from the half-open fruit, ideas ready to burst from the mind under the pressure of the need to express, works ready to tumble from the lips of a mouth, or, more abstractly, the power of language to reveal and disrupt the inner self.[18] The 'rupture' is, however, a luminous one (cf. 'Illumination, largesse!'). It reveals the unity of the mind which is lost or divided through its action, making visible in turn what could not otherwise be seen.[19] The double power of language is present in the curiously tentative syntactical form of the poem ('Si les soleils par vous subis', 'Et que si l'or sec de l'écorce') through which the final discovery is introduced – consciousness awaking to greater memory of itself through the action of inner monologue in relation to sight. Even the homophonous sound of the disparate verbal forms 'jus' and 'j'eus' presents a sense of interchange between the creative sensibility structured by language and the nutritious virtues of fruit – the relationship between substantive and verb. Countless stylistic elements peculiar to the 'forme fixe' of the sonnet[20] magnify the peculiarly enclosed yet suggestive intensity of *Les Grenades* as a self-conscious gesture of literary form.

'A chaque instant, un événement verbal veut répondre à l'événement physique et visuel, et faire passer quelque chose du temps quelconque dans le temps organisé – celui des actes' (P II, 806), Valéry wrote,[21] and 'Ô Langage/Personne n'a fait pour toi/Ce que je vois être fait en toi – /Et nécessairement par toi' (see Part I, p. 16). Far from suggesting that *Les Grenades* is an allegory of poetic language – that poems are pomegranates – I am proposing that its figures of speech render visible the essence of language as a transformational action through which self-awareness and self-presence is increased. The originality of *Les Grenades* lies in its power to reveal the personal art of its 'absent' author through the completely self-contained architecture of its presence as Voice.

(b) Le Vin Perdu, Intérieur, Le Cimetière Marin

Le Vin Perdu

With its marine landscape, first-person speaker, its 'offering to the void' and its elated finale, *Le Vin Perdu* is a 'Cimetière Marin' in miniature. Yet what type of enigma is involved in this limpid yet haunting work? On one level it is simple and anecdotal. The narrative tells of precious wine cast into the sea and 'given back' to the imagination in the form of leaping shapes and 'figures' previously unsuspected. The challenge lies not in deciphering the motive 'behind' the anecdote, but in relating the anecdote and its treatment to the symbolism through which the whole poem speaks as a gesture of form. Indeed, the anecdote is presented as a mystery to the narrator too. The gesture of casting wine into the sea was accomplished in a forgotten place on a day unspecified. The very structure of the poem takes the form of a wondering, Parque-like questioning – what prompted this gesture of libation? asks an inner psychiatrist – and a bemused enchantment at the consequences is its result.

> J'ai quelque jour, dans l'Océan,
> (Mais je ne sais plus sous quels cieux),
> Jeté, comme offrande au néant,
> Tout un peu de vin précieux...
>
> Qui voulut ta perte, ô liqueur?
> J'obéis peut-être au devin?
> Peut-être au souci de mon cœur,
> Songeant au sang, versant le vin?
>
> Sa transparence accoutumée
> Après une rose fumée
> Reprit aussi pure la mer...
>
> Perdu ce vin, ivres les ondes!...
> J'ai vu bondir dans l'air amer
> Les figures les plus profondes...

After a rosy-pink smoke, the sea regains its accustomed 'transparency'; but the wine once lost, that gesture of agitation caused the waves to become drunk and deep shapes to be seen leaping and dancing in the bitter, salty air.[22]

True, the image behind the transformation seems close to the description of the phenomenon of diffusion in physics – one Valéry used as an analogy in the essay 'Crise de l'Esprit' and which can be traced in turn to a passage describing entropy-reversal in the writings of Poincaré:

> Une goutte de vin tombée dans l'eau la colore à peine et tend à disparaître, après une rose fumée. Voilà le fait physique. Mais supposez maintenant que, quelque temps après cet évanouissement et ce retour à la limpidité, nous voyions ça et là, dans ce vase qui semblait redevenu eau *pure*, se former des gouttes de vin sombre et *pur*, – quel étonnement... (P I, 999).[23]

Yet Valéry never uses scientific imagery directly in his poems, feeling that he discovered in the process of poetic composition aspects of mental functioning which resemble the discoveries made by the scientist in method alone, and preferring to embody any such discoveries indirectly in the experience of form. Comparison with the passage in the essay may even be actively misleading if it diverts attention from the simple pattern of loss, transformation and hidden continuity played on in the poem, a pattern far more prominent than that of the apparent reversal of a natural law and one which constantly intrigued Valéry, as it did Coleridge, from the point of view of its persistence in dreams and in the general psychology of genius at work in the imagination conscious of itself. A sense of wondering surprise at the apparent reversal of a natural law – the reversal of an expectancy – does play a part in *Le Vin Perdu*, reinforced by the awed, ballad-like tone with its echoes of, say, Goethe's 'Es war ein König in Thule'.[24] Yet any such reversal surely takes place not in the phenomenon observed, but in the mind of the beholder interpreting it. A sense of a fleetingly experienced bond between the configurations of the outside world and the structure of the perceiving sensibility is conveyed through the curiously 'literal' symbolism of the poem. As in many a sonnet by Mallarmé, the last tercet can be read as belonging to a mental time simultaneous with that of the first quatrain. It is put forward as a recapitulatory description of a complexity which was at the time instantaneous, not as the description of a successive event. Now the 'rose fumée', and the 'figures les plus profondes' can be seen as metaphors of one and the same transforming action, and the miracle is one of ultimate transparency in relation to the 'figures' themselves. The wine is cast into the sea – no image of dispersal is used in the poem – and after a rosy haze *coinciding* with the dancing 'figures', the water regains its accustomed transparency: a transparency to which the poetic stress of the last line has now imaginatively attributed architecture and depth: 'Les figures les plus profondes'.

'[...] dans l'ordre des arts et de la poésie en particulier', Valéry wrote, 'toute la production purement intérieure, si riche ou si profonde soit-elle, ne vaut que pour celui qui en est la source et le lieu: elle ne prend valeur universelle que par les puissances de la forme'.[25] This 'law' of the creative sensibility was exemplified in the process of poetic composition, where he discovered so often the capacity of revelatory self-surprise. To 'sacrifice' or move away from the half-perceived object of expression into the universe of language as an object of attention in its own right – 'cast thy bread upon the waters' – was to re-discover the original impulse, yet illuminated and communicable in a way impossible before. 'J'étais dans ton ombre et dans ta composition', says the 'Idea' to its creator,

> J'étais éparse, près et loin (comme une goutte de vin
>   dans une tonne d'eau claire)
> Dans ta substance. [...]
> Sois pour que je sois, Sois pour être! [...]
> Ma voix est la tienne et tu distingues
> Ma volonté. Mais tu veux...MOI! L'Idée!   (P i, 358).

Without in any way suggesting that *Le Vin Perdu* symbolises poetic composition, I feel it presents the 'law' of the creative sensibility available to us through any constructive experience involving growth in time – love, memory, scientific discovery, artistic creation, and so on. As the most striking feature of that generality, we experience on the one hand a sense of fatality and compulsion (the speaker is drawn to sacrifice the precious substance of his calm in favour of a later illumination over which at the time he has no knowledge or control), and on the other, a sense of liberating freedom through the exercise of risk (the speaker is enchanted by the unexpected yet significant experience of reward). That we do not have to confine such a structure to that of poetic composition is emphasised by the fluid frame of reference of the poem. The setting of the symbolic incident – vague, capitalised 'Océan' and metaphysical 'néant' – encourages the maximum association between abstract concepts such as chance, pattern, the unknown, surprise: in fact a curious blend of the cosmic and intimately psychological reminiscent of Nerval ('J'ai deux fois traversé l'Achéron...'). *El Desdichado* also treats anxiety from the point of view of its maximum generality, also seeks laws in the heart of the arbitrary, also cherishes the chaos and ambiguity which brings about pattern, and, above all, also treats such themes musically through the continuity of an individual voice (P I, 596).

Yet the search for continuity in Nerval's poetry is, like that of Valéry, predominantly an achieved, expressive one, and it is fitting that so much of the deftly chosen vocabulary, sound and syntax of *Le Vin Perdu* can be found to apply – still without confining our interpretation to the theme of poetic composition– to a universe in which communication and literary discovery still hold sway. If we are to respond to the deepening structure of the poem and its characteristic power to complete a cycle of form (xxIII, 180), then we must relate those images of gesture, loss, intoxication, 'dance', transparency, figurativeness and profundity to the transforming action which takes place through language. The terms just used are the ones we have found frequently in a rhetorical context[26] when Valéry is discussing the process of communication in poetry and in prose; and just as the gesture at the beginning of the poem is rewarded by leaping forms capable of illuminatory 'opaqueness', so the destructive sacrifice of the 'transparency' of prose is rewarded in poetic discourse by the ultimate clarity of a form that 'speaks' with greater depth. *Le Vin Perdu* is not a poem *about* poetic discourse, but it is still a gesture of language in which linguistic self-referentiality has been taken to a fascinating extreme. The reversal of accident and significance – the subject of the poem – is also for Valéry the mechanism of true poetic discourse.

'Le réel d'un discours, c'est après tout cette chanson, et cette couleur d'une voix, que nous traitons à tort comme détails et accidents' (P II, 85). Where the voice of the long poems of *Charmes* may seem to render '*l'onde porteuse*' of an emotion (xIII, 822) by their stylistic attributes of resonance, coherence and continuity, I suggest that shorter poems like *Le Vin Perdu* and *Les Grenades* investigate, with their quite different procedures of figurative density and symmetrical reflection, the way in which the searching 'sensibilité intellectuelle' discovers its own analogy in a universe of physical forms or 'figures'.[27]

This is not to say that the smaller poems like *Le Vin Perdu* do not also present the continuity of human consciousness so central to a poetry of voice. Looking back on this curiously exciting poem, so suggestive, so precise, we find that its expressive power is derived not from metaphorical alacrity alone, but from the way in which its vocal dimensions lift and interrelate the elements within it into overall patterns of mood through which an individual response to the process of symbolism can be conveyed (in some ways more powerfully because of the interlocking elements possible in sonnet form). Tone is defined by Valéry as 'l'accommodation du parleur à sa parole-pensée' (VII, 21), imitation of voice-tone in particular as the stylistic key to human unity (XV, 46), and tone is amply present even within the tiny frame of this poem. In the first tercet, for example, word order introduces an intriguingly active structure. We search for the possible meaning of the causal relationship behind the inverted subject and object ('Sa transparence accoutumée' 'Reprit aussi pure la mer...'). And in so doing, we become conscious, partly through the archaïc tone of the inversion,[28] of the symbolic value of the gesture and its gravity for the speaker. The symbolic is being presented as a literal action. In the final tercet, the deliberate tone of the heavily stylised parallel in 'Perdu ce vin, ivres les ondes!' with its interplay of formal and colloquial, exclamatory and analytic, conveys and perpetuates an invisible field of reference through which the grave yet mounting excitement of the speaker is passed. For it is not the event but will-power brought to bear on creative sensibility which 'changes water to wine' (V, 903). Expressive of the pride and trust of the mind in a process outside its own making yet unavailable without conscious intelligence and 'method', *Le Vin Perdu* relates to an affirmation concerning the value of 'substitution' (ibid.) of deep significance in Valéry's creative universe.[29] Hence, as in *Palme*, the individual emotion behind the proverbial tone. 'Le Moi, c'est la Voix [...] la personne qui parle' (IV, 390): if much of the imagery of the poem relates to disruption and uncertainty – boredom, death, sacrifice[30] and the ambiguous mood of its ending (excitement which moves as much away from the celebration of pattern as towards its enchantment?) – then the strong certainty of the vocal elements establishes a further self-identity as the source of continuity. The coincidence of the vocal principle of continuity with the densely figurative in *Le Vin Perdu* shows that Valéry's poems progress not only through 'modulation'. A sense of circularity is also involved, and with it the self-sufficiency of a form capable of checking the infinite regress of meaning available to thought alone.

Intérieur

Une esclave aux longs yeux chargés de molles chaînes
Change l'eau de mes fleurs, plonge aux glaces prochaines,
Au lit mystérieux prodigue ses doigts purs;
Elle met une femme au milieu de ces murs
Qui, dans ma rêverie errant avec décence,
Passe entre mes regards sans briser leur absence,
Comme passe le verre au travers du soleil,
Et de la raison pure épargne l'appareil.

No more and no less confined to its 'outer' literalness than was *Le Vin Perdu* to the physical gesture of wine cast in the sea, *Intérieur* creates a two-way symbolism. It is both a domestic interior and an interior of the mind, the abstraction of the one and the physicality of the other interweaving perpetually, as in the Mallarméan room of the sonnet 'Ses purs ongles...'.[31] Valéry perhaps has much the same relationship of inner and outer space in mind when he writes in the 'Intérieur' of *Mélange*:

Il fait affreux. Pluie et vent mêlés.
Mais je suis en deça du verre qu'ils insultent, au milieu de murs, au sec et au tiéde. Mon regard prend et laisse la tempête, se fixe sur un point d'esprit *qu'il fait parler en moi* [...]. Que de choses et de travaux ont enfin permis que la pensée puisse à l'abri, *durer*, s'assouplir, se perdre, se retrouver et se prolonger [...].   (P 1, 308).

To say that the poem suggests the mental capacity of 'attention' is obviously valid, then. Pure reason is spared from the intrusion of its surroundings, just as the sun's rays are not diminished by a transparent glass. Yet to abstract the conceptual message from the elaborate simile is at the same time to miss the tone which further elements of the poem expressively inject. In the image of master/slave with its humorous domesticity – and hint of male/female stereotyping – arises a paradoxical reversal of strength and dependency which filters into our reading of the poem as an evocation of the part/whole relationship between the intellect and the sensibility. Not necessarily male after all and possibly even contemplating the 'slave' that is the self, if 'une femme' is taken to be the subject's own mirrored form, the narrator depends on that tactful solicitude for the preservation of thought in its separate power. And in this crystalline dialogue – reminiscent of the tender relationship between Faust and Lust, 'la demoiselle de crystal' – we are taken to the heart of the intellect in its 'sensibilised' relationship to the world.[32] The slow, rhythmic phrasing and the handling of the alexandrine in a single self-contained stanza has its own power of contributing to the unity of voice acting through the whole poem. Through it we sense an emotion which appears to have created its theme ('production d'un contenu' [v, 178]).

Rather than analyse the language of *Intérieur* and its humorously allusive periphrases – 'Au lit mystérieux prodigue ses doigts purs' may mean literally 'to make the bed', but allows the everyday notion to recede behind the emotive connotations of its words – we can conclude by allowing the 'figure' of the poem to take over. Patterns of transparency and light, presence and absence, are rendered conceptually 'visible' by the imagery, so that we can extend them as we read to the principle of the voice itself, so often similarly described. 'Comme la lumière est le fait essentiel en peinture [. . .], ainsi la voix est le fait essentiel en poésie. La poésie est *dans* la voix comme les objets dans la lumière' (xxix, 174). Poetry is the presence of the voice, seen and not seen. And if Valéry talks of the spirit of poetry in paradox, then a poem such as *Intérieur* removes the tension of paradox by treating it as a gentle commonplace – hence the choice of domestic interior to describe the master/slave relationship of the intellect and the sensibility: 'je suis le maître si je suis ton esclave' (P i, 1731); 'Oh! ne te laisse pas emporter (comme tant le célèbrent) par la seule force qui n'est pas tienne' (P i, 1731). Like so many of Valéry's poems, *Intérieur* will reveal, to those who need it, a lesson drawn from the complexity of the mind in its attempt to be fully itself. 'Et l'amertume est douce, et l'esprit clair' is not so far from the balance of *Intérieur*, and so to the much longer poem *Le Cimetière Marin*.

Le Cimetière Marin

> Ce toit tranquille, où marchent des colombes,
> Entre les pins palpite, entre les tombes;
> Midi le juste y compose de feux
> La mer, la mer, toujours recommencée!
> Ô récompense après une pensée
> Qu'un long regard sur le calme des dieux!

– strangely familiar even the first time we read them, and with us for the rest of our lives as the reminder of a certain *tone* of experience, 'Où l'amertume est douce, et l'esprit clair', these opening lines take us to what Valéry saw as his most characteristic type of poetry:

> Le 'Cimetière Marin' serait donc le type de ma 'poésie' vraie et surtout les parties plus abstraites de ce poème. C'est une espèce de 'lyrisme' (mi capisco) net et abstrait mais d'une abstraction motrice plus que philosophique.[33]

It is a definition I shall hold in mind when, attempting to appreciate the poem from the point of view of its vocal melody: what Valéry meant by attributing the highest poetic value to the most abstract parts of the poem, and by differentiating their motivating force from the philosophical despite the poem's wide range of intellectual themes: for example the relationship between consciousness and contingency, the thought and the sensation of the passing of time. We shall see how the 'ideas' of the poem are contained musically within its 'song', corresponding to the continuity of the mind as it listens to the flow of inner monologue: 'Tout le corps humain présent *sous la voix*, et support, condition d'équilibre de l'idée...' (P ɪɪ, /49); 'l'être s'écoute, trouve une surpenante suite'.

The poem opens with two separate but closely bound exclamations – the exclamatory mode serving to reinforce the intimate, lyrical tone of the monologue while drawing attention to its simultaneous status as an ode.[34] (We have already noticed that imitation of 'la voix intérieure' is not the only function of poetic discourse for Valéry; the poem must also celebrate and develop the properties of mental transformation made possible in relation to language itself.) The first of these exclamations, with its curious asymmetry of rhythmical groupings (4 + 6, 6 + 4 and 4 + 6, 2 + 2 + 6), is a description of the scene – the sea between the pine trees and tombs of the cemetery sparkling in the midday sun. Yet it is a description in which visual elements are rivalled by the delighted power of the mind making an analogy. The sea is a roof; the midday sun is an intransigent and accurate judge. Above all it is the verbs – 'marchent', 'palpite', 'compose' – which are positioned so as to rise like pure notes of discovery from the surrounding statements. The pride of making an analogy is meanwhile equally the experience of being involved in the movement of the outer world, dynamic despite its relative stillness and similarity of effect. The second exclamation – 'Ô récompense... !' – proclaims, in the form of the rhetorical equivalent of the 'seul soupir' which will enter in stanza 4, that a long glance over the calm sea is the mind's own particular reward after the abstractions of thought. The tranquil roof of the sea palpitates, however; absolute calm belongs to the gods. Already we are aware of the paradoxical component of human consciousness as a form of desire, the condition of separation through which this enjoyment exists. In the course of a single stanza, microcosm of the whole poem, we have moved from sensation to perception and to what Valéry called in his essay *Inspirations Méditerranéennes* the germ of universal thought (Part I, p. 19). Gradually we shall become involved in the drama of sensation and conceptual awareness which takes place in the mind of this 'amateur d'abstractions', 'témoin parleur' of his experience of the three protagonists 'Corps', 'Esprit', 'Monde'. From the lived notion of the sea as change, the cemetery as the confinement of the present with its reminder of death, the sky as relative immobility and the sun as absolute, the voice of 'la Personne qui parle' will weave the song of human possibility at the heart of 'le Moi'.

Still there is no intrusion of the first-person pronoun in the long drawn out apostrophe which opens the poem. It is not until the fourth stanza, prepared by the possessive adjective in 'Ô mon silence', that the first person enters in direct form:

> Temple du Temps, qu'un seul soupir résume,
> A ce point pur je monte et m'accoutume,
> Tout entouré de mon regard marin;

Valéry has delayed the full entrance of reflective consciousness.

Only now with the emergence of the pronoun 'Je' does he signal the presence of a further source of separation from the totally embracing field of the 'regard marin'.[35] 'JE$_1$ et la chose pensée sont symétriques, et non JE$_2$ et la chose vue' (xxii, 122). With the movement towards 'la conscience de la conscience' characteristic of many of the smaller poems of *Charmes*, the speaker now takes stock of his position in the 'miroir parlant' of the scene about him:

> Et comme aux dieux mon offrande suprême,
> La scintillation sereine sème
> Sur l'altitude un dédain souverain.

One of the paradoxes of poetic discourse which the reader is drawn to account for intellectually is the fact that this analytic voice is kept as much part of the aesthetic spell of the poem as the voice of greater involvement at the beginning. The outer world is perceived as the voice of the individual self, and the discovery of that source has not disrupted the 'song'.[36]

It is not difficult to appreciate in the gradual crescendo of sensation, perception, self-awareness of this first movement, the poetic mimesis involved in the metaphor of the soul as a roof which is expressed in the unforgettable invocation of stanza three:

> Ô mon silence!...Édifice dans l'âme,
> Mais comble d'or aux mille tuiles, Toit![37]

Le Cimetière Marin is obviously a masterpiece of harmonic composition, anticipation, repetition, echo, contrast and development. Even its metaphors appear to rise naturally from the movement of the text.[38]

Further brief indication of the overall movements of the poem would reveal the continuation of a form of self-definition in relation to the gradually changing scene and the universal commonplaces of life and death suggested by it. Having identified with its so far motionless and glittering perfection, the beholding consciousness now realises and savours, as change begins to enter the external scene about it, the sensation of its own mortality: 'Comme le fruit se fond en jouissance...'. Now it is the human being who is changing and who takes as arbiter and witness, the relatively unchanging sky: 'Beau ciel, vrai ciel, regarde-moi qui change...': an active, linguistically dependent movement of thought. It is this movement of brave abandonment to the inevitable laws of inner movement – 'la self-variance' as Valéry calls it in the *Cahiers* – which culminates in the first main turning point of the poem: a plunge from contemplation of the outer world and of the position of the mind in relation to it, to contemplation of the depths of the inner self on which this capacity for calm contemplation depends. From the pivot phrase of stanza 7 '. . . Mais rendre la lumière/Suppose d'ombre une morne moitié', we reach the stanza so important to the intellectual coherence of the poem as an investigation and embodiment of the drama of the creative sensibility in its relationship to voice:

> Ô pour moi seul, à moi seul, en moi-même,
> Auprès d'un cœur, aux sources du poème,
> Entre le vide et l'événement pur,
> J'attends l'écho de ma grandeur interne,
> Amère, sombre et sonore citerne,
> Sonnant dans l'âme un creux toujours futur!

Fortified by the plumbing of these depths, a third movement, of greater specificity of thought, might now be said to govern the composition of the poem: thought of the cemetery and the dead within its earth, thought of the pious fiction – proclaimed by the prudent doves and the angels on the tombs – of the soul's survival after death. Yet the sea, like a faithful dog, surrounds the white tombs which now, like mysterious sheep, have the protagonist as their shepherd, and still, the tone is lucid and peaceful, the future suspended in the hot, pure air:

> Ici venu, l'avenir est paresse.
> L'insecte net gratte la sécheresse;
> Tout est brûlé, défait, reçu dans l'air
> À je ne sais quelle sévère essence...
> La vie est vaste, étant ivre d'absence,
> Et l'amertume est douce, et l'esprit clair.

This third movement culminates in an address to the midday sun, poised above the scene, absolute and immobile. Now it is the human self which is looking (not asking to be watched), realising its solitary difference, as principle of change and as a capacity lacking in the perfection of the 'divine':

> Tête complète et parfait diadème,
> Je suis en toi le secret changement.

> Tu n'as que moi pour contenir tes craintes!
> Mes repentirs, mes doutes, mes contraintes
> Sont le défaut de ton grand diamant...

But, as if the absolute perfection of the idea has caused modulation into thought of mortality, again the mind returns to the dead who, also 'absolute', have slowly become vague and undifferentiated, their personality abolished, sunk into the soil.

> Ils ont fondu dans une absence épaisse,
> L'argile rouge a bu la blanche espèce,
> Le don de vivre a passé dans les fleurs!

The poignancy of these thoughts spurs the mind to realisation of its own mortality, the vain hope of immortality included: 'Et vous, grande âme, espérez-vous un songe...?'; and with a tone much nearer bitterness, the thought of the present with its bite of living consciousness returns:

> Le vrai rongeur, le ver irréfutable
> N'est point pour vous qui dormez sous la table,
> Il vit de vie, il ne me quitte pas!

At this point Valéry chose to introduce, in the form of the 'Zénon' stanza,[39] the theme of the intellectual impasse reached through thought alone. It is in relation to this impasse that the conscious mind welcomes the freshness of the wind with its gift of mental renewal through physical sensation. A movement of rejection similar to the movement of mind in *Aurore* thus breaks through immobility:

> Non, non!...Debout! Dans l'ère successive!
> Brisez, mon corps, cette forme pensive!

and the monologue sweeps to its close, the intellect slowly adjusting to the harsh and more daringly exuberant upsurge of being exemplified by the waves dashing themselves on the rocks into leaping particles of spray:

> Le vent se lève!...Il faut tenter de vivre!
> L'air immense ouvre et referme mon livre,
> La vague en poudre ose jaillir des rocs!
> Envolez-vous, pages tout éblouies!
> Rompez, vagues! Rompez d'eaux réjouies
> Ce toit tranquille où picoraient des focs!

The poem has turned almost a complete circle, picking up the image of the sea as a tranquil roof at the beginning and using it to convey the power of the mind to change and align itself with necessity, to retain its illusion of centricity by changing its place. 'Il faut se faire centre, et à chaque instant changer sa position secrète pour qu'elle demeure toujours centrale' (III, 797).

'[...] si l'on s'inquiète [...] de ce que j'ai "voulu dire" dans tel poème', Valéry wrote in his essay *Au sujet du Cimetière Marin*, 'je réponds que je n'ai pas *voulu dire*, mais *voulu faire*, et que ce fut l'intention de *faire* qui *a voulu* ce que j'ai *dit*...' (P I, 1503). Before discussing the rhythmical impulse which undoubtedly had such a large part to play in the 'voulu faire' of *Le Cimetière Marin*, let us concentrate on the architectonic richness of the poem – something which description of its main movements cannot hope to indicate.

One of the most rewarding aspects of the poem is its power to create continuity over and above the different 'moments' of which the monologue is composed – changes of tone held together by the unified resources of 'deux puissances charmeresses', 'La Voix, la Ligne, la Fiction et la Forme' (P I, 597). The theme of death is treated within several different tonalities, for example, yet never do these different tonalities break the melodic thread representing consciousness itself, 'la basse continue'. Or again, attentive to the balance of tones necessary to the composition as an aesthetic whole – an aesthetic balance synonymous with the ideal of mobile equilibrium which we find the intellect recognising and adopting as the source of its own strength – Valéry introduced a tone of philosophical abstraction (in the form the paradoxes of Zeno) at a point where the tone of the poem risked becoming too physically intimate. Complex transitions are likewise established between separate stanzas and between major movements and between minor contrapuntal movements within. Movement from the theme of the relatively static at the beginning to the dynamic at the end is anticipated, for instance, by the image of tiny flecks of moving light – 'imperceptible écume' (stanza 2) – which prefigure the dashing waves at a different moment of the cycle of the day, that great force to which we saw Valéry attribute so much power over the mind (p. 106). In so richly integrated a field with its correspondences between conceptual and physical, inner and outer, images can be used as complex centres of transformation allowing not only formal and thematic but also textual and psychological planes to unite. The early image of the sea as a visible reservoir (stanza 3), becomes a self-referential image of the hidden potentiality which the mind is discovering as its own inner 'silence', and to which language points as to its own inexhaustible centre. ('Ô mon âme, n'aspire pas à la vie immortelle, mais épuise le possible' says the Pindaric epigraph of this mysterious relationship between freedom and form.) Likewise the image of the roof (stanza 3) becomes a metaphor for both the creative sensibility – 'l'âme' – and for the intricate patterns of light and water through which that inner silence is 'spoken' and revealed to the contemplative mind's eye. Likewise the image of the sea as an 'absolute' hydra devouring its own sparkling tail (stanza 23). Appearing to arise from the 'logic' of the mind's encounter with itself and the world, these images are at the same time pieces of splendidly unashamed rhetoric through which Valéry controls both the tone changes of the poem – tone being the adjustment of the speaker to his 'parole/pensée' – and, in non-fictional terms, the response of the reader to the intentionality of poetic form.

In this 'musical' context, the phrase 'Il faut tenter de vivre' (stanza 24) is experienced not as a loosely appended moral platitude, indeed not as a 'thought' at all, but as an intentional element in the cyclical construction of the poem, a means by which the poet signals the separate yet interdependent time-scales of 'être' and 'connaître' which the mind must constantly balance and resolve. 'Présence et intervention du temps dans ces hémistiches', Valéry noted,

> Le vent se lève...Il faut tenter de vivre! La liaison du second au premier – est comme par réflexe. Une sensation éveille brusquement toute une attitude et énergie – ce qui commande un certain 'temps' (de réaction). Ainsi, en dehors des rythmes élémentaires – il y a un 'mouvement' qui doit être *imitation* des *temps* vrais.   (xvii, 310).[40]

Similarly, the ecstatic leap into the waves, symbolic of the mental leap from the Apollonian to the Dionysian within the mind itself, is not a rejection of the intellect, but part of that same cycle of being with which the poem begins: 'Ô récompense après une pensée'.[41] The need for physical action is stimulated by the *thought* of death, and it is this power of psycho-physiological exchange which is poetically conveyed by the revivifying 'inspirational' wind.

If Valéry is making use here of the same principles of harmonic modulation and architectural construction which he used in *La Jeune Parque* and *La Pythie*,[42] then how is it that the effect of this poem is so different?[43] The answer lies partly in the extraordinary 'completion' of *Le Cimetière Marin*, every image carefully integrated and echoed in a form so satisfyingly coherent that no one faculty of the reader's mind is left free to ruin the rest. But above all, I feel, it lies in the way in which the experience of sound has been allowed to penetrate the subject of the poem, making *Le Cimetière Marin* a fully conscious expression of the drama of voice.

Our first approach to sound in this total sense is obviously through the phonetic. The poem is particularly rich in the effects of verbal sound.[44] In the first stanza, for example, the frequently repeated consonants 't', 'm' and 'p', positioned in a way that gives great emphasis to their articulation as dentals and labio-dentals, play a large part in our pleasurable involvement in the sound dimension of the poem and in the unification of the separate elements within: the principle Valéry referred to as 'fils de la divine continuité de la voix'. The alliterations of 'toit tranquille' and 'pins palpite' contribute to this foregrounding of phonetic texture, yet they in their turn take part in a wider system of echoes distributed in long, never quite symmetrical groups throughout the stanza, extending to the plosive [K] and to less obvious echoed sounds. Vowels are equally involved in the patterning: the sharp, light [i] and the dark nasal [ɜ]. The assonance 'colombes' 'tombes' is particularly predominant by virtue of its place at the rhyme and gives resonance in its turn to the words 'compose' and 'récompense', themselves modulating from open to closed vowels in a way which cannot but inject harmonious movement into the potential monotony of the unification principle in itself. Closer analysis than is possible here would reveal many more subtle factors of this kind, and would include the way in which Valéry has used rhythm to set off the phonetic qualities of the poem. To take but one example, the division of the first lines – 4+6, 6+4 – allows phonemic groupings to participate in a further source of dynamic architecture. The tempting alliteration of 'pins palpite' draws us more emphatically towards the cæsura, so that the unit 'où marchent des colombes' appears slower and more isolated, while the partly mimetic repetition 'La mer, la mer' stands out phonetically because of its contribution to the unique grouping $2 + 2$. When the last two lines of the stanza enter with their symmetrical $4 + 6$, returning us to the metrical impulse of the opening line, the effect of achieved symmetry is reinforced by the homophony in 'récompense'/'pensée', and the careful modulation of vowel sounds – particularly in line five, the striking

> o e ɔ̃ ã a ɛ y ə ã e
> O récompense après une pensée

contributes very largely to the contrasting tonality of the final line with its darker sonority.

What are we to conclude about the contribution of sound to the meaning of the poem? (That Valéry treated sound and sense as totally separate variables had already been established [Part I, p. 54] and to speak of 'meaning' here is accordingly to imply the total intentional effect of the poem.) Obviously a poet so sensitive to phonetic sound is not likely to remain immune to its potentially expressive resources. Aware of the richly differentiated tonal qualities of vowels, consonants and phonemes, both singly and in combination, and unusually sensitive to the different musical qualities of pitch, timbre, speed and intensity endowed by the receptive voice in reading aloud, Valéry might indeed be said to utilise expressive effects in his poetry. Although they are capable of yielding quite different effects in other semantic contexts, and although they rarely imitate meaning, sounds in *Le Cimetière Marin* are used to help orchestrate the moods and transitions of the poem in a way which might not after all have disappointed Grammont.[45] The poem is a masterpiece of contrast in unity, where we cannot help but become involved, however unconsciously, at the time of reading, in the tonal differences between, say, the heavy repetitious sonorities of stanza 8 ('Amère, sombre et sonore citerne'), its insistent rhythm reinforcing the knell-like solemnity, and the sharp, light phonemes of 'Chanterez-vous quand serez vaporeuse?' of stanza 17 with its more intimate tone. Within the unusual rhythmical stability of this poem, almost impossible to separate from the phonic in its phonetic sense, certain moods are highlighted or created by sound. And not only in a direct way. Hard and soft sounds can be used to reinforce or to nullify the immediate associations of ideas. In the lines

> Ils ont fondu dans une absence épaisse,
> L'argile rouge a bu la blanche espèce,

gentle sounds seem to soften the harsh content of the idea or alternatively to endow it with a beauty which is in turn horrifying in its compliance, stimulating the intellect to awaken in its turn. Does the liquid 'l' (emphasised by the mute e) exist to illustrate the verb 'boire' or does the pleasure of the sound receive its thematic illustration in the imagery? Whether it be in the accumulated sibilants and 'voyelles éclatantes' of *Ébauche d'un Serpent*, in the contrasting hard/soft sounds of *Les Grenades* and *L'Abeille*, or in the tonal contrasts and echoes of *Le Cimetière Marin*, it cannot be denied that Valéry uses the marvellous expressive resources of language.

Yet is there not something about the intriguing pattern of sounds in the lines just quoted – L RJ, L R J, B/L/BL to isolate the consonants alone – to suggest that 'expressive' use of sound is but one element in a much less tenuous (and more mysteriously effective) sound system? I have already approached this area by mentioning the possible contribution of sound to the architecture of *Le Cimetière Marin*, a region somewhere between formal and psychological effects. Where I consider Valéry's use of sound to reach far beyond the expressive even in the non-mimetic sense referred to by Grammont, is in his particular understanding of harmony and musical continuity of form. Although it undeniably contributes to the expressive qualities of a poem like *Le Cimetière Marin* – both from the point of view of the emotive tones associated with the 'thoughts' of 'la Personne qui parle' and from the point of view of the intellectual architecture of the poem as a whole – sound is used above all to generate in the reader a complex mental sensation, let us call it 'pleasure', by which the mind is aroused to its potentiality as a physical source with 'muscles' of its own in touch with the energy of the body as a whole. It is behind this sensation that the ideas of the poem, still perfectly clear in themselves, seem to recede so that we are looking towards them from a different position than that of abstraction, perhaps what

Valéry meant when he wrote of 'Tout le corps humain présent sous la voix, et support, condition d'équilibre de l'*idée*' (P ii, 549). One of the terms frequently used to describe this state is 'song': 'le chantant, le résonant', a well-known part of Valéry's aesthetic theory and one which has already made us familiar with the notion of a musical harmony whose euphonic presence overrides the thoughts or ideas within (though not the meaning of the poem as a whole). In approaching the subject in this way I hope to affirm the originality of Valéry's handling of the relationship it is possible to establish in a poem between sound and meaning, or, rather, his handling of the capacity of sound to *be* the meaning of a poem ('la forme est le fond'). To see this more clearly, we must turn to the relationship set up between sound as poetic substance, and sound as the thematic material of consciousness ('la Personne qui parle'), in short to the lyrical drama of the voice, 'ce complexe de musique et de sens' (vii, 164). When Valéry writes of the state to be achieved by the poem as 'constitution d'un état *intrinsèque* – sans référence au réel, sans *fin* à atteindre – *même quand une représentation du réel est employée*', he does not imply that the 'real' is subordinate to sound, but that, as he goes on to say, 'Ce *réel* devient alors partie d'un système harmonique – et *ses choses aussi bien engendrées par la forme que la forme par elles*' (xxiv, 365). The way in which the experience of sound overrides the values of words as separate entities for the reader is the equivalent of that process by which the consciousness involved in inner monologue overrides for the speaker the fragmentation involved in perception and thought without the harmonising factor of 'expressive' emotion, 'être' and 'connaître' in perfect accord. 'L'expression et la chose exprimée sont dans le même système' (iii, 707).

The stanza which explicitly synthesises the aesthetic and intellectual aims of *Le Cimetière Marin* from this point of view is the one beginning 'Ô pour moi seul, pour moi seul, en moi-Même...' (stanza 8) where the speaker experiences his own consciousness as a form of void echoing with the sound of the sensibility in its receptivity to the world, 'Amère, sombre et sonore citerne,/ Sonnant dans l'âme un creux toujours futur!'. In stressing the nature of 'le Moi' as an oscillation between the 'absence' of thought and the 'presence' of sensation, 'Entre le vide et

l'événement pur', Valéry is taking us to the dialectic which he felt
to govern the ideal relationship of sound and sense for the reader
(P I, 1332–3), in short to the dialectic of sound and silence[46]
from which the Self is born as the movement and presence of
Voice:

> Le Moi est bien la Personne qui parle. C'est la définition objective
> que j'analyserais ainsi: ce qui *s'entend* excite un acte qui tend à
> produire ou reproduire un bruit analogue.
>
> Cet acte excite à son tour, comme en demande rétroactive,
> quelque chose – ou présence – ou besoin et c'est là la place du Moi.
> Ainsi est-il *trouvé*'.   (xx, 190).

Stanza 8 is grave and bleak in tonality. Yet exactly the same
concept has been prepared in the famous and beautiful stanza
(stanza 5) where the mind savours its mortality as fruit melting in
the mouth:

> Comme le fruit se fond en jouissance,
> Comme en délice il change son absence
> Dans une bouche où sa forme se meurt,
> Je hume ici ma future fumée,
> Et le ciel chante à l'âme consumée
> Le changement des rives en rumeur.

Here, its form euphonically pleasurable to the mind's ear, is the
dramatisation, in terms of the concept of life and death, of that
very same poetic alchemy by which the 'absence' of consciousness
is rendered present by the sound of the voice – 'Comme en délice
il change son absence'. The 'coupure' of consciousness is filled
with the mystery of sound. If we feel we can pierce the secret of
Valéry's use of sound as a 'separate' source of euphony within the
wider harmonics of the poem as a whole,[47] then this is precisely
what the speaker's intellect is suggested to do with regard to the
secret of his own sensibility, dependent for its 'waiting' on the
architecture of the body (P II, 240) – 'Chanterez-vous quand serez
vaporeuse?'. The revelation of that source can no more destroy
the 'charm' of its effect than can our knowledge of the physiological appeal of the euphony in the poem. The Self is Voice, the
soul is body and the poem in its sound/sense harmony is the 'song'
of the soul in its bodily existence. *Le Cimetière Marin* is a poem
supremely conscious of itself and the fragile harmony it extends
and investigates by every possible means.

But there is a further aspect of sound to be mentioned from the point of view of the poem's radical treatment of the 'forme/fond' relationship. In *Au Sujet du Cimetière Marin* Valéry stated that the rhythmical intentions of the poem dictated its existence – the intention in this case being 'une figure rythmique vide, ou remplie de syllabes vaines' then recognised to be decasyllabic. In the hope of renovating a metrical form poor and monotonous in comparison with the alexandrine, Valéry attempted to raise the decasyllable to the power of twelve, envisaging from there a six-lined strophe and a composition assured by the diversity of tones and functions assigned to each group. But the main point of interest for us here lies in Valéry's reference to a 'monologue de "moi" ' in which the most simple and constant themes of his intellectual and affective life – 'Mediterranean' in origin – were subsequently woven together, and which led naturally to the subject of death and pure thought, '(Le vers choisi de dix syllabes a quelque rapport avec le vers dantesque.) [...] *Le Cimetière Marin* était *conçu.* Un assez long travail s'ensuivit' (P I, 1504).[48]

Although there may be an element of oversimplification in Valéry's account of the direct relationship between the rhythmical form and themes of the poem, the idea of a blank form which preceded its subject is no literary extravaganza. Form for Valéry *is* the 'fond' of the poem. The living form behind the poem in this case is that of the voice, 'contour d'une émotion', for we have only to remember that Valéry's most universal monologue was also his most personal, to appreciate the coherent simplicity of this basic myth. The Mediterranean imagery and the 'music' of an ideal voice are the same (Part I, p. 23). In this sense Valéry can write of this most universal poem so dependent on the living physiology of the reader's mind to give it meaning: ' "Le Cimetière Marin" est ma pièce personnelle. Je n'y ai mis que ce que je suis. Ces obscurités sont les miennes. La lumière qu'il peut contenir est celle que j'ai vu en naissant.'[49] In Valéry's conception of 'Poésie' the 'obscurity' of *Le Cimetière Marin* is the equivalent mystery of the sensibility in its relationship to sound, 'le cœur de l'intellect' in its 'singing' relationship to the death-like void introduced by pure thought.[50]

Le Cimetière Marin, perhaps, with *La Jeune Parque,* one of Valéry's greatest poems, certainly one of the great poems of the

European heritage, was composed in the midst of the Surrealist period, 'en pleine crise de modernité'. All the fantastic, even humorous imagery of Surrealism is there in one sense: sails as doves, the soul as a roof with golden tiles, the sea as a faithful dog, and – worthy of Apollinaire – the self as shepherd guarding the sheep-like tombs. And yet what more striking example of a poem in which imagery is totally subordinate to further principles of textual unity and control? As if deliberately to emphasise the notion of constraint so important for human freedom, Valéry has multiplied the literary echoes of the poem, allowing it to act as a kind of centre for all the 'voices' of literature in the past. Thus the lines

> Où sont des morts les phrases familières,
> L'art personnel, les âmes singulières?[51]
> La larve file où se formaient des pleurs

recall the 'Ubi sunt' theme of Villon;[52] the La Fontaine-like 'Chanterez-vous quand serez vaporeuse?' with its striking omission of pronoun is an echo of Ronsard talking to the 'âmelette' of the soul;[53] Voltaire's 'Poème sur le désastre de Lisbonne' is present in the central notion of human imperfection as being creatively superior to the 'divine';[54] Leconte de Lisle's 'Midi' is echoed in 'Midi le juste', and so on. The sense of etymology, too, can be seen as a means of revivifying the general heritage of words, taking us back to the universal operations involved in the metaphor of language itself with its substantialisation of the abstract.[55] The verb 'consumer', for instance ('Quel pur travail de fins éclairs consume...') suggests that the sea is both built up and burnt out by the light of the sun, repeating the central paradox on which the whole poem rests: that of a mobile equilibrium,[56] the 'absence' of consciousness changed to 'présence' through the charm of 'song'. The 'singing' state of the poem is the 'singing' state of the speaker's consciousness in 'central' relation to the universe, a moment of fragile balance which the poem develops and extends. Perhaps this is why Valéry can write of such composed poetry 'J'aime qu'un poème s'élève tout seul à la Poésie...comme une mélodie naissant de la voix' (PII, 72) and 'La vraie création poétique se passe dans le complexe de l'être qui a la voix pour résolution [...]. C'est la voix qui développe le poète, le modifie, lui et sa véritable "profondeur". Il se fait une Voix idéale [...]'

(xxvi, 80). In terms of what is 'said', the voice of 'la Personne qui parle' calls at the end of the poem for the dispersal of the static form through which it discovered its own depths:

> Envolez-vous, pages tout éblouies!
> Rompez, vagues! Rompez d'eaux réjouies
> Ce toit tranquille où picoraient des focs!

Indeed, it is significant that one of Valéry's few 'scriptural' images[57] is set in the context of the infinite dispersal of form. Yet before 'deconstructing' the text in this way – and Valéry's texts are capable of producing such readings – we are returned by the cyclical form of the poem, a quite different voice from that of the speaker's, to the fleeting tranquillity of the first stanza, its peaceful balance still present even now in the harmony of the verse and its 'quasi éternel'. *Le Cimetière Marin* epitomises Valéry's definition of poetry as 'une pensée singulièrement achevée',[58] poetry in which the quality of human silence finds voice.

(c) Ode Secrète, Le Rameur, Palme

Ode Secrète

In Valéry's 'poetry of silence' the title of a poem is far more likely to fit a living capacity conveyed within it than the 'scriptural' reality of the poem itself. We saw this in the case of *Poésie* and there is no reason to suppose that *Ode Secrète* is different. It is unlikely, in other words, that this poem contains reference to a 'secret' necessary to our reading – either an external secret such as that it is an allegory of, say, the signing of the Armistice,[59] or an internal secret to which the title guards the forbidden entrance. The subject of the poem *is* the 'secret ode'. The poem will provide the key to it once its themes, structures and techniques have been allowed to produce in the reader an action of meaningful form. This is not to say that a poem as richly ambiguous as *Ode Secrète* is without the power to suggest alternative readings, as the many critical interpretations based on it confirm.[60] The reading I shall propose is based on the hypothesis that a self-referential use of language as Voice is nonetheless the common denominator through which these alternatives are released and controlled.

'Ô récompense après une pensée': the marvelling apostrophe
which opens *Le Cimetière Marin* is echoed here in the first stanza
of *Ode Secrète*:

> Chute superbe, fin si douce,
> Oubli des luttes, quel délice
> Que d'étendre à même la mousse
> Après la danse, le corps lisse!

This time, however, the 'récompense' is the delicious fatigue after
physical effort, after a 'dance' (it could still be the dance of
thought); and the sensation praised is of gentle abandonment, like
that of one's body stretched out on soft moss.[61] 'One's body'
because the perspective of this point is intimate and yet general-
ised; 'like' because the word-order with its predominant abstract
'chute' and 'fin' attenuates the literalness of the fall, transferring
the physicality of the gesture to a mental context of which it is
perhaps in turn the gesture or act. Hence, too, the qualifying
epithet 'superbe', giving that fall an emotive attribute and a tone
of enthusiastic magnification appropriate to an ode. A fall, maybe, but a proud and splendid one. A proud fall, maybe, but a
gentle end. The oxymoron introduces a paradox still to be
appreciated and only partly explained in the joy of savouring this
projected ending, as if forgetfulness of the struggle involved in its
attainment is a goal in itself. Meanwhile, that by now predictable
(but still mysteriously effective) patterning of sound – extending
here far beyond alliteration and the organisation of the most
obvious vowels and consonants – gives to the reader's mind in-
specting the paradox a pleasurable sense of certainty, not unrelated
to the concept 'quel délice/Que d'étendre...' but by no means
quiescent, since symmetry and surprise are both at work.

> Jamais une telle lueur
> Que ces étincelles d'été
> Sur un front semé de sueur
> N'avait la victoire fêté!

Yes, the note of paradoxical achievement is sustained in the
hyperbole of this second quatrain, and if we link 'front' – the forehead of the person who struggled or danced 'sown' with pearls or
grains of sweat – back to the adjective 'superbe', we are reminded
of those 'fronts souverains' in *Les Grenades*, the wealth and

concentration of thoughts within bursting open the proud brows and revealing the secret conserving structure. Never had victory been celebrated by such a glow as the sparkles of summer on this forehead gleaming with sweat! The phrase reveals an important ambivalence, emphasised by the unconventional word-order ('écart'). Either no victory but this had ever been celebrated with such a glow, or this glow outshines even those which have celebrated victory. I shall return to the possible function of the ambivalence later. It is worth noting, meanwhile, that 'étincelles' is echoed in the more conceptual 'étincellement' at the end of the poem and thus endowed retrospectively with star-like connotations – the 'étincelles d'été' are the stars of the Summer sky reflected on the brow of the fallen body. It is a word with a fine display of associations in Valéry's poetry, ranging from the spark of inspiration or the momentary glow of pleasure, to the tiny, instantaneous details of which a work of art, even the 'work of art' of a human consciousness itself is composed (like the multi-faceted reflections of the sun on the sea in the previous poem). The delayed entry of the other side of the metaphor – the constellations of stars – allows the word a resonance which keeps alive these and other such 'diamond-like' connotations, without our being able to confine our interpretations to them. It acquires, in effect, a halo of meaning which will find its way into other 'secret' areas of the poem. And we note likewise that the similar, more Mallarméan term 'scintillations' – 'Elle jette ses gestes comme des scintillations!...' (P ii, 172) – occurs in the Dialogue *L'Âme et la Danse*, where Valéry describes the flame-like act of the dancer transforming brute reality, struggling to rival the chimerical freedom of the mind in a bodily form (P ii, 171). It is the singing, struggling, transfiguring, flame-like principle of the dance, also the principle of the human voice, which Valéry sets at the centre of his art as an emblem of the mind's desire for self-transcendence:

> Comme la voix chante éperdument, comme la flamme follement chante entre la matière et l'éther [...] – la grande Danse, ô mes amis, n'est-elle point cette délivrance de notre corps tout entier possédé de l'esprit du mensonge, et de la musique qui est mensonge, et ivre de la négation de la nulle réalité?   [P ii, 171].

I do not suggest that the reading of additional texts is indispensable to an interpretation of *Ode Secrète*, or that the possible alliance between their images and those of a particular poem are in any way more than associative – so rich and varied is Valéry's use of an unusually restricted vocabulary. Nevertheless, such texts can often confirm an interpretation possible from internal evidence alone.

> Mais touché par le Crépuscle,
> Ce grand corps qui fit tant de choses,
> Qui dansait, qui rompit Hercule,
> N'est plus qu'une masse de roses!

So much for the great body which danced and 'broke' or, if we take up the invitation of the next stanza, which 'vanquished' Hercules. Touched by the evening light – the setting sun, the Shadow, to use the capitalisation through which, as in *Le Vin Perdu*, Valéry suggests how the mind generalises and conceptualises the physical – it is no more than a mass of roses. 'So much for the great body' if we take that 'Mais' to contradict or qualify the hyperbole of the stanza before. Yet, since this body is obviously the same as that of the first stanza, proudly fallen after the dance or after its labours – now recognised as the labours of Hercules – then is it not possible that the hero remains paradoxically intact in stature for all that he is only a mass of roses? The conjunction has created a curious tension in the flow of otherwise purely descriptive thought. The perception is similar to 'Mais rendre la lumière/Suppose d'ombre une morne moitié' in *Le Cimetière Marin*, proudly accepted by 'la Personne qui parle'. Obviously, as in *Le Cimetière Marin*, a detached as well as involved form of narrative consciousness is at work. 'Roses' meanwhile is plural like 'étincelles', and therefore not simply the rosy colour of the sunset, but the rosy colour of the sunset rendered metaphorically through an image of roses (perhaps as on a tomb, if the hero's crepuscular 'end' has connotations of death).[62] At the same time the stanza raises the much debated question 'whose body?' – that of Hercules himself or that of some other person or presence? – a question to which I shall return later in order to explain a preference for the first interpretation.[63]

> Dormez, sous les pas sidéraux,
> Vainqueur lentement désuni,
> Car l'Hydre inhérente au héros
> S'est éployée à l'infini...

Now the conqueror is adjured to sleep, a conqueror slowly dis-
united from himself (the same 'lentement' occurs in *Le Cimetière
Marin*, where the dead vaguely mingle together in the 'absolute'
state of death, their individuality lost). For the Hydra within him
– the slaying of the hundred-headed Hydra or water-snake of
Lerna was one of the labours of Hercules – has unfolded itself to
infinity. The tone here is almost that of a lullaby – 'Dormez'
picking up thematically the 'fin si douce' and the phonetically
murmuring 'à même la mousse' of stanza 1 – yet a lullaby which
curiously inverts cause and effect, changing natural necessity into
an action accepted for logical reasons: 'Car l'Hydre inhérente au
héros/S'est éployée à l'infini...'. The unfolding of the Hydra –
one thinks of the image of the snake biting its own tail, 'l'hydre
absolu', which Valéry used as a symbol of the human sensibility –
links in our minds with the initial gesture of the body stretched
out on the moss, 'dissolved' in the sunset, or in the flames of the
funeral pyre. The heraldic verb 'éployer', syntagmatically related
to 'à l'infini', prepares and releases the association between the
Hydra and the constellation named after it, and thus the final
image of apotheosis yet to be analysed. Likewise the term 'infini' –
the opposite of those tiny 'étincelles' and of the concentration of
form and effort which takes place in dance (unless we see the
effort itself as infinite in its aspiration, however finite in form).
It announces the concept of formless space to which we are
moving in the next lines:

> Ô quel Taureau, quel Chien, quelle Ourse,
> Quels objets de victoire énorme,
> Quand elle entre aux temps sans ressource
> L'âme impose à l'espace informe!

The ode has progressed tonally in groups of two stanzas –
perhaps with further implicit divisions after the third and fourth
quatrains – all six maintaining a lyrically reflective tone, often in
the form of an apostrophe. Here we have the apparent culmination
of the ode or triumphant song, its wondering morality (reminiscent
of the end of *La Pythie*). What 'objects of victory' – the Bull, the
Dog and the Bear are constellations, the first two being monsters
slain by Hercules – the human spirit imposes on the formlessness
of space.

Fin suprême, étincellement
Qui, par les monstres et les dieux,
Proclame universellement
Les grands actes qui sont aux Cieux!

Here, or so it first seems, is the completion of the circle. That 'chute superbe' is a supreme ending, a sparkling transfiguration of the sleeping or dead hero into the skies – Hercules was so apotheosized. Alternatively, on the symbolic level suggested by the myth, the artistic and scientific wealth of the human mind is blazoned across the skies and mingles its glories with the sun.

Yet is there not, born from those last lines, a deliberate emptiness, a grandiloquent tone more reminiscent of the rhetoric of Pascal and of Bossuet than of Valéry's intimate 'poetry of voice'?[64] Are we not faced with the paradox we found at the end of *La Pythie*, where a form of universality seems to be praised despite Valéry's insistence on the need for re-created individuality, on the counter-effort of the mind towards its own 'absolute' formations? Several subtle elements in the poem remain to be picked up by a further or parallel reading which may suggest that there is another ode, a secret ode, hidden within this more obvious one; an ode much more expressive of a 'poetry of voice' than the paean of praise to autonomy in the final stanzas at first suggests. And while a Mallarméan – perhaps in some ways even an anti-Mallarméan – reading is by no means demanded by the poem, its possibility serves nonetheless to emphasise the presence in *Charmes* of the Symbolist drama of poetic transcendentalism which Mallarmé epitomised for Valéry in its most moving and uncompromising form. Mallarmé's life and work represented the drama of the limits and possibilities of the mind in its creative pursuit of Beauty as an aim in itself. Only this impersonal concept ultimately authorises association of the poem with Mallarmé other than on the biographical level, despite its vocabulary and its possible inspiration in the effect of *Un Coup de dés* and the emotion caused by Mallarmé's death.[65]

To return to the internal evidence of the poem, we have seen how such a close-knit word-structure multiplies associations, both paradigmatic and syntagmatic, and raises questions which, although they remain unanswered, lead us in the direction of paradox.

We have become aware of a compelling bond between the beginning and end of the poem, which keeps its hydra-like structure dynamically incomplete despite its triumphantly progressive form. The curious formal unconventionalities of this 'ode', with its alternating quatrains of all-feminine and all-masculine rhymes, support a thematic movement from intimate to cosmic which is not allowed definite status. We expect to hear a further swing back to a feminine rhymed stanza at the end. 'La Syntaxe, qui est calcul, reprenait rôle de Muse' (P I, 646), Valéry wrote (of Mallarmé's poetry) and 'l'*âme* observe la grammaire autant que possible' (xxIV, 142). The third stanza with its firmly placed 'Mais' prevents us likewise from straightforwardly associating the crepuscular theme with the pleasure theme at the beginning. Perhaps further time has passed during that act of contemplation and the pleasure has dissolved as did the concentrated effort before. The poignant temporal imagery of *La Ceinture* is not so far away. There we find the same theme of dance, the same silent pleasure, contemplated or experienced – not perhaps so separate – the same association of Evening with a universal drama of human limitation and death; above all, the same movement from concentration to dissolution conveyed in the lines 'Car l'Hydre inhérente au héros/S'est éployée à l'infini...'. Taking this image as a metaphor of the inner cycle within the hero's mind, we are led to the sense – as in *La Ceinture* – that someone is watching himself watching; that both Hercules and the body which broke him belong to one and the same being – 'l'autre dans le même' – and that the Hydra is meanwhile the total principle creatively binding body and mind in forever impenetrable form. Hence the 'great body' which danced, which broke Hercules and which is now, the Hydra once unbound, dissolved into a mass of roses: 'Vainqueur lentement désuni'. Does this imply a death or a sleep, or even some further attitude of mind presented to the perceiving mind from within as if it is a death? The dancer, Athikté, we remember, having exhausted 'le trésor le plus caché dans sa structure' (P II, 175),[66] describes herself in the words 'Je ne sens rien. Je ne suis pas morte. Et pourtant, je ne suis pas vivante!' (P II, 176). The answer depends on how we view the relationship conveyed in the poem between the speaking voice, the body, the Hydra and the heroic effort referred to as 'Hercule'. In my opinion these are made curiously synonymous: all are elements of the speaker's own consciousness perceived from within, yet at the same time objectifiable in third person form so as to be available for empathetic transfer – a striking expressive addition to the inner dualism of 'être' and 'connaître' we have discovered in Valéry's poetry in so many forms. It is because of the power of such imagery to convey a form of self-knowledge – perhaps that form of self-knowledge conjured up in the statement 'Je me *vois* quand j'invente – j'ai alors une lucidité *actuelle* – comprendre et créer sont inséparables' (VIII, 226) – which makes it possible for Valéry to move away from a Symbolist principle of transcendence intellectually, while discovering its strength and validity within himself as the source of a universalising desire.

For, to return to the Hydra image and to the suggestions made possible through the skilfully present yet evanescent use of myth in the poem: if Hercules, who fought the Hydra, is fighting something within himself which eventually kills him,[67] then we are justifiably reminded of those texts where Valéry writes of the compulsive urge of the human mind to know – 'comprendre et créer' – in similarly devouring terms. He frequently speaks of Mallarmé's 'Grand Œuvre', for example, as of a passionate dedication of a whole life to something ethereal and improbable, or in 'Discours sur l'Esthétique', he notes that the pleasure of an instant can give rise to a vast, life-consuming quest to capture the fabulous 'monster' of ideal Beauty which such a moment supposed (P I, 1300). No need to point to the obvious relevance of such ideas to the poem – even, perhaps, if we include that of the forest ('Mais c'est une chasse magique que la chasse dialectique. [P I, 1300]), the image of the moss with its veiled echo of some enchanted grove of ideas. Just before in the essay Valéry mentions the way in which aesthetic pleasure 'propose à la pensée une énigme singulièrement spécieuse qui ne pouvait échapper au désir et à l'étreinte de l'hydre métaphysique' (P I, 1299). Entering 'le bosquet des Notions Pures', both types of hunter of the Idea of Beauty, the artist and the philosopher, are haunted by the fabulous monster of which they dream. While the philosopher finds only his own shadow, 'Gigantesque, parfois; mais ombre tout de même', the artist comes closer to creating by his capture the monster for which he seeks. 'Dans la forêt enchantée du Langage, les poètes vont tout exprès pour se perdre, et s'y enivrer d'égarement, cherchant les carrefours de signification, les échos imprévus, les rencontres étranges; ils n'en craignent ni les détours, ni les surprises, ni les ténèbres;' (P I, 1300).[68] Such is the drama epitomised by the Symbolist quest[69] and the drama of 'le dieu dans la chair *égaré*' (my italics) revered at the end of *La Pythie*. Particularly in the case of the philosopher, these writings serve to deprecate a certain failure to recognise that the source of the quest and its metaphors is the sensibility, a knowledge which Valéry's poetry of voice was designed never to forget. 'Ce qui me caractérise, ma vertu particulière, mon don', he writes,

> C'est presque seulement la capacité de percevoir des phénomènes subjectifs *non significatifs*. Je me tiens toujours en relation avec l'informe, comme degré le plus pur du réel, du non interprété. C'est comme le carrefour des métaphores. [...] je conserve [ce don] comme état critique de la conscience.   (III, 364).[70]

Awareness that metaphor and its counterpart, 'l'informe' (a key word in the poem) both have their source in the sensibility surely helps explain the curious 'double' perspective of *Ode Secrète*, from which the speaker sees the body and his own Herculean or heroic properties from an apparently detached position at the same time as empathising with each. The attitude may help explain, too, the strangely circular movement of the poem which, while it works towards the eulogy of metaphor in the final stanzas, undermines – though still 'from within itself' – that 'naïve' position in favour of its own victorious power to perceive 'l'informe':

> Un nuage énorme sur la lune, troubles d'encre et d'argent, masque tordu – qu'entoure le ciel étoilé tranquille, vissé d'astres. Je pense à l'enfantine poésie de chercher mille ressemblances imparfaites de ce nuage, mille chameaux, monstres contrées – tandis que sa valeur, sa poésie puissante et véritablement *illimitée* est justement au contraire d'être informe, lui-même, inaccessible aux mots, sans images.
> (III, 818).

Allowing this text to activate the yeast of paradox already sensed in the poem, we can see that *Ode Secrète* conveys praise of 'l'informe' – the 'pouvoir-excitant' of incoherence which obliges the mind to create (XXVI, 872) – as much as of the order imposed by knowledge on the randomness of the world. Hence the opening paradox through which the moment of abandonment is presented as a greater glory than victory, almost as the victory of defeat (an attitude Valéry associated more with Rimbaud than with Mallarmé). Running beneath the 'public' ode in praise of effort and construction is a 'secret' hymn to the principle of disorder, or at least to the dissolution of the metaphysical hydra of the Ideal at the heart of the Symbolist quest. Perhaps there is even, to probe its secret more deeply in the way the imagery of the poem seems to invite, an ode to the mind's power to accept the ultimate dissolution of death: 'Fin suprême, étincellement'.[71] The placing of these words at the beginning of the final stanza outshadows structurally the 'Grands actes qui sont aux cieux'. They also lead us back to the initial moment of pleasure from the contemplation of which – 'Chute superbe, fin si douce' – everything appears to have unfurled.

Taken as a complete, self-sufficient entity, *Ode Secrète* is no longer a hymn to the opposite principle of creative form. It is a poem which conveys expressively the self-aware 'variation de la certitude' (III, 152)[72] which is the root of metaphor, analogy and myth and their power to reveal to ourselves the glorious 'Mensonge', the monsters of our own desire.[73] It is *this* voice, which, from the empathised delight of the first stanza, through the proud hyperbole of the second, the hesitation of the third, the 'lullaby' of the fourth and the musing reflection of the fifth and sixth, affirms its own life-giving form and continuity, that of individual consciousness, in a context of change and death which runs through it like a ghost. For the dissolution it secretly praises is itself a form of death, throwing it back to the splendour of the form it queries, just as the moment of pleasure between the sun and the shadow – 'à même la mousse' – is changing and formless without the imagination to capture and enshrine it in absence (P II, 647). We are back to the emotion of *knowing* we need the patterns in the stars which the mind creates inevitably, and which poetry recognises and proclaims as our own, the 'glorious lie' of the Ideal. 'Ô quel Taureau, quel Chien, quelle Ourse...'. We are back to the secret ode to the shared revelation of the 'Lie', 'l'état critique de la conscience'.

224

If I have spent an apparently disproportionate time on *Ode Secrète*, it is because the Mallarméan drama at its heart seems to be central to Valéry's poetry of voice from the point of view of its ambivalence of attitude, an attitude which takes us in turn to the paradox of an Apollonian aesthetics consciously based on the strength of Dionysius and able so unusually to integrate the two powers:

> Apollon aime que le tout soit visible et se construise enfin comme un édifice où rien ne manque. Il lui plaît que les images se suivent et que leur système soit imaginable lui-même.
> Mais Dionysios use d'*images dissemblables*. Cette incohérence lui fait mieux posséder l'unité qu'il entrevoit, comme entre les deux mains diverses qui touchent, un seul solide caché aux yeux est saisi.
> Et mêmement il vise des objets si inexprimables que pour les nommer, il dit ce qu'ils ne sont pas – et c'est une infinité de noms...
>
> (IV, 736.

Valéry's poetry does not only musically 'construct' in the face of the idea of death. It expresses the form of consciousness which allows us to 'imagine' life from the greater detachment afforded by the idea of death ('La vie est vaste, étant ivre d'absence'). Just so, when walking with Mallarmé not long before his death, under a Summer sky ablaze with stars,[74] Valéry's mind 'se mit à rêver du moment même'. 'Le soir du même jour', he writes (of the day in 1897 when Mallarmé first showed him the manuscript of *Un Coup de dés*),

> comme il m'accompagnait au chemin de fer, l'innombrable ciel de julliet enfermant toutes choses dans un groupe étincelant d'autres mondes, et que nous marchions, fumeurs obscurs, au milieu du Serpent, du Cygne, de l'Aigle, de la Lyre, – il me semblait *maintenant* d'être pris dans le texte même de l'univers silencieux: texte tout de clartés et d'énigmes; aussi tragique, aussi indifférent que on le veut; qui parle et qui ne parle pas; tissu de sens multiples; qui assemble l'ordre et le désordre; qui proclame un Dieu aussi, puissamment qu'il le nie; qui contient, dans son ensemble in-imaginable, toutes les époques, chacune associée à l'éloignement d'un corps céleste; qui rappelle le plus décisif, le plus évident et l'incontestable succès des hommes, l'accomplissement de leurs prévisions, – jusqu'à la septième décimale; et qui écrase cet animal témoin, ce contemplateur sagace, sous l'inutilité de ce triomphe...
> Nous marchions. Au creux d'une telle nuit, entre les propos que nous échangions, je songeais à la tentative merveilleuse:quel modèle, quel enseignement, là-haut! Où Kant, assez naïvement, peut-être, avait

cru voir la Loi Morale, Mallarmé percevait sans doute l'Impératif
d'une poésie: une Poétique. [. . .]
— Il a essayé, pensai-je, d'*élever enfin une page à la puissance du
ciel étoilé!*   (P ɪ, 625–6).

In this moving and finely controlled passage, inspired by the
intellectually ineradicable sensation of the 'presence' of Mallarmé's
poem *Un Coup de dés* in the night sky, there are many echoes of
the emotion conveyed in *Ode Secrète*. To return to the problem
whether that poem is a homage to or a questioning of the creative
principle which 'devoured' Mallarmé in his quest for perfection
is to realise how facile the opposition really is. Just as Mallarmé
had written his *Tombeau de Charles Baudelaire* in a spirit of
creative independence made possible by Baudelaire, so Valéry's
admiration and love for Mallarmé freed him to be himself. Nor is
Ode Secrète presented as a 'Tombeau de Stéphane Mallarmé',
however much that tempting interpretation is part of its complex
resonance in Valéry's poetic universe. *Ode Secrète* discovers by a
technique of its own – modulation presenting a figurative event
as an example of 'l'informe'[75] – that same movement towards and
away from form which Valéry found at the centre of Mallarmé's
poetry in *Un Coup de dés*. In its own way it attempts to 'donner à
la figure d'un texte une signification et une action comparables à
celle du texte même' (P ɪ, 632). The form which Valéry's texts most
encourage is one which takes into account the power of language
to create simultaneous alternative reactions in its readers to a
single phenomenon. Perhaps – if we must solve a secret – it is
ultimately this power and its philosophical implication for the
mind aware of it, that *Ode Secrète* proposes as its subject[76]

Le Rameur

After the gentle fall and forgetfulness of struggle praised in *Ode
Secrète*, *Le Rameur* seems at first to be praising the opposite or
prior sensation of struggle itself: 'Penché contre un grand fleuve',
the sensations of the oarsman pitting himself against the current of
a great river.[77] And it is the theme of struggle or effort which the
poem has generally been taken to celebrate: the muscular effort of
the body as a symbol of the effort of the mind, perhaps even as a
symbol of the poet at work. But let us look closely at the tone and
imagery through which that theme of obstinate movement is con-

veyed, and in particular at the relationship set up betwen the
consciousness of 'la Personne qui parle' and the theme of the
visual beauty of the natural world.

> Penché contre un grand fleuve, infiniment mes rames
> M'arrachent à regret aux riants environs;
> Âme aux pesantes mains, pleines des avirons,
> Il faut que le ciel cède au glas des lentes lames.

Struggle, yes: that strenuous mental purpose translated into the
body so that the whole sensibility has become an action of oars –
'Âme aux pesantes mains, plaines des avirons' – just as the dancer
in *L'Âme et la Danse* was created through the whirling rhythms
of her feet and the hands of the Pythia were 'pleines de seins
vivants'. Yet 'infiniment' does not suggest a specific goal – not
even, as in the dance, the temporary transcendence of the pure
'ennui' of existence by the sensation of an 'infini esthétique' – and
'à regret' suggests that the action is designed as much to destroy
as to create pleasure. Indeed, it is an action associatively linked
with death, the funereal sound of the oars (echoes of the funereal
sound associations in Baudelaire's *Chant d'Automne*) rhythmically
pulling the speaker away from the 'laughing' environment of the
world, the colourful, differentiated regions of the river banks
perhaps peopled with plants and human forms. Obstinacy of
purpose, yes: 'Il faut que le ciel cède', but a resignation in effort,
a fatality in willpower, as if, for all this power of movement,
perhaps even because of its seemingly infinite potential for desire
and endurance, the human being is not after all so different from
the plane tree stretching its arms 'vêtus en vain de rames' against
the sky. Unlike Athikté, the dancer, absorbed and timeless, the
speaker in *Le Rameur* seems mentally free to examine the movement he takes part in, free to savour in the heart of effort the
presence of a strangely deep, death-like autonomy of pride (the
'grandeur interne' of *Le Cimetière Marin*). For freedom here is
associated not with any aesthetic transcendence, but with the recklessly obstinate alignment of one's being with a monotony of effort
felt to lead further and further from construction and surprise,
further and further from the deceptive appearances of things.

> Le cœur dur, l'œil distrait des beautés que je bats,
> Laissant autour de moi mûrir des cercles d'onde,

Je veux à larges coups rompre l'illustre monde
De feuilles et de feu que je chante tout bas.

No emotion other than the emotion of a lack of emotion passionately channelled into 'negative' purpose: 'Je veux à larges coups
rompre l'illustre monde'[78] – an echo, incidentally, of the creative
action of intellectual 'substitution' we found at the heart of
Valéry's thought through '1892'. Yet that irrepressible 'song' of
the natural world with its flickering light and leaves – the song
of the sensibility necessary to the identity of Narcissus – has already
entered the poem (the seeds of its presence sown in the 'riants
environs' of the first stanza, about to develop still further in the
lovely image of reflected trees in the next),[79] and we are faced with
that paradox of human perception by which deflection from a
source of light enables the eye to see more precisely that which
would blind it in direct contact. 'Oublier insensiblement la chose
que l'on regarde – l'oublier en y songeant, par une transformation
exacte, juste, immobile, locale, naturelle, imperceptible – comme
un morceau de glace échappe à celui qui le serre, correlativement,
contre sa volonté, par sa chaleur. Et l'eau peut redevenir glace.'[80]
So too, the effect of an oblique use of language – Valéry's 'préciosité' – in order to heighten sensuality of effect for the reader, and
so, too, the whole suggestive process by which poetry works: an
obstinate 'refusal' of the immediate referentiality of ordinary
language so that the object, once lost, will reshine the more powerfully through an action of form:

> Perdu ce vin, ivre les ondes!...
> J'ai vu bondir dans l'air amer
> Les figures les plus profondes...

If *Le Vin Perdu* refers to the moment of creativity when the risk
of loss is taken, then *Le Rameur*, yet another of the many varied
'water' poems of *Charmes*, might be said to refer to the sensations
of deflection. Relative to the creative action of the mind epitomised for Valéry in poetic composition, neither poem concerns itself
with this context explicitly or allegorically, and in *Le Rameur* in
particular we find ourselves making such connections purely
tangentially within a context of intensely visual significance, a
phenomenology of sight as the dramatic action-point of the
mingling of mind and world. Indeed, the movement forward

seems but a device to make visible and transmit to the body –
'corps de l'esprit' – the 'Testian' powers of concentration, refusal,
relativisation, which already characterise the speaker's perception
of 'le réel'. Hence the curiously united action of the central metaphor of the oarsman, resonating into several different readings –
psychological, mystical, philosophical, linguistic[81] – at once.

> Arbres sur qui je passe, ample et naïve moire,
> Eau de ramages peinte, et paix de l'accompli,
> Déchire-les, ma barque, impose-leur un pli
> Qui coure du grand calme abolir la mémoire.

Where consciousness of time – 'barque funèbre' – had slipped
between the body of the Parque and the light, awakening as it did
so those vast, taunting 'memories' of lost self-unity, here the
speaker, identifying with the 'barque funèbre' of consciousness
itself – that 'Bateau Ivre' of rebellious resignation – calls on all his
strength to furrow with his keel the vast liquid surfaces representative of calm. The placing of words – 'la mémoire' rhyming with
'moire' at the end of the line – encourages the maximum
association of the term with water, so that it is memory itself
which seems to be revived and refused in the gesture, prepared for
its identification with the terms 'enfance', 'remonte' and 'source'
of the next verse. (In this respect *Le Rameur* exemplifies an
associative technique of Valéry's.) And, of course, the willed
destruction of that calm, 'painted' beauty – the unreality of its
reflection in water allowed to stand for the mental sensation of the
unreality of the natural world as a whole – is made as equivocally
positive as Teste's 'Otez chaque chose que j'y voie' (P II, 38).
Here is an action creatively destructive in its urge to destroy the
mask, to escape from the deceptive lure of total calm. For is not
the static lure of the water – 'l'accompli' – an invidious form of
death for the living soul? ('Pli' is a Mallarméan term, full of an
intimacy both erotic and threatening.)[82]

> Jamais, charmes du jour, jamais vos grâces n'ont
> Tant souffert d'un rebelle essayant sa défense,
> Mais, comme les soleils m'ont tiré de l'enfance,
> Je remonte à la source où cesse même un nom.

Yes, the siren charms of the beauty of the sunlight seem in that
'painted' context to mask the void of reality as they did in *Ébauche*

d'un Serpent ('un sommeil/Trompeusement peint de campagnes')
and the 'hero' fights to withstand them. Yet – the same 'Mais'
present in *Ode Secrète* to prevent the flow of the voice from
coinciding with the logic of an unequivocal affirmation – this
journey moves 'à rebours' in the direction of childhood, as if to
undo all that process of sunlit ripening which shaped the mind in
Les Grenades. It is by definition a journey back not to mature
reward and discovery – 'l'enfance retrouvée à volonté' – but to a
nameless sensation of fluidity, 'la source où cesse même un nom',
an undifferentiated origin as ambiguous as the water which
encourages in the first place the gesture of wilful regression and
search for the unknown.[83] The multi-focused vision encouraged by
such divergent imagery leaves us with no unity other than that of
the strange pride of the speaking voice examining its rebellious
retreat into nothingness. Nor is its proud resolve to break the
stultifying and deceptive calm of nature around it – that 'charme
fermé, [. . .] naïf [. . .] à 1 dimension' which Valéry so mistrusted
– presented as part of a cycle of being, as it is in the imagined leap
into the sea at the end of *Le Cimetière Marin*. Desire, the mind
deprived of its resonance, can have no disruption other than that
of sleep or death.

> En vain, toute la nymphe énorme et continue
> Empêche de bras purs mes membres harassés;
> Je romprai lentement mille liens glacés
> Et les barbes d'argent de sa puissance nue.

Where Narcissus had feared to destroy the calm surface of the
pool – belovedly hoarding his image as that of another person –
the 'negative' action of 'le Rameur' continues triumphantly and
self-sufficiently, its lonely otherness accepted and acclaimed as the
source of an immunity of its own. 'Je romprai' echoes the other
active verbs of fracture, 'Je veux à larges coups rompre', 'déchire-
les', 'impose-leur', yet never, significantly, are these verbs other
than in future, imperative or optative form. The image of 'la
nymphe énorme et continue' seems to render visible the composite-
ness of all those other images of nature ('monde', 'ample et naïve
moire', 'charmes') in contrast to the distinct movement of the oars,
separate, infinite, immobile in their way. Nor – again quite unlike
that plunge into 'l'ère successive' in *Le Cimetière Marin* – is their
action dynamic, dionysian, but slow and patiently controlled, their

repetitiveness designed to conquer (but more as a perpetually sustained direction than an actuality) that ambiguous, naked force to which they harness their strength. Valéry's unified but never quite congruent choice of words conveys a complex gesture neither towards nor away from nature, certainly not Rousseauesque in the popular sense of the term.

> Ce bruit secret des eaux, ce fleuve étrangement
> Place mes jours dorés sous un bandeau de soie;
> Rien plus aveuglément n'use l'antique joie
> Qu'un bruit de fuite égale et de nul changement.

And how to interpret even this 'explicit' stanza with its La Fontaine-like image of silken, passing days ('Jours faits de moments, moments filés des soie')? At first hearing a traditional commonplace of passing time – the river of life – the sound to which the image applies is produced by the time-reversing action of the oars themselves, the experience the speaker imposes on himself. Decidedly the poem expresses no other transcendence than the identification of the mind with its own knowledge of change. For the need conveyed is as much the need to wear out the source of ancient joy, the source of memory, to fracture sensation by sensation, as to be born again with each new stroke of the oars? 'If my aim is to exhaust joy', the speaker appears to be feeling (or, more appropriately to poetry, a feeling appears to be speaking), then let me preserve the sovereign monotony of this rhythm, this total environment of liquid sound, this self-enhancing gesture of retreat (an early draft included the line 'Ce bruit morne [sombre] des eaux que j'aime étrangement').[84] In the total expressive context of the poem, 'Rien plus aveuglément. . .' acquires, overriding its 'linear' syntax, the same potential status of statements such as 'Je veux à larges coups rompre. . .'. Note, too, the mimetic echo of the theme of obstinate monotony of movement in the grave regularity of the alexandrine, ordered progressively and infinitely in carefully rhymed quatrains of 'rimes embrassées', masculine enclosing feminine, many of its regular cæsuras rhyming as well. The 'dante-esque' line of *Le Cimetière Marin*, raised to the power of twelve, was also mingled with a death-like tonality, its lilting balance stopping short of this intense 'chant funèbre'.

> Sous les ponts annelés, l'eau profonde me porte,
> Voûtes pleines de vent, de murmure et de nuit,

> Ils courent sur un front qu'ils écrasent d'ennui,
> Mais dont l'os orgueilleux est plus dur que leur porte.

We are partly, then, in the bleak, echoing landscape of *Le Solitaire*, where the same theme and imagery of exhilarating negation occurs:

> Sonnez, Voix sans parole et Parole sans voix,
> [...]
> Exterminez mystère, énigmes et miracles,
> Vous qui m'avez guéri du nombre des soleils,
> Des stupeurs devant l'ombre et devant les abeilles,
> De l'éblouissement du mirage Infini...
> [...]
> Oh...Passez en moi, Vents superbes!
> Couchez en moi toutes les herbes,
> Rompez les ronces du savoir [...].   (P II, 390–1).

And we are partly back in *La Jeune Parque* where the same image of desire for 'petrification' is used to express a gesture of disdain and retraction in the presence of the ephemeral, the shadowy, the formless, the void. Yet we are also in the metaphorical space of *Les Grenades*, where a sense of wit deflects the theme of the comparison from its expressive source in emotive subjectivity and allows something of the ebullient intellectual mood of comparison to enter the image. It is the theme of pride in this case which is enforced through analogy between the hard forehead of the oarsmen and the curved stone bridges above it, a pride which offers more than negative transcendence in its identification with the deep, liquid element to which it is opposed, but by which it now seems to be borne triumphantly along like a form of dark hope, 'l'eau profonde me porte'. In a sombre, inverted key similar to stanza eight of *Le Cimetière Marin*, are we so far after all from the last stanza of *Aurore* and the joyful 'onde porteuse' of the mind in its inwardly expressive energy?

> Leur nuit passe longtemps. L'âme baisse sous eux
> Ses sensibles soleils et ses promptes paupières,
> Quand, par le mouvement qui me revêt de pierres,
> Je m'enfonce au mépris de tant d'azur oiseux.

No longer the same mystery of Nerval's sonnet, where the image of an eye and of stone are so mysteriously fused,[85] here the only mystery is that of human endurance in its uncompromising movement of detachment from both sunlight and shadow. Surely the subject of *Le Rameur* is none other than 'le Moi pur' experienced from within.

Enigmatic in one sense, *Le Rameur* is a poem where enigma is not a riddle to be solved, but an effect – achieved by the forcefully harmonised and coherent but always multi-focused use of words. Indeed, there are a multitude of elements in the poem which put us on our guard against limiting psychoanalytic, philosophical and mystical interpretations, even while the themes and patterns central to those visions – the 'maternal' element of water, appearance and reality, mystical withdrawal, and so on – are intriguingly present. For what counts above all about this technique is Valéry's expression of the complexity of a gesture on the part of the mind entertaining it, or, if this sounds too closely confined to the 'fictional' consciousness speaking in the poem, on the part of a poetry of Voice itself. Is there not in *Le Rameur* a sense in which, in this still most reflexively sustained poetics of language, the gesture of rowing releases metaphorically through its widening 'cercles d'onde' the conscious experience – 'le Moi pur' – of the drama of voice ('Le Moi, c'est la Voix')?

> Arbres sur qui je passe, ample et naïve moire,
> Eau de ramages peinte, et paix de l'accompli,

– this is the world of flame and foliage which the speaker sings softly – 'chante tout bas' – in an interior monologue available only to himself: to use the terms with which Valéry characterises such an action, 'presque à soi-même' (P I, 623), 'au plus près de sa source' (P I, 623–4).[86] Indeed, by keeping their secret, by refusing to be lured by their charms, the oarsman could be said to be refusing to 'voice' their presence, and thus refusing to enter that journey away from silence, away from the 'source', away from reality, which the immediate appearances of phenomena invite (away from ordinary language, if one were talking linguistically). Hence the journey *against* the current, the gesture of withdrawal into strong, disdainful silence: 'la source où cesse même un nom'. Yet this very movement of negation is vibrant with a human presence, a pride, which the gesture of the oars seems itself to articulate and modify as its movement proceeds and that very source, as we have also seen, is always distant, a goal rather than

an actuality, and one expressively tinged in the poem with an aura
of threat, dissolution and death. For is not consciousness itself, in
Valéry's psychodrama of inner acoustics, an 'interval', a diver-
gence, a listening ear, the shutting of an eye?[87]

> Tandis que je m'attache à mon regard de pierre
> Dans le fixe et le dur "Pourquoi?",
> Un noir frémissement, l'ombre d'une paupière
> Palpite entre moi même et moi...   (P. i, 160).

But to take the discourse of the poem as a whole, it is the very
'song' of the world that the speaker rejects which we hear increased 'tout bas' in the phonetic sound-patterns of the poem –
the flickering symmetries of nasals and plosives, 'p's and 'm's, in
the description of the 'rejected' trees in the water. And the whole
action of the poem, in its imagery and structure as well as in its
sound dimension, expresses the inner thoughts and emotions of
that 'silent' voice which creates by its separate actions a duration,
a flow. For the curiously intense movement of the poem, a kind of
sustained gathering of all possible elements – sounds, cæsuras,
rhymes, quatrains, word echoes – into a rhythm of its own, is
mimetically expressive not simply of the sound of oars, but of the
inner sensations of the mind responding to rhythm and expressing
the emotion of rhythm in turn: the subordination of the semantic
to the euphonic, but the euphonic endowed with a semantic
power of its own. There are thus two creative 'directions' in *Le
Rameur*,[88] the one away from expression and towards reality, and
the other towards expression and away from reality; and it is the
strange congruence of these two directions in the Voice of the
poem itself – the voice of consciousness, 'le Moi pur' realised in
language – which we hear and are made to realise we hear in the
poem as the source of 'le réel' in humanised form. As Valéry
writes in the 'elegy' of *Équinoxe*, 'Mon silence a perdu ses voix'
(P i, 159). The same paradox was present in *Le Solitaire* where
Faust discovers that his own voice is the source of his identity:
'En somme, je pourrais bien tirer au sort qui je suis ou plutôt qui
je fus...C'est la même chose. Après tout, je ne suis que la personne qui parle...Mais qui Parle à qui?...' (P ii, 394).[89] In that
the notion of an 'origin' is shown in *Le Rameur* to be as ambiguous and 'meaningless' as the river itself against which the oarsman
works, defining himself by his gesture, and in that the notion of a

source is related to an action of naming, then here is the drama of 'L'Être et le Néant' which constitutes the drama of the voice itself, a gesture of silence whose action is sound. 'Toute poésie gît dans le commencement, ou plutôt est tout le temps *un commencement* – et comme. . . *du* commencement – *commencement* est sa matière! [. . .] *Car* (dit le voyant) – au commencement est la Voix' (xxiv, 862).

Aurore opened *Charmes* with a movement of hopeful identification with 'l'onde porteuse' of the voice from the perspective of its dawning hope, the source of desire. *Le Rameur* is more the thematic counterpart of that poem than its metrical twin *Palme*, which is the joyful coda of the volume with its theme of creative surprise, and it could be said to complete the movement 'crepuscularly', the symbolic shadow of the bridges and the shutting of the eyelids suggesting the treatment of the same theme in darker key. For the cognitive movement of the mind in its hope for knowledge is a movement towards the discovery of the death of the body and hence of itself, 'la source où cesse même un nom'.

> Que sais-tu? L'ennui.
> Que peux-tu? Songer.
> Songer pour changer
> Chaque jour en nuit.
> [. . .]
> Où vas-tu? À mort,
> Qu'y faire? Finir,
> Ne plus revenir
> Au coquin de sort.
> Où-vas-tu? Finir.
> Que faire? Le mort.   (P i, 163).

We have only to compare the amplitude of the expressive gesture of *Le Rameur* and its leisurely alexandrines with the brevity of this impudently truthful 'Chanson à part' to feel once again the discrepancy between the content of a voice and its existence as form, its existence as a dark joy which that death-like message of consciousness perpetually haunts. *Le Rameur* discovers and presents this discrepancy consciously as the most precious enigma of the voice itself. For the voice and the capacity it symbolises is all we have with which to move 'against the current', expressing as we do so greater and greater distance from the 'charms' we inevitably reject and recreate. It seems therefore fitting that in that 'barque funèbre' floating above the tree-tops which have played so much a part in his poetry as a locus of exchange between language and desire,[90] Valéry is moving 'above' the images of his own poems and thus expressing once more the self-made language of a poetry acting through what is said with a greater and greater 'action de présence' of its own.

Palme

It is no accident that the metre and imagery of the final poem of *Charmes* resembles that of *Aurore* at the beginning. Composed together, both are poems of hope, both contain metaphors of fruition. Yet where the heptasyllable of *Aurore* is light and impatient, the same metre here is slow and deliberate, speed and lightness contained within by other means; where the metaphor of fruit occurs only spasmodically in *Aurore*, here it is sustained throughout the whole poem, and not in terms of pain and plundering but in terms of slow maturation. The hope expressed through *Palme* is not violently dynamic but patient and accepting: itself part of the theme of ripening: 'Une espérance éternelle/Monte à la maturité'. *Palme* is a poem of and about calm and simplicity, yet it is a poem which relates for that very reason into the deepest themes and purposes of Valéry's poetic universe.

> De sa grâce redoutable
> Voilant à peine l'éclat,
> Un ange met sur ma table
> Le pain tendre, le lait plat;
> Il me fait de la paupière
> Le signe d'une prière
> Qui parle à ma vision:

An angel, a gift, a sign which seems to 'speak' to the mind through sight: this exciting poem opens as if with an Annunciation scene in an Italian painting – Sassetta *and* Leonardo – its forms mysterious and dynamic yet solidly real. For the gift is a humble, homely one, 'tender' bread, 'flat' milk, familiar things seen for themselves yet cherished as if we are seeing them clearly and simply for the first time. 'Le signe d'une prière/Qui parle à ma vision': nothing is said, for it is vision itself, the conscious experience of sight, which produces the discovery of reality and thus the

236

sense of a voice speaking a message of importance for the mind.
An angel – popular metaphor for a well-doer and complex symbol
of the 'grace' of a privileged moment – announces the certainty
of what in accordance with reality it is possible to be: as calm and
as present to oneself as a palm tree bearing its fruit. An astonishing
number of tones and levels: metaphorical, literal, perceptual,
visionary, popular and proverbial, have already perfectly combined in one outwardly simple opening stanza, and the rest of the
poem proceeds to render in visible linguistic form the 'song' of
that message of silent inner sight:

> Pour autant qu'elle se plie
> A l'abondance des biens,
> Sa figure est accomplie,
> Ses fruits lourds sont ses liens.

Born from analogy with a mental state which its exemplary
description restores in turn, the palm tree is evoked in its own
reality, real and present in its biological principles, yet absent from
the literal action-space of the poem except through the wondering
admiration of the message which understanding and empathy
with its principles conveys: 'Admire comme elle vibre'. Balanced
between sunshine and shadow like the plane tree of *Au Platane*
and the great Tree of Knowledge in *Ébauche d'un Serpent*, symbol of the relationship between 'être' and 'connaître', the palm
tree is 'chosen' as arbiter of human experience, the simulator, to
the mind perceiving it, of wisdom and peace:

> Ce bel arbitre mobile
> Entre l'ombre et le soleil,
> Simule d'une sibylle
> La sagesse et le sommeil.

Its golden fronds lightly sounding in the clear air which stirs it
like a finger (impossible to pin down the sound/sight synaesthesia
of these lines, made possible by the emotive and symbolic associations of the word 'or': treasure, ring, colour), it charges the soul of
the desert with its imperishable voice:

> L'or léger qu'elle murmure
> Sonne au simple doigt de l'air,
> Et d'une soyeuse armure
> Charge l'âme du désert.
> Une voix impérissable

> Qu'elle rend au vent de sable
> Qui l'arrose de ses grains,
> A soi-même sert d'oracle,
> Que se chantent les chagrins.

The palm tree itself is unaware. Each day simply increases its unconscious sweetness. Yet it is still the real, physical embodiment and revelator to human awareness of the patient expenditure and co-ordination of natural forces in time. As if to extract the treasure of this creative principle, Valéry now makes even more explicit the 'human' side of the message: 'Parfois si l'on désespère' ending:

> Ces jours qui te semblent vides
> Et perdus pour l'univers
> Ont des racines avides
> Qui travaillent les déserts.
> La substance chevelue
> Par les ténèbres élue
> Ne peut s'arrêter jamais,
> Jusqu'aux entrailles du monde,
> De poursuivre l'eau profonde
> Que demandent les sommets.
> Patience, patience,
> Patience dans l'azur!
> Chaque atome de silence
> Est la chance d'un fruit mûr! [. . .].

And the message finally over, as if relieved by the shedding of its fruit, there now comes the final proverbial address to the palm tree itself:

> Qu'un peuple à présent s'écroule,
> Palme! . . . irrésistiblement!
> Dans la poudre qu'il se roule
> Sur les fruits du firmament!
> Tu n'as pas perdu ces heures
> Si légère tu demeures
> Après ces beaux abandons;
> Pareille à celui qui pense
> Et dont l'âme se dépense
> À s'accroître de ses dons!

Does the mind of the thinker wear itself out in acquiring its talent or does it exercise itself in growing from its gifts? The equal metrical stresses of 'se dépense' and 's'accroître' allow a poignant ambiguity, making both interpretations equally necessary; while the main tone of the poem emphasises 'victoriously' – the palm is

the emblem of victory – the latter tone of generosity and fulfilment. If Valéry omitted an explicit human comparison from the
final version of *Au Platane*, the analogy is perfectly justified here
by the proverbial perspective on the natural. And we remember
the 'wisdom' of Valéry's own intellectual endeavour – 'Gladiator'
(Part I, p. 257, n.8), his ideal system of 'educating' by drawing out
natural possibility: 'L'homme "supérieur" n'est pas l'homme
doué d'un don, et qui restitue cette fortune; c'est celui qui s'est
organisé dans toute son étendue' (vii, 119). Human heroism is
ultimately a 'natural' process too, free to create, but not to refuse
to transform its creative powers through the universality of form.

Throughout *Palme* it is the imitative embodiment in language of
the calm, balanced 'message' of order and equilibrium which
gives the poem meaning and power. Neither a statement of a
moral message nor a description of a palm tree would suffice to
make the message of song part of our minds. Not to want to say
but to want to make – 'vouloir faire' – Valéry had written in
relation to his most 'personal' poetry of voice, *Le Cimetière Marin*,
and it is as though *Palme* explicitly embodies this same principle
of creation by form. And here, of course, it is sound above all that
plays its part. The rhythmical balance of the lines, the odd number
of syllables helping to create a marvellously live swing of alternating stresses from line to line (for example 4/3, 4/3, 2/4 in the
central lines ' – Calme, calme, reste calme!/Connais le poids
d'une palme/Portant sa profusion'). Throughout the poem, the
ear picks up a set of unresolved sound-symmetries perpetually
seeking equilibrium and yet perpetually thrown back to their
original position of departure as by a slight over-emphasis on a
pair of weighing scales.[91] Under the heading 'Psaume S' in a part
of his notes published as *Mélange*, Valéry wrote:

> *Au commencement fut la Surprise,*
> *Et ensuite vint le Contraste;*
> *Après lui, parut l'Oscillation;*
> *Avec elle, la Distribution,*
> *Et ensuite la Pureté*
> *Qui est la Fin.*
> (P i, 337),

– a 'fable' of poetic genesis similar in its typographical layout to the pictorial principle of branching lines Valéry once contemplated for *Palme* itself.[92] The 'fable' reminds us above all of the morphological principles present throughout the poem and extending not only to its rhythmical stresses, but to alliteration and rhyme.

Yet how can it be that principles of aesthetic symmetry in language seem to embody the 'message' of the palm tree itself, swaying between the earth and the firmament? However strikingly simple in tone and impact, *Palme* is based on a complex analogy between principles of natural growth – the biological laws which govern the tree's cycle of growth and fructification (indeed its existence to the eye too as a symmetrical yet irregular form) – and those principles governing the poem itself, its existence as a linguistic structure designed to be of maximum appeal to our inner sense of harmony and form. Thus it is not only figuratively through its metaphorical devices, but in a far-reaching sense extending to its own existence as a total metaphor of mind that *Palme* affects us. *Palme* has as its subject that same process of enriching self-discovery in the presence of natural form dreamt of by the narrator in *Les Grenades*. Where in *Les Grenades* the basis of the discovery is explained, here in *Palme* it is given indirectly, yet paradoxically more completely in the terms of the sight/sound synaesthesia felt by Valéry to be the basis of our inner dialogue with the world, the silent 'voice' of consciousness 'hearing the message of sight. Poetry is 'L'accord de la Voix qui est un acte, et de l'Ouïe qui est sensation' (P I, 596), and *Palme* accordingly is no mere allegory of poetic creation, but the poetic principle of the sensibility metaphorically transposed into impersonal form: 'Une voix intarissable/[. . .]/A soi-même sert d'oracle'.

What, then, is the relation between the human hope embodied by the palm tree and poetry itself? The first point to establish is surely that the hope expressed in *Palme* does not apply, or rather is not confined to the coming of a work of art itself. The lines

> Chaque atome de silence
> Est la chance d'un fruit mur!
> Viendra l'heureuse surprise:

apply to a general sense of the privileged moment – 'inspiration' – to the coming of that same experience of delightful potentiality which the angel signals at the beginning of the poem by a mere glance of the eye.[93] As in *A la Recherche du Temps Perdu*, the privileged instant is unreliable, however; intelligence and will-power are needed to incorporate it, to be fully receptive, and, accordingly, much of *Palme* explores the general human need to be ready to act on a moment's inspiration, when

> Une colombe, la brise,
> L'ébranlement le plus doux,
> Une femme qui s'appuie,
> Feront tomber cette pluie
> Où l'on se jette à genoux!

Valéry's poetry explores, as we have so often seen, the emotions of the intellect and its power to deepen the 'musical' continuity of experience. By a characteristic circularity here, the 'femme qui s'appuie', leaning on the imagined tree, can also be seen as the 'angel' of the beginning (the poem, dedicated to Valéry's wife, Jeannie, resembles in tone the gentle presence of exchange between two aspects of the Self in *Intérieur*). Here, however, the angel's presence is given such certainty – 'voilant à peine l'éclat' – that it is no mere filter sparing the full light of the intellect. Instead it is with the certainty of a command of absolute assurance that the message is given, a source of being that the mind must turn to in order to fulfil the evidence of its understanding of its own laws, to realise itself.

It is not through analogy with the genesis of the work of art that the theme of the poetic enters, then. It enters through the deep bond set up between poetic possibility and the mental power to extend the privileged moment by a lived metaphor of memory – a 'figure' which the image of the palm tree serves to emphasise *within* the poem as well as for ourselves. 'Ces jours qui te semblent vides...': the palm tree like the poem encourages as well as expresses human power to trust in a process of growth beyond the present instant. Like the angel, it speaks to our vision by allowing greater understanding of ourselves, the 'possible'. To align oneself with nature and to do so in such a way that, as in a certain kind of human love, the power of the mind is increased rather than diminished, that is the 'ethic' of *Palme*.

To extend the symbolic frame of reference of *Palme* to the genesis of the poem is to find moving confirmation of the generality of its message. Riddled with variants and even whole rejected stanzas,[94] the manuscripts reveal that same process towards the rejection of 'ideas' and extraneous images in favour of simplicity of form. 'Gloire du long désir, Idées', wrote Mallarmé in *Prose pour des Esseintes*. Of that and other poems there are many echoes in *Palme*,[95] and the same process of maturation towards ultimate simplicity of form is the message of *Palme*. To be excited and 'inspired', but to reject that immediate excitement in favour of the calm necessary to its full realisation – 'vouloir, vouloir et même ne pas excessivement vouloir' (P i, 489) – it is as if the final stanza of *La Pythie* were heard all over again. For to rely on the natural enthusiasm of the mind without critically channelling its diversity, is to fail to make the full human *use* of its own internal laws. 'The expense of spirit in a waste of shame' – in Valéry's terms 'les effets sans cause' – has no place in the economy exemplified here. 'En toute chose, il faut trouver la *Musique des actes*' (xii, 637).

Palme is a fitting conclusion to *Charmes* as a volume, though not an 'end' to the message of creative possibility it conveys: that precise sense of the nature of 'l'inchevé – 'l'infini est défini' – which Valéry tried to communicate as the very structure of thought.[96] We have seen how, for Valéry, a text once relatively complete falls like fruit from a tree of still growing possibility, a tree preparing more acts of expression, more poems, more fruit. The concept does not deny the completed text significance for the reader, but for the reader to become producer of the state of 'Poésie', it is important that the relationship between the virtual and the instantaneous be somehow signalled in the poem itself. In *Palme*, the image of the growing tree enriched through the loss of its fruits is the expression of this very paradox, the signal of a silence expressed through language but which the finite structures of language cannot contain. The tree is ignorant of the truth of its own life-principle – 's'ignore' – and it grows 'sans mystère' between the opposing claims of the earth and the sky. Yet by making this ignorance explicit, by comparing the knowing growth of the mind with the unknowing growth of the tree, Valéry has thrown into relief the invisible domain of the mind as a storehouse of constructive possibilities aimed at the greater achievement of reality, once poetry – the discourse of the possible – has conveyed

them to us. 'Tout est sur table – Pas d'ombres', he once wrote of
the music of Bach, 'Pas de sentiment, pas de mystère, autre que
celui (qui est le suprême-) de l'existence par soi' (xiv, 751).
We are back to 'le pain tendre, le lait plat', perfectly themselves
without turbulence or shadow and thus, in the linguistic universe
of the poem, talismans of the mental possibility of a similar
simplicity on the part of the mind in touch with its own natural
life, 'le réel'. 'Et maintenant, voici que je suis ce que je suis, et que
je ne crois pas être autre chose', says Valéry's Faust likewise in
words of great relevance to *Palme*: 'Il fallut tant d'espoirs et de
désespoirs, de triomphes et de désastres pour en venir là...'
(P ii, 321). The human vision celebrated in *Palme* is no mere
message of natural parallelism, but of the capacity to recognise in
the simplicity of the natural universe laws which it is the ultimate
goal of the mind to achieve by conscious effort in exchange for its
own particular capacity for anxiety and pain. Thus it is the
classical values of Faust's monologue that *Palme* appropriately
introduces as the culmination of *Charmes*:

> Serais-je au comble de mon art? Je vis. Et je ne fais que vivre.
> Voilà une œuvre...Enfin ce que je fus a fini par construire ce que je
> suis. Je n'ai plus aucune autre importance. Me voici le présent, en
> échange parfait avec quoi qu'il arrive. Point de reste. Il n'y a plus de
> profondeur. L'infini est défini. Ce qui n'existe pas n'existe plus. Si la
> connaissance et ce qu'il faut produire par l'espir pour que SOIT ce
> qui EST, te voici FAUST, connaissance plein et pure, plénitude,
> accomplissement. Je suis celui que je suis. Je suis au comble de mon
> art, à la période classique de l'art de vivre. Voilà mon œuvre: vivre.
> N'est-ce pas tout? Mais il faut le savoir...Il ne s'agit pas de se
> trouver sur ce haut plateau d'existence, sans le savoir. Que d'aven-
> tures, de raisons, de songes, et de fautes pour gagner la liberté d'être
> ce que l'on est, rien que ce que l'on est! Qu'est-ce que la perfection,
> sinon la suppression de tout ce qui nous manque[Ce qui manque est
> toujours de trop...Mais, à présent, le moindre regard, la moindre
> sensation, les moindres actes et fonctions de la vie me deviennent de
> la même dignité que les desseins et les voix intérieurs de ma
> pensée... (P ii, 321–2).

In this wonderful monologue, written near the end of his own life,
Valéry has taken the rôle of Orpheus – 'inventeur de ce qui est' –
to its poetic conclusion: the acceptance of life as a masterpiece of
the human mind: 'VIVRE...Je ressens, je respire mon chef-
d'œuvre' (P ii, 322). All the voices of existence expressed in

Charmes are contained within it, transmuted into a key which coincides with that of 'classical' balance and calm. On that plateau of consciousness, poetry is no longer necessary, yet it is poetry which is the constant instrument necessary to the transformation of 'être' by 'le faire'. Poetry founded on this goal is constantly drawn to convey the fragility of its own harmony and the necessary pain of the sensibility which its magic transforms, the moment when 'l'ouragan des songes' must always enter the mind sustained by knowledge of itself. For whereas the palm tree is ignorant of its 'double' nature – its 'voix impérissable' speaking to the mind's eye of the beholder alone – the tree of the human sensibility can know its own nature, expressing it in fulfilment of its own inner law:

> Illumination, largesse!
> Voici parler une Sagesse
> Et sonner cette auguste Voix
> Qui se connaît quand elle sonne
> N'être plus la voix de personne
> Tant que des ondes et des bois!

The most intimate voice of *Charmes* is still the voice of Narcissus listening to the 'emptiness' of his own sensibility in the 'miroir parlant' of the natural universe and discovering 'cette puissance de motilité' (xxii, 304) which Valéry felt was never sufficiently expressed. 'Narcisse – Substitution d'un être autre et indépendant à la partie spontanée du moi' (vii, 248) (see Chapter 6, n. 29). Approached in this light, *Palme* offers the reader an image of the 'unconscious', but at the same time (there *is* no 'unconscious' for Valéry) it is a splendid metaphor of the sensibility illuminated by awareness,[97] the mysterious source which for Valéry poetry develops in all its natural resonance: 'le Langage issu de la Voix'.

Conclusion

Je crois que le ressort de ces possibilités de double effet est dans la puissance de motilité [...]. (XXXI, 304).

Mais il ne faut pas croire que ceci soit nouveauté. Ce n'est que faire consciemment ce qui est nécessairement fait inconsciemment dans tous les cas où le langage intervient. (XVI, 645).

Ton discours, ton raisonnement vont à leur fin. Mais ta voix en moi, veut encore ta voix. (XXVI, 203).

Curiously repetitive and persevering in its aims and preoccupations, Valéry's theory and practice of poetry is nevertheless excitingly expansive in depth and possibility, so that any ending to this book must seem arbitrary. Yet certain questions of critical perspective impose themselves. No pale imitator of Mallarmé, is Valéry still best described by the phrase 'classique du Symbolisme'?[1] What is the most radical contribution of a theory of Voice to our conception of poetic language?

That we can talk of theory at all is striking in the case of a thinker so wary of the danger of systematisation, and whose whole effort of creative invention can be appreciated as an attempt to keep the intellect in touch with 'l'informe', the source of its own virtuality and power. Convinced that prejudice against theory can be as damaging as its misuse, Valéry developed a method of thinking in which lucidity and a sense of the limits of cognition are perfectly compatible. The key to this paradox seems to lie in an unusually sustained sense of the interdependence of freedom and constraint in the living organism; it is not unconnected that Valéry attempted to treat his own sensibility as finite in order to 'substitute' creatively for its uncontrollability a conception of awareness with its own sense of identity and growth. Indeed, it is in relation to this goal of creative self-harmony that we discover the roots of a poetry of voice based on 'ornamental' principles:

245

the combined musical and architectural expression through language of the total bodily gesture of thought. No study of Valéry's poetry would be correctly balanced without reference to the immense rôle of the sensibility not simply as an element which the poet must master, but as an experience which totally determines the intellectual methods and intentions rationally developed to tap its resources. The sensibility for Valéry is the prime mover of the mind in its closed 'demande/réponse' relationship to the universe, and the human individual 'listens' to himself according to this same law of inner 'delay'.[2] In poetic terms, we are of the same 'creative' substance as the universe, and it is the nature of consciousness to be drawn to create in turn.[3]

Valéry became aware of the 'echoing' source of consciousness through an acute sense of his own functioning – 'Ce "cœur" d'autant plus transparent qu'il est plus troublé' (xxii, 323) – and it was an experience which the 'self-listening' activity of poetic composition epitomised for him above all other as a general law which the intellect could learn to exploit for purposes of its own (the imitation and development of natural resources is often the strength of Valéry's 'poétique'). We have seen how this possibility ('Bouchoreille') was particularly present in relation to phonetic sound, and I have suggested that the discovery resulted not only in the choice of particularly euphonic combinations of sound in poetry, but in one of the most far-reaching studies of the psychophysiology of poetic effects yet produced. Wishful thinking only when we approach Valéry's ideal of 'harmonics' as if it were designed to transmit to the reader the precise equivalent of initial perception in its creator, this ideal becomes convincingly realistic, in my opinion, when we approach it instead as an action of discovery through which the poet uses words to stimulate and increase that same sense of virtuality made possible through inner monologue: 'Trouver l'être qui chante' (xxvii, 811). Indeed, the sound/sense harmony for which Valéry is famous relates precisely to this latent virtuality of experience in the reader rather than to the impossible equation of sound and content. Here Valéry makes his most radical contribution to the possible interpretation of the much misused critical terms form and content.

The concept of voice has had many parts to play in this powerful self-generating theory of expressive communication. First and foremost – and this is unusual in a theory of literature – voice has meant the sound produced by the human larynx in speaking, singing or other utterance. We have seen how, with his acute sense of the physical conditions which regulate as well as permit the higher faculties of the human being, Valéry was sensitive to those aspects of phonation and articulation in poetry which can be made to utilise and draw attention to our Janus-like nervous system with its power to stimulate the conscious mind through the physiological aspects of sound. For the human voice is not sound alone, and Valéry's second main use of the term in the context of the 'production' and 'consumption' of poetry relates to our capacity for meaningful speech and for expression, not simply through words themselves, but through use of the voice as a musical instrument, capable of inflection, speed, pitch, accent and tone. Moved in his youth by the quality of a contralto singing-voice – though this should not be used as a reductionist explanation of the complex intellectual and aesthetic use he made of the event – Valéry became particularly conscious of the way in which sensation and emotion interact with one another 'irrationally': so much so that he treated poetry in part as an attempt to create and make use of this irrational and affective power. Hence the 'myth' of the lost source – 'Poésie' – which the poet would reconstitute by using language in a particular way. Yet poetry for Valéry exploited and developed *all* the properties of language, its medium, and the third major use to which we have seen him set the term Voice is in the context of poetry conceived as a total action of expressive form involving and integrating every faculty of mind. This is as far removed as possible from the language of ordinary speech and the unstructured flow of inner monologue; nonetheless Valéry sets the mental capacities involved in the action of inner and outer speech at the centre of his conception of poetry as the natural discourse of 'L'Être *vivant* ET *pensant (contraste, ceci)* – et poussant la conscience de soi à la capture de sa sensibilité [. . .] sur la corde de la voix' (xxii, 435–6).

What, then, finally, of the relationship between this, I believe, uniquely sustained analytic practice of poetry as 'le *Langage* issu de la *Voix*' and the conception of poetic language which may be said to have dominated modern European literary poetics? What contribution has Valéry made in particular (we have already noted his radical re-expression of the relationship between 'forme' and 'fond') to a special literary discourse concerned with the development of capacities sensed in 'privileged' moments of experience?

Two main conceptions of poetic language might be said to have dominated a literary poetics concerned with the primacy of language: the 'Hermetic', where the poet's activity is directed towards the creation of a self-contained linguistic structure through which language offers itself as an object of experience, and the 'Orphic', where the poet attempts to bring the world and man to language within an order of 'presence'.[4] We have seen Valéry's highly developed sense of the first of these possibilities in his admiration for the poetry of Mallarmé. A poet in Valéry, too, would destroy the process of signification of ordinary discourse in order to substitute for the universe of meaning a universe of pure figures. Yet we have also seen Valéry's uneasiness concerning Mallarmé's dedication of these impersonal poetic resources to the 'Voice of Language', and his own equal insistence on the second, 'Orphic' possibility through which, by using the corporeal and dynamic aspects of language in its transformational relation to consciousness, the poet is tapping a source of 'Being'. Orpheus is a constant figure in Valéry's poetic universe, playing upon the lyre of the human sensibility, its chords those of the voice itself, and inventively discovering the 'music' of form.

Yet before concluding that Valéry substitutes an 'Orphic' for a 'Hermetic' conception of poetry, and certainly before assuming we hear echoes of Heidegger's notion that not Language but Being speaks through us in poetry,[5] it is essential to make use of our discovery that poetry for Valéry is the voice of 'l'Être *vivant* ET *pensant*', the qualifying emphasis '*contraste, ceci*' reminding us of an art which aspires to develop the natural power of language to unite conscious and unconscious levels of the mind from the point of view of the ever absent 'témoin parleur' (a 'Self' whose 'absence' poetry renders expressively present in form). It might seem that where Mallarmé devoted the resources of a 'Hermetic' conception of poetic art to the experience of Beauty (an aim re-establishing its own contact with the subjective), Valéry explicitly combined the resources of *both* conceptions of poetic form. This he attempted by creating a form of poetry which harnessed the dynamism of the action of speech in its relationship to processes of mind wider than those of signification ('La parole est la langue en acte' [vɪɪ, 677]), while transferring these processes consciously and visibly – often in the form of the awareness of 'la Personne qui parle' – to a form of 'music' by which the whole human universe becomes open to the expressive action of poetic speech.

From Russian Formalism through Anglo-American structuralism to present-day French literary semiotics, all the main language-based conceptions of our time maintain a distinction between the body of utterances we call literature and other utterances.[6] Returning to the question of Valéry's attitude to a special literary discourse, we are led to the striking conclusion that although he cultivates the notion, inherited from Mallarmé, of isolating a particular function of language (as opposed to a special area of experience), Valéry ensures that the closed form of poetry relates to the rest of our experience by means of the reality of language itself. Yet does this mean that he denies the discourse of poetry intrinsic value? I think not, and in order to answer this question in the light of the evidence drawn together in this study, I shall turn briefly to the question of difference between the written and the spoken, taking as a convenient critical focus the contemporary theoretician Jacques Derrida's *La Voix et le Phénomène* – a work particularly relevant in that Derrida, like Valéry, stresses the primacy of the voice in a way which contemporary phenomenology has failed to do.

To put the matter schematically, Derrida could be said to maintain that the primacy of the voice in Western literature – the notion that the written is the shadow of the spoken – is based on a 'metaphysics of presence' or idealisation of voice falsely conceived as a principle through which we have access to objects in direct form, a 'wholeness' of meaning in our relation to the world. Where the phenomenologist Husserl makes written language a mere dress of the spoken, its own limitations relegated to a secondary level of experience, Derrida insists, on the contrary, that the spoken is itself already at a far remove from the fiction of presence, and, consequently, that the separation of phenomena does not exist prior to language.[7] Hence – if we study the written language 'scientifically' ('la grammatologie') – the possibility exists of learning about the myths (particularly that of 'whole-ness', 'human nature' or 'being') governing our relationship to the world.

Comparison with Valéry's position is immediately complicated by the fact that 'voice' for him and for Derrida means different things, quite apart from the fact that theory for Valéry arises directly from the practice of poetry, where Derrida is a theoretician alone. Agreeing that the spoken is already removed from presence (it seems a commonplace), Valéry turns, like Derrida, to the written as an extension of the spoken, but only, we remember, as an imitation of the principle of 'Being' related to language itself. Here his insistence on poetry as a specifically *written* medium comes into its own.[8] Is this a further 'metaphysics of presence'? Not at all. As we have seen both stated and 'proved' through his poems, language for Valéry has a unique rôle in actualising what is purely virtual and dialectical. Superficially opposed in that Valéry at first sight welcomes voice where Derrida decries it, the two reach a similar position in that both intensify the specificity of the written; yet in the course of reaching this similar position, Valéry has travelled a completely different route ('La voix est la voie') and one with different consequences for a theory of litera-ture. Because he has stressed the potential relationship of 'Être' and 'Connaître' by means of the written, Valéry could be said to have maintained the humanist notion of individual unity which Derrida denies.[9] Is this what Derrida implies when he writes that Valéry's critical formalism is by no means disqualified by his creative position? 'Peut-être touchons-nous ici à une limite où l'opposition de la forme et du sens, avec tous les partages qui s'y ordonnent, perd sa pertinence et appelle une toute autre élaboration.'[10] Indeed. And might not that 'toute autre élaboration' already be contained in Valéry's work with its extraordinary power of syn-thesis of the 'classical' and the 'new'? 'Il reste alors à *parler*, à faire *résonner* la voix dans les couloirs pour suppléer l'éclat de présence', Derrida continues,

> Et contrairement à ce que la phénoménologie – qui est toujours phénoménologie de la perception – a tenté de nous faire croire, contrairement à ce que notre désir ne peut pas ne pas être tenté de croire, la chose même se dérobe toujours.
> Contrairement à l'assurance que nous en donne Husserl [...], 'le regard' ne peut pas 'demeurer'.[11]

Nor can the voice itself 'remain' for Valéry ('Chanterez-vous quand serez vaporeuse?'). Where Derrida deprives writing of the victory of maintaining something of its author after death (in the same way as it is deprived of the victory of retaining something of its object), Valéry's lack of interest in such victories means that for him literature survives as an action of language which re-echoes within the reader the same 'fiction' of subjective presence operative in the action of speech. 'Chanterez-vous quand serez vaporeuse?' retains in this context the full expressive irony of this emotion, the purely 'bookish' immorality of the poem until it is awoken from sleep by the right tongues and ears.[12]

Perhaps the most striking conclusion to emerge from Valéry's particular appeal to the voice model in the context of the written is that he becomes the least Symbolist of poets, despite the strong echoes we have discovered in his poetry of the drama of 'poésie pure' and the relation of art to transcendental form. Indeed, his stress on the potentiality of poetry as the 'exercise' of a universal capacity for self-unification often makes Valéry seem more like the English Romantics than the French Symbolists. Listen to Words-worth describing 'The dangerous craft of culling term and phrase/From languages that want the living voice/To carry meaning to the natural heart',[13] or to that natural structuralist, Coleridge, insisting on the way in which an atomic use of language destroys the 'immediate presence' of the word as an instrument exciting thought in all its energy of flesh and blood.[14] Yet *whose* is the voice speaking in poetry for Valéry and what is its relationship to the world? In order to highlight what makes Valéry's poetry essentially as different from the poetry of the English Romantics as from that of the French Symbolists, it would seem necessary to return finally to the concept of 'silence', the paradoxical fruit of a poetry of voice. Although it is a subject too rich and complex to be treated here specifically, it is to be hoped this study has prepared the reader to appreciate it.

A sensation of the inexhaustible nature of reality (centred on the unavoidable oscillation in the conscious mind between 'being' and 'knowing'); the conviction that these phases of the sensibility are too intricate to be communicated in words ('Un homme qui souffre ou qui jouit se sépare' [xxII, 323]); a sense of the richness

251

of moments where the urge to express and expel – in tears, in speech, in gestures of the body – is balanced by the sense that to do so is to destroy the balance of mental impulses towards and away from language: all these universal experiences constitute what Valéry so often refers to as 'l'ineffable', a concept which he defines as deeply related to inner monologue and the predominant urge of the mind to seek, to understand and to know. We have seen how 'l'ineffable' is the very aim of Valéry's poetry, which he defines as an attempt to convey 'l'état du manque de mots' in words.[15] It was in relation to this paradox that we met the concept of 'silence', a term used almost as frequently as voice itself.

'Silence' in Valéry's poetic theory is no mere code-word for a myth of 'Being'. It is closely related to the nature of poetry conceived with the nature of language in mind, 'être' and 'dire' being related in a particularly convincing way.[16] We found this relationship explored in, for example, the passage headed 'Station sur la Terrasse' – referred to at the end of the analysis of *Charmes* (p. 290, n.96) – where Valéry notes that his work has given him the precisely defined sensation of what has not been said: not simply what he had failed to create, not simply the result of any cynicism about language,[17] but that which *still remains to be expressed because the language of poetry has made it more present*. The quality of this silence, so closely bound to the experience and aspirations of poetic Voice, is present throughout Valéry's poetry, becoming explicit in lines like 'Le silence au vol de cygne/Entre nous ne règne plus' of *Poésie* – 'poésie' being Valéry's term for the state of silent virtuality that the poet seeks to convey in the poem whatever its subject – or in a line like 'Mon silence a perdu ses voix' of *Équinoxe* (P I, 159), and many more. Indeed, we remember that the famous words of *Le Cimitière Marin*: 'Ô pour moi seul, en moi seul, en moi-même...' have behind them the concept of the human sensibility as that which consciousness 'speaks' in its perpetual search for the unity of self-definition ('Auprès d'un cœur dont je suis le poème' [P I, 1684]). This being so, Valéry's poetry fulfils the condition of 'communication transnarcissistique'[18] – 'Il faut donc construire de soi en soi, ce soi qui sera l'instrument à faire telle œuvre' (XVIII, 29) – and we can now better understand how that famous preference for process over product is no disparagement of poetry on his part, but rather a sign of his insistence that however intrinsically conceived in its special discourse, the poem relates to a virtuality of experience outside itself. Without allegorical symbolism, he thus achieves a self-referential language where a line like 'Le silence au vol de cygne' comes to denote and convey for the reader the 'meta-linguistic' aspirations of the voice of consciousness in its most intimate relationship with what Valéry calls, in moods of both frustration and of joy, 'le cœur'; 'l'âme':

> Écoute la nuit...
> Tout devient merveille:
> Le silence éveille
> Une ombre de bruit...
>
> Une ombre de voix
> N'est-ce point la mienne
> Dont l'âme te vienne
> Si loin que je sois?   (P I, 1699).

Space does not permit discussion of Valéry's relationship to the twentieth-century poets who have succeeded him, other than to suggest that his approach to poetry, never afraid to cherish the resources of traditional rhetoric, and very far from being a mere restatement of Mallarmé's distinction between two separate functions of language, has a potential we are only beginning to appreciate – a question quite independent of the minor consideration of imitation or development of Valéry's own style. This 'poétique du langage' is not without its dosage of literary subversion,[19] yet the remarkable result from the point of view of Valéry's own poetry is that it could be said to deepen the 'ciel intérieur' of Baudelaire as much as the 'espace linguistique' of many contemporary poets.[20] Yves Bonnefoy bases his challenge 'Nous avons à oublier Paul Valéry'[21] on a total misunderstanding of the nature of Valéry's 'forme close' and the relation of a poetics of 'fabrication' to the material world, 'miroir parlant' of the human self. As I hope to have shown, this relationship involves a radical re-expression of the rôle of cognition in constituting emotion and of the nature of the expressive sensibility in relation to language. Consciousness for Valéry is the emotion of knowingly taking part in a living action of contrast 'dont l'autre pôle est: *tout ce qui est*' (XXII, 309). It is these two poles of experience *within* the sensibility that the poetry of *La Jeune Parque* and of *Charmes* unites *expressively* in the form of 'song'. For there are not two rhetorics in Valéry's poetry: 'music' and 'meaning'. 'Le Moi, c'est la voix', 'La voix, clef de la poésie.' The sceptical[22] intelligence he brought to bear on the practice of poetry contributes in a uniquely thorough way to our understanding of the dynamic relationship between language, mind and world which literary communication exploits.

Notes

Preface

1 There is no full-length single study of Valéry's poetry and poetic theory in English (F. Scarfe's *The Art of Paul Valéry* [1954] and C. Whiting's critical edition of *Charmes* [1973] are part exceptions). In French, readers of Valéry's poetry must remain indebted to the pioneering studies of P.-O. Walzer, J. Duchesne-Guillemin, J. Hytier, and, more recently, J. Lawler and M. Parent (see Bibliography). Even here, P.-O. Walzer's study is the only general one.

2 See Introduction, n. 5. By 'communication', I do not mean the transmission or exchange of ideas in the informational sense, which Valéry reserves for a non-poetic use of language, but rather the poet's inventive discovery of generality through expressive form. The critical challenge of reconciling 'incommunicability' with a theory of poetry as the production of effects in the reader is posed by Jean Hytier in *La Poétique de Valéry* (Paris, Armand Colin, 1953), 240–1. The solution I am adopting is a somewhat different one.

3 Broadly speaking, I have followed Valéry in using an initial capital – Voice — to indicate poetic discourse, as opposed to the natural phenomenon of the voice on which his poetry was modelled for its own distinctive purposes. Many usages fall between these two extremes or refer to a complex mode of psychic energy which activates the virtuality of consciousness and speech. It is hoped that their meaning will be clear from the context.

4 See J. Jackson, *La Question du Moi, Un aspect de la modernité poétique européenne* (Neuchâtel, la Baconnière, 1978). The pre-occupation in twentieth-century French poetry with the problem of accommodating self, world and language to a literary mode is described by Roger Cardinal in his Introduction to *Sensibility and Creation, Studies in Twentieth-Century French Poetry* (London, Croom Helm Ltd, 1977), 10. See also the discussion 'Man, Things and Poem' by Ian Higgins in *Francis Ponge* (London, The Athlone Press, 1979).

5 E.g. 'Celui qui *parle* doit *vivre*, et cette vie passer à celui qui écoute. Vivre, ce n'est pas seulement penser [...]. Mais la pensée réelle [...] revient toujours à un "présent" qui est son lien avec corps et sensations. [...] Forme identique, valeurs différentes' (VIII, 544); 'La *forme* en art serait ainsi de suggérer/communiquer à x qu'il a le corps (le fonctionnement, souffle, tension) qui convient à la pensée exprimée. [...] Communiquer au spectateur-auditeur, les conditions

255

physiologiques qui sont en accord avec l'intention et la pensée de l'auteur' (VIII, 552).

6   See E. Kris, *Psychoanalytic Explorations in Art* (Schocken Paperback Edition, 1964 [1952]), 248. Further discussion of ambiguity – a term inaugurated as a general critical tool by W. Empson in *Seven Types of Ambiguity* (London, Chatto and Windus, 1930) – can be found in W. Nowottny's *The Language Poets Use* (London, The Athlone Press, 1962).

> 'The term "ambiguity" now has wide currency as a means of referring to diverse ways in which the language of poetry exhibits a charge of multiple implications and fits itself to contain within the form of discourse aspects of human experience whose difference or distance from one another might seem such as not easily to permit their coherent assembly in linguistic form' (ibid., 146).

I am suggesting that Valéry's poetry becomes communicative when the link between linguistic ambiguity and the reader's sensibility is rationally and even transparently achieved.

7   A possible link between narrative modes and the physiological function of the voice is made in Guy Rosalto's essay 'Voice and Literary Myth' (*The Structuralist Controversy*, ed. R. Macksey and E. Donato [Baltimore and London], The Johns Hopkins University Press, Paperback edition 1975 [1970], 207–9). A major work in the area of literary voice in the first sense is W. Booth's *The Rhetoric of Fiction* (Chicago, University of Chicago Press, 1961).

8   See Conclusion. The terms are used by G. Bruns in *Modern Poetry and the Idea of Language* (New Haven, Conn., and London, Yale University Press, 1974).

9   A study of this kind is Kirsteen Anderson's forthcoming thesis: *The Idea of Voice in Valéry's Writings*. I am particularly grateful to have seen this work in preparation. The following voice-oriented articles have also come to my attention since beginning this study: W. Ince, 'La voix du Maître ou Moi et style selon Valéry', *R.S.H.*, 129 (jan.–mars, 1968), 29–39; N. Bastet, 'Valéry et la Voix Poétique', *Annales de la Faculté des Lettres et Sciences Humaines de Nice*, 15 (1971) and K. Anderson, 'Valéry et Tomatis: étude sur la conscience auditive du poète', *B.E.V.*, 20 (mars 1979), 27–44. See also in part M. Lechantre, 'L'hiéroglyphe intérieur', *M.L.N.*, 630–43 and 'P(h)o(n)étique', *C.P.V.* I, 93–119; H. Laurenti, 'Musique et monologue – notes pour une approche valéryenne du poème', *R.L.M.*, I, 49–66 and the section 'Je me parle' in N. Celeyrette-Pietri's *Valéry et le Moi, des Cahiers à l'œuvre* (Paris, Klincksieck, 1979).

10 For Guy Rosalto (op. cit., 214) this voice is capable of delimiting the literary myth in relation to the work of fiction, thus enabling the subject to sustain its own internal division and the work its power to charm us. I believe Valéry's poetry leads to the appreciation of a similar position vis à vis the 'myth' of Voice.

11 Baudelaire's description of Poe which came to mean so much to Valéry (see p. 30).

Introduction

1 Sensitivity to the 'magical' sound of the human voice over and above the meaning of words is a theme treated by Flaubert and Nerval (see Alison Fairlie's comments in 'Sentiments et sensations chez Flaubert', *C.A.I.E.F.*, 26 [mai 1974], 246).

2 For full discussion, see J. Hytier, *La Poétique de Valéry*, 233–99.

3 *'Celui qui parle, entend; celui qui entend, parle. C'est la loi fondamentale'* (xxvi, 381); 'Le moi est ce qui entend et comprend la parole intérieure, le seul spectateur des visions' (ii, 645); 'Je crois que le ressort de ces possibilités de double effet est dans la puissance de motilité – laquelle on ne médite jamais assez' (xxii, 304).

4 Introductory works on Structuralism are listed in the Bibliography under Culler, Hawkes, Jameson, Scholes, Sturrock.

5 The term 'communication' has two senses, everyday and critical (see A. Wilden, 'Language and Communication' in *System and Structure* [London, Tavistock Publications, 1972]). When Valéry denies the possibility of communication in art except indirectly through ambiguity (see Preface, notes 2 and 6), he is using the term in its everyday sense as that of complete understanding, yet suggesting that, unless conceived as dialogue (a frequent concept in his thought), such a possibility is an 'illusion of the reduction of difference to identity' (ibid., 433). Communication in art takes this into account: "La valeur art...dépend essentiellement de cette non-identification, de cette nécessité d'un intermédiaire entre le producteur et le consommateur. Il importe qu'il y ait entre eux une chose irréductible à l'esprit, qu'il n'existe pas une communication immédiate, et que l'œuvre, ce médium, ne puisse apporter à celui qu'elle touche de quoi se réduire à une idée de la personne et de la pensée de l'auteur' ('Réflexions sur l'art', quoted by Jean Hytier, op. cit., 240).

6 Valéry's *Cahiers* were published in facsimile in 29 volumes by the C.N.R.S. from 1957–61. A classified anthology has more recently been compiled and edited by Judith Robinson in the series 'Bibliothèque de la Pléiade': *Paul Valéry, Cahiers I*, 1973 and *Cahiers II*, 1974 (quoted here in the form of 'C i' and 'C ii' only when reference is made to 'passages inédits').

7 E.g. *'L'homme du fini* – /C'est moi. Celui qui enveloppe le *tout*, les *touts*, sachant que le fonctionnement exige que les *touts* soient traitables, et enfin traités, comme *parties*' (xiv, 322). 'Sensibilité' is Valéry's term for the wider 'possible' set of mental relationships of both 'intellect' and 'emotion' (different mind/body states of the same phenomenon) and for the consequent oscillation of 'being' and 'knowing' within consciousness itself.

8 Cf. 'Représentation *totale*. B. Utilisation de cette fonction et dressage' (xiv, 868). By association with the training of a horse, the term 'dressage' relates to the notion 'Gladiator' (the name of a famous racehorse), Valéry's ideal of training and developing the natural

257

resources of the mind once it is experienced as a finite organism. The poetic ideal of developing the sensibility 'sur la corde de la voix' – see the quotation central to this study (p. ix) – is directly relevant in this context.

> Cf. 'L'intelligence dirige les divers inconscients qui sont les bêtes sans elle; et elle rien, sans eux: identiquement rien. [...] Le cheval ne concevrait pas de franchir des obstacles, et il ne sait pas qu'il les puisse franchir, jusqu'à ce que l'éperon, la voix, les aides, contraignent ce brillant système de muscles à faire ce qu'il n'avait jamais fait' (vi, 603).

We shall meet the motif of the horse again in *La Pythie* and *Au Platane* (see Part II).

9   See Chapter 1, pp. 23–8.

10   See in particular the relevant chapters of J. Robinson's *L'Analyse de l'Esprit dans les Cahiers de Valéry* (Paris, Corti, 1963) and N. Celeyrette-Pietri's *Valéry et le Moi* (Paris, Klincksieck, 1979). Valéry's power to grasp the importance of developments in nineteenth-century mathematics is described by John Amson in *C.P.V.E.*, 233–7. He was particularly concerned with the problem of handling discreteness in a continuous way, and his ability to visualise a function as a single entity comprising all its possible values, enabled him to make use of the increased generality of the theory.

11   Cf. Nicole Celeyrette-Pietri's comment: 'La double affirmation que l'individu récèle la généralité de l'Homo, et qu'on ne peut rien reconnaître qu'à partir de la référence/Moi fonde la recherche psychologique et le rapport à l'écriture' (ibid., 367).

12   Cf. N. Bastet, 'L'expérience de la Borne et du Dépassement chez Valéry', *C.P.V.*, i, 59–90. By conveying the will to express in the face of the impossibility of understanding, poetry might be said to accept and make use of the inevitable centre of the Self in the 'miroir parlant' of desire: 'Le MOI est la réponse instantanée de chaque incohérence partielle qui est excitant' (P ii, 69); 'Ce qui n'est pas *moi* – devenir *moi*' (iii, 483).

13   In the context of a theory of communication, see Anthony Wilden's chapter 'Montaigne and the Paradoxes of Individualism' (op. cit., 88–109).

14   I have discussed certain creative implications of Valéry's thermodynamic analogies in *Paul Valéry and Maxwell's Demon, natural order and human possibility*, Occasional Papers in Modern Languages, 8 (University of Hull Publications, 1972).

15   Valéry called this random state of the sensibility the 'cours naturel'. This and other mind/body concepts used in the context of the 'Cours de Poétique' are described by Walter Ince in *The Poetic Theory of Paul Valéry*, 56.

16   In *Poetic Drama as Mirror of the Will* (London, Vision Press, 1977), 12, Michael Black suggests that 'the "will" does not necessarily express itself immediately in either words or music: it is very often

internal, silent, non-verbal. Both words and music are in areas immediately adjacent to that central silence, so that expression may then come, as words, or music (or both): but it may also come as bodily movement or dance or pictorial art or any other expressive form.' The idea of gesture was very important to Valéry and he frequently considers these further expressive forms: theatre, the physical gestures of a speaker, the dance, the Guignol, and so on. Although poetry has a privileged rôle in revealing the nature of that 'central silence', it was still important for him to relate language itself to gesture: 'Le langage articulé verbal part du geste – et l'exige *une fois pour toutes*' (xxiii, 807); 'Le verbe est acte de celui qui parle' (viii, 77). I shall suggest that it is the specific nature of the verbal that emerges most strikingly from Valéry's thought, not its commensurability with other expressive forms.

17   See J. Robinson, *L'Analyse de l'Esprit*, 9–27. For comparison between Valéry and Wittgenstein see R. Piétra, 'Valéry, Wittgenstein et la philosophie', *B.E.V.*, 20 mars 1979, 47–65.

18   A. Rey, 'Sens et discours poétique', *P.V.C.*, 39–48. For discussion of Valéry's contribution to linguistics see J. Schmidt-Radefeldt, 'Valéry et les sciences du langage' (*B.E.V.*, 8 jan. 1976, 16–33), and *Paul Valéry, Linguiste dans les Cahiers* (Paris, Klincksieck, 1970).

19   Compare with the approach to language of the language-philosopher John Searle (*Speech Acts*, Cambridge, Cambridge University Press, 1969). In both cases, refusal to reify language enables emphasis to be placed on the intentional action of the mind – determined by but not confined to the forms of its exchange – and for the written to be approached in terms of the same intentionality as the spoken (see conclusion). Valéry would have approved of Michel Deguy's comment 'La langue est affaire trop sérieuse pour être abandonnée aux linguistes' (quoted by Henri Meschonnic in his preface to *Poèmes, 1960–1970*, Paris, Gallimard, 1973).

20   T. Todorov, 'La "poétique" de Valéry', *C.P.V.*, i, 125–32.

21   *Yggdrasill*, lx–xxxiv, 25 déc. 1937–fév. 1939 – notes taken by Georges Le Breton during part of Valéry's lectures (for the first lecture, see P i, 1340–58). In 1939–40 Valéry seems to have been particularly concerned with the function of inner language and its relationship to self-awareness and intellectual creativity.

22   Valéry does not refer here to Saussure's now famous *Cours de Linguistique Générale* of 1913, but to Michel Bréal's *Essai de Sémantique* (1897).

23   In many other ways Valéry's thought is similar to that of I. A. Richards, particularly on the relation of the aesthetic to the psychophysiological (cf. W. Ince, *The Poetic Theory of Paul Valéry* [Leicester University Press, 1961], 48–50).

24   Valéry's refusal to be manœuvred by language – 'ne pas me laisser manœuvrer par le langage' (xxiii, 221) – still allows the public conventions of language a major rôle in its own 'destructuring'.

25   *Écrits* (Paris, 1966). For a stimulating account see Malcolm Bowie's

essay in *Structuralism and Since, From Levi-Strauss to Derrida*, ed.
J. Sturrock (Oxford University Press, 1979), 116–53.

26 Valéry's notion of 'Being' can be compared with that of Heidegger,
but also strongly contrasted (see p. 248). In relation to the notion that
'man is dead' and that it is 'language which speaks us', see P. Kurz,
*Language and Human Nature, A French–American Philosopher's
Dialogue* (St Louis, Mo., Warren H. Green, Inc., 1971) – including
Derrida's 'The Ends of Man' (180–206). It is noteworthy that Derrida
– whose notion of voice I shall contrast with that of Valéry (p. 249) –
has recently crossed swords with the 'illocutionist' language philosopher John Searle (see n. 19, above) (*Glyph*, John Hopkins Textual
Studies, 1, 2).

27 Significantly, André Breton relates 'écriture automatique' to lack
of sound in inner speech ('Le message automatique', *Point du
Jour* [Paris, Gallimard, 1970], 167, quoted by M. Lechantre in
'(P(h)o(n)étique', *C.P.V.*, I, 104). A comparison with the theoretical
implications of Nathalie Sarraute's technique of 'sous conversation'
would reveal, in my opinion, essential but far less radical differences.

28 See F. Jameson, *The Prison-House of Language* (Princeton, N.J.,
Princeton University Press, 1974).

29 Cf. the final lines of *La Pythie*: 'Et sonner cette auguste Voix/Qui se
connaît quand elle sonne/N'être plus la voix de personne/Tant que
des ondes et des bois' (P I, 136). Valéry's the ' "Moi pur" est le
Zéro [. . .] qui n'est pas *rien*' (XXI, 62) can be compared with the 'moi
zérologique' of Kristeva and Barthes.

30 For Barthes, the writable ('scriptible') text, as opposed to the readable
('lisible') work is one where the reader enjoys the pleasure of production by having been led to mimic the processes by which the text
was written.

31 Amongst the writings of Barthes which helped give rise to this
fashionable notion are *Le Degré zéro de l'écriture* (Paris, 1953);
Essais Critiques (Paris, 1964); *S/Z.* (Paris, 1970); *Le Plaisir du Texte*
(Paris, 1973).

32 Valéry's use of the action of speech as a model by no means implies
that poetry imitates the language of ordinary speech. Deliberately
stylised, the discourse of poetry achieves the appearance of naturalness
where ordinary language is at a far remove from the 'natural'. It is
thus at a far remove from Flaubert's 'beau style' (which Valéry felt
to be based on a contradiction). His often aggressive writings on the
novel can perhaps best be read as a re-emphasis of his poetic theory
by contrast.

33 See G. Genette, 'Vers une poétique' in *Les Critiques de notre temps
et Valéry* (Paris, Garnier, 1971).

34 The Rousseauesque paradox of freedom as constraint is treated partly
in relation to language by Felicity Baker in 'La Route contraire',
Reappraisals of Rousseau, Studies in honour of R. A. Leigh (Manchester, Manchester University Press, 1980), 133–62.

35 'La richesse d'une œuvre est le nombre des sens ou des valeurs

qu'elle peut recevoir tout en demeurant elle-même' *Vues* [Paris, La Table Ronde, 1948], 357).

36 See the chapter 'Consciousness, emotion and the nature of love' in C. Crow, *Paul Valéry: Consciousness and Nature* (Cambridge, Cambridge University Press, 1972), 48–65 and P.-O. Walzer, 'Fragments d'esthésique', *A.J.F.S.*, 230–42.

37 '*Charmes*: Il faut me lire comme on danse' – quoted by Nicole Celeyrette-Pietri from a MS of *Charmes* (op. cit., 351). Cf. In *Philosophie de la Danse*: 'Cette résonance, comme tout autre, se communique: une partie de notre plaisir de spectateurs est de se sentir gagnés par les rythmes et virtuellement dansants nous-mêmes' (P ɪ, 1400). Barthes and the pleasure of creative reading may not be so far away after all.

38 Whether the Structuralists' championing of Mallarmé is fair would be the subject of another book. Is his polyvalence so open-ended or do his symbols contain the drama of polyvalence? Is the voice of language proposed as the voice of the universe or the voice of an individual's creative perception of Beauty?

39 Quoted from a Cahier of 1942 by Régine Piétra, op. cit., *B.E.V.*, mars 1979, 62.

1 Poetic development

1 See in particular the introduction compiled by Agathe Rouart-Valéry for the Pléiade edition of Valéry's collected works.

2 The influence of Rimbaud is less central to the thesis of this book. The reader is referred to general studies of Valéry's work for suggestions on his mathematical and architectural reading and interests. The subject of ornamentation (Valéry had read Owen Jones' *Grammar of Ornament*) also inspired his imagination as a means of linking the abstract principles of mathematics and the natural principles of plant growth, both models in poetic composition. 'Il est remarquable que les mathématiques ont de commun avec la poésie et la musique que chez elles – le *fond* devient l'*acte* de la forme' (xv, 881).

3 Examples can be found in the section 'Poèmes et PPA [Petits Poèmes Abstraits]' of *Paul Valéry: Cahiers II* and in 'Poésie brute' (P ɪ, 351–9). See also the many prose poems in Jean Hytier's notes (P ɪ, 1718–31), where there is also invaluable information on the place of publication of poetic works other than those of *Album de Vers Anciens*. Concentration on the poems of *Charmes* has precluded study here of this major aspect of Valéry's poetic works. The reader's attention is drawn to works by U. Franklin and R. Pickering listed in the Bibliography. See also the introduction to *Poems in the Rough*, trans. H. Corke, *The Collected Works of Paul Valéry*, ed. Jackson Mathews (London, Routledge and Kegan Paul, 1970) and J. Levaillant, *La Jeune Parque et poèmes en prose* (Paris, Gallimard, 1975).

4 See also the chapters 'Nature and imagination', 'Living things',

'Growth and decay' in C. Crow, *Paul Valéry: Consciousness and Nature* (Cambridge, Cambridge University Press, 1972), 69–122.

5 See S. Yeschua, *Valéry, le roman et l'œuvre à faire* (Paris, Lettres Modernes, Minard, 1976) and P. Laurette, *Le Thème de l'Arbre chez Paul Valéry* (Paris, Klincksieck, 1967).

6 On the possible link between the voice theme and 'Mme. R' (p. 24), see N. Celeyrette-Pietri, *Valéry et le Moi*, 341. Cf. the early poem *Le Navire* of 1889 where Valéry wrote: '...Revenant de l'Amour lointain – ainsi mon Âme/Conserve la senteur des rêves d'autrefois,/ Et ne peut oublier une certaine *Voix*' (P I, 1597). 'Voice' in the early poems is an explicit concept designated within the poem (cf. P I, 1579, P I, 1585). Later its presence is diffuse and inexplicit.

7 See p. 91. Cf. the concept of 'Narcisse' fundamental to all Valéry's interests as a poet, and which summarises the sensation that what is seen speaks like a mirror of the Self. 'Entendre parle. La conscience est une bouche qui écoute. Parler écoute. Et là aussi, voir être vu; ce qui est vu, voit, ce qui voit est vu' (VIII, 378). This is the 'confuses paroles' and 'regards familiers' of Baudelaire's *Correspondances* translated into extreme psycho-physiological terms.

8 E.g. the Parque's 'poetic' statement 'Car je tremblais de perdre une douleur divine' can be compared with the following passage in the *Cahiers*:
'Le *diabolique* le plus raffiné [...] consiste dans la profonde peine, la répugnance que cause à la victime l'*idée qu'elle pourra être délivrée de son mal*, par changement de sa sensibilité aux imaginations ou aux constatations qui la causent. *Elle en meurt*, mais croit sentir que ne plus le ressentir *serait ne plus vivre*! elle ne peut se résigner à perdre [...] l'immense valeur de ce dont la perte [...] fut l'origine du mal [...]. Ceci est énorme' (XXIX, 841).
By comparing the tone of the *Cahiers* with the tone of the poem, we can see that the voice of the Parque often coincides with 'le Moi sensible', identification with the inner 'divinity' of that which seems diabolical to the intellect alone. A further study along these comparative lines seems necessary, complementing the important work by Hartmut Köhler in *Paul Valéry Dichtung und Erkenntnis, Das lyrische Werk im Lichte der Tagebücher* (Bonn, Bouvier Verlag Herbert Grundmann, 1976).

9 See S. Yeschua, '"Substitutions" et poétique chez Valéry', *C.P.V.*, I, 133–48.

10 Like 'communication', the term 'expression' must be strongly differentiated from *direct* lyrical transmission of personal feelings.

11 See C. Crow, 'Valéry, poet of "patiente impatience"', *F.M.L.S.*, III (1967), 370–87.

12 See n. 7, above, and N. Celeyrette-Pietri, 'Je Jeu du Je', *P.V.C.* 10–25.

13 See D. Moutote, 'L'égotisme poétique de Valéry dans Charmes', *R.L.M.*, I, 29–48.

14 See p. 16: '[...] j'ai appris du moins la continuité de cette chaîne de tourments [...]' (VIII, 41). I have discussed the important distinction

in Valéry's thought between 'knowing' and 'understanding' in Chapter 3 of *Paul Valéry: Consciousness and Nature*.

15   See P.-O. Walzer, *La Poésie de Valéry* (Genève, Cailler, 1953) (Chapter 3, 'Le Temps des Idoles') and C. Whiting, *Valéry, jeune poète* (Paris, P.U.F., 1960).

16   *Lettres à Quelques-uns, 1839–1943* (Paris, Gallimard, 1952), 40.

17   Where for Mallarmé the poet's task lay in the greater and greater realisation of impersonality in a Work, perfection for Valéry lay in the potential of the mind itself, the poetic work being purely instrumental. Always incomplete by definition, the work would present 'le *possible-à-chaque-instant*' (P I, 1467). What he admired most about Mallarmé's ideal goal was its power to separate intellectual certainty from belief.

18   Valéry's writings on Poe should be read in conjunction with those of Baudelaire and Mallarmé. Details can be found in R. Gibson's anthology *Modern French Poets on Poetry* (Cambridge, C.U.P., 1961).

19   'J'ai posé cette question, il y a plus de 50 ans – *Que peut un homme?* (Teste)', Valéry wrote in 1945, 'Et dans ma pensée cela vint à la suite 1. d'une intensité de ma volonté de conscience de moi;/2. de la remarque que peu ou personne n'allait jusqu'*au bout*... – Certains ont cru que *ce bout pouvait être la mort*' (xxix, 765). That the body is the limiting force of the pure intellect was one of Valéry's deepest intellectual discoveries. Thus, '*Le présent est le sentiment de la permanence de l'organisation du corps*' (viii, 544).

20   Poe's cosmogony appealed to the formalist side of Valéry's imagination in that it made possible a conception of the universe as a reversible thermodynamic system (see N. Celeyrette-Pietri, op. cit., 64–70).

21   See P.-O. Walzer, *La Poésie de Valéry* (Genève, Cailler, 1953).

22   James Lawler describes Valéry's relationship with Mallarmé in *The Poet as Analyst, Essays on Paul Valéry* (Berkeley and Los Angeles, University of California Press, 1974).

23   See in this connection Georges Mounin's 'Mallarmé et le langage', *Europe* (avril–mai, 1976), 10–17. Lloyd Austin reminds us how Mallarmé's alchemical urge is related metaphorically to poetry as the only authentic 'magic'. ('Les moyens de mystère chez Mallarmé et chez Valéry', *C.A.I.E.F.*, [mars 1963], 103–4). Valéry's own 'alchemy' is discussed by Céline Sabbaghe in 'Quelques aspects alchimiques de l'œuvre de Paul Valéry', *B.E.V.*, 18 (juin 1978), 29–48. (Cf. 'Gladiator', Introduction, n. 8.)

24   Rimbaud's revolutionary rhetoric attained for Valéry 'ce point extrême, paroxystique de l'irritation volontaire de la fonction du langage' (*Lettres à Quelques-uns*, 240).

25   Quoted by J. Lawler, *The Poet as Analyst*, 132.

26   The speculative tension of Mallarmé's poetry and its ability to create doubt is explored, however, by Malcolm Bowie in *Mallarmé and the Art of Being Difficult* (C.U.P., 1948). See also *Ode Secrète*, p. 222 ff.

27   Images of whiteness and sterility seem to occur more in a 'scriptural' than a 'vocal' poetics. The graphic dimension of Mallarmé's *Coup de*

Dés nonetheless caused Valéry an excitement which he expresses by a synaesthesia of sound and vision: 'murmures, insinuations, tonnerre pour les yeux' (P i, 624).

28 See Gerald Bruns' chapter on Mallarmé in *Modern Poetry and the Idea of Language* (New Haven, Conn., and London, Yale University Press, 1974).

29 The poem *Valvins* (P i, 85) is an obvious example of a direct homage (Valvins was Mallarmé's home, where the two poets often rowed together on the river, perhaps inspiring *Le Rameur*). The resonance of Mallarmé's vocabulary can be found throughout Valéry's poetry (see P. Guiraud, *Index du vocabulaire du symbolisme*, vol. ii. *Index des mots de poésies de Paul Valéry* [Paris, Klincksieck, 1953]).

30 See J. Lawler, op. cit., 127. Hearing Mallarmé reading *Un Coup de Dés*, Valéry wrote '[. . .] il se mit à lire d'une voix basse, égale, sans le moindre "effet", presque à soi-même. . ./J'aime cette absence d'artifices. La voix humaine me semble si belle intérieurement, et prise au plus près de sa source [. . .]' (P i, 623). This low voice, the contrary of the Homeric epic where the voice thunders, may be compared with that of Monsieur Teste (P ii, 18–19) (see C. Crow, '"Teste parle": a study of the potential artist in Valéry's M. Teste', *Y.F.S.*, 44 [1970], 157–68). An idea of Valéry's own quiet reading voice can be gained from the record 'Leur œuvre et leur voix', Disques Festival, FLD, 81. Mallarmé's poetry is nonetheless 'tonnerre pour les yeux' (see n. 27).

31 The quotation begins with Valéry's salutation to Wagner for accomplishing 'le vrai Poème – dans lequel la claire vue et conscience du problème de l'action de l'art [. . .] s'allie aux ressources naturelles, s'alimente de l'énergie de la vie passionnée'. But see Chap. 2, n. 28.

32 The not insignificant influence of Heredia on Valéry's poetry is discussed by Walter Ince in 'Valéry et Heredia', *C.P.V.E.*, 119–37.

33 The double urge of the artist towards submission to reality and towards the transfiguration of reality is noted by Alison Fairlie in 'Flaubert et la conscience du réel', *Essays in French Literature*, 4, November 1967, 3.

34 Studies of the geneses and variants of Valéry's poems are listed in the Bibliography under Austin, Ireland, Pratt, de Lussy, Nadal, Lawler.

35 See, J. Robinson, *L'Analyse de l'Esprit*, 'Foi et mysticisme', 200–16 and W. Ince, 'Être, connaître et mysticisme du réel', *E.N.C.*, 205.

36 Lucienne Cain reports that Valéry considered this poem ' "entièrement symboliste", entendant par là, suivant une des rares définitions qu'il ait données de ce mot, que, plutôt que d'imposer en elle un "état d'âme", elle incitait le lecteur à "créer" le sien, quel qu'il fût' (*Trois Essais sur Paul Valéry* [Paris, Gallimard, 1958], 36).

37 See the notes to *Paul Valéry : Œuvres*, vol. i, 1527–718.

38 A. Fairlie, *Baudelaire : Les Fleurs du Mal* (Edward Arnold [1960], 1972), 1.

39 See Bruce Pratt's study of 'Les premiers états de la Jeune Parque': *Rompre le Silence* and *Le Chant du Cygne* (Paris, Corti, 1976, 1978).

2 Poetic theory

1 See in particular the rich and indispensable studies by J. Hytier, *La Poétique de Valéry* (Paris, Armand Colin, 1953) and by W. Ince, *The Poetic Theory of Paul Valéry – Inspiration and Technique* (Leicester University Press, 1961).

2 Valéry's meditations on the rôle of consciousness can be fruitfully compared with those of Karl Popper and John Eccles in *The Self and its Brain* (Berlin, Heidelberg, New York, Springer International, 1977). For Popper, conscious and intelligent activity has a biological function related to the integrative and adaptive evolutionary needs of the organism. For Valéry, too, consciousness maintains the *status* of an epiphenomenon while still being dependent on the physical brain of which it is a function. He would seem, however, to interrelate 'Corps', 'Esprit' and 'Monde' very differently from Popper's World One, Two and Three.

3 'La personne qui parle est déjà autre que moi – et je suis fait autre qu'elle, par cela seul que cette *personne qui parle m*'engendre *personne qui entend*' (xx, 15). Valéry is often concerned with the pathological conditions through which can be glimpsed the inverse of the balance of faculties necessary for self-identity. Loss of the power to identify with the strangeness of one's voice is conveyed in *La Pythie*, whereas in *La Jeune Parque* an overall awareness recognises and examines the sensation of division ('Qui parle...?'). Cf. Rimbaud's famous 'Je est un autre.'

4 Cf. M. Lechantre, 'L'hiéroglyphe intérieur', *M.L.N.*, 633; 'Valéry bouchoreille', *Le Langage et l'Homme*, 18, 1972, 49–53, and 'L'analyse du langage: le Moi Bouchoreille' in N. Celeyrette-Pietri, *Valéry et le Moi*, 298–303.

5 Valéry notices how during the 'phénomène étrange de l'extériorisation' of the action of speech 'on franchit un seuil imperceptible et dès lors l'air vibre' (iii, 483), an image kept in *Palme*. External speech differs from the 'secret' inner one by virtue of conventions of association and co-ordination which subject it to their greater solidity and binding power (to the detriment of its lightness and speed). To preserve the inner impulse without losing the advantages of convention, the poet is advised not to bound too impetuously from inner idea to outer form.

6 See J. Schmidt-Radefeldt, *Paul Valéry linguiste dans les Cahiers* (Paris, Klincksieck, 1970).

7 In psychology, this sense of bodily totality is known as 'cœnesthesia', a general sense of existence arising from the sum of bodily impressions. Its apparent lack in children deprived of social contact (e.g., the wild boy of Aveyron) suggests that it is dependent on the same sense of self that is related to the birth of inner language (xxvii, 393). The distinction between merely living and consciously existing is a central one in Valéry's poetic theory, precisely because of the relation between

language and 'le sentiment que nous avons d'une substance, de notre présence' (P ɪ, 927).

8 Communication by speech is one of the most demanding interdisciplinary subjects, requiring a knowledge of anatomy, physiology, physics, psychology and linguistics (see P. Denes and E. Pinson, *The Speech Chain – the Physics and Biology of Spoken Language* [New York, Anchor Books, 1973]). With his Leonardo-like imagination, Valéry might be said to have spanned all these approaches to some degree. His main strength lies in their integration in that area of communication related to consciousness in its most specifically human form.

9 Valéry was immensely sensitive to sound. He considered that it related to a fundamental level of our being, 'l'âme instant'. For a comprehensive study of this whole area of his poetry and thought the reader is referred to the article and forthcoming thesis by Kirsteen Anderson (see Preface, n. 9).

10 'N + S – Qu'un simple son, ou timbre de son, *émeuve*... Qu'une certaine émotion cherche dans telle note grave, dans l'attitude phonomusculaire qu'elle détermine – son acte et sa *vérité* [...] que *la toute-puissance soit toujours irrationnelle*' (xvɪ, 101). The rubric 'N + S' ('nombres plus subtils') was Valéry's shorthand term for the mysterious relation between sensation and sentiment, formal and significant (ɪ, 467) – 'Poésie' – which his conception of poetry as an art of language is designed to exploit. It is thanks to this conception that, however specific, the 'monde à part' or aesthetic state achieved in the poem is not isolated from the organism in its natural capacities.

11 'Un poète [...] n'a pas pour fonction de ressentir l'état poétique: ceci est une affaire privée. Il a pour fonction de le créer chez les autres' (P ɪ, 1321).

12 '*Toute sensation éveille une virtualité*, un implexe que j'appelle *harmonique*' (xxɪx, 50). Cf. W. Ince, '"Infini esthétique" et poésie selon Valéry', *Poétique et Communication*, 69–81.

13 In that the reader also 'dances' (see p. 261, n. 37), poetry involves the integration of our mental faculties. See *L'Âme et la Danse* (P ɪɪ, 148–76).

14 *Œuvres Complètes* (Paris, Gallimard [Bibliothèque de la Pléiade], 1951), 368.

15 The image of the lyre is also used in relation to love, from which Valéry thought it possible to construct, as in poetry, a human masterpiece (xxɪv, 239–42). I have suggested the link between love and aesthetic emotion in *Consciousness and Nature* (Cambridge University Press, 1972), 62–5.

16 Valéry mentions in this connection his famous predilection for the mute 'e': 'En tant que poète je suis spécialiste des sons: é, è, ê, C'est assez curieux' (see M. Gauthier, 'L'architecture Phonique du Langage Poétique dans la poésie de Valéry', *P.V.C.*, 377–97). I shall return to the question of favoured sound-patterns when discussing *La Jeune Parque* (p. 81).

17 Passage inédit, Cahier L, 1911, p. 11 (Quoted by Claude Valéry,

'Valéry, le Langage et la Pensée', *Poétique et Communication*, 13–21).

18 'Que de résonances, que d'échos, que de battements, que d'harmoniques dans cet empire!' (C i, 396). Cf. the humorous description 'Bouche' in which Valéry evokes the cavernous home of the voice (P i, 323) or, less humorously, the horrors of the blocked nasal passage when thought wishes to be free, yet moves within this contingency (vi, 824). We shall see in relation to *Poésie* (p. 144) how the mouth becomes almost a synonym of inspiration, while in *Aurore* (p. 124) the creative sensibility is an 'Universelle oreille'. Ears are 'ces entremetteuses aux portes de l'esprit' (P ii, 85).

19 E.g. 'Il me semble que l'âme bien seule avec elle-même, et qui se parle, de temps à autre, entre deux silences *absolus*, n'emploie jamais *qu'un petit nombre de mots*, et *aucun d'extraordinaire*' (P i, 453).

20 See the chapter on 'Maturation and poetic composition' in C. Crow, *Consciousness and Nature*, 177–215.

21 The notion of restraint is vital to Valéry's conception of poetry. 'Les œuvres à grandes contraintes exigent et engendrent la plus grande liberté d'esprit' (x, 731). Together with its further elaboration in 'formes fixes', rhyme is one of the most striking means by which fluidity and stability are imposed, and Valéry approaches the subject with a cavalier disrespect for the popular notion that rhyme should always serve an idea, or that an idea is necessarily deeper than a convention (P i, 1452). 'Formes fixes' serve the function of alerting and training a mental animal whose blood is semantically and formally one and the same (ix, 576).

22 See M. Gauthier, 'La décomposition poétique du mot', *Poétique et Communication*, 241–59. Where the function of ordinary language might be said to be to bring words together, Valéry diffuses or displaces the syntactical functions of words so that the outer, unifying voice of the poem contains a multiplicity of distances. The function of sound is thus to bind with pure relations syntactic and semantic elements which are at the same time held in abeyance. Cf. 'Presque tout le grand art est de créer du temps, – du retard gros de substance émotive (qui doit être réduite ou compenseé par voie rythmique –)' (xiv, 427). A poetry of voice is based on the maximum diffusion of meaning and the maximum conservation of form.

23 For examples in *La Jeune Parque*, see p. 81.

24 On the interpretation of semantic and structural values Valéry writes 'La musique verbale (vers et rythme) entraine la quasi-nécessité d'introduire (*car elle le fait désirer*) dans le "contenu" (le signifié – le substitué φ) des relations d'idées "harmoniques" – des complémentaires, des symétriques, etc. [...] Le *sens* ici veut les qualités du *signe*' (xxviii, 414). A major part of my study of the poems (Part ii) will be devoted to suggesting how certain themes are generated by the form of the poem, thus making visible the expressive action by which meaning is articulated.

25 Cf. 'La puissance des vers tient à une harmonie *indéfinissable* entre ce qu'ils *disent* et ce qu'ils *sont*. "Indéfinissable" entre dans la

définition [...] L'impossibilité – ou du moins la difficulté, – de définir cette relation, combinée avec l'impossibilité de la nier, constitue l'essence du vers' (VII, 151). The combination of analytic procedures with recognition and use of the 'undefinable' (cf. 'l'ineffable') constitutes one of the greatest strengths of Valéry's poetic theory and practice.

26 Cf. La Voix. L'Échange de signaux avec l'Autre *devient partie intégrante du Même* – s'y développe. Le *langage intérieur crée un Autre dans le Même*' (XXIV, 321). In reading we hear another's voice inside us as our own. These natural 'facts' of language use are accentuated by Valéry poetically, so that we become aware of them and their power is increased.

27 The idea was Mallarmé's, but Valéry adapted it (P I, 1272).

28 See p. 38, n. 31. Valéry makes the following qualification, however: 'Du moment que R.W...a organisé les moyens d'agir, ad libitum sur le système nerveux général par sa musique sans inertie – c'est-à-dire où les changements s'introduisent indépendemment les uns des autres [...] comme dans un système vivant – il faut aller plus loin et faire de cette musique, le langage, mais langage du système nerveux' (IV, 206).
Compare with his famous saying that the greatest possible poet is the nervous system (P I, 335).

29 See *La Jeune Parque* (chapter 3).

30 Because it can accentuate the 'irrational' power of sound to stir the emotions, the 'charm' of poetry is sometimes linked to 'black' magic (XVII, 678). Perhaps Valéry is also holding in mind the power of art to establish a lost source as real: 'On l'oublie et il n'en reste que le sentiment d'un degré dont la vie ne peut jamais approcher' (IV, 587). From a need 'vers 91' to create a state of enchantment 'sans référence au *réel*' (XVIII, 281), he moves nearer the goal of communication through exchange.

31 Cf. 'En toute chose, il faut trouver la *Musique des actes*, et, elle *rencontrée* – tout chante et se fait merveilleusement' (XII, 657).

32 Quoted by J. Hytier, *La Poétique de Valéry*, 215–16.

33 'Poésie' is thus related to a state 'antérieur à l'écriture et à la critique' (P I, 651). 'Poésie' is not to be confused with poetic discourse, however, a highly elaborate *written* form. I shall return to the question of the written and the spoken in the Conclusion.

34 Composing *La Jeune Parque*, Valéry became interested in an account of the diction of the actress Rachel which gave him insight into the relationship between physiology and melody (see J. Lawler, *Lecture de Valéry, une étude de "Charmes"* [Paris, P.U.F., 1963], 9). *La Jeune Parque* was to be 'presque une seule phrase, longue et pour contralto' (P I 1629).

35 The quietness of this voice can be compared with that of Mallarmé (see Chapter 1 n. 30). In direct contrast to poetic voice as declamation, poetry is thus linked to the interiority of 'la voix subjective' (XXVI, 382). It is characteristic of the obliqueness of deep emotion with its

corresponding art of understatement that it should be the music of
the *speaking* voice which reminds Valéry most of the emotion engendered by the singer and which he takes as his poetic model.
'La *voix* est l'instrument pathétique et dramatique par excellence./Fait
sentir entre les extrêmes de son registre, le niveau normal [...]'
(xix, 885).

36   '[...] En quoi le parlé se distingue du chant? Ici grand sujet pour
la diction des vers' (xix, 471). Like Rousseau in the *Dictionnaire de la
Musique*, Valéry answers the question by pointing to the characteristic
power of the singing voice to form appreciable sounds joined by
harmonic intervals, whereas in the speaking voice, sounds are not
sufficiently single to be appreciated (see M. Dœuff, 'Le philosophe
dans le gosier', *La Quinzaine Littéraire*, 284 [1–3 aout, 1978] special
number devoted to *La Musique, le Mot, la Voix*). '*Alors le rythme
[...]* les actes en liaison – en loi – d'où sensation de *prévision,
d'attente* [...]. Le chanteur tout entier est modification d'une colonne
d'air, mais colonne continue et modifications claires – Attentif à cette
colonne, fluide invisible, – porteur respectueux, support de ce courant
d'air' (viii, 421). Despite his mention of 'poètes ténors' and 'poètes
contr'alto' (x, 31), however (his own preference being for the contralto
tone), Valéry insists that the voice of poetry should contain the
instantaneous, non-analytic quality of speech as well as the continuity of song.

37   Tone is of vital importance in Valéry's poems, the unifying factor of
all the different aspects of style (xv, 46) and the means by which the
speaker adapts to his 'parole-pensée' (vii, 21). 'Le *ton* de la voix est
la signification d'une attitude par le rythme et par les intensités et les
mesures' (vii, 164). Tone is thus a means of simulating personality
within the impersonality of poetic discourse.

38   For a general study of the 'poésie pure' debate to which Valéry con-
tributed so much, see D. Mossop, *Pure Poetry. Studies in French
Poetic Theory and Practice: 1746–1945* (Oxford University Press,
1971).

39   Of his favourite writer, Racine, Valéry writes '[...] éprouvez à loisir,
écoutez jusqu'aux harmoniques les timbres de Racine, les nuances, les
reflets réciproques de ses voyelles [...] les liens souples de ses con-
sonnes et de leurs ajustements. Et donc et surtout, ne vous hâtez point
d'accéder au sens' (P ii, 1258). He even proposed that the quality of
Racine's voice could be reconstructed from his verse.

40   Valéry's writings on style are extremely far-reaching and very often
connected with the special characteristics of the author's use of voice.
He writes, for example, 'La poésie résulte d'une turgescence d'une
tonalisation de la voix articulée, dans toutes ses propriétés phoniques
et psychiques et motrices et ses modes résultent d'une analyse très
subtile de cette voix et de ses effets' (x, 858); 'Le style est la marque
du ton dans la façon de l'œuvre' (xv, 46).

41   Metaphor represents a 'multiformité du changement possible' (iii,
244) and as his reason for not abusing it, Valéry states that 'Entre

autre choses interdites, je n'ai voulu jouer sur la surprise systématique, ni sur l'emportement éperdu, car il me paraissait que c'était réduire les effets d'un poème à l'éblouissement de l'esprit sans atteindre et satisfaire sa profondeur.'

42 I.e. the notion of 'écart' as introducing order.

43 His own and Mallarmé's poetry is seen as empty only if one is 'un esprit *à la moderne* pour qui (conséquence lointaine de Platon et du Christianisme) *esprit* et *corps, fond* et *forme, sens* et *symbole sont* choses 1. *opposées*, 2. *exclusives* l'une de l'autre, 3. non *équivoques*' (xv, 799).

44 The 'provisional' is a literary lesson par excellence:
'Le "devoir" de ne pas croire – c'est-à-dire de n'attacher aux *paroles* venant des autres ou *de soi* (en Soi) qu'une "valeur" provisoire – laquelle, d'ailleurs, est vraie valeur; de ne donner ou consentir aux mots que leurs poids probable d'origine [...]./Rien n'enseigne plus cette nature provisoire que le travail littéraire' (xv, 179).

45 Cf. the prose poem *Amateur de Poèmes*, where Valéry conjures up the effect of the poem on the reader: 'UN poème est une durée, pendant laquelle, lecteur, je respire une loi qui fut préparée; je donne mon souffle et les machines de ma voix; ou seulement leur pouvoir, qui se concilie avec le silence' (P i, 95).

3 *La Jeune Parque*

1 There have been many versatile studies of *La Jeune Parque*. For details, see Bibliography under Chisholm, Duchesne-Guillemin, Laurenti, de Lussy and Sørensen. See also the essays in *Recherches sur "La Jeune Parque"*, *R.L.M.*, série "Paul Valéry" n. 2, sous la direction de Huguette Laurenti, Paris, Minard, 1977.

2 Francis Scarfe has treated a cretain aspect of this subject in *The Art of Paul Valéry: a study in dramatic monologue* (London, William Heinemann Ltd., Glasgow University Publications xcvii, 1954). See also H. Laurenti, 'Les Langages de La Jeune Parque', *B.E.V.*, 6, juillet 1975, 18–30.

3 For the way in which inner monologue relates to the dialectical 'presence' of the Self, see p. 11 and p. 46. To this subject can be added Valéry's comment that 'Le mot Sensation peut tantôt être remplacé par le mot Origine, ou Implusion, ou Présence, ou Intervention, ou Modification' (viii, 41). The modificatory presence of sensation is of great importance as part of the subject-matter conveyed in *La Jeune Parque*.

4 E.g. P i, 1630, P i, 1636.

5 In the course of the time-span evoked in the poem the Parque could be said to wake from sleep, fall asleep and re-awaken. The poem joins the poetry of sleep explored in *Agathe* (P ii, 1388–92).

6 It is not difficult to see how Valéry's own experience of '1892' pro-

vided much of the material of the poem. Fear of the real mental energy generated by the imaginary intensified for Valéry as it does for the Parque the natural safety-valve of thought (xviii, 105).

7   I have treated certain aspects of the swan theme – connected only superficially with the theme of a lover – in ' "Le silence au vol de cygne": Baudelaire, Mallarmé, Valéry and the flight of the swan', *Baudelaire, Mallarmé, Valéry: New Essays in Honour of Lloyd Austin*, ed. M. Bowie, A. Fairlie and A. Finch (Cambridge University Press, 1982).

8   See C. Crow, 'Valéry and the Image of the Tree-top', *Sensibility and Creation, Studies in Twentieth-Century French Poetry*, ed. R. Cardinal (London Croom Helm Ltd., 1977).

9   Only those of us without the habit of self-awareness will find the poem clear, says the Parque to her philosopher. 'Les plus profonds humains, incompris de soi-mêmes,/D'une certaine nuit tirent des biens suprêmes/Et les très purs objets de leurs nobles amours./[...]/Un silence est la source étrange des poèmes' (P I, 165).

10 '[...] jouer au plus fin avec ce système étrange', Valéry wrote in 1913 of the relationship between the primitive sympathetic nervous system and the cerebral system,

> 'Passer entre l'excitation et la réponse, ou entre deux réflexes. Tromper ce trompeur dont le cerveau, son fils a fini par se dégouter à demi. Quelle situation! Mythe et drame possibles!...Le cerveau loyal, nu, pas *profond*, toujours trompé par la clarté, cocufié mais honnête – enchaîne à ce serpent ou femme nerveuse – qui en sait plus que lui moins que lui [...] s'alimentant s'aidant et s'entre-tuant...' (v, 11), quoted by Peter Boa – see bibliography.

Such is the drama of 'being' and 'knowing' whose repercussions are staged in the poem as within consciousness as a higher level of 'sensibilité', part to whole.

11 'La plus belle poésie a la voix d'une femme idéale, Mlle Âme' (vi, 170). 'Âme' is Valéry's poetic term for the sensibility.

12 The poet is miraculously 'taken over' by the law he sets in motion: 'De même un enfant finit par donner à son père [...] la forme de la paternité' (vi, 818). This existential discovery will be celebrated in *Palme* where the giver is enriched by the giving of gifts. It is a central part of Valéry's poetic theory of communication.

13 Greatly indebted to J. Levaillant's 'La Jeune Parque en question', *P.V.C.*, 136–51, I still feel that a form of psychological realism is involved *through* 'textuality'. For the psychological is itself treated formally by Valéry. As in music, however, our experience is enlivened by the perception of choice of interpretation.

14 Thinking of the difference between this poem and the two great preceding poems by Mallarmé (*Hérodiade* and *L'Après-Midi d'un Faune*), Valéry suggests that whereas Mallarmé's poems were created by a formal procedure superior to their subject, his own were derived from the intention of making the reader experience 'une connaissance de l'être vivant, qu'il ne suffit pas de reconnaître mais qu'il faut

apprendre' (xxiv, 117). Once more, the emphasis is on the power of the poem to point outside language itself.

15 Valéry often sought to understand certain states of attentiveness through their inverse, the dream state, for instance (see J. Robinson, 'Dreaming and the Analysis of Consciousness in Valéry's Cahiers', *F.S.*, xvi, 2 [April 1962], 101–23, and *C.P.V.*, 3, 'Questions du rêve'). The 'crisis' or transition experience of waking is chosen to convey the essence of self-awareness as a form of self-listening in accommodation to change. Sleep, one of the most extreme phase-changes of consciousness, is chosen to modify the Parque's consciousness at its most intense point of refusal.

16 The thermodynamic notion of a closed system was used by Valéry – like that of the Gnostic symbol 'ouroboros' – to describe the complete poem (as well as conservation of possibility in the context of mental functioning). For more general discussion see N. Bastet, 'Faust et le cycle', *E.N.C.*, 115–28.

17 See J. Levaillant, op. cit.

18 'C'est que Mallarmé recherche toujours l'effet d'orchestre.. comme effet orchestral *L'Après-Midi d'un Faune* me paraît un chef d'œuvre qu'on ne surpassera pas. Pour moi, au contraire, l'unité musicale dans le vers, c'est le son, la voix, le récitatif de Gluck, de Wagner parfois, mais par-dessus de Gluck' (quoted by J. Hytier, *La poétique de Valéry*, 279, n. 2).

19 Cf. P ii, 1257. The considerable influence of Gluck's opera *Orpheus* on *La Jeune Parque* has been studied recently by Pauline Roth-Mascagni in *Musique et Géométrie de Trois Poèmes Valéryens* (Bruxelles, André de Roche Éd., 1979), 13–79. It was not only the Italianate contralto voice which moved Valéry so much, but the art of modulation by which Gluck overcame the convention of an abrupt contrast between melodic aria and dry recitative. To this ideal of musical continuity – '*la ligne de la voix*' (vi, 350) – Valéry brought his own specifically verbal solutions, such as that of relating the themes and 'masses' of the poem by as many links as possible (xiii, 273). Orphic themes and images (e.g. the snake and the 'descente aux enfers') fuse with his own poetry of voice (see above, p. 6).

20 The term 'volume' is used in a poetic context for the depth of relationships through which the reader's voice is to be reached (vii, 6).

21 Pauline Roth-Mascagni distinguishes as sources of modulation metaphors, syntactical figures, rhythm and *leitmotif*. For a more general discussion see Lloyd Austin's 'Modulation and movement in Valéry's verse', *Y.F.S.*, 32.

22 Quoted by W. Ireland in his important study ' "La Jeune Parque", Genèse et Exégèse', *E.N.C.*, 91.

23 A favoured 'étymon euphonique' appears to be the combination 'P', 'R', 'S' as in 'paresse', 'présence,' 'poreuse', 'repose', 'espère', 'esprit' (see M. Gauthier, 'L'architecture phonique dans la poésie de Valéry', *P.V.C.*, 394). Recent study has gone so far as to perceive graphic or visual emblems in the sound architecture (see the daunting

article by J.-P. Chausserie-Laprée, 'Deux figures de la Jeune Parque: une approche architecturale et musicale du texte poétique', *B.E.V.*, 13, mai 1977, 19–31).

24 Mallarmé's different use of sounds is discussed by Malcolm Bowie in *Mallarmé and the Art of Being Difficult* (Cambridge University Press, 1978). See in particular his comments on rhyme. In 'Mallarmé's "Toute l'âme résumée"' (*Neophilologus*, LX, 1976, 364), Anthony Hunt points out that 'There is no question of seeing the sounds of the poem as "inherently" suggestive of particular meanings, but rather of perceiving how the development of ideas and the deployment of sounds are co-extensive and mutually enlightening.' Valéry's sound 'mnemonics' – often confused with 'inherent' meaning in H. Sørensen's study (see Bibliography) – can be said to enlighten the development of ideas only if we see the ideas as figures making visible the sound/sense relationship itself.

25 The whole first unit (to 'extrêmes') is heard as two melodic parts of roughly equal length (9 + 8), articulated by the pivot of 3 + 1; then, with its gentler nasals, the third line composes itself into two symmetrical hemistiches (6 + 6), only the end sounds – 'pleurer' – rising to link back to the beginning and to link forward with the next rhyme.

26 *Œuvres Complètes*, 364.

27 Mental self-presence is increased (see Chapter 2, n. 7) if an image of our bodies is available in our minds, and this is partly the effect of poetic sound. Cf. the humorous lines in *Ébauche d'un Serpent*, 'Ils roulaient depuis le béryl/De ma crête, jusqu'au péril!' (P I, 144) and, at the end of *Aurore*, 'Et frémit depuis l'orteil' (P I, 113). Many of the themes and images in Valéry's poetry seem to make explicit what is happening to the sensibility in the presence of poetic language. Bodily sensations in *La Jeune Parque* are no exception.

28 Valéry referred to *La Jeune Parque* as the 'croissance naturelle d'une fleur artificielle' (P I, 1632) and he reflects frequently on the relationship between 'Passages et modulations – le secret le plus fin de l'art' (XIX, 824) and processes of growth and continuity in nature. He achieves a relationship between 'forme' and 'fond' like that in Baudelaire's 'Thyrse', where the dual principle of the priest's baton – stiff rod and trailing vine leaves – is made an emblem of artistic form.

29 See M. Gauthier, 'La décomposition poetique du mot', *Poétique et Communication*, 241–59.

30 The bond of thirst and source is central to a poetics in which desire is given presence through voice ('Fais que ma soif se fasse source').

31 The vocative imperative is an image of 'le détachement de *moi* de ce corps, ce navire' (IV, 223), Valéry noted. Once more a basic understanding of the mental operations behind language usage invigorates his poetic practice.

32 The reader is referred to Pauline Roth-Mascagni's study (see n. 19, above) for suggestions on the way in which the spiralling movement of consciousness lends its design to the logical and musical composition

of the poem. Present most obviously in the image of the serpent referred to by the Parque as 'Thyrse' [see n. 28, above]), it determines the way in which the major and minor modes of the poem (the urge towards consciousness and death and the urge towards life and being) interrelate in a cyclical rotation never quite closed, 'Succession d'*arc de spire*, réversion sans fin composant l'espace et le temps' (op. cit., 26). We think again of Valéry's reference to 'nœuds' (p. 74).

33 In A. R. Chisholm's view these are processes of 'differentiation' and 'individuation' (*An Approach to 'La Jeune Parque'* [Melbourne University Press, 1938]).

34 See M. and P. Parent, 'Réflexions sur la valeur des motifs de l'eau et du vent dans *la Jeune Parque* et dans *Charmes*', *R.L.M.* ı, 67–102.

35 'Nature, Humanisme, Tragédie' in *Pour un Nouveau Roman* (Paris, Gallimard, N.R.F., 1963).

36 The process of revivification of the physical operations at the roots of abstract words is not so much etymological as physical (see p. 19, 'Inspirations Méditerranéennes'). This in the line 'QUE DANS LE CIEL PLACÉS, MES YEUX TRACENT MON TEMPLE', Valéry allows the Latin association with temples (brow) to come to the surface by association with other parts of the body ('J'ai de mes bras épais environné mes tempes' is in turn a literal gesture from the mental 'comprendre').

37 The famous passage of the slow coming of the tear ('Je n'implorerai plus que tes faibles clartés...') is a poetic exploration of what Valéry calls the 'expulsive' gestures of the organism in the face of the 'ineffable' (to weep or to speak being different ways of restoring equilibrium to the system overpowered by the weight of sensibility in its creative relationship with the world [ııı, 722]). In a comment of great interest from the point of view of the relationship between his poetic principles and those of Rimbaud and Mallarmé, Valéry relates the art of ornamentation (so much a part of the form of *La Jeune Parque*) to the organisation of a superabundance of mental impressions. The *loss* of initial richness turns to gain when this order restimulates the sensibility in its turn (xxvııı, 362).

38 See Sørensen, op. cit., 156, for a complete list of sound words included in the poem.

39 The notion of seeking a lost name in the noise of the sea is referred to by Nicole Celeyrette-Pietri, *Valéry et le Moi*, 301 ('Quelle conque a redit le nom que j'ai perdu?').

40 The relationship of the early drafts of the poem to the important theme of a cry breaking the silence has been studied by Bruce Pratt (see Chapter 1, n. 39). Only partly retained in these lines, yet basic to the whole drama of the poem and its genesis, is the concept of a mysteriously revelatory voice (cf. the poetic cry by which Valéry 'betrayed' the earlier years of silence and distance from emotion). The personal source of the poem is nearer the surface in the earlier drafts, where the voice theme is more frequent (e.g. 'Cette voix transparence' (ibid., 22), 'miroir formé par cette voix – /facile

enfance/secrets/timbre/voix intérieure' (22); 'mon oreille/actuelle/
écoutait' (23); 'Ce timbre m'étonne comme d'un étranger' (23);
'Comme pour mêler les machines de ma voix/A ma pensée' (27); 'mais
si mal retenu/Cette parole née une dernière fois' (27); 'Alors d'un cri
fatal j'ai voûté le silence' (28); 'Encore dans mes os vibre la violence
Du cri dont j'ai plongé le fer dans le silence/Val de toutes mes chairs
au plus haut de ma voix' (95).

41 E.g. *La Jeune Parque commentée par Alain* (Paris, Gallimard, 1953
[1936]).

42 Lloyd Austin writes that '*La Jeune Parque*, like *Le Cimetière Marin*,
is built up on the central interplay between the vision of the absolute
and the realisation of the limits of human existence. Each of these
attitudes is divided into two opposing extremes. The four themes
interpenetrate with a crescendo of enriching modulations, precisely in
the sense of transitions, each of which introduces a new emphasis but
also recalls and modifies the previous themes' (*Y.F.S.*, 32).

43 Quoted by Hartmut Köhler in 'Transparenz und Konsistenz, Ein
Kommentar von La Jeune Parque im Lichte der "Cahiers"', *Paul
Valéry Dichtung und Erkenntnis*, 252.

44 Cf. Teste's 'La première chose est de parcourir son domaine' (P II,
69). The Parque is not the 'female equivalent' of Teste, as we read so
often in commentaries insisting on objectifying a male and female
consciousness. Teste's consciousness provides one tone of the capacities
she represents and he in turn dreams 'Si le moi pouvait "parler"'
[cf. 'Tu es voix de ton inconnu' (P II, 71)].

45 See H. Laurenti, 'Les langages de la Jeune Parque', *B.E.V.*, 6, juillet
1975, 25.

46 In his *Cours de Poétique*, 14 janvier 1938, Valéry noted 'Il y a trois
grands objets: le monde, notre corps, l'esprit. Lorsque s'éveille
l'homme, ces trois grandes masses d'événements se distinguent'. For
Judith Robinson, the rediscovery of identity coincides with the re-
discovery of the separation of the outside world (*L'Analyse de l'Esprit*,
123–4).

47 'Expiant quoi', Valéry wrote of his own emotional suffering at the
time of his play *Mon Faust* (written in the 1940s long after the poem):
'Le crime peut être d'avoir pendant des années exalté de toute ma
sensibilité un sentiment, élevé de toutes mes forces jusqu'au zénith de
l'absurde un monument de tendresse sous toute la masse, tout d'un
coup me tombe sur ma vie' (*B.E.V.*, 10, juillet 1976, 5 [Collection
Carlton Lake]). James Lawler suggests how closely the tears in the
poem were connected with Mallarmé's death (*The Poet as Analyst*,
148).

48 'La voix est à la poésie sa lumière' (VII, 6); 'Comme la lumière est le
fait essentiel en peinture [...] ainsi la voix est le fait essentiel en
poésie. La poésie est *dans* la voix comme des objets dans la lumière'
(XXIX, 174). The scientific description of light as either wave-motion
or a stream of particles is present analogically in Valéry's poetic
theory (e.g. XVI, 237; XVII, 66). So rich is the analogical field in

La Jeune Parque, that the islands could be said to be bathed in the 'light' of her own voice.

49   Cf. Valéry's frequent descriptions of bird-song as a form of gratuitous energy: '[...] ainsi l'Oiseau, jusque dans sa voix, est plus libre de ce qui le touche' (P ɪɪ, 660). The voice is an 'équilibre mobile', a spinning top both 'soutien et propagation' (xxɪx, 150): a possibility deeply and consciously reflected in poetic form as the harmonisation of separate details (effective yet transparent).

50   Quoted by Hartmut Köhler, op. cit., 276.

51   Cf. a comment headed 'Eros' where Valéry writes 'Il était parti pour franchir...et il est vaincu, consolé, inondé de volupté [...] Mais quel but était celui de son être? Quel extrême? quel suicide?' (P ɪɪ, 752). The parallel between 'Eros' and consciousness with its 'soif de désastres' allows us to see how the sexual and erotic motifs in the poem relate to the drama of the mind. At the same time the sexual elements in the poem – which Valéry described as 'surajouté' – are designed to soften ('attendrir') its intellectual tone (P ɪ, 1630).

52   For the poet this state corresponds to one of emotional freedom, 'le jour de céder à son cœur', while the work 'looks back at its author as if his thought fades with it: 'Ce que je pensais, mes images demeurant les mêmes ne sont plus regardées de moi, mais me regardent...' (vɪ, 195).

53   The notion of the difficult as opposed to obscure poem is discussed by Malcolm Bowie in *Mallarmé and the Art of Being Difficult* (Cambridge University Press, 1978).

54   Cf. 'Qui donc es-tu? – Je suis la Personne qui Parle! Celle qu'on nomme JE, et qui, de corps en corps, de visage en visage et même en toute vie/forme, a le moment pour acte et ne sait faire qu'Être' (xxɪx, 54).

55   Adapted from the remark by Lacan quoted by Barthes in *Fragments d'un discours amoureux* (Paris, Éditions du Seuil, 1977). *La Jeune Parque* brings alive a multiplicity of insights about the nature of language which have their echoes in contemporary terminology, the 'fiction' of Self in particular. At the same time it could be said that the unificatory action of poetry interests him most: e.g. 'Poésie est formation par le corps et l'esprit en union créatrice de ce qui convient à cette union et l'excite ou la renforce./Est poétique tout ce qui provoque, restitue cet état *unitif*' (xɪ, 289).

4   *Charmes – L'Abeille – Aurore*

1   *Lettres à Quelques-uns,* 184.

2   P ɪ, 1654. The text reproduced by Jean Hytier and quoted here is that of 1933 (reproduced in the edition of *Charmes* of 1941). The 1922 text is the basis of Charles Whiting's edition *Paul Valéry: Charmes ou Poèmes,* Athlone French Poets (London, The Athlone Press, 1973).

3   Quoted by James Lawler in *Lecture de Valérv: une étude de 'Charmes'* (Paris, P.U.F., 1963), 12.

4 J. Lawler's study (ibid.) makes detailed use of the manuscripts of *Charmes*. See also Lloyd Austin's work on the genesis of *Le Cimetière Marin* (Bibliography).

5 In 1921, Valéry wrote (partly in Greek) 'Tu m'as imprimé avec une force infinie cette importance du corps que l'analyse de mon esprit avait peu à peu constituée et que j'avais poussée, moi vivant toujours en esprit jusqu'à la percevoir dans le pur intellect' (VIII, 862), quoted by Nicole Celeyrette-Pietri, *Valéry et le Moi* (Paris, Klincksieck, 1979), 378. Earlier he noted 'Ce paradoxe, le mien, de subir une espèce de poète, en somme, en moi; et de posséder à un degré singulier le sentiment du fonctionnement' (V, 131).

6 Jean Hytier reproduces differently disposed tables of contents in which 'on a cru parfois discerner l'intention de distinguer entre *poèmes* (en romain) et *poésies* (en italique)' (P I, 1652).

7 The controversy is described by Lloyd Austin in 'Modulation and movement in Valéry's verse', *Y.F.S.*, 44, n. 21. Émilie Noulet partially defends her original hypothesis of the birth of a poem (*Paul Valéry* [*Études*] [Brussels, 1951]) in '"Aurore", essai d'exégèse', *R.L.M.*, I, 104. Valéry explicitly denied the *thematic* architecture of *Charmes* (XIV, 768).

8 Valéry goes on to suggest that the justification of such rhythms would constitute the true analysis of *Charmes* – an approach adopted by Jacques Duchesne-Guillemin in *Études pour un Paul Valéry* (Neuchâtel, La Baconnière, 1964).

9 See Alison Fairlie, *Baudelaire: Les Fleurs du Mal*, Studies in French Literature, 6 (London, Edward Arnold, 1972 [1960]).

10 E.g. *Commentaires de Charmes* (P I, 1512).

11 In the 1922 edition (see P I, 1652).

12 'Faust IV – la lettre' (C II, 1608). Valéry's play *Mon Faust* was unfinished and there are many notes for a further act (e.g. the moving passage on tenderness as the mute exchange of two 'unknowns' beyond all possessive glories [P II, 1413–14]).

13 Cf. the poem 'Abeille Spirituelle' or 'Ambroisie' (P I, 1694–5). ('Ambroise' was Valéry's middle name.)

14 See C. Crow, *Paul Valéry: Consciousness and Nature* (Cambridge University Press, 1972), 95–101 ('The insect').

15 See Valéry's admiring essay on the poetic craft of La Fontaine: *Au sujet d'Adonis* (P I, 474–95).

16 E.g. *L'Âme et la Danse* (P II, 151); *Ébauche d'un serpent* (P I, 143).

17 Valéry has still chosen a heavier line for *L'Abeille* than the rapid pentasyllable of *Le Sylphe* (with its 'Le temps d'un sein nu...') and the rhyme scheme makes it more the Elizabethan sonnet than the light rondeau. Many phonic elements in *L'Abeille* break down this stability, however, in particular the 'vocal' elements which override the classical exterior. For detailed analysis, see Michel Malherbe, '"L'Abeille", poème euphonique?', *B.E.V.*, 24, juin 1980, 17–29.

18 Valéry describes the 'cogito' of Descartes not as a syllogism but as a reflexive desire on the part of the intellect, 'un vivant et pensant qui

crie [...]' (P i, 80ff). The theme of the 'cry' of the mind is of central importance in his thought (see Nicole Celeyrette-Pietri, *Valéry et le Moi*, 311 ['je crie/j'écris'] and the study of the manuscripts of *La Jeune Parque* made by Bruce Pratt [see Bibliography]).

19 The reciprocity between 'soif' and 'source', 'donner' and 'recevoir', 'parler' and 'entendre' is the basis of Valéry's notion of the sensibility.

20 Cf. Lacan, 'Le désir est une métonoymie', *Écrits*, 528.

21 E.g. 'Sur qui' changes to 'Sans qui', 'Mal' to 'tourment', 'prompt' to 'vif'.

22 'Impatience' is the instinctive and passionate urge to create and to understand (cf. 'La sainte impatience meurt aussi' in *Le Cimetière Marin*). It is also connected for Valéry with a hatred of repetition and thus with the need to exhaust the possibilities of life 'une fois pour toutes'.

23 Cf. the notion of mobile equilibrium (see Chapter 6, n. 56). Valéry compares the intricate labour of the artist creating poetry from separate details, with the movement of an insect or bird suspended over flowers by the rapid movement of its wings.

24 Vocal seduction is distinguished from demagogy by the call to the mind to awaken in its circle of charm. At the same time Valéry draws attention to the hypnotic sensations of consciousness itself.

25 *Aurore* was first published in 1917 and subsequently in *Odes* (1920), which consisted of *Aurore*, *La Pythie* and *Palme*.

26 Something in the speaker is the hare in Rimbaud's *Après le Déluge* (*Les Illuminations*) where the same matinal prayer ('oraison') occurs. The delicately controlled potentials of the dawn image are explored by Ursula Franklin in *The Rhetoric of Valéry's Prose Aubades* (University of Toronto Press, 1979).

27 Cf. in *Ébauche d'un Serpent* the themes of mask, trap and lie (stanzas 3–4), where the sun encloses the human race in 'un sommeil/ Trompeusement peint de campagnes' (P i, 139). Such concepts have an ironically positive rôle and relate to the poetic concept of 'Charm'.

28 See C. Crow, ' "Le silence au vol de cygne": Baudelaire, Mallarmé, Valéry and the flight of the swan', *Baudelaire, Mallarmé, Valéry: New Essays in Honour of Lloyd Austin* (Cambridge, 1982).

29 Cf. Mallarmé's poetic aim of 'nomination': 'donner au lys le mystère d'un nom' ('rien ne demeurera sans être proféré'). The difference between an aesthetics of 'naming' and of 'greeting' relates to the central thesis of this book.

30 'Quand l'ombre menaça de la fatale loi/Tel vieux Rêve, désir et mal de mes vertèbres', *Œuvres complètes*, ed. H. Mondor and G. Jean-Aubrey, 'Bibliothèque de la Pléiade' (Paris, Gallimard, 1951), 67.

31 Cf. Diderot's image in *Le Neveu de Rameau* (*Œuvres Romanesques* [Classiques Garnier, 1951], 395). ('Mes pensées ce sont mes catins.')

32 Cf. 'Chant de l'Idée-Maîtresse' (P i, 357).

33 '[...] les fils déjà sortis de mon esprit', *Œuvres complètes*, 678. Valéry's image of the spider (see p. 128) – also used by Keats and

Ponge – relates to the same self-referentiality (the conscious mind 'fatally' carries on in its own terms the creative work of the sensibility, 'matière même d'Orphée'). For discussion of the central concept of 'attente' in Valéry's poetry see J. Hytier, *La Poétique de Valéry*, 138–41.

34　'Être' and 'connaître' are defined strictly within the context of mental functioning – i.e. as self-implicating modes of the 'omnipresent' sensibility (xxiv, 304) in its 'spherical' relationship with the world. Otherwise 'Être' is one of the 'trombone' or 'parrot' terms Valéry refused to use in his prose writings without qualification, yet employs to give resonance in poetry on condition that this resonance is controlled in its turn (part of the poem's precisely defined sense of 'l'inachevé' and 'l'ineffable').

35　See A. Henry, *Langage et poésie chez Paul Valéry* (Paris, Mercure de France, 1952), 71–2.

36　See, for example, W. Stewart, 'Le Thème d'Orphée chez Valéry', *E.N.C.*, 163–78.

5

(a) Au Platane, Cantique des Colonnes, Poésie

1　Yet a further echo of Rimbaud (see Chapter 4, n. 26) and of Mallarmé (ibid., n. 29).

2　Cf. 'Bel Canto' (viii, 38).

3　See *Inspirations Méditerranéennes* (Part I, p. 19).

4　Cf. L. J. Austin, 'The Negative Plane Tree', *E.C.*, 3–10.

5　A further echo of La Fontaine ('Le Chêne et le roseau'). These lines are seen by Lacan as an example of metonymic condensation in which an invisible relationship springs from 'tête' and 'tempête' (*Écrits*, 504).

6　I have developed the theme of the tree's limitations in *Paul Valéry: Consciousness and Nature*, 117–20. A connection between the dynamic principle of the voice and of flame is established in *L'Âme et la Danse*, where tree, voice and flame are 'ivre de la négation de la nulle réalité' (P ii, 171).

7　Cf. Ponge: 'Il faut, à travers les analogies, saisir la qualité différentielle' (quoted by Ian Higgins in 'Francis Ponge', *The Language of Poetry: Crisis and Solution – Studies of Modern Poetry of French Expression, 1945 to the Present*, ed. Michael Bishop [Rodolpi, 1980] 49).

8　Cf. '[...] Ma voix ne suit qu'une ombre de pensée. Mais pour toi, grand Lucrèce, et ta secrète soif, qu'est-ce que la parole, une fois qu'elle chante? Elle y perd le pouvoir de poursuivre le vrai' (P ii, 179). *Au Platane* reveals and integrates the tensions between a Symbolist 'denial of reality' (see n. 6, above) and a classical conception of form.

9　Hence the lyrical title 'Au Platane' rather than the Parnassian title 'Le Platane'. Valéry's poetry combines passion for revealing the potential of the inner world – 'l'âme' – with a voluptuously precise grasp of external reality inherited from, amongst others, Leconte de Lisle.

10 See Part One, pp. 29–30.

11 See J. Jallat, 'Valéry et les figures de rhétorique', *C.P.V.*, I, 167.

12 A. Henry, *Langage et poésie chez Paul Valéry* (Paris, Mercure de France, 1952), 71.

13 Compare with Hugo's use of the same image.

14 We have seen the horse as emblem of training the mind and 'riding' the unconscious (Part I, p. 258, n. 8).

15 See in relation to *La Jeune Parque* (Part I, p. 92).

16 See the thesis developed in Part I (Chapter 3 in particular).

17 Cf. Jeaninne Jallat's reference to 'deux rhétoriques valéryennes, tournées vers les deux côtés de notre modernité: le système, la structure, – la Poétique; la dissemblance, la traversée, la différence, – ce nouveau mode du langage dont il faudra bien un jour, nommer la rhétorique' (op. cit., 181). *Au Platane* seems to combine the two in a single action of poetic form.

18 The theme of speaking stone relates to the drama of Orpheus/ Amphion.

19 Jacques Duchesne-Guillemin suggests how the regular stanza divisions create the spirit of a solemn procession through time (*Études pour un Paul Valéry* [Neuchâtel, La Baconnière, 1964], 139).

20 Cf. 'Qui parle à ma vision' (*Palme*). There is a constant interchange of faculties in Valéry's poetry and thought. Here 'parle' is a metaphor for the silent eloquence produced by inventively discovering within oneself the interdependence of inner and outer world ('Le réel est mon équivalent' [VII, 31]).

21 Cf. *La Jeune Parque*: 'Moi si pure, mes genoux/Pressentent les terreurs de genoux sans défense.../L'air me brise [...]'.

22 The dancer, symbol of the pure, flame-like movement of the 'poetic' imagination, is evoked in *L'Âme et la Danse* in terms of ephemeral columns and branches swayed by the 'musical' breeze.

23 Cf. Keat's *Ode to a Grecian Urn*. An interesting study in this area of aesthetics is Anton Ehrenzweig's *The Psycho-analysis of Artistic Vision and Hearing* (New York, George Braziller, 1965).

24 Valéry's debt to Gautier was inherited from Baudelaire and Mallarmé, yet it suggests his own sensitivity to the precise rendering of intellectual sensation through attention to the physical world (see n. 9 and n. 20, above).

25 For an imaginative account of the significance of architecture to Valéry, see *Eupalinos ou l'Architecte* (P II, 79–147). Architectural terms in the poem – 'Bandeau', 'lit', 'nez' – have been humorously transposed to the human.

26 A haunting Orphic image of the early Symbolist period is Nerval's 'Modulant tout à tour sur la lyre d'Orphée/Les soupirs de la sainte et les cris de la fée' ('El Desdichado', *Les Chimères*).

27 See Chapter 4, n. 36 (above).

28 See Part One, p. 45

29   The theme of sound in *Poésie* is treated by Kirsteen Anderson in 'Valéry et Tomatis : étude sur la conscience auditive du poète', *B.E.V.*, 20 (mars 1979), 31–3.

30   See C. Sabbaghe, 'Les Disparitions de Narcisse', *P.V.C.*, 155.

31   *Le Rameur* (Chapter 6, n. 83).

(b) Les Pas, La Ceinture, La Dormeuse, Fragment du Narcisse

32   See S. Bourjea, 'L'Ombre-Majuscule, une exégèse de "La Ceinture" ', *R.L.M.*, I, 137–8.

33   *Romans, récits et soties* (Paris, Gallimard, 1958), Chapter VII.

34   The theme is developed by Elizabeth Jackson in *Worlds Apart* (Paris, Mouton, 1976), 4–9.

35   'Dons' often acquires a sexual connotation in Valéry's poetry (e.g. in *Le Cimetière Marin*, 'Le sang qui brillent aux lèvres que se rendent,/ Les derniers dons, les doigts qui les défendent').

36   Cf. Valéry's comparison between the poetic state and the delicate oscillation of a pendulum between 'son' and 'sens' (Part I, p. 55).

37   The reader is referred to James Lawler's rich study of this important poem: 'L'Ange frais de l'œil nu. . .', *The Poet as Analyst* (Berkeley, Calif., University of California Press, 1974), 74–116.

38   *Le Spleen de Paris* (*Œuvres Complètes* [Paris, Gallimard, 1961], 232).

39   See L. J. Austin, 'Modulation and movement in Valéry's verse', *Y.F.S.* (44), 30. The tmesis provides a striking example of how a syntactical constraint helps create the expressive deviation it contains.

40   See M. Parent, 'La fonction poétique du langage dans "Charmes" ', *P.V.C.*, 64.

41   See L. J. Austin, op. cit., 29.

42   See J. Lawler, *Lecture de Valéry*, 86.

43   ibid., 84.

44   See J. Searle ed., *The Philosophy of Language* (Oxford University Press, 1971), p. 5.

45   See C. Crow, *Paul Valéry: Consciousness and Nature*, 53–65.

46   The 'distancing' involved in Valéry's use of sexual imagery leads in my opinion to a very different approach from that adopted by Charles Whiting in *Paul Valéry: Charmes ou Poèmes*, 8–17.

47   The poem first appeared as a unity in 1926. Details of its various stages can be found in J. Hytier's notes (P I, 1664).

48   See F. Scarfe, *The Art of Paul Valéry: a study in dramatic monologue* (London, William Heinemann Ltd., Glasgow University Publications XCVII, 1954).

49   See N. Celeyrette-Pietri, 'Métamorphoses de Narcisse', *R.L.M.* I, 19 (also the section 'Le Moi au Miroir' in *Valéry et le Moi*, 129–77).

50   In the legend, Echo forfeited the use of her tongue except to speak the last of others' words. Through unrequited love of Narcissus, her form faded with grief and her bones changed to rocks, leaving nothing but her voice.

51 For the 'whole/part' relationship of consciousness and the sensibility, see Part I, p. 73.
52 For further details, see C. Whiting, *Paul Valéry: Charmes ou Poèmes*, 115–23.
53 See Part I, p. 22.
54 Part II and III were added in the 1926 edition of *Charmes*.
55 I have illustrated these principles briefly in relation to *La Jeune Parque* (see Part I, p. 81).
56 Cf. 'Fais que ma soif se fasse source' (XXIV, 283).
57 Compare and contrast with the remark by Derrida in *La Voix et le Phénomène* (Paris, P.U.F., 1967), 15–16.
58 See E. M. Elder, 'Le finale fragmenté des "Narcisses" de Valéry', *C.P.V.*, I, 187–206.
59 See Part I, p. 27.
60 H. Köhler, 'Quelques poèmes de Valéry interprêtés par ses "Cahiers"', *P.V.C.*, 359.
61 Cf. the difference between 'le *langage* issu de la *Voix*' and 'la Voix du *Langage*' on which this study is based.
62 Lettre à Leautaud, 1905 (quoted by Céline Sabbaghe, 'Les Disparitions, de Narcisse, *P.V.C.*, 154–5).

(c) La Pythie

63 For a comprehensive study, see Maka-de Schepper's *Le Thème de la Pythie chez Paul Valéry* (Paris, Société d'Édition 'Les Belles Lettres', 1969).
64 Valéry has kept much of the local colour connected with the Greek oracle, for example the burning herbs ('empyreumes' [stanza 12]) whose intoxicating odour was used to bring on the trance. However it was essential for his poetic purposes that he should change the more usual version of the legend according to which the priest or 'pontif' acted as intermediary between the oracle and the god.
65 'Monstre-animal intellectuel/Ce corps instrument de musique, de netteté' (a comment on *La Pythie* quoted by James Lawler, *Lecture de Valéry*, 135).
66 The rôle of the octosyllable is treated by Jacques Duchesne-Guillemin in *Études pour un Paul Valéry* (Neuchâtel, La Baconnière, 1964), 114. Valéry wished to demonstrate its versatility to Pierre Louÿs, and tells us that the sonority of the line 'Pâle, profondément mordue' 'se composa d'elle-même' (P I, 1338).
67 'Logique de la Pythie, Chemin de l'idée. Employer le corps à *former* les idées' (quoted by James Lawler, *op. cit.*, 134).
68 See Part One, p. 6.
69 E.g. 'Crois-tu, quand se brise les cordes/Que le son jaillisse plus beau?/Ton plectre a frappé sur mon torse,/Mais tu ne lui laisse la force/Que de sonner comme un tombeau!'. The funereal emptiness of this sound will be picked up in transmuted form at the end of the poem in the lines 'Qui se connaît quand elle sonne/N'être plus la voix

de personne'. Valéry refers to the body as a musical instrument by virtue of its mingling of the animal and intellectual (see n. 65, above). In the half-willed experience of creative 'attente', the 'chords' of the sensibility are like secret harps (see p. 141).

70 Cf. 'Pour la poésie – ayez une idée très vague du poème à faire, et une notion aussi précise que *possible de la poésie même* [...] Le fil de la poésie est Voix' (vii, 402).

71 Valéry described both *La Jeune Parque* and *La Pythie* as a poetic attempt to follow the physiological sensations of consciousness 'perçu par le Moi' (see Part i, p. 74).

72 Appropriate to the mountainous cavern of the legend, the image also fits the 'vibrante demeure' described in relation to *Aurore* (see p. 107). Valéry has transferred an archetypal symbol of the unconscious into a 'vocal' image of his own: the sensibility made transparent by the intellect recognising its own source in the law of 'parler/entendre': a law which cannot be altered but which can be *used*. Cf. 'couper les racines de la douleur' (v, 903).

73 Cf. Lacan's notion of entry into the symbolic order through language, and the impossibility of a private language in the thought of Wittgenstein.

74 Cf. in *La Jeune Parque* the urge for petrification ('QUE DANS LE CIEL PLACÉS...') and the lines 'Je pense, sur le bord doré de l'univers,/A ce goût de périr qui prend la Pythonisse/En qui mugit l'espoir que le monde finisse' (P i, 101). The head of Medusa on the lyre is associated with the severed head of Orpheus (e.g. in Moreau's painting, admired by the Symbolist generation), his voice still calling for Eurydice. These and other myths – e.g. Jason and the golden fleece – contribute indirectly to the rich associative texture of the poem and its concentration on the individual as a source (and product?) of universal form.

75 Cf. James Lawler sees these waves as the Pythia's tears, bringing her, like the Parque, to the self-acceptance necessary to the final deliverance through form (*op. cit.*, 131).

76 Valéry was particularly interested in the phenomenon of 'la voix interne étrangère' (see Part i, p. 45). Seduced by his echo, Narcisse still knows the voice projected by the woods and streams to be his own.

77 E.g. the poem falls, the tree remains, Valéry wrote, but also 'un enfant finit par donner à son père la forme de la paternité' (vi, 818). He frequently makes use of an analogy with giving birth, e.g. 'Ce qui ne me coûte rien ne me donne pas la sensation d'avoir vécu – Pas plus que d'engendrer ne donne de mal et fait moins auteur qu'enfanter. En quoi je suis femelle [...]' (xv, 140). Note also his comment on the discrepancy in labour between the pain of passing the baby's head and the rest of its body: 'La légende commence' (vi, 168) (quoted by Nicole Celeyrette-Pietri, *Valéry et le Moi*, 342). This image seems particularly relevant to the birth of form in *La Pythie*.

78 E.g. P.-O. Walzer, *La Poésie de Valéry*, 296.

79 Quoted by J. Lawler (op. cit., 133) and C. Whiting (op. cit.). Cf. 'et que l'œuvre fût rigoureusement impersonnelle [...] ni ne fût pas l'acte *d'une* personne tant que d'un "esprit", c'est-à-dire d'un *système complet potentiellement*' (x, 154). For discussion of the concept of impersonality in Valéry's poetics, see Part i, p. 14. 'Absolute' language pertains to the 'pensée singulièrement achevée' of poetry.

80 *Umbra* in *Toute la Lyre* (quoted by J. Duchesne-Guillemin. op. cit., 115). Acknowledging the influences of Hugo (P i, 1657), Valéry has also retained the ten-lined stanza of his verse and the disposition of rhymes *ababccdeed* used in *Aurore*.

81 See I. Gheorghe, *les images du Poète et de la Poésie dans l'œuvre de Valéry*, 25.

82 Cf. 'Pauvre système – arbre de vie, platane branlé par ses propres fureurs élémentaires inexplicables. Cela donne une drôle d'idée du "Moi"' (xxv, 571); 'L'arbre souffle des fruits si lourds, qu'il ne les peut retenir: il les perd ou il se brise. Va-t-il gémir qu'il y a deux *arbres* en lui?' (P ii, 577).

83 For the concept of 'attributed inspiration' see W. Ince, *The Poetic Theory of Paul Valéry – inspiration and technique* (Leicester University Press, 1961), 89–94.

84 James Lawler quotes from an earlier version of *La Pythie* the line: 'Je suis enfin sauvé des ondes...' (op. cit., 122). At the same time as it reinforces the idea of sound, the image reinforces the idea of birth. Kirsteen Anderson discusses the 'intra-uterine' theme of sound and liquidity in 'Valéry et Tomatis: étude sur la conscience auditive du poète', *B.E.V.*, 20, mars 1979, 32–3.

85 Quoted by Ned Bastet, 'Valéry et la Voix Poétique', *Annales de la Faculté des Lettres et Sciences Humaines de Nice*, n. 15, 1971, 44.

6 (*a*) About *Ébauche d'un Serpent*

1 Style conscious of itself is described in *Mon Faust* (P ii, 298) (cf. Baudelaire's aspiration for the *Petits Poèmes en Prose*).

2 See J. Lawler, *Lecture de Valéry* (Paris, P.U.F., 1963), 154. It has been easier to discuss the three small poems preceeding *Ébauche* as related pieces (see pp. 187–93).

3 For discussion of the Gnostic heresy used in Valéry's poem, see J. Cocking, 'Towards *Ébauche d'un Serpent*: Valéry and Ouroboros', *A.J.F.S.*, vi (1969), 187–215.

4 What Mallarmé called the glorious 'lie' of the soul, Valéry sees as the music of poetic Voice endowing with presence the 'fiction' of the total Self.

5 Cf. 'Musique très belle, je sais que tu me mens' (P ii, 704).

6 *Lettres à Quelques-uns*, 184.

7 ibid. Note in particular the 'exaggerated' alliteration of dentals and sibilants ('Dore, langue! dore-lui les', 'plus doux des dits que tu connaisses!'; 'Sitôt pétris, sitôt soufflés/Maître Serpent les a sifflés').

8 The Socrates of *Eupalinos* was born 'plusieurs' – the infinite lives of which we are capable – but died 'un seul': 'se détacha le Socrate qui était dû aux magistrats et à la ciguë' (P II, 114).

9 The strangeness of *knowing* this state is different from the disturbing strangeness of *La Pythie*.

10 Although Valéry was rarely free from stereotyping by gender, his poetry is unaffected at least in so far as that the Animus/Anima stereotype is used in the context of a single mind.

11 See J. Lawler, op. cit., 167 n. The image of stone – its 'pâleur' linked to the Virgilian theme of religious awe or silence – is frequently used in *La Jeune Parque* and *La Pythie*. See also C. Whiting's note on the link between the epigraph of *La Pythie* and *Cantique des Colonnes* (op. cit., 96).

12 Cf. 'Que serait-il, Amour, sans le Serpent qui parle? Une monotone et périodique combinaison des sexes selon l'histoire naturelle...Fi! Quelle sainte et sotte simplicité' (P II, 332).

13 The change to third person (the reverse of the procedure in *Les Grenades*) creates a change of perspective in which greater intimacy with the reader is involved.

14 Cf. Lacan's translation of Freud's 'Wo es war, soll Ich werden' as 'Là ou c'était, là comme sujet dois-je advenir' (*Écrits*). Poetry for Valéry increases 'ce qui fait le Moi' (see Part I, p. 5).

15 The fruit image is constantly present in Valéry's poetry and thought (see C. Crow, *Paul Valéry. Consciousness and Nature*, 80–1, 131–3, 171–5). Image of the sensibility, it is noted above all for its 'vectorial' power, carrying forward the potentiality of form.

16 See W. Ince, 'An Exercise in Artistry: Valéry's "Les Grenades"', *The Romanic Review*, LV (1964), 190–202.

17 Valéry was notoriously opposed to imitative sound-use. The independent sound and sense values of language are made to create an indissoluble unity, a self-contained 'charm' (see pp. 21 and 55).

18 Compare with the proud silence symbolised by Monsieur Teste (cf. *César* [P I, 79]) and with the image of rupture in *Poésie*, where the mouth is diverted from its harmonious unity. Valéry often dwells on the enforced change from eloquent inner silence to outer public sound.

19 See J. Jallat, 'Valéry et les figures de rhétorique', *C.P.V.*, I, 161.

20 For discussion of Valéry's varied use of the sonnet form see J. Hytier, 'L'Esthétique valéryenne du sonnet', *A.J.F.S.*, 6 (1969), 326–36.

21 This can be compared and contrasted with the relationship between words and things in the poetry of Ponge (see the work by Ian Higgins listed in the bibliography). Valéry writes 'On peut prêter aux choses tous les mouvements humains non volontaires et même les paroles échappées explosives' (IV, 11). Even here, the resemblance with Ponge seems deceptive, however.

(*b*) *Le Vin Perdu, Intérieur, Le Cimetière Marin*

22 Cf. the 'Orphic' line in *La Pythie* 'Soit l'eau des mers surprise'.

23 The image is from Poincaré (see W. Ince, 'The Sonnet "Le Vin Perdu" of Paul Valéry', *F.S.*, x [1956], 40–54).

24 See K. Maurer, *Interpretationen zur späteren Lyrik Paul Valérys*, (Munich, Lehnen Verlag, 1954).

25 *Lettres à Quelques-uns*, 233–4.

26 Cf. 'Le langage lui-même est plein des louanges de l'EAU. Nous disons que nous avons SOIF DE VERITÉ. Nous parlons de la TRANSPARENCE d'un discours. Nous répandons parfois un TORRENT de paroles. . ./Le temps lui-même a puisé dans le cours de l'EAU pure la figure qui nous le peint' (P I, 204).

27 See Valéry's essays on Leonardo (P I, 1184; P I, 1221).

28 See Monique Parent, *Cohérence et Résonance dans le Style de 'Charmes'* (Paris, Klinksieck, 1970), 145.

29 This important subject and its relation to an art of ornamentation, music and architecture is briefly treated by Silvio Yeschua in ' "Substitutions" et poétique chez Valéry', *C.P.V.*, I, 135–48.

30 Perhaps an association with the theme of suicide running through *La Jeune Parque* (see H. Köhler, 'Quelques poèmes de Valéry interprêtés par ses "Cahiers" ', *P.V.C.*, 372).

31 See Chapter 4, no. 30.

32 'La pensée intellectuelle grossie à la structure d'une sensibilité' (see the 'incident' related by H. Köhler, op. cit., 364).

33 *André Gide-Paul Valéry, Correspondance 1890–1942*, 489 (P I, 1687).

34 See H. Morier, 'La motivation des formes et des mètres chez Valéry', *P.V.C.*, 327.

35 'Au dela, en deça des noms/Sont les pronoms, qui sont plus – vrais déjà, et plus près de la Source' (XXI, 870); 'Toute proposition implique la parole et la connaissance, c'est-à-dire un *témoin parleur* et articulé/ Le je ou moi indique que ce témoin est aussi un élément de la proposition. L'expression et la chose experimée sont dans un même système' (III, 707). For discussion of this important subject see N. Celeyrette-Pietri, *Valéry et le Moi*, 304–8. I have treated the notion of interior monologue in Part I, p. 44.

36 'Le chant (le cri etc) actes en quoi, par quoi, l'être se croit source, origine et centre personnel de choses' (VII, 99). By artificially instituting the state of 'le chantant, le résonnant', the poem keeps us in a state which the speaker's consciousness maintains only through a constant action of inner voice, 'témoin parleur' of a changing self.

37 'Pas de "moi" sans toi' (XXII, 304), Valéry wrote, and there is a phonetic echo of the second person emphatic pronoun here in the word 'Toit'. Above all, the metaphor works through its startling sound sequence. Cf. the image of the sensibility as a roof in stanza 4 of *Aurore* (followed by 'Dans les ténèbres de toi').

38 'Dans tous les cas une métaphore d'ordre sensible est à la pensée ce qu'une illustration est au texte. Elle sort du texte (ceci est important). Elle contient dans un complexe, d'un moment, d'une portion indéscriptible du texte' (I, 357), quoted by Jürgen Schmidt-Radefeldt in 'Intuition et inspiration, analogie et métaphore', *Poétique et Com-*

munication, 188. Stylistically, a metaphor for Valéry offers a 'multi-formité du changement possible' and a means of retaining a sense of 'l'informe' (III, 364).

39 See R. Champigny, 'The Zeno Stanza' *E.C.* IV, n. 1 (Spring 1964), 11–18.

40 Quoted by Jean Hytier in 'Les Cimetières Marins dans la poésie française', *B.E.V.*, 4, janvier 1975, 35.

41 Valéry suggested that thought had no end in itself other than through chemistry or action (XXIX, 841; '[...]Point de pensée qui épuise la virtualité de l'ésprit' (P I, 1219).

42 Valéry attempted to convey the way in which the functioning of the body gave rise to ideas and to a physiological sensation of conscious-ness ('perçu par le Moi' (Part I, p. 74). The idea of a fugue-like construction with 'la basse' representing 'l'attention' (XVII, 60) is discussed by Huguette Laurenti, 'Musique et Monologue', *P.V.*, 1 (see 66, n. 12 in particular).

43 See H. Laurenti, ibid., 58.

44 The 'muscular' pleasure of this use of language is discussed by Michael Gauthier, 'La décomposition poétique du mot', *Poétique et Communication*, 255.

45 See Maurice Grammont, *Petit Traité de Versification Française* (Paris, Armand Colin, 1965). An interesting and controversial article on this subject is George Mounin's 'Paul Valéry et Maurice Grammont', *E.M.* (1972), 125–34.

46 Silence here ('silence en musique, en parole') is based on the hidden but poetically conveyed concept of equilibrium, 'élément positif-productif-transitif, et non final' (XX, 69). For the counterpoise of the urge towards and away from expression see Part I, p. 17. In an early verse of *Aurore* Valéry wrote 'La lyre universelle/Je la touche et vais cherchant/Dans ma forêt sensuelle/Les silences de mon chant' (quoted by Ida-Marie Frandon in 'Le Poème: déguisement et transitivité', *Poétique et Communication*, 136). It is in this expressively 'non-final' sense that 'Le silence est la source étrange des poèmes'.

47 Michel Gauthier suggests that the 'secret' of Valéry's euphonic com-positions can be penetrated through analysis (L'architecture phonique du langage poétique', *P.V.C.*, 377–97). See also Michel Malherbe, ' "L'Abeille" – poème euphonique?', *B.E.V.*, 24, juin 1980, 25.

48 For evidence of this 'long travail' see the relevant works by L. J. Austin listed in the Bibliography. (P I, 1686).

49 From a letter to Jacques Doucet (quoted by E. Jackson, *Worlds Apart* [Mouton, 1976], 27).

50 See the variant 'Auprès d'un cœur dont je suis le poème' (P I, 1684).

51 Valéry's insistence that poetry should supplement the 'absence' of the author and the inertia of the written (through a 'personalised' style linking it to the individual being) might be said to spring from the same emotion as is implied by the phrase 'l'art personnel'. In his own case, certain favoured groups of sounds create this intimate tone or 'euphon'.

52 Also Gautier (see J. Hytier, 'Les Cimetières Marins dans la poésie française', *B.E.V.*, 4, janvier 1975, 34).

53 Ronsard and Mallarmé both represented the art of 'le chanté' for Valéry.

54 Stanzas 13 and 14 make explicit the concept (central not only to the poem, but to Valéry's whole conception of the creative sensibility) that human limitation – i.e. the body – is the necessary condition of creativity. It is lacking in the static perfection of the 'divine', ironically equated in the poem with death and the extinction of 'la sainte impatience' (in Voltaire's poem 'hope'). Cf. *'L'incomplet est fondamental'* (xxi, 65).

55 See Graham Martin's edition: *Le Cimetière Marin (The Graveyard by the Sea)* (Edinburgh Bilingual Library, University of Texas Press, Austin, Texas, 1972.)

56 The rôle of the voice, too, is as of a spinning top (xxix, 150), an 'anneau tourbillon-système quasi *éternel'* (xii, 579).

57 Again the contrast with Mallarmé's concept of silence.

58 *L'Amateur de Poèmes* (P i, 75).

59 The idea that the poem refers to a pyrrhic victory – the Armistice of First World War – is discussed by Graham Martin in 'Valéry's "Ode Secrète": the enigma solved?', *F.S.* xxxi (Oct. 1977), 432.

60 These interpretations are described by Lloyd J. Austin in 'Les Moyens du mystère chez Mallarmé et chez Valéry', *C.A.I.E.F.*, 15, 1963.

61 For the sexual or erotic connotations sometimes involved in Valéry's use of moss see *Le Bois Amical*, 'Et puis, nous sommes morts sur la mousse' (P i, 80).

62 Cf. the 'bûcher' of Hercules if we bring in the classical allusions poetically present in the poem (L. Austin, op. cit.).

63 Cf. 'Elle met une femme aux milieu de ces murs' in *Intérieur*.

64 See Hartmut Köhler ('Quelques poèmes de Valéry interprêtés par ses "Cahiers"', *P.V.C.*, 365–76).

65 E.g. the Mallarméan verb 's'éployer'.

66 Cf. the passage in *L'Âme et la Danse*: '[...] comment la nature a su enfermer dans cette fille si frêle et si fine, un tel monstre de force et de promptitude? Hercule changé en hirondelle [...]' (P ii, 161). Leonardo is also referred to as 'Hercule' (P i, 1232). Valéry's tone in the essay is admiring as in the poem.

67 See the thesis put forward by Graham Martin, op. cit., 425–36.

68 See I. Gheorghe, *Les images du Poète et de la Poésie dans l'œuvre de Valéry* (Paris, Minard, 1977), 68.

69 The crepuscular drama of Valéry's poetry is contrasted with that of Mallarmé by Serge Bourjea, 'L'Ombre-Majuscule, une exégèse de "La Ceinture"', *R.L.M.*, i, 144.

70 See H. Köhler, op. cit., 368.

71 See James Lawler's interpretation of the phrase 'temps sans ressources', (op. cit., 233), a phrase we can associate with 'la source où cesse même un nom' in *Le Rameur*.

72 See H. Köhler, *P.V.C.*, 369.
73 Ibid., 372 and G. Martin, op. cit., 430.
74 The only constellation not included in Hercules' Labours is the Great Bear (whose seven stars are associatively present in 'De scintillations sitôt le septuor' of Mallarmé's 'Ses purs ongles...').
75 Cf. *Le Vin Perdu*.
76 Valéry's reaction to the famous 'spaces' of Pascal is discussed by Judith Robinson in 'Valéry, Pascal et la censure de la métaphysique', *C.P.V.E.*, 185–208.
77 'Ramer contre' is one of the many popular expressions which Valéry poetically 'extends'.
78 Compare with the rebellious aesthetic of Rimbaud's *Illuminations* and *Une Saison en Enfer*. Valéry frequently admires the integration of metaphor in Rimbaud's work (in contrast to the different use of Mallarmé).
79 Cf. the Narcisse theme.
80 Quoted by H. Köhler, *Paul Valéry Dichtung und Erkenntnis*, 311. The same aspect of 'attention' is treated in *Intérieur*.
81 See J. Onimus, 'Lectures du "Rameur"', *P.V.* i, 147–60.
82 Cf. 'azur', 'soie', 'oise'.
83 Cf. the 'Source' in *Poésie*. 'Il faut donc se désaltérer, redevenir, avoir recours à ce qu'exige tout ce qui vit' (P i, 204). See also on the concept of the indefinable 'source' J. Derrida, 'Les Sources de Valéry, "Qual, Quelle"', *M.L.N.*, 563–99.
84 See J. Lawler, op. cit., 237.
85 'Un pur esprit s'accroît sous l'écorce des pierres' ('Vers Dorés', *les Chimères*) – a line phonetically close to 'l'or sec de l'écorce' in *Les Grenades*.
86 The word 'soie' – rhyming with 'voix' – was used in Valéry's description of the sound of Mallarmé's voice (see Part i, p. 37).
87 Cf. *La Ceinture* where the coming of night symbolises the loss of the visual bond which links the mind and its 'souffle' to the world. (In *Ébauche d'un Serpent* the sun subjects 'la présence obscure de l'âme' to the sensation of sight.)
88 James Lawler writes of two main parts in the poem's composition (op. cit., 237).
89 Here the identity is negative. Yet it is this discovery which forms the basis of 'le Moi pur'.
  'L'œuvre capitale et cachée du plus grand esprit n'est-elle pas de soustraire cette attention substantielle à la lutte des vérités ordinaires? [...] Ce n'est pas sa chère *personne* qu'il élève à ce haut degré, puisqu'il la renonce en y pensant, et qu'il la substitue dans la place du *sujet* par ce moi inqualifiable, qui n'a pas de nom, qui n'a pas d'histoire, qui n'est pas plus sensible, ni moins réel que le centre de masse d'une bague ou d'un système planétaire, – mais qui résulte de tout, quel que soit le tout...' (P i, 1228).
90 See C. Crow, 'Valéry and the image of the tree-top', *Sensibility and Creation*, ed. R. Cardinal (London, Croom Helm, 1977), 16–35.

91 See Pauline Roth-Mascagni, *Petite Prose pour 'Palme'* (Paris, Minard, 1977).
92 Ibid., 60, n. 37. For discussion of the typographical in Valéry's poems, see M. J. Minard, 'Typographie et littérature – notes de méthode', *R.L.M.*, I, 161–85.
93 Cf. the popular expression 'Dans un clin d'œil'.
94 P. Roth-Mascagni, op. cit., 33.
95 E.g. 'azur', 'vue', 'visions': the vocabulary of *Prose pour des Esseintes*.
96 The sensation of having precisely defined what could not be done is described in a moving passage in the *Cahiers* called 'Station sur la Terrasse': 'Voilà ton œuvre, me dit une voix [...]', ending 'Si tu veux, ma Raison, je dirai...que mon âme...se sentait comme la forme creuse d'un écrin [...] et ce vide (s'éprouvait) attendre un objet admirable. [...] Mon œuvre était cela' (xxv, 618–19). Valéry's poetry could be said to be concerned with 'l'inachevé', 'l'état de manque de mots', which the poem allows the mind consciously to 'hold' as its own universal form.
97 Many images in *Palme* can be linked back to *Aurore* with its theme of the creative sensibility (in particular the lines 'Dans la vibrante demeure/Il n'est de souffle qui meure/Sans avoir semé l'amour.' from the 'rejected' Orphic stanza [P I, 1658]). The 'donner/recevoir' paradox underlies Valéry's theory of both 'Poésie' and mental functioning.

Conclusion

1 M. Raymond, *De Boudelaire au Surréalisme* (Paris, Corti, 1940), 153.
2 The importance of this discovery in Valéry's thought cannot be overestimated. He shows empirical awareness of a 'law' in the human sensibility common to many systems in biology and physics which can be modelled mathematically as a recursive filter (where 'delay' enables each new event in a stream of data to be modified by the previous one).
3 'Je suis cette créature/Dont la fatale nature/Est de créer à son tour' (P I, 1658).
4 Here I am indebted to the argument put forward by Gerald Bruns in *Modern Poetry and the Idea of Language* (New Haven, Conn. and London, Yale University Press, 1974).
5 Ibid., 235.
6 See M. L. Pratt, *Towards a Speech Act Theory of Literary Discourse* (Bloomington, Ind., Indiana University Press, 1977), x–xi.
7 *La Voix et le Phénomène* (Paris, P.U.F., 1967), 14.
8 For discussion of Valéry's attitude to the medium of the written in contrast to the spoken, see, for example, M. Lechantre, 'L'hiéroglyphe intérieur', *M.L.N.*, 630–43 and N. Celeyrette-Pietri, 'L'écriture et la voix', *Poétique et Communication*, 207–27.

9 The context of this humanism is the perception of extreme discontinuity (see Introduction).

10 'Les sources de Valéry. "Qual, Quelle" ', *M.L.N.*, 563–9.

11 *La Voix et le Phénomène*, 117.

12 See the poem where books in libraries are seen as sleeping 'charms' (P I, 1701).

13 *Prelude*, IV (quoted by G. Bruns in the chapter 'Eneregi: The Romantic Idea of Language', op. cit., 51).

14 Ibid., 55.

15 Wittgenstein's famous dictum that one should remain silent about that of which one cannot speak is partly negated by the whole enterprise of poetry (Mallarmé's 'nier l'indicible'), yet Valéry conceives of literature as an attempt to convey and use 'l'ineffable' ('La littérature essaye par des *mots* de créer *l'état du manque de mots*' [XVIII, 350]; 'Il faut donc placer l'excitant dans l'incompréhensible' [XXVI, 524]).

16 See the chapter 'Être et dire' in M. Raymond's *Le Poète et le Langage* (Neuchâtel, La Baconnière, 1970).

17 Valéry's poetic 'silence' is very different from silence as it is existentially conceived in the work of, say, Beckett. This view can be contrasted with silence in relation to words as it is conceived in immediate experience (see what Judith Robinson calls 'Words and Silence in "L'Idée Fixe" ', *M.L.N.*, 647).

18 H. Meschonnic, *Pour la Poétique*, II (Paris, N.R.F., Gallimard, 1973).

19 See G. Genette, 'La Littérature comme telle', *Figures* I (Paris, Seuil, 1966), reproduced in *Les Critiques de notre temps et Valéry* (Garnier, 1971), 175–85. Genette also writes of 'ce renvoi du discours à son envers silencieux, qui est, pour nous, la littérature même...' (*Figures*, 242, quoted by J. Robinson, op. cit., 647).

20 See C. A. Hackett, 'Les grandes tendances de la poésie française depuis 1950', *C.A.I.E.F.*, 30, mai 1978, 198 (see also *New French Poetry*, ed. C. Hackett [Oxford, Basil Blackwell, 1973], xxvii).

21 'Faut-il oublier Paul Valéry', *L'Improbable* (Paris, Mercure de France, 1959), 137–45.

22 Valéry's scepticism finds many echoes in the adventurous spirit of a post-structuralist investigation of literature. At the same time his critical practice of poetry appears to confirm only those contemporary theories which treat the literary work dynamically and retain at least a form of intentionality as the hard-won fruit of their questioning of subject-object relationships in language and thought. The reader becomes the subject of the Poet's 'listening' art.

Bibliography

A. Works by Valéry

Paul Valéry: Cahiers, vols. I–XXIX (Paris, C.N.R.S., 1957–1961).
Paul Valéry: Œuvres, vols. I, II, ed. J. Hytier, coll. Pléiade (Paris, Gallimard, 1975, 1977).
Paul Valéry: Cahiers, vols. II, ed. J. Robinson, coll. Pléiade (Paris, Gallimard, 1973, 1974).
André Gide–Paul Valéry, Correspondance 1890–1942, ed. R. Mallet (Paris, Gallimard, 1953).
Cours de Poétique (Yggdrasill, IX–XXXIV, 25 déc. 1937–25 fév. 1939).
Lettres à Quelques-uns, 1889–1943 (Paris, Gallimard, 1952).
Vues (Paris, La Table Ronde, 1948).
Poems in the Rough, tr. Hilary Corke, ed. Jackson Mathews; vol. II of *Collected Works of Paul Valéry* (Princeton, University Press and London, Routledge and Kegan Paul, 1970) Bollingen series, No. 25.

B. Critical works on Valéry

Alain, *La Jeune Parque commentée par Alain* (Paris, Gallimard, 1953 [1936]).
Anderson, K., 'Valéry et Tomatis: étude sur la conscience auditive du poète', *B.E.V.*, 20 (mars 1979), 27–44.
Austin, L. J., 'Genèse du Poème', *Le Cimetière Marin*, vol. 1 (préface H. Mondor) (Grenoble, Roissard, 1954).
  'La Genèse du "Cimetière Marin"', *C.A.I.E.F.*, III–V (juillet 1953), 235–69.
  'The Negative Plane Tree', *E.C.*, 3–10.
  'Modulation and movement in Valéry's verse', *Y.F.S.*, 44 (1970), 19–38.
  'Les moyens de mystère chez Mallarmé et chez Valéry', *C.A.I.E.F.*, 15 (mars 1963), 103–4.
Bastet, N., 'Faust et le cycle', *E.N.C.*, 115–28.
  'Valéry et la Voix Poétique', *Annales de la Faculté des Lettres et Sciences Humaines de Nice*, 15 (1971), 41–50.
  'L'expérience de la Borne et du Dépassement chez Valéry', *C.P.V.*, I, 59–90.
Boa, P., 'Valéry's "Ego Poeta": Towards a Biography of the Authorial Self', *Neophilologus*, 62, 51–62.
Bonnefoy, Y., 'Faut-il oublier Paul Valéry', *L'Improbable* (Paris, Mercure de France, 1959), 137–45.

Bibliography

Bourjea, S., 'L'Ombre-Majuscule, une exégèse de "La Ceinture"', *R.L.M.*, I, 121–45.

Cain, L., *Trois Essais sur Paul Valéry* (Paris, Gallimard, 1958).

Celeyrette-Pietri, N., 'Le Jeu du Je', *P.V.C.*, 10–25.

Valéry et le Moi, des Cahiers à l'Œuvre (Paris, Klincksieck, 1979).

'Metamorphoses de Narcisse', *R.L.M.*, I, 9–28.

'L'écriture et la voix', *Poétique et Communication*, 207–27.

Champigny, R., 'The Zeno Stanza', *E.C.*, IV, 11–18.

Chausserie-Laprée, J.-P., 'Deux figures de "La Jeune Parque": une approche architecturale et musicale du texte poétique', *B.E.V.*, 13, mai 1977, 19–31.

Chisholm, A. R., *An Approach to 'La Jeune Parque'* (Melbourne University Press 1938).

'Valéry's "Ébauche d'un Serpent": Valéry and Ouroboros', *A.J.F.S.*, VI (1969), 187–215.

Crow, C., *Paul Valéry: Consciousness and Nature* (Cambridge University Press, 1972).

Paul Valéry and Maxwell's Demon: natural order and human possibility, Occasional Papers in Modern Languages, 8 (University of Hull Publications, 1972).

'Valéry poet of "patiente impatience"', *F.M.L.S.*, III (1967), 370–87.

'"Teste parle": a study of the potential artist in Valéry's Monsieur Teste', *Y.F.S.*, 44 (1970), 157–68.

'Valéry and the Image of the Tree-top', *Sensibility and Creation, Studies in Twentieth-Century French Poetry*, ed. R. Cardinal (London, Croom Helm, 1977).

'"Le silence au vol de cygne": Baudelaire, Mallarmé, Valéry and the flight of the swan', *Baudelaire, Mallarmé, Valéry: New Essays in Honour of Lloyd Austin*, ed. M. Bowie, A. Fairlie, A. Finch (Cambridge University Press, 1982).

Derrida, J., 'Les sources de Valéry. Qual, quelle', *M.L.N.*, 563–99.

Duchesne-Guillemin, J., *Études pour un Paul Valéry* (Neuchâtel, La Baconnière, 1964).

Essai sur la Jeune Parque de Valéry (Paris, Itinéraires, 1947).

Elder, E. M., 'Le finale fragmenté des "Narcisses" de Valéry', *C.P.V.*, I, 187–206.

Frandon, I.-M., 'Le Poème: déguisement et transitivité', *Poétique et Communication*, 129–53.

Franklin, U., *The Rhetoric of Valéry's Prose Aubades* (University of Toronto Press, 1979).

Gauthier, M., 'L'architecture phonique dans la poésie de Valéry', *P.V.C.*, 377–97.

'La décomposition poétique du mot', *Poétique et Communication*, 241–59.

Genette, G., 'La Littérature comme telle', *Figures* I (Paris, Seuil, 1966) (*Les Critiques de notre temps et Valéry* [Garnier, 1971], 175–85).

Gheorghe, I., *les images du Poète et de la poésie dans l'œuvre de Valéry* (Lettres Modernes, Langue et Style, 6 [Paris, Minard, 1977]).

293

Bibliography

Guiraud, P., *Index du vocabulaire du symbolisme*, vol. II *Index des mots des poésies de Paul Valéry* (Paris, Klincksieck, 1953).

Henry, A., *Langage et poésie chez Paul Valéry* (Paris, Mercure de France, 1952).

Hytier, J., *La Poétique de Valéry* (Paris, Armand Colin, 1953).

'L'Esthétique Valéryenne du sonnet', *A.J.F.S.*, 6, (1969), 326–36.

'Les Cimetières Marins dans la poésie française', *B.E.V.*, 4, jan. 1975, 13–35.

Ince, W., *The Poetic Theory of Paul Valéry – Inspiration and Technique* (Leicester University Press, 1961).

'La voix du Maître ou Moi et style selon Valéry', *R.S.H.*, 129 (jan.–mars 1968), 29–39.

'The sonnet "Le Vin perdu" of Paul Valéry', *F.S.*, x (1956), 40–54.

'An Exercise in Artistry: Valéry's "Les Grenades"', *The Romanic Review* IV (1964), 190–202.

'Être, connaître et mysticisme du réel selon Valéry', *E.N.C.*, 203–22.

'Valéry et Heredia', *C.P.V.E.*, 119–37.

'"Infini esthétique" et poésie selon Valéry', *Poétique et Communication*, 69–81.

Ireland, G., '"La Jeune Parque" – Genèse et Exégèse', *E.N.C.*, 85–101.

Jackson, E., *Worlds Apart: Structural Parallels in the Poetry of Paul Valéry, Saint-John Perse, Benjamin Péret and René Char* (Paris, Mouton, 1976).

Jallat, J., 'Valéry et les figures de rhétorique', *C.P.V.*, I, 149–85.

Köhler, H., *Paul Valéry Dichtung und Erkenntnis. Das lyrische Werk im Lichte der Tagebücher* (Bonn, Bouvier Verlag Herbert Grundmann, 1976).

'Quelques poèmes de Valéry interprêtés par ses "Cahiers"', *P.V.C.*, 353–76.

Laurenti, H., 'Musique et monologue – notes pour une approche valéryenne du poème', *R.L.M.*, I, 49–66.

'Les langages de "La Jeune Parque"', *B.E.V.*, 6, juillet 1975, 18–36.

Laurette, P., *Le Thème de l'arbre chez Paul Valéry* (Paris, Klincksieck, 1967).

Lawler, J., *Lecture de Valéry: une étude de 'Charmes'* (Paris, P.U.F., 1963).

The Poet as Analyst, Essays on Paul Valéry (Berkeley and Los Angeles, University of California Press, 1974).

Lechantre, M., 'L'hiéroglyphe intérieur', *M.L.N.*, 630–43.

'P(h)o(n)étique', *C.P.V.*, I, 93–119.

Levaillant, J., 'La Jeune Parque en question', *P.V.C.*, 136–51.

Lussy, F. de, *La Genèse de "la Jeune Parque" de Paul Valéry, Essai de chronologie littéraire* (Minard, Lettres Modernes, coll. Situation, 34, 1975).

Maka-de Schepper, M., *Le Thème de la Pythie chez Paul Valéry* (Paris, Société d'Édition 'Les Belles Lettres', 1969).

Malherbe, M., '"L'Abeille", poème euphonique?', *B.E.V.*, 24, juin 1980, 17–29.

Martin, G., *Le Cimetière Marin (The Graveyard by the Sea)*, Edinburgh

Bilingual Library, University of Texas Press, Austin, Texas, 1972.

'Valéry's "Ode Secrète": the enigma solved?', *F.S.*, xxxi (Oct 1977), 4.

Maurer, K., *Interpretationen zur späteren Lyrik Paul Valérys* (München, Lehnen Verlag, 1954).

Minard, M. J., 'Typographie et littérature – notes de méthode', *R.L.M.*, i, 169–85.

Morier, H., 'La motivation des formes et des mètres chez Paul Valéry', *P.V.C.*, 325–52.

Mounin, G., 'Paul Valéry et Maurice Grammont', *E.M.*, (1972), 125–34.

Moutote, D., 'L'égotisme poétique de Valéry dans Charmes', *R.L.M.*, i, 29–48.

Nadal, O., *La Jeune Parque; étude critique* (Paris, Le Club du Meilleur Livre, 1957).

Noulet, É., *Paul Valéry [Études]* (Brussels, La Renaissance du Livre, 1951).

'"Aurore", essai d'exégèse', *R.L.M.*, i, 103–19.

Le Ton Poétique (Paris, Corti, 1971).

Onimus, J., 'Lectures du "Rameur"', *R.L.M.* i, 147–60.

Parent, M., *Cohérence et Résonance dans le Style de "Charmes" de Paul Valéry* (Paris, Klincksieck, 1970).

'La fonction poétique du langage dans "Charmes"', *P.V.C.*, 61–73.

Parent, M. and Parent, P., 'Réflexions sur la valeur des motifs de l'eau et du vent dans *la Jeune Parque* et dans *Charmes*' *R.L.M.*, i, 67–102.

Pickering, R., 'Energy and integrated poetic experience in the abstract poetic prose of Valéry's *Cahiers*', *A.J.F.S.*, xvi, 244–56.

Piétra, R., 'Valéry, Wittgenstein et la philosophie', *B.E.V.*, 20, mars 1979, 46–65.

Pratt, B., *Rompre le Silence: Les premiers états de 'La Jeune Parque'* (Paris, Corti, 1976).

Le Chant du Cygne (Paris, Corti, 1978).

Rey, A., 'Sens et discours poétique chez Valéry', *P.V.C.*, 39–48.

Robinson, J., *L'Analyse de l'Esprit dans les Cahiers de Valéry* (Paris, Corti, 1963).

'Dreaming and the Analysis of Consciousness in Valéry's Cahiers', *F.S.*, xvi, 2 (April 1962), 101–23.

'Valéry, Pascal et la censure de la métaphysique', *C.P.V.E.*, 185–208.

'Words and Silence in "L'Idée Fixe"' *M.L.N.*, 644–56.

Roth-Mascagni, P., *Petite Prose pour 'Palme'* (Paris, Minard, 1977).

Musique et Géométrie de Trois Poèmes Valéryens (Bruxelles, Andre de Roche, éd., 1979).

Rouart-Valéry, A., 'Introduction Biographique' (P i, 11–71).

Sabbaghe, C., 'Quelques aspects alchimiques de l'œuvre de Paul Valéry', *B.E.V.*, 18 (juin 1978), 29–48.

'Les Disparitions de Narcisse', *P.V.C.*, 153–72.

Scarfe, F., *The Art of Paul Valéry: a study in dramatic monologue* (London, William Heinemann Ltd., Glasgow University Publications xcvii, 1954).

Schmidt-Radefeldt, J., *Paul Valéry linguiste dans les Cahiers* (Paris, Klincksieck, 1970).

Bibliography

'Intuition et inspiration, analogie et métaphore', *Poétique et Communication*, 169–90.

'Valéry et les sciences du langage', *B.E.V.*, 8, jan. 1976, 16–33.

Sørensen, H., *La Poésie de Paul Valéry: étude stylistique sur 'La Jeune Parque'* (Copenhagen, A. Busck, 1944).

Stewart, W., 'Le Thème d'Orphée chez Valéry', *E.N.C.*, 163–78.

Todorov, T., 'La "Poétique" de Valéry', *C.P.V.*, I, 125–32.

Valéry, C., 'Valéry, le Langage et la Pensée', *Poétique et Communication*, 13–21.

Walzer, P.-O., *La Poésie de Valéry* (Genève, Cailler, 1953 [Slatkine Reprints, Genève, 1967]).

'Fragments d'esthésique', *A.J.F.S.*, 8 (1971), 230–42.

Whiting, C., *Paul Valéry: Charmes ou Poèmes*, Athlone French Poets (London, The Athlone Press, 1973).

Valéry, jeune poète (Paris, P.U.F., 1960).

Yeschua, S., *Valéry, le roman et l'œuvre à faire* (Paris, Lettres Modernes, Minard, 1976).

' "Substitutions" et poétique chez Valéry', *C.P.V.*, I, 135–48.

C. General works

Baker, F., 'La Route contraire', *Reappraisals of Rousseau, Studies in honour of R. A. Leigh* (Manchester University Press, 1980), 133–62.

Barthes, R., *Le Degré zéro de l'écriture (1953) suivi de Nouveaux Essais critiques* (Paris, Seuil, 1972).

Fragments d'un discours amoureux (Paris, Seuil, 1977).

Baudelaire, C., *Œuvres complètes*, ed. Claude Pichois, Vol. 1, 'Bibliothèque de la Pléiade' (Paris, Gallimard, 1975).

Black, M., *Poetic Drama as Mirror of the Will* (London, Vision Press, 1977).

Booth, W., *The Rhetoric of Fiction* (University of Chicago Press, 1961).

Bowie, M., 'Jacques Lacan', *Structuralism and Since, From Lévi-Strauss to Derrida*, ed. J. Sturrock (Oxford University Press, 1979), 116–53.

Mallarmé and the Art of Being Difficult (Cambridge University Press, 1978).

Bréal, M., *Essai de Sémantique* (Paris, 1897).

Breton, A., 'Le Message automatique', *Point du Jour* (Paris, Gallimard, 1970), 167.

Bruns, G., *Modern Poetry and the Idea of Language* (New Haven, Conn. and London, Yale University Press, 1974).

Culler, J., *Structuralist Poetics* (London, Routledge and Kegan Paul, 1975).

Deguy, M., *Poèmes 1960–1970* (preface by H. Meschonnic) (Paris, Gallimard, 1973).

Denes, P., Pinson, E., *The Speech Chain – the Physics and Biology of the Spoken Language* (New York, Anchor Books, 1973).

Derrida, J., *La Voix et le Phénomène* (Paris, P.U.F., Épiméthée, 1967).

Diderot, D., *Le Neveu de Rameau* (in *Œuvres Romanesques*, Classiques Garnier, 1951).

Bibliography

Dœuff, M., 'Le philosophe dans le gosier', *La Quinzaine Littéraire*, 284 (1–3 août 1978), special number: *La Musique, le Mot, la Voix*.

Ehrenzweig, A., *The Psycho-analysis of Artistic Vision and Hearing* (New York, George Braziller, 1965).

Empson, W., *Seven Types of Ambiguity* (London, Chatto and Windus, 1930) (Second edition, 1947).

Fairlie, A., 'Flaubert et la conscience du réel', *Essays in French Literature*, 4, November 1967, 1–12.

Baudelaire : Les Fleurs du Mal (London, Edward Arnold, 1972).

'Sentiments et sensations chez Flaubert', *C.A.I.E.F.*, 26 (mai 1974), 233–49.

Gibson, R., *Modern French Poets on Poetry* (Cambridge University Press, 1961).

Gide, A., *La Porte Étroite* (*Romans, récits et soties* [Paris, Gallimard, 1958]).

Grammont, M., *Petit Traité de Versification Française* (Paris, Armand Colin, 1965).

Hackett, C. A., *New French Poetry* (Oxford, Basil Blackwell, 1973).

'Les Grandes Tendances de la Poésie Française depuis 1950', *C.A.I.E.F.*, 30, mai 1978.

Hawkes, T., *Structuralism and Semiotics* (London, Methuen, 1977).

Higgins, I., 'Francis Ponge', *The Language of Poetry: Crisis and Solution – Studies of Modern Poetry of French Expression, 1945 to the Present*, ed. M. Bishop (Rodolpi, 1980).

Francis Ponge (London, Athlone Press, 1979).

Hunt, A., 'Mallarmé's "Toute l'âme résumée"', *Neophilologus*, LX, 1976, 357–66.

Jackson, J., *La Question du Moi, Un aspect de la modernité poétique européenne* (Neuchâtel, La Baconnière, 1978).

Jameson, F., *The Prison-House of Language* (Princeton University Press, 1974).

Kris, E., *Psychoanalytic Explorations in Art* (New York, Schocken Paperback Edition, 1964 [1952]).

Kristeva, J., *La Révolution du langage poétique* (Paris, Seuil, 1974).

Kurz, P., *Language and Human Nature, A French–American Philosopher's Dialogue* (St Louis, Mo., Warren H. Green, Inc., 1971).

Lacan, J., *Écrits* (Paris, Seuil, 1966).

Mallarmé, S., *Œuvres complètes*, ed. H. Mondor et G. Jean-Aubry, 'Bibliothèque de la Pléiade' (Paris, Gallimard, 1951).

Meschonnic, H., *Pour la Poétique*, I–IV, Collection 'Le Chemin' (Paris, N.R.F., Gallimard, 1970–8).

Mossop, D., *Pure Poetry. Studies in French Poetic Theory and Practice: 1746–1945* (Oxford, Clarendon Press, 1971).

Mounin, G., 'Mallarmé et le Langage', *Europe* (avril–mai, 1976), 10–17.

Nerval, G., 'El Desdichado', *Les Chimères* (*Œuvres:* texte établi par A. Béguin et J. Richer, 'Bibliothèque de la Pléiade' [Paris, Gallimard, 1970–4].

Nowottny, W., *The Language Poets Use* (London, The Athlone Press, 1962).

Popper, K., Eccles, J., *The Self and its Brain* (Bonn, Heidelberg, Berlin, Springer International, 1977).

Pratt, M., *Towards a Speech Act Theory of Literary Discourse* (Bloomington, Ind., Indiana University Press, 1977).

Raymond, M., *De Baudelaire au Surréalisme* (Paris, Corti, 1940).

Être et Dire (Neuchâtel, La Baconnière, 1970).

Rimbaud, A., 'Après le Déluge', *Les Illuminations* (*Œuvres complètes*, 'Bibliothèque de la Pléiade', Paris, Gallimard, 1963).

Robbe-Grillet, A., 'Nature, humanisme, tragédie', *Pour un Nouveau Roman* (Paris, Gallimard, 1963).

Rosalto, G., 'Voice and Literary Myth', in *The Structuralist Controversy*, ed. R. Macksey and E. Donato (Baltimore, Md., and London, The Johns Hopkins University Press, paperback edition 1975 [1970]).

Saussure, F. de, *Cours de Linguistique Générale*, 1913.

Scholes, R., *Structuralism in Literature: an introduction* (New Haven, Conn., London, Yale University Press, 1974).

Searle, J., *Speech Acts* (Cambridge University Press, 1969).

Glyph, John Hopkins Textual Studies, 1, 2.

Sturrock, J., ed. *Structuralism and Since, From Lévi-Strauss to Derrida* (Oxford, University Press, 1979).

Wilden, A., *System and Structure* (London, Tavistock Publications, 1972).

Index

Abeille, L', **109–15**, 117, 143, 156, 186, 189, 210, 277, 278
Agathe, 270
Air de Sémiramis, 38, 39
A la Recherche du Temps Perdu, 241
Album de Vers Anciens, 38–40
Amateur de Poèmes, L', 270, 288
Âme et la Danse, L', 217, 227, 266, 277, 279, 280, 288
Amphion, 141, 280
Amson, J., 258
Anderson, K., 256, 266, 281, 284
Ange, L', 27, 95, 124, 165
Animus/Anima, 73, 285
Anne, 38
Apollinaire, G., 214
Apollonian, 139–40, 176
Après-Midi d'un Faune, L', 100, 153, 271, 272
Au Platane, 104, 107–8, **131–7**, 139, 141–2, 156, 237, 239, 258
Aurore, 104–10, 115, **116–30**, 131–2, 137–8, 142, 144, 149, 155–7, 167, 171, 174, 205, 232, 235, 267, 273, 278, 279, 280, 283, 286, 287, 290
Austin, L. J., 263, 264, 272, 275, 277, 281, 288
Avranches, 106

Bach, J. S., 56, 93, 108, 163, 243
Baker, F., 260
Barthes, R., 14, 16, 260, 261, 276
Bastet, N., 256, 258, 272, 284
Baudelaire, C., 5, 20, 28, 30, 32, 34, 40–1, 43, 47–8, 56, 61, 85, 90, 109, 134, 151, 227, 253, 256, 262, 263, 273, 280, 284
Beckett, S., 291
Bergson, H., 7
Black, M., 258
Boa, P., 271
Bois Amical, Le, 288

Bonnefoy, Y., 253, 291
Booth, W., 256
Bossuet, 184, 220
'Bouchoreille', 7, 45, 52, 53, 246
Bourjea, S., 281, 288
Bowie, M., 259, 263, 273, 276
Bréal, M., 259
Breton, A., 260
Bruns, G., 256, 264, 290, 291

Cahiers, 3, 6, 7, 10, 20, 29, 31, 96, 159, 204
Cain, L., 264
Cantate du Narcisse, 158, 165
Cantique des Colonnes, 104, 131, **137–42**, 156–7, 174, 285
Cardinal, R., 255
C.E.M., 3, 10, 76
Ceinture, La, 146, **150–3**, 155, 163, 221, 289
Celeyrette-Pietri, N., 256, 258, 261, 262, 263, 265, 274, 277, 278, 281, 283, 286, 290
César, 38–9, 285
Champigny, R., 287
Chant d'Automne, 227
Chant de l'Idée-Maîtresse, 15, 278
Charmes, xviii, 6, 18, 22, 39–41, 58, **103–9**, 115, 117–18, 121, 124, 129–31, 136, 141–3, 146, 149, 156–7, 172, 175, 177–8, 180, 188–9, 197, 203, 220, 228, 235–6, 242–3, 252, 254
Chausserie-Laprée, J.-P., 273
Chénier, A., 28, 61
Chimères, Les, 197, 289
Chisholm, A., 270, 274
Cimetière Marin, Le, xv–i, 3, 19, 21, 23, 28, 63, 68–9, 104, 107–9, 149, 164, 176, 180, 187, 194, 200, **201–15**, 216, 218–19, 227, 230–2, 239, 252, 278, 281
Cocking, J., 284

Index

Coleridge, S. T., 195, 251
'Confiteor' de l'Artiste, Le, 151
Conque, La, 28
Corot, G., 151
Correspondances, 127, 145, 262
Un Coup de dés, 100, 220, 225, 226
Cours de Poétique, 9, 275
Cratyllism, 54
Crow, C., 258, 261, 262, 266, 267,
    271, 277, 278, 279, 281, 285, 289
Culler, J., 257
Le Cygne, 134

Dante(-esque), 93, 231
Deguy, M., 259
Denes, P., 266
Derrida, J., 249–51, 260, 282, 289,
    291
Descartes, 277
Dialogue de l'Arbre, 64, 131
Diderot, D., 278
Dionysius, 139, 140, 152, 171, 176,
    207, 225
Dœuff, M., 269
Dormeuse, La, 104, 109, 146, 153–5,
    156, 187
Duchesne-Guillemin, J., 255, 270,
    277, 280, 282, 284

Ébauche d'un Serpent, 104, 107, 109,
    148, 180–7, 189, 210, 229, 237,
    273, 277, 278, 284, 285, 289
Eccles, J., 265
Ehrenzweig, A., 280
Elder, E., 282
Élévation de la Lune, 28
Empson, W., 256
Équinoxe, 38, 234, 252
Éros, 115, 156, 276
Été, 38, 40
Eupalinos ou l'Architecte, 123, 125,
    128, 171, 280, 285
Eurêka, 32
Eurydice, 283
Eve, 181

Fairlie, A., 257, 264, 277
Fausse Morte, La, 187, 188–9
Faust (see Mon Faust)
Feu distinct, Un, 38–9
Fileuse, La, 38
Flaubert, G., 257, 260
Fleur Mystique, 28
Fleurs du Mal, Les, 109

Fragments du Narcisse, 109, 131,
    146, 157–66
Frandon, I.-M., 287
Franklin, U., 261, 278
Freud, S., 12, 170, 285

Gauthier, M., 266, 267, 272, 273, 287
Gautier, T., 140, 280, 288
Genette, G., 260, 291
Gheorghe, I., 284, 288
Gibson, R., 263
Gide, A., 31, 38, 147, 158, 281
'Gladiator', 6, 239, 257
Gluck, 22, 41, 57, 79, 88, 272
Goethe, J. W. von, 195
Grammont, M., 210, 287
Grenades, Les, 187, 189–93, 197,
    210, 216, 230, 232, 240, 285
Guiraud, P., 264

Hackett, C. A., 291
Hawkes, T., 257
Heidegger, 248, 260
Henry, A., 279, 280
Hercules, 218–21
Heredia, J.-M. de, 38, 264
'Hermetic', xviii, 248
Hérodiade, 29, 271
Higgins, I., 255, 279, 285
Hugo, V., 61, 175–6, 180, 280, 284
Hunt, A., 273
Husserl, E., 249, 250
Hytier, J., 255, 257, 261, 265, 268,
    272, 276, 277, 279, 281, 285, 287,
    288

Ince, W., 258, 259, 264, 265, 266,
    284, 285, 286
Insinuant, L', 15, 109, 187–8
Inspiration, 177–9
Inspirations Méditérranéennes, 19,
    202, 279
Intérieur, 199–200, 241
Ireland, W., 264, 272

Jackson, E., 281, 287
Jackson, J., 255
Jallat, J., 280, 285
Jameson, F., 257, 260
Jason, 121, 283
Jeune Parque, La, xviii, 4, 18, 21–5,
    41, 57, 60, 66–102, 103–6, 110,
    113, 116–19, 121, 124, 145, 156–8,
    163–4, 167–8, 186, 194, 208, 213,

Index

229, 232, 254, 262, 265–8, 270–6, 280, 282, 283, 285, 286
Jeune Prêtre, Le, 28, 33
Jones, O., 261

Keats, J., 278, 280
Köhler, H., 262, 275, 276, 282, 286, 288, 289
Kris, E., 256
Kristeva, J., 260
Kurz, P., 260

Lacan, J., 12, 13, 276, 278, 279, 283, 285
La Fontaine, J. de, 112, 127, 214, 231, 277, 279
Lamartine, 33
Laurenti, H., 256, 270, 275, 287
Laurette, P., 262
Lawler, J., 255, 263, 264, 268, 275, 276, 277, 281, 282, 283, 284, 285, 288
Le Breton, G., 259
Lechantre, M., 256, 260, 265, 290
Leconte de Lisle, C.-M.-R., 28, 214, 280
Leonardo, 236, 266, 286, 288
Levaillant, J., 261, 271, 272
Linguistics, 7–10
Louÿs, P., 28, 33, 282
Lucrèce, 64, 131, 133, 135, 279
Lussy, F. de, 264, 270
Lust, 200

Maka-de Shepper, M., 282
Malherbe, M., 28, 277, 287
Mallarmé, S., xvi–ii, 9, 13–14, 16, 19, 24–6, 28–31, 33–8, 40–1, 43, 48, 51, 53, 55–9, 61, 81, 83, 91, 100, 113, 120, 122, 153, 165, 175, 195, 199, 217, 220–2, 224–6, 229, 242, 248, 253, 261, 263, 264, 268, 270, 271, 272, 273, 274, 275, 278, 279, 280, 284, 286, 288, 289, 291
Martin, G., 288, 289
Mathews, J., 261
Maurer, K., 286
Medusa, 172, 283
Mélange, 199, 239
Méphistophélès, 180, 181
Meschonnic, H., 259, 291
Minard, M., 290
Molière, 162

Mon Faust, 2, 15, 22, 110–11, 115, 200, 243, 275, 277
Montaigne, M., 5, 258
Moreau, G., 283
Morier, H., 286
Mossop, D., 269
Mounin, G., 263, 287
Moutote, D., 262
Musset, A. de, 1, 33

N + S, 266
Nadal, O., 264
Narcisse, 23, 26–7, 146, 158, 188, 228, 244, 262, 281, 283, 289 (see also *Fragments du Narcisse*)
Narcisse Parle, 33, 38, 158
Navire, Le, 262
Nerval, G. de, 197, 232, 257, 280, 289
New Criticism, xvii, 10, 14
New Novel, 74
Noulet, É., 277
Nowottny, W., 256

Ode Secrète, 104, **215–26**, 230
Onimus, J., 289
Orpheus/'Orphic', xviii, 6, 12, 38, 97, 103, 106–7, 141, 143, 157, 184, 186, 243, 248, 272, 280, 283
Ouroboros, 272, 284

Palme, 105–6, 108–9, 180, 198, 235, **236–44**, 271, 278, 280
Paradoxe sur l'Architecte, 141
Parent, M., 255, 274, 281, 286
Parent, P., 274
Parnassians, 28, 38, 61, 279
Pas, Les, 146–**50**, 155, 187–8
Pascal, 79, 184, 220, 289
Pegasus, 135
Philosophe et la Jeune Parque, Le, 72
Philosophy of Composition, 31
Pickering, R., 261
Piétra, R., 259, 261
Pinson, E., 266
Poe, E. A., 15, 19, 29, **30–3**, 34, 40, 256, 263
'Poèmes et PPA', 20, 261
Poésie, 7, 36, 41, 44, 47–8, 51, 57, 60, 76, 119, 125–6, 130, **143–6**, 155–6, 213, 252, 267, 285, 289
Poésie et Pensée Abstraite, 47
Poincaré, H., 195, 286

301

Index

Ponge, F., 279, 285
Popper, K., 265
Porte Étroite, La, 147
Pratt, B., 264, 274, 278
Pratt, M., 290
Pre-Raphaelites, 28
Profusion du Soir, 38, 150
Prose pour des Esseintes, 242, 290
Proteus, 89
Proust, M., 48, 67, 241
Psaume sur une Voix, 36
Psyché, 73, 156
Pygmalionism, 73
Pythie La, 74, 104, 106, 108–9, 121, 131, 163, 166–79, 180, 186, 192, 208, 219–20, 223, 242, 258, 260, 265, 278, 282, 284, 285

Rachel, 268
Racine, 28, 61, 79, 82, 87, 269
Rameur, Le, 109, 226–36, 281, 288
Raven, The, 31
Raymond, M., 290, 291
Realism, 23, 40
Renoir, 39
Rêve, 28
Rey, A., 259
Richards, I. A., 259
Rimbaud, A., 24–6, 28, 31, 40–1, 61, 91, 224, 261, 263, 265, 274, 278, 279, 289
Robbe-Grillet, A., 74, 90, 274
Robinson, J., 257, 258, 259, 264, 275, 289, 291
Romanticism, 5, 40, 53, 70, 177, 251, 291
Ronsard, P. de, 28, 89, 112, 214, 288
Rosalto, G., 256
Roth-Mascagni, P., 272, 273, 290
Rouart-Valéry, A., 261
Rousseau, J.-J., 231, 260, 269
Russian Formalists, 13, 249

Sabbaghe, C., 263, 281, 282
Sarraute, N., 260
Sassetta, 236
Saussure, F. de, 9, 10, 14, 259
Scarfe, F., 255, 270, 281

Schmidt-Radefeldt, J., 259, 265, 286
Scholes, R., 257
Schopenhauer, A., 184
Searle, J., 259, 260, 281
Sète, 18
Siegfried, 30
Socrates, 140, 285
Soirée avec M. Teste, La (see Teste)
Solitaire, Le, 232, 234
Sørensen, H., 270, 273, 274
Stewart, W., 279
Structuralism, xvii, 2, 8–16, 249, 257, 261, 291
Sturrock, J., 257
Suave Agonie, La, 28, 33
Surrealism, 13, 214
Sylphe, Le, 105, 109, 187, 277
Symbolism, xvii, 28, 30, 39–40, 55–7, 100, 220, 222–4, 251, 280, 283
'Système', 6, 12, 29

Tales of Mystery and Imagination, 32
Teste, 2, 3, 17, 25, 28, 50, 95, 183, 229, 263, 264, 275, 285
Tityre, 64, 131, 133, 135
Tombeau de Charles Baudelaire, Le, 226
Todorov, T., 259

Valéry, C., 266
Valvins, 38, 264
Variété, 49
Verlaine, P., 28, 34
Villon, F., 28, 214
Vin Perdu, Le, 194–9, 218, 228
Voltaire, 214, 288
Vue, 38

Wagner, 19, 41, 56–7, 79, 88, 141, 157, 184, 264, 268, 272
Walzer, P.-O., 255, 263, 283
Whiting, C., 255, 263, 276, 281, 282, 284
Wilden, A., 257, 258
Wittgenstein, L., 7, 259, 283, 291
Wordsworth, W., 251

Yeschua, S., 262, 286